THE SOURCE
OF LIGHT

REYNOLDS PRICE

THE SOURCE OF LIGHT

NEW YORK

ATHENEUM

1981

*Parts of this novel appeared, in earlier
forms, in* ANTAEUS *and in a limited edition
from* SYLVESTER & ORPHANOS.

Library of Congress Cataloging in Publication Data

Price, Reynolds, 1933–
    The source of light.
    I. Title.
PS3566.R54S6   1981   813'.54   80-69650
ISBN 0-689-11136-3

FOR
DAVID CECIL
AND
STEPHEN SPENDER

That angelic language has nothing in common
with human languages is shown by this—
that angels cannot utter one word of human language.
They have tried but could not, for they cannot
utter anything that is not in
perfect agreement with their nature.

SWEDENBORG, *Heaven and Its Wonders and Hell,* 237

ONE

THE PRINCIPLE OF
PERTURBATIONS

MAY–AUGUST 1955

HUTCHINS Mayfield had stripped and faced the water, intending to enter before his father and stage the drowned-man act to greet him. But turning in the half-dark cubicle, he was stopped by sight of another man, naked also, close there beside him. He took two quick steps to leave, then knew—a dressing mirror he'd failed to notice hung on the pine wall. He went back and looked, not having seen himself for a while—not alone and startled, fresh for study. (In fact, except for negligent shaves, it had been two weeks—his twenty-fifth birthday. He'd been in Richmond that night with Ann; his grandmother tracked him down by phone to wish him luck. He'd borne her rambling a little impatiently; so she closed by saying, "Have you checked your looks now you're over the hill?—twenty-five is the downside in our family, Hutch, whatever doctors say. Twenty-five, we're *grown*." He'd checked in Ann's bureau mirror and confirmed it.) Now he studied his groin, full in the warm day, and thought how little it had caused but pleasure—a grown man's first means of work hung on him, an aging toy. But he smiled and reached a hand toward the cool glass, stroked the dim image. It bobbed in gratitude—pony, pet turtle—and Hutch laughed once, then heard his father's voice at the pool.

"What things will this cure?" Rob Mayfield said.

"Sir?"—the Negro attendant.

Now an exchange was promised in the earliest consoling sound of Hutch's life—a white voice, a black voice twined and teasing. He stood to wait it out.

"Which one of all my many troubles will this spring cure?"

"They tell us not to make big claims no more. Used to say kidneys, liver, eczema, the worst kind of blues, warts, falling hair. Whatever they tell me, it cured my feet. I was born flat-footed."

Rob said "Bathing fixed them?"

"No, never. I drink it. But it sure God jacked these feet off the ground.

Born glued to the floor; now my kids play under em—run in and out, hide all in the shade. This your first time here?"

Rob said, "Yes. Thirty years ago I lived in Goshen, but I never got over the mountain somehow."

"Shame on you then," the Negro said. "Goshen ain't nothing but sand and cold river. Warm Springs would have helped you, just twenty minutes west."

"It seemed farther then. The road was bad."

"Beautiful now. Go on; step in—never too late."

Rob laughed but said "Oh it is." Then he moved.

Hutch came to the door of the cubicle to look—Rob Mayfield's back. His father stripped was something he really hadn't seen, not for years.

Fifty-one years old but still white and firm in waist and hams, Rob stooped to grip the rails of the stairs and descended slowly into eight feet of clear water bubbling from the earth, precisely the heat of a well human body. Then he swam four strokes to the center of the pool; embraced the ridgepole and looked back, smiling, to his only child. "I should have found this thirty years ago. Might have changed some things."

Hutch also gripped the rails but paused at the top. "What things?"

Rob continued smiling and paddled his hair back, still barely gray, but said no more.

Hutch looked for the Negro. He was back out of sight with his radio; so Hutch could say, "You might not have had me." He grinned but was earnest.

"I didn't say that."

"I've been the main trouble for most of those years."

"Never said that either."

Hutch nodded—it was true—but he stood on, dry in the thick warm air of late afternoon, and looked at what seemed the only block in his path: this middle-sized man, drenched and curling. The main thing he'd loved, that might yet stop him.

Rob clapped his hands once. "Were you ever baptized?"

"Not in my recollection."

"Then descend," Rob said and raised his right arm. The smile never broke, but he said "Father. Son—"

Hutch slowly descended. They laughed together as Hutch's head sank. But he didn't rise. He went straight into the drowning tableau—emptied his lungs so he fell to the smooth rocks that paved the spring and sprawled there, lit by green light that pierced the water.

It worked. Rob saw him as dead, that quickly—dead limbs gently flapped by currents, the long hair snaky. Yet he didn't move; he called the Negro. "Sam, step here."

The man was named Franklin, but he came at a trot.

Rob pointed down.

Franklin nodded. "Dead again." He stared a long moment. "Looks real, don't it? He do that a lot, every time he come—like to scared his young friend to death last week."

Hutch jerked to life and thrust toward the surface. He broke out, streaming; faced his father, and said "—Holy Ghost."

Rob said "Welcome."

They swam, sank, floated for the hour they'd purchased. No other bather joined them, and Franklin stayed off in his own little room. Within three minutes of the drowning, they had calmed. The water's constant match of their own body-heat soon made it a companion—gentle, promising of perfect fidelity: the craving of both men, in different ways. To Hutch it seemed a large faceless woman—spread and open, inescapable—into which he inserted his whole free body; four times in the hour he stiffened and fell. To Rob it finally seemed a place—the original lake in which he had formed, which he'd left insanely but had now found again, and in which he'd dissolve. They scarcely spoke, only fragments of pleasure. They felt no need, for the first time ever in one another's presence. When the hour was up and Franklin came, they were deep in separate dreams of safety.

Franklin said "You shriveling yet?"

Rob looked to Hutch.

Hutch looked at his own right hand. "A little."

"Then time to get out. Hour's all you can stand." Franklin held white towels like gifts more tempting than the spring itself.

Hutch swam the strokes that put him by his father. That whole charged body was covered with beads of air like an armor. He reached out and wiped his hand down Rob's chest, clearing a space.

Rob took the wrist and, not releasing it, swam back an arm's length to focus the face. "I'll try not ever to forget this," he said. "You please try the same."

"I can promise," Hutch said.

"No, just try."

Hutch nodded and they swam together toward the stairs.

In the safe dreamy hour, Rob had found no way to tell his son what he'd had confirmed two days ago—that Rob Mayfield, early as it was, would be dead by winter; that the body which had served him unfailingly till now had conceived and was feeding in a lobe of its right lung a life that would need nothing less than all. At the stairs he said "You first. You're slower." He wanted that instant of sight to decide.

Hutch gave it. He climbed out strongly but paused on the top step, not looking back; then he cupped his face in both large hands and shuddered hard—only once but enough.

Rob saw that to tell him now before the end would be to stop the trip he'd planned, that he'd leaned his life on mysteriously. Or, if he should still leave in face of the news, to show him as the final demon of dreams—faithless after decades of smooth deceit. Rob took the rails also. Against the lovely pull of the spring—its promise of care—he hauled himself and his fresh partner up.

2

THEY ate a good supper at the Warm Springs Inn (mountain trout, new lettuce) and set out at eight in clear cool darkness to drive the pickup on to Hutch's near Edom—some sixty miles north through mountains and valleys, and they both were tired. Rob had started up from North Carolina at noon to meet Hutch at five. Hutch had thumbed down from Edom; the bath was his idea. So Hutch drove now and—through the first mountain, cross the Cowpasture River—they said very little. Past the river Hutch realized his whole idea would force Goshen on them—on his father at least, who had not been there in eight or nine years. They had already passed two signs naming Goshen, but it still lay a quarter-hour ahead, and Rob had not mentioned it since talking to Franklin. So Hutch said, "Tell me what you want me to do" (meaning, stop at the grave or drive on past).

Rob said, "Be a better man than me at least."

Hutch started to explain but accepted the delay. "Tell me how to go about it."

"I expect you know. You've lived a quarter-century; you've hurt nobody, not that I know of."

Hutch said "I killed my mother."

"You couldn't help that. I couldn't keep you from her. Rachel pulled you out of me by main force, Son; and she held on to you, but you had to come out. Rachel died of bad luck. Your luck was better—and my luck, to have you."

"Thank you," Hutch said, "but still tell me how."

Rob turned to the dim profile beside him. "I was answering politely, just words to say. I couldn't tell a dog how to bury a bone, much less a grown man how to live. I don't even understand your plan."

Hutch glanced across. "The trip?"

"Well, no. I did a little wandering myself—sooner than you, on a smaller map: a few whistle-stops in southwest Virginia. Europe was torn up all through my freedom. No I meant what comes once you've seen the world and are back here, ticking through the numerous years. You're counting on the ravens to feed you apparently; they often renege."

Hutch smiled at the road. "I can do two things that'll tide me over if the ravens fail—teach children English and make women think they've been rushed to Heaven before their time." Since he was grown he had hardly mentioned love to his father.

Rob remembered that and waited. Then he said, "How many would you estimate you'd rushed?"

"Sir?"

"Women, to Heaven—how many have you sent?"

Hutch said "I was joking."

Rob said, "I'm not. I'd like to know. It would help me to know what women mean to you. It's a danger that runs in your family, you've noticed —the Mayfield side."

Hutch also waited. His window was open on the loud spring night; it spoke at their silence—incessant jangle of small life *signaling*, no one creature mute in solitude, even the fox that crossed before them musky with lure. He thought that awhile; then said, "It would help me too. I doubt I know. I've liked two or three women more than anybody—Alice Matthews, Polly. I may need Ann Gatlin—she hopes I do; I hope I do."

"But you haven't asked Ann to marry you yet?"

Hutch said, "Worse—I've asked her not to visit me in Europe. She'd started on plans to join me for Christmas."

"What made you do that?"

Hutch waited again, then tried the answer he'd offered Ann. "I think I need air."

"To do what in?"

"—Need stillness around me."

Rob said, "Nine-tenths of the world's population works eight or ten hours a day more than you. You've rested, Son. Lie back and be grateful."

Hutch laughed. "You hit it. I'm so well-rested my mind is souring but *grateful* I'm not. I'm an aging boy, as you point out. I need to work and I think I'm going toward it."

"Ann Gatlin sounds like a nice job to me, a fine evening shift—the one shift that pays."

Hutch said "She'd like that."

"What's wrong with that?"

"I didn't know you rated Ann very high."

Rob said, "Now I do. She wants you around. She means to last."

Hutch said "I think you're right."

"But you're holding her off?"

"For now. No choice."

Rob said "There you're wrong."

"I can't take her with me."

"Then ask her to wait. Hell, beg her." Rob looked away.

They let another patch of silence spread. By now the river was steady beside them in the unseen gorge. Its chilly clatter blanked all other sounds; and when the patch had lasted three minutes and Hutch had thought of nothing but fear—fear of failing his kin, fear of finally knowing no work to do, fear of solitude—he said, "You can see I have brought you to Goshen." The meanness was instant filth on his tongue.

But Rob answered calmly. "I noticed you had. I figured you would." He leaned forward, opened the glove compartment, drew out a flashlight, and shone it on Hutch. "So I came prepared. Stop by Rachel's grave."

Hutch nodded. "Two miles."

Rob said, "Time enough to tell you this story. May prove useful someday. It's named 'Little Hubert.' Little Hubert used to like the girls in kindergarten. One day the teacher sent his mother a note—*Hubert runs his hand up all the girls' dresses. Please tell him to quit*—so his mother said, 'Son, do you know what girls have under their dresses?' Hubert said 'No ma'm.' She said, 'A pink mouth with a lot of sharp teeth. Remember that.' Hubert said, 'Yes ma'm. Thank *you* for the tip.' And he acted on it—never touched a girl, though he did a lot of dreaming and a lot of self-service. Twenty-five years of good behavior passed. Then a woman named Charlene chased him down—flat wouldn't let Hubert say No, even Maybe—and they got married. Went to Tampa on their honeymoon, palm trees and moonlight; danced till near-dawn when Charlene asked him if it wasn't time for bed. Hubert said 'O.K.' and they went upstairs. It took her about an hour, but finally Charlene came out of the bathroom all sweet and ready in a peach satin gown. Hubert was long since under the covers in flannel pajamas, more than half-asleep. But she slid in beside him and commenced to stroke his arm till Hubert said, 'I thought you were *tired.*' She said, 'But Sugar, you haven't even touched me' and pulled his hand toward you-know-where. He jerked back fast and said 'No you don't!' She said, 'What do you mean? This is my first night!' Hubert said, 'Go to it. But count me out. I know what you're hiding down there.' She said 'Just what's *normal*, silly.' He said, 'So right!—the normal set of teeth. I'm not risking my good fingers on you.' And he was about to head back into sleep when she said, 'Sugar, you're out of your mind—my teeth are in my head. Look here.' She threw back the sheets and raised that gown. So Hubert sat up and bent over gradually and took a long look. Then he said, 'No wonder! Good night, Charlene! Just look at the condition of those poor *gums!*' "

Hutch laughed; he'd never heard it.

Rob sat like a stuffed Baptist preacher through the laughter; but when Hutch subsided, he said, "Don't forget it, especially in Europe. The gums over there make ours look healthy." Then he switched the flashlight on, at his own face, and turned to his son—a wide bright grin. "You know he was wrong, little Hubert—don't you?"

Hutch smiled. "Yes sir—"

"Very sadly wrong."

Hutch said, "Yes sir, I have reason to know."

"You're not afraid, are you?"

"Not of that," Hutch said. Then he slowed to turn left.

In a Stepin Fetchit voice, Rob said, "You mean you scared of dead folks, cap'n?"

Hutch said "I may be."

"And you may be right."

They had stopped at a pair of shut iron gates. The headlights showed the nearest stones, which were also the oldest—marble tree-trunks, lambs, the locally famous seated-boy-with-birddog (an only son, self-shot while hunting). Hutch doused the lights but made no move, though the plan had been his.

At last Rob opened the door in darkness and stepped to the ground. He stood a minute while his eyes adjusted; when Hutch didn't move, he took a long leak. Then he looked back once at the truck—only outlines— and went on to climb the easy gates. On the other side he lit his flashlight and walked a knowing path forward, fairly straight.

Hutch sat and watched him, held in place by feelings that had waylaid him unexpected—reluctance to pay this farewell homage to his mother by night; a small seed of dread to visit at night a mother he'd never seen alive, whom his own life had canceled; and worse, to visit her this last time with Rob who had cared so little for her memory as not to have been here in nearly a decade. Rob's light had vanished. *Well, let it. Let him bear full-force what he'd tried to deny—the physical locus of his own worst damage: the strip of earth which held in solution all that remained of a lovely girl gone twenty-five years, kept from her son.* The darkness continued, no further light. Then shame replaced the harsher knowledge, and Hutch was freed to go. He cranked the engine, switched on the headlights (which didn't reach Rob); and climbed out to find his father, wherever. He had been here often in recent years; so he had no trouble finding the way, though he entered black dark within fifty feet, and still there was no sign or sound but the river. His feet had struck the low rock-border of the Hutchins plot before he saw pale wavering light and heard what seemed an animal scrabbling. The one large tombstone blocked his way; Hutch stepped round it slowly.

The flashlight was propped at the base of the stone, rapidly failing. Rob was kneeling on the head of Rachel's grave, digging with his nails in the ground above her face. Or filling a hole the size of a softball with what seemed fresh dirt. Rob didn't look up or speak but finished the little job, replacing a lid of turf at the end. Then still not looking, he reached for the light and slammed it once on the stone—pure black. Then the sounds of him rising, stepping toward Hutch; a hand that found Hutch's shoulder, no fumbling, and gripped it hard. His calm voice said, "You've chosen this, have you?"

Hutch said "Sir?"

"Home—you think of this place as home?"

Hutch had not thought that. He'd spent no more than an hour here
in short rare visits, no more than two or three weeks in the town. But now
he said, "I may, yes sir. I think I may."

"Then once you decide—if you ever decide, decide soon enough—bury
me here. Bury me wherever you think is your home."

Hutch said, "Yes sir. But by then I'll surely be senile myself; you'd do
well to leave some written instructions for somebody younger than both
of us."

Rob said "You'll do." His hand came down from shoulder to wrist;
he gripped Hutch's wrist.

So Hutch raised the joined hands—a sizable weight—and searched over
Rob's dark face with dry fingers. They found tears of course.

3

THOUGH they'd been nearly midnight reaching Hutch's in Edom, they both
woke easily at dawn—a bright sky but cool still. Under compulsion Rob
had slept in the bed; Hutch had slept on the ample davenport. Each knew
the other was awake by silence (mouth-breathers both, they slept like seals
—steadily announcing their vulnerability); but for twenty minutes neither
one spoke. Hutch was thinking of ways to get Rob out of the house for
the morning; he needed calm for his final packing. It didn't occur to him,
huddled on himself, that his father was colder and thinking too. Despite
his age Hutch rested in the standard child's assumption that a parent's
mind is a marble wall, uncut by a single urgent requirement or even impatience.

But in those minutes Rob firmly decided his answer to the question
he'd faced all yesterday. He wouldn't tell Hutch. He would not ask himself to bear the boy's response, whatever—the man's; he could seldom believe he had made at least half of what was now a man. Today he would
help the man load his boxes of books and records, his desk, in the truck;
then he'd leave as cheerfully as he could manage. The man would be in
England in a week, for at least a year. Rob would be underground before
that ended. Now for the first time, it seemed desirable—sleep as blank as
the heart of a potato or some unimaginable form of reward. Whatever his
sins, none of which he'd forgot, Rob Mayfield didn't anticipate punishment. But he found he was hungry. Having always been a famished riser,
he saw no reason to abandon the habit; so without sitting up he suddenly
spoke. "Have you got your pencil handy?"

Hutch also stayed down and said "No sir."

"Then listen carefully, remember perfectly, and execute at once—"
Hutch said "I'll try."

"—A small glass of sweetmilk, three eggs scrambled in butter (keep them soft), country sausage, hot biscuits, fig preserves, and strong coffee."

Hutch said "Coming up" but made no move.

Rob recalled he'd neglected to say any prayer; so he said to himself what, a boy of twelve, he'd seen was the heart of Jesus' prayer (the only one that didn't seem a showoff, and even that could be trimmed to two words— "Your will"). Then he sat up in the cold air and looked.

Hutch was still drawn tight beneath his quilt, head turned away.

For a moment Rob felt a strong desire to be served for once, to lie back and let this child start the day—warm the space, cook the food, soothe the sick, earn the keep. He even fell back on his elbows and beamed the wish toward Hutch—*Stand up and take over. Do everything for me. You'll be amazed how little that will be, how soon I won't need anything at all.* But he thought of the end the doctor had outlined three days ago—"You'll begin to cough; no syrup will help. Then you'll have trouble breathing, worse and worse till your lungs fill steadily with fluid and drown you. No pain." He'd asked if the doctor was promising no pain. Humorless as Moses, the doctor said, "No. If it spreads into bone, then we'll have real pain" (Rob had let the *we* pass). That would no doubt come to more than a little service before the end. He would ask nobody but his mother to give it. Though he still hadn't told her, there was no chance of doubt that Eva Mayfield would say any word but Yes—and mean it, have the full strength to mean it. So he stood to the cold bare floor in his underpants, walked to the front room, and lit the oil heater. Then he parted the curtains and looked to the woods. In a high black pine, a young owl sat on a limb near the trunk, beginning its rest. A gang of blue jays quarreled at it with no effect, then flew on their way. Then the only sound was the tin stove warming, cracks and booms.

From the quilt Hutch said a muffled "Blessings on your head."

Rob said, "I accept them and will use them in your name. Now haul your precious white ass to the ground and feed this hollow old man you invited."

Hutch said, "Back to sleep. I've packed all the food."

"Unpack me an egg."

"I'm leaving, remember?"

Rob said "Goodbye."

4

By nine Hutch had managed to get Rob out. He'd given him a choice of the local sights—a self-conducted tour of the school or the New Market battlefield twelve miles north or Endless Caverns. Rob had said, "The caverns sound more like me. I'll be back at noon and we can load up—if I don't get lost; I'll try to get lost." He'd laughed and gone. Hutch had sat and drunk a third cup of coffee, consuming the quiet as if it were a suddenly discovered vein of some scarce mineral his bones required. (That he'd been with his father only sixteen hours, six of them asleep, and still craved solitude shamed him a little; but it came as no news. He was coming to see that all his conscious life—from four or five on—he had moved to a law which required him to take equal time alone for every hour of company, however amusing.) Then unwashed he started the last packing in a small footlocker, the final choice of what would accompany him on the trip. The rooms were already lined with boxes of the clearly expendable things, for storage in Fontaine. It was part of his purpose to go as nearly clean as he could, stripped of all but the vital minimum of the thicket of props he'd set round himself. Clothes were simple (he owned very few and they meant nothing to him, though he kept them neat). He laid out two changes of winter and summer clothes, then turned to hard choices.

Music—he would have no phonograph, but he chose two records he felt he might need when he got near anyone else's machine: Brahms's *Alto Rhapsody* by Marian Anderson, Purcell's *Dido and Aeneas* with Flagstad.

Books—a Bible, which Rob had given him (it had been his Great-grandmother Kendal's); *The Diary of a Country Priest* by Bernanos; *Anna Karenina* (World's Classics edition, four inches by six, miraculous compression); a tattered pamphlet of pornographic photographs he'd found in a garbage can at college (a beautiful, and beautifully joined, young couple); his notebook and the daily log he kept.

Pictures—his mother and father, young together; his Grandmother Mayfield, Alice Matthews, Ann Gatlin, a postcard view of the marble head of a girl from Chios (Boston Museum).

Objects—the five-inch marble torso of a boy he'd bought in New York for fifty dollars three summers ago (sold for Greek but more likely Roman, though gentled by elegance); a box of drawing pencils, pen points, erasers; a box of watercolors; a pad of drawing paper; a pinebark carving of a human body which had once been a man but was now finished smooth.

It took him two hours to make the choices, stow the rest, set the boxes on the porch; but when he had thrown the last food to the birds, the house was effectively free of him. The three years he'd lived here—mostly happy—had altered it only by a few extra nailholes, a few strands of hair in unswept corners (he'd paid a woman to clean it tomorrow). He walked to the center of the house—the short hall—and stood in the emptiness for maybe two minutes, regretting and fearing. Then he stripped off his work clothes, folded them into a box bound for storage, walked to the shower, and bathed very carefully. Only then did he see that the wide gold band—tight on his left hand—was the main thing he carried, except for his pleasant and pleasing body.

5

To fill the half-hour till Rob was back, Hutch drove the four green miles in to school. He had said his farewells two days ago—and received the Headmaster's valedictory sermon—but there might be some mail; and whatever the woes of teaching three years in a rural Episcopal Virginia boys' school, he was nudged already by a sudden posthumous love of the place; nostalgia for a time which had been (he hoped) the end of childhood, delayed but calm. He passed no visible human on the drive; and even as he swung through the campus gates and parked by The Office, he could see nobody, though he actively searched—no colleague or town-boy, no yardman mowing. Monday's commencement had emptied the space as thoroughly as war; so he sat a moment, accepting the favor. Little as he'd moved in his life till now, he already knew the shock of returning to find loud strangers banging on the sets of his former life. Then he entered the dim cool hall of the Office. On his way to the pigeonholes, he passed the Master's open outer room and Fairfax Wilson there, fervently typing. She hadn't seen him—good. He could go out the back and miss her completely, no need to hear-out today's diatribe. But his name was already gone from the slot. Competent to organize vast migrations of nations cross oceans or nuclear blitzkrieg, Fairfax had done her duty by the school (and by herself; she resented his leaving)—the quitter was effaced. She would have any mail that had come today. When he stopped in her door, ten feet from her, she didn't look up but pounded on. So he tried to turn her, concentrated in silence on her rapt profile—lean sister to a class of moviestar (Kay Francis, Barbara Stanwyck) who had shaped her looks twenty years ago, then moved beyond her into fleshy surrender while Fairfax had kept her virgin strength: a little withered but still a banner, proud flag of choice and loyalty-to-choice.

Finally she cut her big dark eyes toward him, no more smiling than a stork. "I thought you were strolling on the Left Bank by now."

"No ma'm, England. And not for eight days—I've got five days on the water first."

She hiked a black brow. "Water? I thought anybody rich as you would be flying first-class."

He'd explained it fully some months ago; but in the slack time, he was willing to rally with her awhile (if you let her discharge her excess life in keen exchange, you might be spared a monologue on the fools she dealt with, the dog's road she trod). "No ma'm, I told you I'd be eating rat cheese and soda crackers."

"They may not even have cheese and crackers—they don't have *heat*—and what's this *ma'm*? I just age a year at a time like you. My friends call me Fair." She smiled at last, broad smile that drew real beauty to her face.

As always Hutch was a little startled by the urgent beauty and by his own quick but reluctant sense that they'd missed a chance at one another. Twenty years between them seemed a flimsy screen. He'd have given her something she'd maybe never had; she'd at least have taught him how to burn on *high* for forty-five years and show no scorching. He said, "Miss Wilson, are you saying I'm a friend?"

She swiveled the chair to face him, then looked to the Headmaster's door. "He's not here today—in Lynchburg buying a new ballplayer; some eight-foot child that can't write his name." She'd whispered that much but straight at his eyes, her own eyes burning. Then she raised her voice to its normal power—a carrying richness—and said, "Hutchins Mayfield, I consider you the finest young man now residing in the Old Dominion; and you know how stuck I am on Virginia."

Hutch smiled and nodded but said, "I'm leaving in an hour, sad to say. Will Virginia survive?"

She refused the fun. "You'd better go now. An hour wouldn't give me time to say how far above the run you are. There are plenty people here who think you're crazy as a duck-in-love to be throwing yourself on fate like this, but you know what I tell them?—I tell them 'Lucky fate!' "

As always half-convinced by her force, Hutch could only thank her.

"Don't thank me. Just send me a Christmas card from some famous spot—nothing naked please—and in your first book put a lunatic maiden-lady from Virginia who types to perfection and knows what's what."

Hutch laughed. "A promise."

6

HE returned with his trifling mail to the car, looking down in hopes of seeing no one; so he'd reached for the door before he saw a man lying back on the hood. A boy—Strawson Stuart, long for his age, Hutch's pupil for two years. He lived in town; his eyes were shut. Hutch said, "I heard you had died Monday night at Morse Mitchell's party, but I didn't know I'd get the body for disposal."

Straw sat up solemn. "Well, you have." He extended his arms cruciform and held the pose. Then he smiled, the second dazzler of the day. "No I've risen and come by to help you load. Saw the note to your father; he's still not back."

"He may never be. He went to Endless Caverns."

Straw said, "Then carry me to Warm Springs quick."

Hutch said, "I scared you so bad last time, I doubted you'd ever want to go again" (he had drowned for Straw; even more than Rob, it had shaken the boy who'd seemed unshakable).

Straw said "But I do."

Hutch studied him long enough to know a true answer. "So do I, very much. There's no chance at all. I've got to load the truck, see Father off, then drive on to Richmond by suppertime. You said you'd see me in England."

"I will."

Though Straw had graduated and Hutch resigned, the place itself—the campus in sunlight, its order—had kept Hutch from thinking of the hours that followed their bath in the spring. Now the different place which Straw constituted, in power and need, demanded homage. The sight of the stripped boy asleep in his arms last Saturday dawn stood clear in Hutch's mind. He watched it gladly with no regret. "We'll drive down to Cornwall —Tristan, Tintagel. You liked that in class."

Straw nodded—"I liked it"—still grave as an arbiter.

Or a god—young god of Want and Use, no more kind or cruel than electric current. Hutch thought that also, then said "Let's pack."

7

THE three-hour silence of the drive to Richmond—across the Shenandoah and the last line of mountains in afternoon light—had come over Hutch like total sleep, an apparently endless depth of rest into which he could dig with easy hands, no dreams to meet. Welcome as food, though he hadn't thought of the past few days as trial or punishment. He accepted the rest, drove his old Chrysler gently but fast, and managed an almost perfect exercise of his kindest skill—life in the present. The future vanished before him, no trace—his father's life without him; the choices Ann would face, the bid she awaited; the thousand accidents of settling in a strange place; the cold fear that soon his promise to work would uncover only empty shafts in himself and in plain view of the friends and kin who held his promise, a tangible note. The past existed only as happiness, snatches of memory of childhood peace—whole summer hours in the swing by his grandmother, hearing her life; carving bark with Grainger, drawing hills with Alice. No agonized mother; no father drunk and stripped on a bare floor, dribbling piss; no need to choose one person from the world and love only that. The present was all—his serviceable self borne on through evening and country peaceful as a child asleep, its own reward, toward nothing at all.

Yet of course toward Ann. When he entered her door at half-past six, there were no lights on; and he couldn't hear her. He set down his small bag and stood to listen—still nothing. Was she gone on an errand? Gone for good? How much would he care? He waited to know but no news came, no feeling at least. He only hoped for the quiet to continue, and without conscious stealth he managed to walk the length of the hall with no board creaking. Then he stopped just short of the open kitchen door; there were small sounds there—scraping, small splashes. He leaned out to see.

Ann was at the sink, looking west through the window, scraping potatoes. The light that was left fell in around her and lit her at the boundaries —the line of her head and hair, her shoulders. She seemed to burn, very hot at the core; sunlight was only the breeze that fanned her and heightened her flare.

Hutch felt that he should be responding to her action, her work for him—this living Vermeer unconsciously staged for no one but him; a loving and lovely woman in daylight, worked by love as by coal or steam. And he did feel grateful; but much more strongly, he felt the pity of the line she made—the deceptive stillness of a human body which seems enduring when of course it is swept by time like a wind. He thought again that what set him off from others his age—here at least; would it be true in Europe?—was the fact he'd always believed in death, his mother's main gift. He'd always known that individual people *leave* apparently forever; that the hope of knowing, really knowing, any single person must be exercised *now*. And the only means of knowledge was touch. Rob had taught him that. Right or wrong, it was one more conviction which set Hutch firmly off from ninety-five percent of the people he met. They saw their bodies as hoards of treasure to be guarded unsleepingly; Hutch saw his as a nearly bare room, doors ajar.

Ann turned and made a few signs in the air with one empty hand.

Hutch said "Meaning what?"

She smiled. "—Meaning I thought you had gone deaf and dumb, standing there so long."

"You heard me?"

"Yes."

"Why didn't you look?"

She said, "I couldn't think of anything to say."

"That's a new problem, right?"

A born narrator, she laughed once. "Right. But it's also new being left four thousand miles behind, typing letters for a lawyer and peeling potatoes for just myself."

The depth of the room—twelve feet—was still between them; and in those few words, the sun had set, blue dusk had risen. Hutch felt a powerful need to leave; to say a plain "Sorry," then turn and go.

But Ann made another set of signs, both hands.

He recalled she'd learned sign language as a girl—Girl Scouts or school. "Are you really spelling words?"

"Yes." She made the phrase again.

"Still lost," he said.

So she came on toward him, a finger to her lips. One step away she stopped and said, "The young lady said, 'Leave me something to remember.' You got anything you could spare to leave her?"

Hutch smiled. "Tell her yes."

She led on past him through the darkened hall.

He followed. She shared his trust in touch, the body's hunt for ease and honor.

In a speechless half-hour, they each found both—the ease that follows successful grounding of a long day's chagrin, the mutual honor two satisfied bodies award one another for candor and nerve. Then Hutch fell asleep in the dark beside Ann, and her arm on his chest became in three minutes the dream of the tunnel. He'd endured the dream from early childhood, though not for some years. Not a story but a trial—far underground he must dig for his life through a tunnel no bigger than his own clothed body, inching forward only with the strength of his nails which he knew to be bleeding, though he couldn't see.

When he'd spasmed and whimpered more than once, Ann shook him. She knew the dangers of stopping a dream, and she shook too gently.

So he dug on awhile.

Ann let him go but pressed her mouth forward till she brushed his ear; then whispered her menu, "New potatoes, Swiss steak, snap beans—"

Hutch was still.

Ann said "Banana pudding."

Hutch said, "Let me leave you this one green banana for future use." His hand found her fingers and set them on his crotch. It was simple to turn and meet her lips.

She said, "I accept it and will name it for you," though the sense she had in her warming palm was of sleeping birds, blind and bare but close in a nest and shielded by her.

8

THE whole last hour of the long drive home, Rob pushed for speed to make it by dark. But even the light load of Hutch's belongings strained the old engine and defeated the plan. When he saw he couldn't be there much before eight, he concentrated on a second small chance—that Grainger had come out as promised to check, feed Thal, and leave a few lights on (she still dreaded dark). So he made that his aim—the lighted house; the nine-year-old Boston bulldog, fed and gassy. And it drew him on successfully, hardly thinking; only seeing those two modest hopes, both likely. He got to the mail box at ten to eight—just the paper and a bill from the freezer-locker plant—then geared down to climb the half-mile of drive, still rutted from winter. But at the bend, past the last stand of pines, the house was black as the sky behind it. Rob actually stopped in disbelief and tried to recall the last time Grainger failed him—never before. Was he sick or was Eva? Was he in there dead (Grainger was sixty-two, with high blood-pressure)? It took main force to start up again and finish the trip.

The flashlight was also dead, from last night. Rob stepped to the ground in thick dark and hurled it far as he could; if it crashed, he never heard it. He felt his way slowly, feet low to the ground, through the yard to the steps. Then he climbed carefully. On the porch he waited in final hope someone was inside—Grainger or a drunk or an angel of death. Not even the scrape of Thal's claws at the door. He called once "Grainger." Then "Thal." Then he whistled. Still as slate.

So he went to the door. The knob turned freely; warmer air rushed to meet him but nothing else. He could hear Thal though, her disastrous lopped-snout struggle to breathe now quickened by fright. He knew she was sitting in her gunshell box at the back of the hall, shuddering hard; but he didn't try the light. He stood on the sill and said, "Thal, please explain why it's dark like this."

Thal snorted and sneezed but held in place.

"Are you starving?" Rob was hoping she knew him by now (she wouldn't have barked at a stranger with an axe unless he struck Hutch).

But she stayed and her shivers had the rabies tag jingling at her neck like a midget dancer—terrified or glad?

Rob took a step in and reached to his left for the light switch. Nothing. He flipped it three times, then felt his way to the low hall-table and found the lamp. Nothing. He said, "Miss Thalia, have you eaten the wires?"

She was suddenly still.

He found the table drawer where he kept his only matches safe from mice, then cupped his groin against bumps and groped with the free hand for the oil lamp waiting on his bedroom mantel. He hoped there was oil. His hand found the pistol—his Grandfather Kendal's loaded revolver now fired just six times a year, on Christmas day, to prove it worked. It had never failed but had never been needed, not in Rob's recollection. Now he read it like a blind man, from the scored wood butt to the cooler barrel, tamping the open bore—too small for a finger to probe, though he tried it calmly. Then he found the lamp and only then struck a match— yes, half-full. He lit it. Quick white flame, the hot smell of coal oil, yellow light as loving as any one hand that had ever touched him. He faced the door. "Thal, we're safe now. Light."

Silence still.

"*Light,* old lady. Come here and see." He even slapped his thigh.
Nothing. Was she gone?

He took the lamp and, cradling the chimney, entered the hall again and took enough slow steps to let the glow reach her.

At its touch she snorted, stood up fully, and did the little horizontal welcome-home shimmy with her wide spayed rear.

Rob wanted her to meet him. "Step *here,*" he said and whistled through his teeth.

Gradually she came, still a-dance but looking down, no longer afraid but not yet clear of the doze and dream of two days alone.

When she got up near him, he squatted and set down the lamp and scratched her throat—vigorous digs. "Has Grainger been here?"

She loved it, threw her head back as if plunged into some serious bliss more welcome than rest, and peed a small puddle in token of thanks.

"I see you're not perishing for water at least." He stood and went to the screen to let her out. As he passed the table, he could now see enough to notice a white sheet of paper he'd missed, propped against the phone. Thal took her time debating the wisdom of going, then went; and Rob brought the lamp back to read the note.

Rob, I was out here at 5 o'clock. Fed Thal and left you and her some lights on. Miss Eva expecting you for dinner tomorrow at 12:30. Then I'll come out with you and unload Hutch's stuff. Hope he was well and you gave him a kick in the tail from

Grainger

He needs it.

Rob lifted the receiver of the phone; it hummed. So he found the number and called the power company. A young woman answered, a girl's voice really. He told her he had got home to find his lights out.

"All over?"

"Yes ma'm."

"You checked your fuses?"

"No but it's failed on at least two circuits, and I don't want to play with a house old as this."

"How old?" she said.

"A hundred-ten years and dry as east Egypt." Then he laughed. "What the hell has that got to do with anything?"

She said, "Let it burn. And you take pictures—make lovely Christmas cards."

Rob laughed again. "Have I got the power company?"

"No the firebug-ward at the State Hospital."

"Who are you?"

"Matilda Blackley."

"When are visiting hours?"

"Every Sunday all day. I wear pink and wait." Then she laughed at last. "*I'm* sorry," she said. "It's been a hard evening and you sounded nice. No, power is off all out your way. Lightning hit a substation."

"Has there been a storm?"

"Lord, where have you been? Thought the world was *over*."

"—In Virginia," he said. "Just now drove in. It doesn't even seem to have rained out here."

"You out near Essex?"

"Yes."

"No wonder," she said. "You all are deprived in general out there."

"Would you like to help?" In the pause that followed, Rob gave no thought to whether he'd angered her; he spent some seconds realizing that he was actually killing himself—this racing tumor—out of pure need for help: the help of close company, lacking ten years. He was building a little partner in his chest, which would stop when he did.

The girl said, "Shoot, I'm worse off than you. You know what a girl makes, starting down here on the weekend switchboard?"

She'd chosen not to freeze; Rob felt thankful but afraid he'd lost her now. Not that he thought any meeting was likely, only that her bright voice had propped him when he'd had no hope of a prop.

"You got you a lantern?"

"A kerosene lamp as old as the house; but it works, yes ma'm. Nice gentle light. Worst mistake ever made, bulb-light on human faces."

"You're older than you sound. You must date back." There was still the tug of interest in her voice, beyond politeness.

"Old enough to have sense," he said.

"Then tell me something true to see me through the night. I've got four calls blinking at me right now."

Rob didn't need to think but gave it to her truly the moment she asked. "You've helped one deprived soul out near Essex."

"No charge," she said. "I'm glad to have talked to a courteous voice."

"My name is Rob."

"Thank you, Mr. Mayfield. I was Tilda King. I knew you at school— never took your class but watched you from a distance. You'll have light soon." She winked out quick as a fallen star.

By then Thal had drained and was back at the screen door, yipping for entry.

The lights stayed out while he ate a cold supper of cheese and white bread. He tried to read the paper; but kind as it was, the oil light strained his eyes before he got far. He read a last sentence on the lower front page—"Mistaken for a turkey, Roscoe Bobbitt was shot in the face Tuesday evening at his home"—then thought he might phone his mother to confirm he'd see her tomorrow. She didn't need a call; she knew he'd be there. For all the nearly seventy years of reasons life had offered her for doubting a future, she went on trusting that her plans would unfold—and if not, she'd survive. Or Hutch—he doubted he could bear to hear Hutch this soon again (when Hutch had said he'd phone from New York Sunday, Rob had said, "We've made a nice personal goodbye. Let's don't string it out down the seaboard on wires"); he was anyhow with Ann now, hardly waiting for his father. Or sleep—could he sleep? He sat at the kitchen table and wondered—testing his body for sufficient exhaustion; its agreement to acquiesce in a few hours, prone and not dreaming.

It did seem weary but it made him no promise. What else was there though?—to go out with Thal and walk them both senseless in an evening still warm and close as a loft, to drive in to Fontaine and see his mother early or chance finding Grainger awake at his radio; or step ten feet to the pantry and take the pint of bourbon he kept there, sealed, as test and proof of his vow not to drink; then drink himself out. He weighed each of them; wanted no single one more than sleep, if that would come.

He wanted his son here with him to the end. He wanted his wife, dead twenty-five years. He wanted Min Tharrington, who'd wanted him for years; then had left him when he chose to rear his son here. He wanted not to die—well-behaved so long, still young as men went in his dogged family, still lonely as he'd been from the day he was born (excepting odd stretches which, counted end to end, might make a few weeks from a life of—what? —two thousand-six hundred weeks). He bedded Thal down in her box, let her lick the last salt from his thumb; then fumbled toward his own room, stripped, slept at once—no substantial dream, only moments of gratitude in which he tasted the grainy brown blankness of the rest and managed to think *If where I'm headed is the least like this, I can gladly go.*

Hours later—2:40 by the clock—he was waked by Thal at the edge of his bed. She couldn't reach high enough to see him fully; but she hadn't jumped or barked, only propped on the side rail and watched till he turned. They were scalded in light. The naked bulb suspended over Rob was burning. He sat up. "You scared?"

She wasn't; she'd only been waked herself and had come to show him. Ears back, grinning with the excess joy which seized her several times a day and would long since have worn a human flat-down, she strained to kiss him.

He rolled near to let her, not touching with his hands but repeating her whole name—"Thalia" (Hutch had named her as a puppy for the muse

of comedy, in honor of the ease with which simple pleasures exalted her).
When she'd had her fill, he said, "Hours till day. Please turn out the
lights and go back to bed."

She considered it.

Then Rob hauled himself from the damp sheets and stepped to the
hall. Grainger at least had kept his promise—there was light from the
kitchen, the front bedroom, the porch, the hall. It was not till he moved
toward the porch and caught himself in a mirror that he saw his dick
wagging solid before him, half-gorged with the sham immunities of sleep.
He stopped and turned full-face to the glass. He could hardly remember
using it before (mirrors were quick resorts for shaving; this big one hung
here because, when his mother was furnishing the house, she said, "Any
man teaching schoolchildren needs to check at least his buttons as he runs
out the door"). Despite the lights and the unshaded windows by the door,
he took himself in hand and stroked till he crested hard again above his
curly navel—the bare head as eager as ever and sleek with the same purple
blood, same hope. The belly and chest it pointed to were still lean and
white, the nipples high and flat. Thal had gone to her box, but he spoke
to her now. "I'm grateful to you, Thal—never say I'm not—but keep this
in mind when you outlast me: it was some kind of shame and disgrace to
life that Rob Mayfield was left here with you. He refuses the blame."

She didn't look up.

He took the phone again, dialed the operator, and placed a call to
Min Tharrington in Raleigh. They hadn't met since Christmas, hadn't
spoken since he called to thank her for a birthday card in March; but late
as it was, he had no question of his right to wake her. Four rings—she
was gone, never took more than two (she lived in three rooms). In an
instant he felt what he hadn't felt till now—*I will not bear this.*

But she answered, her voice drugged with something—surely sleep.

"I woke you up."

"No you didn't."

"You're lying." He was already smiling—some chance of reprieve, his
old delight in her lifelong refusal to admit anybody had ever caught her
sleeping when mostly after ten she would answer like a mummy or a
child waked to pee.

"I was stretched out reading"; she paused as though gone. "Even if I
wasn't you could say you were sorry."

"But I'm not," Rob said.

"That's nothing new."

By then she was clearing; he could hear little puffs as she propped up
in bed. "There is something new," he said.

"Can I stand to hear it?"

"You'll have to judge that. Will you be there Sunday?"

"I'll be here, Rob, till they wheel me out."

"Sunday then about four o'clock?"

"Is that the new thing?—you paying me a visit?"

He knew that it was. He didn't want to tell her anything, only see her, touch her if she'd let him after so long. "Yes," he said.

"Come at five. I might even fix us a meal."

"Too hot," Rob said.

"Might change by then."

There was nothing else to say—not now, this late—but the sweetness of having one familiar voice answer when he spoke (even sixty miles off) was almost sufficient to rescue this day, the day that had passed. "Will it be just you?" he said.

"What's that meant to mean?"

"On Sunday. Will there be anybody there with us?"

"Just the ferns." Min laughed. "You remember the ferns; they've multiplied. Glad something here has."

"Only checking," Rob said. "Now go back to sleep. See you Sunday at five."

"No, wait," she said quickly; then stopped a moment. "Let me say just this—I'm here alone now, I will be Sunday and every day after. We chose that, remember?"

"I remember *you* chose it."

"Rob, it's too late to fight. You know what I mean."

He nodded.

"*You* sleep." She hung up then.

Even dropped that suddenly, he still felt reprieved. He stood with the dead receiver at his chest as if to broadcast a set of heartbeats to whoever might listen—strong, a little fast. Then he said again "Sunday," louder than before.

Thal looked up, jingling. She took his rising inflection to be some sort of invitation; and game as ever, she jumped to the floor, shook once, sneezed, watched him—more closely than anything else had watched him except his young wife and Min as a girl.

He said, "I'm sorry. False alarm—for you anyhow, old lady. Back to bed."

She held her place and shook again, happy.

"You feel like a ride to Raleigh on Sunday?"

She felt like anything but pain or fright.

"You'd wait in the car though—you understand that? Couldn't have you, at your age, witnessing what I hope to witness. Might finish you off."

She was losing interest; she turned to gnaw a flea.

Rob smiled. "May very well finish *me* off, finish all involved." He doused all the lights and slept again easily.

9

THAT morning—Friday—Hutch breakfasted with Ann, drove her to work;
then headed south on the turnpike for Petersburg, twenty-five miles in
full hot sun. By quarter to ten he had found the building, a 1920s brick
apartment-house with limestone Chinese lions at the entrance and dragon
rainspouts. He'd never been here before but climbed to the third floor and
found with no trouble the bell labeled *Matthews*. He heard its dim ring
and the quick response—sharp steps forward from several rooms back—
and felt the delight of hope.

She had felt the same and opened smiling—Alice Matthews, his
mother's friend. She studied him a moment; then said, "Dear God, when
have I seen you?"

He said, "Labor Day, almost nine months."

"You're grown," Alice said. With both long hands she stroked her
own cheekbones, to show him the site of the change in himself. "What
happened?"

Hutch laughed. "Is it that bad?"

She waited. "Oh no. It's fine; you're gorgeous. I was just surprised."

"You're always surprised."

"So I am," Alice said. "It keeps me young." She stood back finally to
beckon him in. "You haven't seen this."

He hadn't. She had moved in January (her father having died at
ninety-three and left her well-off, she'd quit her teaching after thirty years
and improved her quarters). The first room was long and light with high
arched ceilings, rough rabbit-gray walls on which squads of pictures hung;
the old davenport and chairs were freshly covered in umber velvet and
stood on a deep wine-colored rug. The lean new grandeur was startling
after years of the crowded teacher's-rooms she'd camped in—wardrobes
and hotplates.

Alice said, "You hate it. You think it's wrong."

Hutch went to the sofa and sat by the table, which bore only one
book—*Etchings of Rembrandt*. Then he said "No it's right" and knew
he was honest. She'd earned the space surely as if it had waited here, a
visible goal through all the years but sealed till now.

She smiled. "It is. I hoped you'd see it. Everybody else of course
thinks I'm flat crazy—'You'll die if you quit; you've been teaching too long.'
I'll say I have. In thirty-odd years of public-school art, I taught some
sweet children—a few of them beauties so stunning you longed to freeze
them on the spot in their one perfect day—but I never taught a single
one that wanted what I knew, the little I knew, and thanked me for it."

Hutch said, "Not so. I've been thanking you steadily since I was fourteen."

Alice nodded. "You have. You shame me, fairly. But I never taught you."

"Just everything I know."

"What's that?" Alice said. She still hadn't sat but stood before him, straight and attentive as though this were more than a courtesy call—some final chance to break through screens and see truth plain. The money and ease had not cooled her fervor.

"The thing I know now is, I'd like a cup of coffee."

She balked a moment, loath to stop in her search. Then she grinned. "It's ready. Sit still and I'll bring it."

He sat, to give her a pause for calm, and looked round the walls—mostly familiar. At his left a few old reproductions—Giorgione's cave "Nativity," Henner's "Fabiola," a big Gainsborough girl's head, the Kritios boy. On the broad wall opposite, landscape drawings and watercolors by Alice and her friends—among them, his own laborious copy of a mountain and trees in the country near Goshen, done the day he'd met Alice eleven years ago. At his right something new—eight portrait photographs, men and women, different ages, some smiling, some sober (he recognized only himself and his mother). He walked toward those. The older man and woman would be her parents; they showed bits of her. But the other three—two men and a woman, all young, in their twenties. Kin or friends? He knew Alice had one long-lost brother, but neither of these boys was like her at all. The younger in fact was younger than he'd first thought, seventeen maybe. The girl was fine, her shoulder to the camera with the sideways glance so popular thirty years before and so likely to show any face at its best—the line from forehead to chin that mimicked the line of a straight back and good high buttocks. He straightened her frame.

Alice entered with a tray. "Do they break your heart?"

"Ma'm?"

"They still break mine. That's why they're in here." She set down the coffee and stood beside him. "I carried them round in a folder for years, thinking someday I'd have space to hang them. So when all this space opened wondrously, I framed them and hung them by my bed back there." She pointed behind her, then studied the pictures a moment. "Couldn't *take* it." She sat to pour coffee.

Hutch joined her. "Take what?"

She shook her head, looking down, as though she wouldn't speak. But when she gave him his cup, she said, "—The fact that they're gone."

"Not me."

"Sure you are."

"I'll be back."

"No you won't, not for me. You left me when you were fifteen years old."

Hutch smiled. "I really don't see it that way."

And by then she was smiling. "Doesn't matter how you *see* it. I know how it *is*. We spent a good part of two summers together when you were a boy. Then you'd got all I had and were grown and went elsewhere."

"I thought I'd been taking from you right on; I know I have. But I had Rob to see to and my Grandmother Mayfield."

Alice shook her head again.

"Did you want me to stay?"

When she looked up her face was clear and young, taut with deprivation. "I wanted everyone of you to stay and you knew it. I asked you all daily, every day you knew me." She drank a long draft of very hot coffee.

Hutch could see two choices—to stand at once and leave without speaking (what his father might do, half the men in his family) or to deal calm hands and play them out. The first was his preference, but he looked to the pictures again and was held. "Who are they?" he said, "—the ones I don't know."

She waited awhile, then decided to tell him. "My mother and father, then Rachel Hutchins Mayfield, Hutchins Mayfield, Marion Thomas, York Henly, Callie Majors."

"How many are dead?"

"My parents and your mother. The rest are no more than three hours from here, in a well-tuned car—which my car is."

"You know where they are?"

"Sure. They're all three chained-up to glum or dumb mates."

Hutch remembered her speaking of Marion Thomas the morning they'd met—a boy she loved in high school and never told. So he said, "You told me who Marion was a long time ago. Which one is he?"

"On the lower left there."

Hutch saw it was the young one—a foursquare face looking gravely out, clipped straight hair, a celluloid collar, Scotch-plaid tie. "If he never knew, how did you get the picture?"

"From the paper at home. He had won a trip to Washington for selling the *Grit*, and our paper ran his picture. I saw my chance. I wrote in and asked to buy the original, not thinking that it surely belonged to his mother and would be retrieved; and you know they sent it to me—next day, free, not a word of comment. Just as if it was my due." She took another draft. "For once they were right."

Hutch said "York and Callie?"

"Callie's the girl who's not your mother; York is the boy who's neither you nor Marion."

"They were friends?" Hutch said.

Alice laughed. "Oh *enough!*—too much about me. Yes sir, they were friends I worshiped and loved (two different things); but they're no longer active in my present, shall we say? Now tell me what matters. Tell me all your plans."

Hutch said, "I can't remember what I've written you."

Alice laughed again. "Precious little, dear bean. Your letters are as generous as a Christmas box from Hetty Green."

He nodded. "I'm sorry. I'll do better in England."

"That's a promise?"

"Yes ma'm." She had slipped off her shoes and curled in the chair; Hutch could see she meant to hear him out. They'd always had this right over one another—permission to ask any question and be answered. Despite the twenty-six years between them, they'd never lied or bent or held back. He suddenly knew he'd tell her now—anything; she must only ask.

She started. "So it's Oxford?"

He nodded. "Has to be. When we sold that timber of Mother's last fall, I thought I could take my part of the money and buy at least a year in Europe—to roam round; then settle maybe, start my work finally."

"Writing?"

"Whatever. I'm still scared to say. In any case the Draft Board said No to that. With a teacher's deferment they can't let me off—there's a risk I might enjoy it—but they said if I planned to do further study (a little guaranteed pain), they'd back me to the moon. So I sent a few letters and found to my surprise that any American smart enough to tie his shoes and willing to pay can get into Oxford or Cambridge in a minute. And in fact they're cheap, cost a lot less than here."

"So you'll study what?"

"As little as possible; I'm not sure yet. Their letters are sublimely uninformative—little handwritten notes: *Dear Mayfield, You'll be assigned rooms in college. No need to seek digs.* I like the *Mayfield*; makes me feel I'm a soldier in the desert campaign with Rommel bearing down."

"Is it Magdalen College?"

"No they didn't want me for some secret reason, maybe not rich enough; they're famous snobs. Merton did and it's oldest; and Eliot was there, hiding out from the *First* War, so that's a good omen. Far as I can see, once you get past their looks, all the colleges have the same good and bad points. The good is—they leave you very much to yourself. The bad is—they all have pleistocene plumbing, no heat, and hog food."

"Have you got your long johns?"

"Grandmother bought those the day I was accepted."

Alice nodded. "Fine. I bought you a chain."

Hutch smiled but plainly didn't understand.

"—To chain yourself down."

"Will I need that? Why?"

She shook her head. "I'm sorry. Is your coffee too cold?"

"No, tell me what you meant."

"Just jealous," she said.

"No you aren't. I need to know."

She sat up, extended her feet to the floor, and faced him straight. She looked her age again, not tired but worn from unrewarded waiting. "This is not fair," she said. "I know we've been friends. I know you were glad as a child to find someone who'd read a book or two and could halfway draw and was lonely as you. You've gone past that and I really don't mind—I'm a small-town spinster with appropriate resources; never once thought I was Rosa Bonheur or wanted to be. So you were not mine, and I made very few claims on you through the years. But here now lately, with your mother's face near me, I see I was wrong. Or wrong not to state what I knew all along—you're mine as much as Rob's, more than anyone else's. I'll tell you how. I loved your mother before you were born. When she came to Lynchburg to Father's sanitarium, nineteen years old and out of her mind—wild as a panther, thinking she had a growing child in her womb and had never touched a man—I loved her on sight. I was one year older and had already winnowed through a big hill of evidence that I'd live life out alone as a waterhole in deepest Death Valley. Poor Marion there was my main indication—barely knowing I existed, he showed me I was cursed to choose every time, from any room I entered, the person who possessed two distinguishing traits: some odd startling beauty which many would miss *and* the utter inability to love Alice Matthews. I sound self-pitying. I'm not. I'm honest. And I know I'm a fool, a fool the size of the Gobi Desert—I've tried to change; they've tried to bleach Negroes —but here was your mother, grand as a spring storm, and she loved me back. For more than a month in the spring of 1925, when she was nearly well, she loved only me. Or clung to me; I called it love—still do, since the ways she found to cling to me (whole nights) were the final ways we ever love." Alice stopped and waited a moment, still facing him. "You still want to know?"

"Yes."

"I'm not upsetting you? You don't think I'm crazy?"

"No."

She said, "I'm not lying anyway. Count on that."

"I do," Hutch said. "I have for years."

She nodded. "Fine. You're what we made." She stopped again, then thought she had finished and stood to take the cups.

He touched her arm, bare and cool. "I don't understand."

So she sat on the edge of the chair, looking down, and said, "I didn't know how odd it would sound—worse, *crazy*: a cracked old maid inventing life backward."

"It's the only kind of life there is."

Alice laughed. "O Diogenes, praise to thy wisdom!" Then she looked, saw him shamed in his innocence, was sorry, and laid out the rest of what mattered. "What's hard to say but true is this—I loved your mother before you were born. For some weeks I gave her the care and attention she'd craved and lacked. I was too young to ask her to stay with me, too young to know we would never find better—or half as good. Rob stepped in and asked. In the silence round her, she answered Yes. But through the four years they had together, she still turned to me for all he couldn't give— steady care, I mean (I could watch her, not blinking, for days on end and never be tired); we never touched again except to greet and part, with Rob looking on. Then you were born, which ended her. Half-ended me too. I saw you when I came to her funeral of course; but after that, not till we met again in Goshen. You were what?—fourteen. Within six hours I knew you were mine—the thing that was left of your mother and me, mine at least as much as Rob Mayfield's, *made* out of me sure as mountains are made out of hot blind rock." She waited, then held out her hands as if for shackles. "Lead me to the madhouse." She laughed again.

Hutch closed her wrists in his own dry fingers, then kissed her forehead.

"Don't fail us," she said.

"What would failing be?"

"Not honoring us, the courage we had—your mother and I as girls, dumb girls—to take what food the world provided and make life from it."

"I won't," Hutch said, knowing he meant it and grateful for the order but warned by the heat of her solitude, the speed and spin of her self-intoxication. He'd come here the way he came as a boy, to tell one sane unshockable soul his clattering secrets of need and fear and fevered hope. She'd asked him nothing more serious than where he'd sleep for the next twelve months. Well, he'd answered that—on a no doubt narrow cot in south-central England. He could head toward that now, clean, unencumbered, also callow and cruel.

10

Rob's mother said *"Summer"* as she opened for him; as usual she was right. Here two-thirds through spring was a broad summer day; and though the yard oaks were already full-leaved and shaded the porch, enough of the dry light reached down to show her unchanged in her ease—Eva Mayfield, born Kendal in this same house sixty-eight years ago, gone from here only the twelve months it took her to marry, bear Rob, and learn that her own life required this place and service to her father long as he lived (with young Rob a watcher at the rim of the work). In all that mattered—the line, eyes, smile—she was still the girl he had first known and needed. Only the brown hair was pure white; the skin slightly thinner, more porous to sun.

"Yes beautiful," he said.

She waved him in and reached up to kiss him in the notch of his jaw. "You're twenty minutes late. Sylvie may want to kill you."

Rob said, "About time—no I'm sorry. Had to stop by the superintendent's office." (He'd stopped by to say that, barring intervention of a personal nature by the right hand of God, they should not count on Rob Mayfield teaching school again—September or ever.)

"You're done at least." She had already turned and stepped toward the dining room.

He could not help a laugh.

Eva didn't stop but said, "All your paper-work in? Every grade on every dummy?"

"Yes ma'm."

"Then you're all set to help me now."

She meant the list of chores she always gathered through the winter to lay straight on him the day school closed (she feared few things; Rob-at-leisure was one). Yet what he thought as he followed her back was not how high the ironies were stacking but that so far she hadn't mentioned Hutch, the satisfactory object of her gaze for twenty years. And he thought of explanations—she was jealous that Rob had had last sight of Hutch as he wandered off, or Hutch had phoned her last night or today and fed her curiosity; or now Hutch was gone, she was forcing herself to relearn the strokes of a solitary swim in cold water otherwise empty of life. It didn't matter which, maybe some of each. Let her ask for Hutch then if she wanted news. Behind the short tale of Warm Springs, Goshen, the Caverns, the packing, stood Rob's own news—the first real freshness he'd brought her in years, since he claimed he'd finished drinking. It was only a question—would she see him through? He wanted to know today, no later (Monday Hutch would be past recall). He wanted to stop in his tracks in the hall and say, "Mother, help *me*. I strongly suspect I can finally show you a need even you won't wave off, smiling." But he went on, begged pardon of Sylvie in the kitchen, then sat to let them gorge him again.

11

AND afterward, cooling on the porch by Eva, he'd still found no way to start and tell it. Never having mentioned the early signs or his visits to the doctor, whatever he said now must be total news—nothing gentler than "Watch me. One more man is leaving," though it hadn't escaped him that the shock might also be a kind of gift, another stripping-off from her life that had sought simplicity avidly as ships' hulls or wings. Leaving only Hutch—and he nearly launched, wherever he landed. So against his vow, he started with Hutch. "Don't forget to tell Grainger to come before dark. Got to unload the truck before another rain, and I don't feel up to doing it alone."

Eva nodded. "He promised he'd be back by three. I can't fathom why he's starting rabbits again" (he'd gone thirty miles in her car to buy a pair of rabbits).

Rob said "Hutch has left him."

She studied his face, the first time today, but could see no wish to harm in his eyes. Then she looked to the street, now softening in glare. "Hutch left every one of us three years ago. Grainger knew it good as me."

Rob smiled. "Many thanks for keeping it from me. I guess I thought he was mine till now, till yesterday anyhow at 2:15."

Still facing out she said, "He has been. I'm sorry. You were what he hung onto, harder than he knew. He set down the rest of us gentle as birds; he's holding you still."

Rob saw it was the only defeat she'd conceded in a life of wins, only one he'd witnessed. He knew what it cost her; and though he doubted her accuracy (he'd ceased understanding Hutch a long way back), he also saw his chance and took it. "Now he'll have to let go, even me."

"He won't. You made him."

"I did. I remember—upstairs in this house. But Mother, his wishes in this don't count."

Eva searched him again and found nothing new. "He'll be back; you watch."

"*You* watch." He half-smiled.

"Then you had a falling-out?"

"No." Rob was stopped by a bubble of laughter. "You could say that."

"You say it. You're the cryptic clown today."

"Yes ma'm. I'm the one; I'm the fall-out, Mother."

"Have you taken a drink?"

"Would to God I had. I'm dying instead."

"*All* are, darling."

"Look, please ma'm."

She looked. There was something new, just now—a fullness that pressed on his face from within, excess power. She thought it was early sorrow for Hutch; it left him anyway younger than she'd seen him since Rachel's death, an odd rebirth in the impeded light. So she smiled. "Look fine."

"Thank you," Rob said, "but it's not the case."

Eva said, "Let's end the little mystery-hour. What's happened please?"

"I'm pretty bad off." With flat palms he struck both knees twice silently and breathed out hard. With the breath went a sizable quantity of pleasure, to be giving her at last the bedrock demand. His face dulled and shrank.

She saw it and believed him. "What can I do to help?"—the simplest offer she'd ever made.

He couldn't say it straight but said it to the nearest tree, the maple that still showed rusty nailheads by which his Aunt Rena had measured his growth every birthday for twenty years. "I'm very much afraid that by fall I'll have to ask you to tend to me."

Eva nodded. "I can start today. Say the word."

"The word is my lungs. I've got extensive tumors, nothing left but to wait."

"Dr. Simkin says so?"

"—And the best men at Duke; he sent them the X rays. It's in my spit."

"Do they want to operate?"

"No ma'm, it's scattered—little shadows all over." He scrubbed his upper chest and then looked toward her.

"Get Grainger to move you in here today."

"Thank you, not yet—six to nine months, they say. Let me do a few things."

"You didn't tell Hutch?"

"I wanted to but No."

"That was right," Eva said. "Tell him when it's time."

Rob could smile again. "When will that be, Mother?"

"I'll tell you," she said.

Rob nodded.

Eva stood.

12

THE fan belt had broken in Delaware, so they got to New York on Saturday evening too late to use their tickets to *Bus Stop* (twelve dollars wasted); but their rooms at the Taft were ready, side by side. Neither of them had much experience driving north of Washington, and they both were flat and glazed by heat and the hours of rudeness that stretched like yellow unbreathable fog north from the Susquehanna. They washed and agreed on separate naps; then supper, a walk, a late movie maybe.

Hutch had slept an hour when he woke in the close dark—a noise at his door. Someone repeatedly turned the locked doorknob and rattled the frame. He was naked but sat up and called out "Ann?"

No answer; then the door was still.

Could he have dreamt it? He found a wet towel in the blackness, draped it round him, walked to the door, and said again "Ann?" Nothing. So he opened it. Nothing. He leaned out. No one in sight on the long dim hall. A dream then or possibly the house detective (from previous trips he remembered them checking on trusting out-of-towners who left rooms open to the whole five boroughs). He shut it quietly and, awake by now, could see red light straining through the thin curtains. He went to the window and looked down the twelve floors to Seventh Avenue, surprisingly empty. Its emptiness always surprised and pleased him—pockets of vacancy every few yards through the crammed blistered city. The first time he'd come here alone, four years ago, he'd walked everywhere and especially late at night with a growing exultation as he saw what was new and vital for a child reared in family webs—that you truly could live among human people but not live with them; that endless swarms of unthinkable variety would pour from the ground and grant you license to study them forever, provided you never addressed or touched them. He wanted to dress and go straight down and walk till morning, but he went to the phone and asked for Ann's room. In a moment through the wall, he could hear the bell. Again and again.

The operator came on—a chromium voice—and said "No reply."

He said, "Please try again, 1232; must have got the wrong room," though he knew they hadn't—in the bathroom maybe.

After nine more rings the operator said, "Your party's out, sir."

He said "No she's not"; but he hung up, chilled. Who was leaving who? Not lighting the room, he found his traveling clothes and dressed quickly, stepped to Ann's door, knocked, and called her name. No reply. Again. He tried the knob—locked.

Far down the hall a man in his undershirt looked out and went on looking.

Hutch returned to his room, sat on his bed, turned on the reading lamp—his mouth foul with bafflement about to be fear—and said to himself as plainly as at school, "Something has started which you can't stop, and you are the cause." Then he took hold and tried to consider chances. She had waked up, tried to rouse him at the door, then gone down for coffee. She had left for home (why?—he'd refused to let her wear his ring and register for one room as man and wife). She was still in the room, angry or dead. Having laid those out—pieces on his board—he gained the genuine competence of dread. He knocked once more and said "Ann, I'm worried." Then he phoned the operator and gambled on candor—he was worried; could she help?

"Certainly," she said, her voice still hard. "Hang up and I'll call you back in five minutes."

He propped himself on the wooden headboard, shut his eyes, and tried not to think. But in twenty seconds he'd gone again through the list of chances, deepening the dangers. So he tried to seize control by asking, "Suppose each has happened—then so what?" If she'd gone downstairs a page would find her. If she'd gone outside she'd be back soon. Independent as she was, she didn't court trouble; not from strangers at least. If she had died (strokes ran in her family but not this young), then the trip was off for another month maybe; an elegant stickhouse of plans would tumble. "*Jesus*," he thought. He meant his own blank monstrosity—his amazement at that—but it made him see that he'd asked no help from anything stronger than a telephone voice. He said his father's prayer and opened a drawer on a Gideon Bible. Then he shut his eyes again, opened the book at random, blindly ran a finger down the page, and stopped—"Therefore night shall be unto you, that ye shall not have a vision; and it shall be dark unto you, that ye shall not divine." Her safety, her life close up by his seemed suddenly the urgent need of the world. For another two minutes, still stretched on the bed, he felt nothing else.

The telephone rang. "Sir, I get no response to a page in the lobby or the coffee shop. Any news up there?" With the last her voice was assuming life.

"Nothing. No."

A long wait passed in which it seemed she had no other hope or had disconnected. Then she said, "I could put you through to Mr. Amsler, the night assistant-manager—"

Hutch said "All right" but as the ring started, he thought how helpless and absurd he'd sound. After two more rings he'd hang up and wait.

"Leonard Amsler speaking."

Hutch paused an instant with the sense that a broad wheel, oiled and poised, was waiting only for the sound of his voice to turn and plunge on a course it had already chosen and yearned toward. He said, "Mr. Amsler, this is Hutchins Mayfield, room 1230. I may have a problem. Miss Ann Gatlin and I checked in here at eight this evening—she's in 1232. We were tired and agreed to nap for an hour, then meet for supper. I've had my nap but I can't contact her. Her phone doesn't answer. I've knocked on her door. We've paged downstairs."

"Then she must have gone out."

"Not without me, no."

Another long wait, then Amsler's voice descended in pitch and volume and slowed—the professional clerk's preparation for trespass. "You seem to be worried. Any reason to think she'd behave untypically?"

Reasons flew up like bats; but Hutch said, "She'd been a little blue, yes."

He'd thrown the right switch, yielded crucial ground. Amsler jerked into gear, a galvanized frog. "I'll come right up and check her room. You're in 1230?"

"Yes, I'll wait for you here."

By then Hutch was more than half-sure they'd find her dead—natural causes, murder, suicide. Once listed, the means of death didn't concern him, only the need to settle the fact and free in his locked throat the years of feeling—tenderness, thanks—he'd stored for this girl. He combed his hair, repaired his quick dressing, stepped into the hall. He didn't knock again but waited at his own door and, working his mind, tried to separate strands of the odor that filled all hotel corridors—talcum, cold cigars, drying rubber goods, wallpaper glue.

The elevator opened; two men stepped out—one in business clothes, the other a bellhop with a brass hoop of keys. When they reached Hutch, Amsler extended a hand—"Len Amsler, Mr. Maitland"—and the bellhop grinned.

"This is standard," Hutch thought. "They do this hourly." So he didn't delay them to hear his right name.

Amsler said, "Let's see what we have in the room. Mike, open the door."

Mike found his passkey, advanced on the lock with a hunched squinting stealth, and labored to turn it. "Sometimes these things take awhile to work"—Irish as cold rain.

Hutch stepped toward the door. "I'd better look first."

Amsler said in his solemn telephone voice, "Mr. Maitland, you may be glad to have witnesses."

Hutch barely allowed himself to understand. What he suddenly felt was the laughter of trust; he trusted in some easy answer to this. And he actually smiled as he nodded to Amsler.

Mike opened the door on hot solid dark.

Amsler leaned in far enough to switch on a light. The room took a left turn; the bed was hidden. All they could see was Ann's open suitcase, her scuffed-off shoes. Amsler stepped back and said to Hutch, "We'll be right behind you."

Hutch tried once more to forestall discovery. He called "Ann Gatlin."

Amsler laid a firm hand against his back.

She was there on the bed, stretched on her stomach in a blue quilted robe, no other cover—feet and calves bare. Her face was averted, hands palm-down at the sides of her head as if in surrender to whatever she'd met or was meeting now.

Hutch stood at the edge, in the hope of seeing breath.

Amsler stood beside him.

Mike, at the end of the bed, reached out and held her foot a moment. "She's warm, O.K."

Too late, Amsler waved to restrain him.

But Ann extended the touched foot farther, paddled it twice.

Mike giggled.

Hutch bent and took her shoulder; rocked it gently, calling her back.

She said, "I'm sorry. I thought I locked my door." Then she craned her neck and looked round, wincing in the raw yellow light. Her face was latticed with the damask of the covers, the muscles slack in the chaos of sleep. She was still too dazed to be puzzled by strangers.

Hutch said "Are you all right?"

She nodded and smiled, then noticed Mike and Amsler.

Hutch said, "We've been trying to rouse you half an hour. Thought maybe you were dead."

She nodded again. "I was." Then she smiled again. "Needed to be."

Hutch saw the men out, explaining she'd never done this before. He was dazed himself, by anger and thanks.

13

THEY ate downstairs—club sandwiches and French fries—then walked out into the warm damp night and laughed their way through a tour of Times Square. Once the scare had receded, Hutch was tired again; but Ann was ready to look till dawn (they'd agreed a movie was a waste of time). So he trudged on with her through open-fronted jazz bars, Ripley's *Believe It Or Not!* Museum, pinball arcades, bookshops, junk shops. Finally she insisted on paying three dollars to have Hutch photographed alone at a baize table playing out a hand of poker, chips stacked before him. In the finished print, ten minutes later, he was shown at play with three solid partners, all wearing his face at appropriate angles—accomplished with mirrors and surprisingly good. They laughed and he ordered a second print to mail to Rob, but he knew something crucial had been stumbled on, and he knew Ann knew. He also knew he could ask her now to head back in. The sight of his four faces bluffing each other had drawn a firm line to the tawdry hour. Ann was suddenly quiet. Hutch was gray with exhaustion and the picture's news—an unlosable game—but also ringing in every cell like summer woods with the need to lay his skin on hers, to risk a partner.

14

ANN welcomed him in, but in her own room—her one condition, that they be in her bed. And once he agreed and came back to join her, they didn't speak again for more than an hour. As they worked through the dark time, Hutch realized the splendor—that they'd built this much in seven years together: the mutual right and total competence to please one another through measurable and surely memorable spaces as empty of words as the pith of a tree. And better than *please*—the mitigation they could press from one another by the simple motions which practice had taught them, practice in the deepest courtesy of all.

When they'd each come to that at separate speeds, Hutch kissed her eyes, lay flat beside her, and slept at once.

As Ann heard his breathing shift to the helpless rate of surrender— his daily change into what she dreamed all their days might be—she rolled to her left side, huddled against him, burrowed her head in the curve of his arm, and laid her right hand flat on his belly.

In the dream Hutch was having—he'd dreamt in a moment—he was still free to move his hand to cover hers.

She accepted that awhile, then questioned her right. *If someone you've spent seven years of your life steadily learning like a hard foreign language—learning to use, serve, honor, protect and three-fourths succeeding—if that someone can one day decide to walk flat away and give no reason, having asked for you every day of those years or at least never told you to haul-ass home, and you can't stop him—don't know another way, have all but forgot everything you knew before him—what right do you have to lie in a hot room high in the black air of New York City, the biggest collection of quitters and leavers ever gathered on one slim spit of land since land began, and bear the dead·weight of your own private quitter's five resting fingers? To hell with* right—*why be* fool *enough?* She drew her hand out, spread it at her lips, and quietly puffed cool air across it. It seemed the first service she'd done herself in weeks, maybe months. Slowly not to wake him, she turned back apart till her body touched him nowhere. She would surely not sleep; she could lie alone though. In another two minutes he felt as far as Burma.

Hutch had waked when she claimed her hand. He'd understood at once and honored the withdrawal. He didn't move or speak. He had hoped to go—and maybe return—without ever trapping the act in words. He'd thought they could both resume, or forget, much easier without the nets of apology, blame, analysis, and hope that he (and all his kin) spun naturally as spider silk. But the evening's skirmish with possible disaster or comic abandonment had shown him he owed her as full an explanation as he knew and could give. He lay there till he knew it. Then he listened for her sounds. Silent as wax—she was surely awake. He said, "May I talk for just two minutes?"

Ann paused long enough to give him doubts. "You can talk till noon, Demosthenes; but I don't guarantee Miss Gatlin will hear more than fifteen words."

"Tired?"

"Amen."

"After that last nap I thought you wouldn't need sleep for weeks."

"Yes, well—stop a moment in your rush toward progress and think how hard Miss Gatlin has *lived* in recent weeks. She should go underground and curl-up till Groundhog Day at least."

"Two minutes—I promise."

She slid still farther away, then propped her head on the pillow but looked only up at the vanished ceiling. "Sure. Deal," she said, though she sounded gentle.

Hutch turned to face her, keeping the distance she'd set between them. He said it to the edge of her profile, where it caught the last of the light pumped toward them from the street. "I'm not leaving now because of any wish to lose you. I'm as grateful to you as to anyone alive, except maybe my father, and you understand that. But I'm twenty-five years old—the way I figure it, more than a third of a normal lifespan— and the trouble for us comes out of that. I've known you for only a part of that time, seven mostly good years. There were long years before you, and several more people; and what you and I've made cannot cancel that. I never meant us to; I never felt cursed or really burdened by, you know, all the layers of Mayfields and Kendals and Hutchins piled on me. What I have felt is full, *crowded* even. I'm the place where a good deal of time comes to bear, and several lives—the only place on earth. You remember in the war they were always telling us not to waste a crumb or an atom of steel. I took them seriously then and still do. My people abandoned so much on my doorstep—or had it snatched from them and set down here. There's no one but me left to use it at all, consume it, convert it, redeem back all my people pawned away—their generous starved hearts." He paused, not feeling he'd lied or bragged but sure that his words built the statue of a fool, sure as Tar built the Baby. So he thought he'd finished. .

Ann seemed to agree. She lay quiet a good while, though still propped and breathing attentively. Then she said, "You've got one whole minute left."

Hutch laughed. "I yield it."

"Then the question-and-answer period can start?"

"Yes ma'm—one minute."

"Thank you, sir. I may need two of my own." She faced toward him slightly but kept her limbs clear. "This plan of redemption—just how will that run?"

He laughed again as he felt himself slam down, wing-shot. "Slow as Christmas, I'll bet, with backfire and smoke. No, you know what I mean —the work I'm planning." He saw her nod.

"You're stopping your own life to sit in a cold room with only your-self and chew on the little you know or have dreamt about a dozen dead people who mostly never saw you, surely never wished you harm— that's as much as I know."

"And it makes us even—it's as much as I know."

"Then I beat you," she said. "I know something else."

"What?"

She faced him finally. "You're crazy."

Hutch laughed. "May very well be. It would be quite appropriate, another family custom."

"I was serious," she said.

"It's crazy to want to be a grown man at work? Ann, grown cattle *work*."

"Making milk"—she nodded—"for calves they've made. Bulls just eat and screw and have temper tantrums."

"In Spain they work."

"To get killed."

"Or free." He could see that her right hand lay extended on the crest of her thigh. It had offered—he well knew—to hold no one but him. He knew that the natural thing on earth would be to reach toward it, accept, take her with him. And the wish to touch her flooded him now, this soon again—but *touch* not *hold*. He'd surrendered the right; only Ann could renew it.

Ann lay very still, transmitting nothing but the single dim line— shoulder, arm, legs (her head was all dark, her feet in the linen).

It seemed again a sensible goal, near and possible but endless in promise. Hutch quivered with want but kept his place and studied what was visible, all it might mean. It was clearly the best chance offered any-one in his family for years to have what, with all his marginal hopes, he had never doubted was the central aim—a well-paired life. But the aim for *whom?* Well, the animal world and, within it, that part of the hu-man race that was not somehow lame or scared. Or *designated* by what-ever hand of God, Fate, The Past to stand on the edge alone and stare inward steadily. Was he designated? For ten years at least he'd sus-pected so; and for all his native buoyancy, his huge but sporadic needs for the time and touch of others, he had more than half hoped so. In his own childhood he'd often felt like the low but well-built cooking fire round which, at distances carefully gauged, the members of his own blood-family wheeled—for the sight and warmth, with occasional startling forays toward him (where he lay alone also). But when his own manhood flared up in him, it consumed his fuel and, though his family had never understood it, changed him to a member in their own ring of prowlers, impelled by hunger. He'd made his own forays, seized his own food— none of which had lasted long, most of which had left him burned. Ann had been the exception. For almost a third of his life—patient, funny, and as nearly inexhaustible as anyone he'd known or heard of ever—she'd volunteered to want him and to want more of him than any other asker. Surely her knowledge was as usual right; he was crazy to go, to risk her absence whenever he returned. And risk it for what?—for clear space and time in which to prove he was either a born outrider capable of calling in useful reports or a driven scout on solitary missions of value to groups huddled nearer the fire or a wheyfaced fool fed on flakes of his own dry skin and nails: an ordinary Mayfield, the latest of hundreds.

Ann sat up and fished for her half of the sheet, pulled it to cover her, then lay back and settled into what was her usual posture for sleep—flat on her back, face rightward; hands laddered on her belly, which was calm now.

In a minute she'd be gone. Hutch slipped from his left hand the ring that had started as his great-grandmother's. He'd had it stretched when he reached his full growth; so he knew it would swallow any finger of Ann's, strong as she was. He closed it in his palm; then laid that fist on Ann's right hand, opened it slowly, and left the ring. It was warm as the air; he doubted she could feel it.

And she didn't move or speak for a while. Then she slid her left hand down to cover her right. "What does this change?" she said.

Hutch knew he didn't know. He had mainly acted to forestall her sleep—feeling that tomorrow would be a new thing, that one night's sleep might build the last courses of a final wall between them. So he said "Nothing really."

"Then it's just a gold string."

"Ma'm?"

"—The string to keep me on till you know your plans."

"I think you know the ring means more to me than that."

"I know it's some heirloom."

They'd talked enough; he wouldn't tell her now. "It has a little history attached to it, yes. But for now what it means is, come to Rome at Christmas." They'd discussed a Christmas meeting when he first planned to leave; last month he'd told her No.

Ann stayed in place, quiet. Then slowly she found the proper finger on his hand and replaced the ring.

Hutch said "What does this change?"

"Nothing really," she said. "It means I am still on a string, my own string. I plan to stay on it till Thanksgiving Day, which gives us six months. If the transatlantic postal system pulls the string hard and steady between now and then, I'll come to Rome at Christmas and hope for you there."

Hutch laughed once. "I *fold*."

They kissed, cool as cousins.

15

SUNDAY morning Sylvie showed up an hour late—eight o'clock. She opened the back screen on Eva, fully dressed, drinking coffee at the table. But before she could comment on the oddness of that, she had to ask the question that had bothered her all night. She stood on the threshold with good sun behind her and said, "Miss Eva, how old am I?"

"The same age as me nearly, twelve days younger."

Sylvie stepped on in and set down the bag of ginger snaps she would eat through the day. Then she turned her back, took off her sun hat (a man's, wide-brimmed), and slipped on the red knitted skullcap that covered her gray hair entirely. Then she ran the cold faucet to clear the pipes—she hated pipe water—and said, "That don't help me one bit."

"You know my age. You fixed my last cake."

"I fixed every cake you had but one—or watched Mama fix it. I've still forgot."

"I'm three score and ten minus two; so are you. Why is that so important?"

Sylvie didn't answer. Now the water was pure, she filled the percolator and plugged it in.

Eva said, "I've had all the coffee I need."

"That instant mess—eat your stomach right out. You ain't the only one; Mr. Grainger got to eat. He ain't eat, is he?"

"Not that I know of. Haven't seen him since he left here for Rob's yesterday."

"The car is back. He'll come pulling soon." She sliced thick bacon and laid it in a cold pan, careful as a nurse. Then she turned to cracking eggs.

Eva said "You didn't answer."

"Must be I didn't want to. I may be making plans."

"What plans?"

"To leave *here*. I ain't sticking round here for this integration, plan to save my skin for a lovely funeral."

"You know something I don't? You heard of any trouble?"

"Ain't saying what I heard. Don't need ears though to know mean white folks making *they* plans."

"Name two white people that were ever mean to you."

"If I gave you the list, I'd ruin this bacon—you want some bacon, don't you?"

"And where would you go that didn't have trash of all shades, with their meanness?"

"New York," Sylvie said.

"Great Jonah! New York is the sink of the earth; they use colored people for *sausage* meat."

"May do," Sylvie said, "but they settled this integration long ago."

"Yes. You know what it means in New York City? It means that, for money, they'll let you sit your poor tired tail by a rich white woman on the bus for six blocks till she gets off at her air-conditioned house, leaving you to ride to Harlem and sleep with rats running cross your body big as dogs in the heat."

Sylvie turned her bacon. "Sound safer than it going to be down here when *cutting* start." She knew she was teasing, and fairly near the quick, but it suited her this morning; Miss Eva understood.

Eva didn't answer though.

And when Sylvie turned she saw what she hadn't seen for twenty-six years, since Eva's father died.

Eva faced the door, the warm sun, her eyes cupping water. It spilled down her cheeks, and she said "Be good to me."

"What's wrong with you?" But Sylvie stood her ground—never go to Eva till Eva called you.

She didn't call. She dried her face and waited and then said, "I've got another dying to manage. I doubt I can do it."

"I don't," Sylvie said. She laid the perfect bacon on a brown bag to drain. When she poured in the eggs, she would ask for the name. But she heard Grainger's door open back in the yard, so she quickly said "Who sick?"

"Rob. Cancer. By Christmas."

Sylvie couldn't turn again. She said "Oh Jesus" for herself, for Rob. Then she said "Grainger know?"

"I doubt it. Rob just told me yesterday—after lunch; you'd left."

Sylvie stirred seven eggs into flecked bacon grease and said "We'll do it." When Grainger stepped in and Eva stood to set his place, Sylvie said, "Radio saying peace coming soon."

Eva said, "Good morning, Grainger. Peace coming where, Sylvie?"

"All over. Any day."

Grainger said "Who said?"

"Some preacher," Sylvie said. "Big smart man, raking in money by the peck. Count on him to be telling it straight."

16

FROM the moment Min met him at the door, Rob had worked at re-
claiming her—his sense of her; whatever within her had held him six or
seven years and had sent her to him since her own girlhood. Was it in
her at all, a radiance, or simply a route his own desolation found and
took? And the same for himself—what had he shown her that made him
a goal? Why had she found the means, after years of waiting, to wait no
longer? Had they been plain fools? Or had they been right, till time canceled whatever signals they'd flown at one another? Were the signals gone
forever? He felt no urgency to answer the questions; only to uncover from
the debris of years enough of the girl he had sometimes wanted, then to
want her again and ask for the chance—just once, tonight, first time in
ten years.

And though she'd disguised her former body in a uniform fifteen
pounds of flesh, she did throw occasional messages of promise that time
had not passed but had drifted like snow round one standing obstacle—
the first Min he'd known. In the dim alcove she used for a kitchen, Rob
had stood three steps back and watched her assemble their supper—
chicken salad, lettuce, crackers, canned snaps barely warmed on her doll-
house stove. When she'd got it on the tray, she'd turned and said, "You
can take this in please and lay it out prettier than it deserves. I thought
a cold feast was called for to damp such raging hearts." Then she'd
laughed for the first time, eyes flaring wide—her perfect feature, now
mostly hooded. And when she'd offered him the second slice of icebox
lime pie and he'd accepted, she'd returned with an equal second for herself—"You're only middle-aged once; never waste an instant's chance
at help. Food's the surest consolation, in a plentiful land." Yet after they'd
finished and had sat back to rest, what Rob still hunted was some trace
Min might want him after so long a gap for more than talk—a slow
Sunday killed.

She talked about work though. In recent years she'd lived as an independent genealogical researcher, mostly at the State Library and Archives
in the interests of mainly northern women in their sixties and seventies
who were either demonstrating to husbands and children that the family's
roots plunged south for water or were rushing to plait some net against
age—made of dates, blank names, wills conveying mules and bedticks.
She sat at the far end of her ruined sofa and said, "I've been working for
a New Jersey lady with a Carolina past or so she hoped; it's turned out
poorly so far, Baptist preachers stretching back toward *Palestine*. But
anyway she's put endless money behind me, so I drove up last week
around Mount Airy to look for graves. I was lost in short order and stopped

for directions on the far edge of town at a low white four-room house with forsythia piled to the eaves. As I got to the porch, a tan dog ran right at me from the bushes, silent as cotton. I stopped of course to let him decide on mangling or welcome. But he never had time; he was still smelling ankles when an odd voice said, 'You come to get him?'—not quite a cleft palate but something badly wrong in the roof of her mouth. A squat woman not much older than me, in a wash dress and sweater, was at the screen, smiling. I thought she meant the dog; and since he still was silent, I wondered whether everything on the place had voice trouble. But I said, 'Oh no I've come for directions. I'm afraid I'm lost.' The woman stamped her foot, drummed hard on the tight screen; and the dog flew off—he'd dug a deep hole beneath a crepe myrtle, so he hid in that and watched me. Then she unhooked the screen and opened it to me and said, 'No ma'm. You're at the *place*.' A wonderful smell—gingerbread, I still think—was pouring out round her, which was why I went in. I was half-scared of her—her eyes were such a light gray they seemed all but white, and her hair was fine as fur—but the fact she was clean and the comforting smell made me go in. When I'd got in the living room and rearranged my eyes—unpainted pine walls, hard chairs, not a picture—I said, 'I'm looking for the homeplace of Stilby Warren or his family graves.' She went on smiling and pointed to the rocker and said, 'I'll find him for you. Just rest.' She'd seen I was tired; and peculiar as it all was, I actually rested—ten minutes maybe. Not a sound from her. I don't think I slept, but I did shut my eyes. I know that for sure because, when I opened them, they'd adjusted even further to the cool dark air; and I saw that the far wall was papered, top to floor, with magazine pictures of children, trimmed neatly and glued without wrinkles. Every size and color—the children, I mean (black as grapes, pink, yellow)—though none were just babies, none too young to walk. Then she reappeared, quick and quiet as the dog. She had put on white anklet socks but was otherwise the same. 'He was almost packed,' she said. 'I just helped him some.' I noticed she was carrying a little tan suitcase, a child's case really with brass stud-nails and a curious lock." Min stopped and looked up; had she carried Rob with her this far?

He said, "You were scared at that point."

She waited to consider. "Funny thing is, no. She was too kind-looking, and I was still hoping her gingerbread was ready and would be my reward."

"For what?"

"Being there, having found her somehow. I'd already figured I was her only company since the war at least."

"What made you think that?" Rob said.

"The bareness, I guess—the age of the pictures: every child but one was dressed in '30s clothes." Min moved to stand.

Rob saw his chance failing. "No, finish," he said.

So she sat back, laughed, and said, "I saw I had to stop her. I told her, 'I'm sorry but you misunderstood. The man I'm hunting died ninety years ago.' I stood but she stepped toward me and opened the valise. Laid in it was a doll—a brown-headed boy—dressed neatly in a handmade blue chambray shirt and black felt overalls with big pearl buttons. He was packed in tight with wads of what looked like baby underclothes and socks, a child's yellow toothbrush."

Rob said "You ran."

"No I didn't."

"—Crazy as her. I'd have been halfway back to Raleigh by then."

Min nodded. "You would have."

He saw he'd offended. *Good*—he had the power still. *Bad*—she'd close against him. She'd started this, laughing, but she'd struck something more as she dug through the story in his presence and for him. He must take the small gift or be ready to leave. He said, "Any signs of a man on the place?"

She said "I wasn't looking." But she thought it through. "No I don't think there were. Signs of nobody really but I told you that."

"Were you dreaming?"

Min laughed. "Oh no I touched the boy. She raised up his hand."

"Was the lady a dummy?"

"A moron, you mean?"

"They keep dolls sometimes when they've got nothing else. I've seen morons sixty years old with dolls."

Min smiled. "Well, this one was just my age. No she looked all right. She was giving it to me."

"Why?"

"I didn't ask."

"Can I see him?" Rob said.

"If you want to drive to Mount Airy, sure. You don't think I took it?"

"Might have been the right thing—polite anyhow: don't refuse a kind giver."

She said, "I didn't. I held the open case and asked his name. She said she hadn't named him, so I named him then and asked her to go on keeping him for me till I had a real place of my own to take him. She had to think a minute but finally agreed. The last thing she said was, 'He'll wait happy here.' I said I didn't doubt it and then I left. The dog made another mute run at my heels, but I got out intact. She was standing at the door still waving, last I looked."

Rob said "What's the name?"

"Sir?"

"—The name you gave him."

She smiled. "That's the secret. I have to save something."

He made a little ring with his thumb and middle finger to signal O.K., then he saw her through the ring and brought it to his eye as if it were a lens. She was looking down, yawning; and though her smile survived, Rob saw for the first time how much worse her luck was than his. In a good many things, they were fairly even—the central people they'd loved had vanished; their daily work had mostly been *jobs*, little handfuls of money their only reward. But Rob saw himself as continuing. Despite Hutch's leaving now in grinning indifference, he was leaving alive with whole tracts of Rob's face copied in his. For all the big differences which Rob hardly fathomed, he knew he'd made one thing that had its own chances—and made it on a girl he'd finally loved. Min was stopped; she ended here, in her own four walls, her thickened body. Kind as she'd been at her best— and even now—nothing would survive her but a mixed crate of knickknacks, the muffled gratitudes of a few aging schoolchildren and her old-lady clients. He was partly responsible, he'd always known—unable as a boy to bear her worship, unable after Rachel's death to pardon himself long enough to marry Min, then bound to Hutch so closely as to ease and grad- ually cancel the separate will of a ravenous body which had sent him to her. By then—thankful, pitiful, hoping to bless—he wanted her again. So he made the long reach, through air that seemed numb, to take her right hand.

Her hand was palm-down on the cushion beside her. She turned it to accept him, wove her fingers with his. But she didn't face him. Being tired and calm, she laid her head back and shut her eyes.

"Name it Rob," he said. "—A dressed-up baby still waiting in a box."

"For what? *I'm* the waiter."

"You quit," Rob said. "You told me you were tired."

"I was, when I told you. You never checked again."

"Hutch needed me," he said.

"He's gone now surely." She said it so gently as to leave it half a question.

Rob conceded her rightness. "He thinks so, yes."

"How long will he stay?"

"That won't concern me." It was literally true and he'd said it quickly to end this tack. In the few little meetings they'd had since parting eleven years ago, he and Min had silently agreed to ration all reference to Hutch severely. Though Hutch stood between them thoroughly as a mountain, they'd chosen to ignore him—in respect, fear; and maybe on the chance he'd someday vanish, leaving them free again for one another. To ease the warning Rob raised their joined hands and turned them in the light. But they didn't bear looking at, not this late. The lamp was at his shoul- der; he switched it off. Then he sat back and waited for his eyes to open to whatever flow seeped up from the street through Min's gauze curtains. Considerable—in a while she was back there beside him. Were they some kind of tragedy, linked like this but with no time before them? He couldn't feel that. Was it some unforgivable waste, to be punished, that they'd lost ten years they might have spent together? Here just now, he couldn't think that, though he carefully tried. He could only want to reach her entirely again, down all their length (he had asked the doctor if he was dangerous to others—none at all, at last). He began, as always at their best, with her face—exploring it lightly.

When he reached her dry mouth, her lips moved silently once to greet him. Then she said, "Do you think we are starting anything?"

"No ma'm—confirming."

Min nodded. "That's better."

"So it's fine by you?"

She waited. "Not fine exactly but friendly."

Rob laughed and, though they continued then more closely by the moment, Min never felt his few glad tears—never mentioned them at least.

17

WHEN he'd thanked her and told her goodbye (but no more), Rob went down to the street at half-past eleven and found both Grainger and Thalia dozing in the car at the curb. The air was still close, and the windows were down. Thal heard him first and sat up grinning, but he had to speak to Grainger. He leaned in and said in a disguised voice, "Would you be kind enough to tell me the way to the local White Citizens' Council Office?"

Grainger's head stayed back, his eyes stayed closed; but he said, "Step in. I'll drive you to the door. I work for them."

"Doing what?"

"Mailing colored babies back to Africa, fast as they cry. Driving white gentlemen round for little visits to old ladyfriends."

Rob opened the door, slid in, reached to Thal.

Grainger sat up and reached for the starter.

"You tired?" Rob said. "I'll be glad to drive."

Grainger cranked the engine. "No me and Thal are fine. I been to two shows, she snored and pooted for six good hours." Before he drove off he glanced to Rob. "You rejuvenated?"

Rob smiled ahead. "Very nicely, thank you." Then he knew he was thoroughly drained of strength, though he felt no pain or desperation. "But I may need a few minutes' sleep myself."

"Sleep on," Grainger said. "This old man's awake."

He slept to within ten miles of home, another peaceful hour (was the tumor consuming his dreams as well?—when he woke he couldn't think when he'd dreamt last). He looked to Grainger, calm as a post. Thal was buried on the floor in the back, hardly breathing. For a mile he was happy —having left an old friend in perfect understanding; being driven safely toward his own good place by a Negro who was not just his half first cousin but the one wholly trustworthy human he'd known, and for thirty years. Then like an inspiration, he felt in his upper right chest not a pain but a sudden sense of *white*, a knobbed patch of whiteness blank as his nap and the size of a monkey's hand. He lay back and waited; the hand stayed in place, extended, still, nerveless. He could not know it would never close again or stay still long—it was now a declared component of his time—but he felt stunned enough to say, "You made your summer plans?" (Grainger spent a month or six weeks, most summers lately, at the house he owned in Bracey, Virginia).

Grainger nodded. "Yesterday."

"About the first of July?"

Grainger waited a space. "Staying here this summer."

Rob recalled Eva saying he'd gone to buy rabbits two days ago. "I'll watch your rabbits for you."

"Scared Sylvie might kill em."

"She might," Rob said. "I'll watch her too, been watching her forever."

Grainger nodded. "I'm staying."

That came as another assurance, whyever, that the weeks ahead were a crossable distance. Rob said "You got some project?"

"Guess so."

"What is it?"

Grainger faced him finally. "You going to make me tell you?"

Rob laughed once. "Not if it's against your religion."

Grainger said, "I'm moving out to stay with you, long as you stay there."

Rob said "Not long." Then he waited and looked. "You know what I mean?"

Grainger seemed to nod.

"Mother told you?"

"This morning—me and Sylvie, at breakfast."

"What did Sylvie say?"

Grainger said, "She heard it before I came in. By the time I got there, she won't saying nothing."

"What did you say?"

"You're the one love to talk."

Rob laughed (Grainger with him). "You can rest your ears by New Year though."

Grainger said "I can wait." Then he said, "How long you be keeping your strength?"

"To move around?"

"Yes."

"Doctor didn't say. I'm counting on another four or five months at most."

"Let's take us a trip."

Rob said "How far?"

"Our old places, not far—just round Virginia."

"Hutch took me by Goshen."

"I didn't mean there—maybe Bracey, Richmond. Haven't seen Miss Polly in a good while; have you?"

Rob thought and said "Two years, maybe three."

"She still alive, ain't she?"

"Was at Christmas; I heard from her then."

"Me too," Grainger said. "Sent me that dollar bill she sends every year. Me and her live long enough, I'll be a rich man."

Rob said, "She'll live. She may never die. She likes it too much."

Grainger said "Good." Then he said "You disagree?"

Rob didn't know at once. He looked to his right. By their glare he could see they were coming to the turn-off for Stallings Mill Pond, the site of numerous early drunks and of his first serious quarrel with Min when she'd been strong enough to walk off rather than beg him for care (he'd asked her to beg). She'd thought he was taunting; he'd thought he was taunting—but if thirty-four years had shown one thing, they'd shown he was earnest. All he'd ever wanted was care not control, not strength but safety. Little stretches of that had come in his youth from his Aunt Rena, Sylvie, his father, Polly, Grainger. Only Hutch, in the four close years they'd had, built real walls for him. Tomorrow by noon Hutch would have sailed, the gate of the first wall floated away. Rob looked back to see if the pond showed at all in the thin moonlight. No the woods were too dense. So he said "Not really."

Grainger said "Beg your pardon?"

Rob laughed, "I'm not really head over heels in love with the world, if that's what you mean. I never really was. I loved a few people. I wish Hutch was here."

"He'll be back in time."

"How?"

"We'll call him back in time."

Rob said, "Oh no. He's left it to us."

18

Hutch dreamt. In his own room alone at four (that stretch, not quite an hour long, when New York is silent enough for thought), he saw himself enter a sizable building the walls of which were solid glass. He felt it was England, but the indoors was warm; and the man who came down a hall to meet him was certainly Rob, by look and voice. He said a short welcome, though he gave no sign of recognition or special relation. Then he led Hutch forward on inspection of numerous rooms and yards—all empty as robbed graves, flooded with light; no picture on the walls, no place to sit. More and more, as the man named off the rooms, Hutch wondered if he'd somehow changed past knowing; and he hoped for a mirror but no mirror came. Finally as they rounded back to the entrance, Hutch thought he would call the man *Father* when he left. But he wasn't leaving. The man put his hand out, smiled very broadly, and said, "I'd worried that you wouldn't show up. More than one said you wouldn't. But you kept your word. You're here and I'm thankful. It's safe in your hands." When he'd pressed Hutch's right hand warmly and firmly, he walked out the door into light even brighter than the prismatic rooms. Hutch stayed in place and watched him out of sight.

Then on the street below, garbage men sounded Monday—his departure.

He woke and lay still, cool and afraid, for half an hour till natural light first stroked at the curtains. Then he stood, stepped into his underpants, opened the curtains on grimy glass, went back to his bed, and knelt beside it. Facing the window and the straining dawn, he asked for strength to do what he should—this day and later—and he named every person he remembered loving and commended them to care. He mentioned no regrets and asked no pardon. It took him ten minutes. Then he stood again, washed his face and teeth, dressed lightly, and went next door to join Ann. By then there were six hours left till he sailed.

19

May 28, 1955

Dear Hutchins,

I think you said the Queen Mary. *If it's the* Elizabeth *I hope they'll somehow read my addled brain and get this to you on your sailing day— to say "Fare well," also that I'm sorry I talked so much yesterday and listened so little. It's been one of the permanent intentions of my life not to finish as the kind of bore I knew so many of when young—old crocodiles utterly trapped in their leather, satisfied as fed babies, pouring out the sweet songs of Self Self Self or the Dreadful World (I've never liked myself but have treasured the world).*

No, two things were working. One I see so few people that, when one turns up, I forget I'm susceptible, imbibe too fast, am drunk with company in under ten minutes and raving like a parrot on Spanish rum; Two in sight of your eyes, which are your mother's eyes, I suddenly felt I should tell you the last things you didn't know—how I wanted your mother, how nearly you are mine. Hence my curious outburst, not quite uncontrolled as I hope you know.

I listened to you at the right time to listen—that summer you were fourteen and we stayed in Goshen. That was when you knew all you needed to know, with no contradictions—who had loved you, who you thanked, who you missed and needed, what you meant to make in the long time you had. The first day you and I were ever together, standing up to walk back from drawing the mountain, I asked you how you felt about the morning (meaning what we had done, our separate pictures); and you said, "Well, objects seem to have a lot of patience." I recall I laughed. You took no offense and even joined in. Now I see that was what you needed to know and are acting on now.

Go to it, dear bean; look all you can, and the best luck ever. May I add only one small qualification, which you already know?—people are objects surely as hills but they last a bit less and are thus less patient. Be as true to them as you've been to the ground and to various trees—and gentler, Hutch.

Send any reports you care to show. I'll respond or not, as you tell me to. Whatever—I'm here, patient as bread.

Love from
Alice

May 28, 1955

Dear Hutch,

You were sweet to call me up and tell me goodbye. It would have also been good to see your face one more time at least, but I know you were busy as a demon at Judgment. Men in your family have been telling me goodbye for over fifty years so by now I ought to be grateful for the distance—don't you think? We had our good visit at Easter anyway. I went back to the cemetery two weeks later and know you'll be as surprised as I was to know that your azalea was blooming right on at your grandfather's headstone—and your great-grandfather's—in spite of a hard late frost and much wind. They were always warmers though in very different ways as your own father is and I trust you will be.

England is a place I can't picture well. I hope you will have a roof for your head since I read they haven't rebuilt from the war and I hope you like hot tea better than me. If you don't and if they sell any coffee, I am sending five dollars. Buy some on me and when it keeps you up in the late cold night, wing a thought my way. I will no doubt be right here sewing some lace tent for a rich stout lady with a daughter altar-bound but I'll feel the compliment and bless your name. My blessings work.

Blessings on you, son,
Your friend,
Polly Drewry

6:10 AM   MAY 30 1955

AWAKE ALL NIGHT HUNTING RIGHT FIFTY WORDS TO SAY WHAT I THINK. ALL I FIND IS FOURTEEN. SPEND EVERYTHING YOU TAKE. BRING HOME NEW LUGGAGE. YOU WILL ONLY REGRET YOUR ECONOMIES.

LOVE AS LONG AS I LIVE
GRANDMOTHER

June 1, 1955

Dear Rob,

Three days on the water now, and none of it has been quite what I expected—which is good, I guess. Especially since nothing has been bad but the heat, and that only lasted through one long night. The day we left New York was hot—nearly ninety by noon—and this old boat was hot as a locked-up Buick in Texas by the time we backed out and breasted the sea. Since nothing English is air-conditioned, we carried the heat—a pocket of Hell—for eighteen hours. My cabin did at least. Cabin is a serious exaggeration—this one makes Abe Lincoln's look like Pennsylvania Station—and mine it's not; I share it with two men. One is a German Jew who seems to have lived in Buffalo for ten years and learned no English (won't answer me anyhow); he's going back to Frankfurt where he'll be understood. The other—Lew Davis—is a fellow my age who grew up in Wales but has been in Canada traveling with a circus in recent years. He'll be visiting his family "to see if I can stick it for more than two weeks without falling down dead from laughter or tears" and has asked me to join him. I may once I've got my bearings and a car. I think he's a gypsy, but he swears he's not.

He and I walked the deck that first night in search of air (the German stewed downstairs in flannel pajamas). Then by dawn things cooled off, and ever since I've given my famous imitation of the Great Tree Sloth— long bouts of hard sleep and overtime dreaming, interrupted briefly by mammoth British meals. I met a London surgeon in the bar last night and eventually told him I'd been mostly unconscious for seventy-two hours; was anything wrong? He said, "Nothing worse than carbohydrate shock." I laughed but he said, "A very real condition, prevalent on sudden contact with British food. Many prisoners of war, brought home to pure starch, were felled like poplars. Lost two myself." So time may be short; remember me in prayers. In another half-hour I'll be summoned by a gong to eat mushroom tarts, well-done roast beef, Yorkshire pudding, roast potatoes, Brussels sprouts, white bread, boiled pudding, and a toasted cheese savory to finish. Finish! is the word.

Otherwise the threats consist of fellow passengers. I boarded in hope of high-toned couples in evening dress with sunset breeze in their hair as they sauntered the polished timbers, faintly smiling at the herds in steerage. So far all I've seen is twenty-odd Congressional secretaries, traveling together at budget rate and famished as yuccas. They're all thirty-eight, all single at present. They've run through assorted legislators, pages, colonels —or been run through like sieves—and see no objection to trying on a Fledgling Southern Writer (I slipped and told them the first night out; they all read Thomas Wolfe in junior high school and pray I'm his ghost). But I cling to the memory of Little Hubert's wisdom and guard my digits, something T. Wolfe neglected.

Next morning. Read over, that seems too dumb to mail. But I'll mail it to show you how hard I've been huffing and puffing to cheer myself up in this odd high leap I find myself taking. What we didn't discuss last week were the things I am scared of. The main thing is me—that once I've paid for and found this famous stillness around me, filled my fountain pen, and faced the window, then there'll be no work: not a thing I know that'll prove big enough to hold any human eye but mine and no words to say even small things in. With all my need to get space and air, get away from friends and home, I neglected to see how thoroughly all of you screened me from the chance that stares at me now on the east Atlantic in a tacky old hotel that happens to float—I may be a fraud. Last night Lew Davis said "Say me a poem." We were up at the bow—clear sky, many stars. I said him Hopkins' "Starlight Night," a favorite of mine; pretty hard, no doubt. He nodded and said "Good work," maybe thinking the poem was a sample of me. I held back from giving him a speech on Hopkins and said nothing at all. Then he said,

> *"Assuming those stars are holes*
> *Punched through a high tent*
> *Onto some brand of light*
> *That heals most pain,*
> *Assuming I could swim my arms*

Three times and pass through a hole
Into nothing but light—
I'd stand on here."

I asked him who wrote it. He laughed—"Nobody. I said it. Now it's gone" (wrong—I learned it as he went). I'm not standing Lew Davis up by Father Hopkins, but see what I mean? Lew had a thing to say, a little odd but plain. I had this funny performance to give, of another man's dare. And I never told him better, though I will today.

So scared, yes. But hoping.

We're due in Southampton tomorrow afternoon about four o'clock. Assuming I'm not detained as a hoax by H. M. Immigration, I'll take the train to Oxford and be there by bedtime—if I find a bed. I'll look the place over, store my trunk in college, take delivery of my car, and hit the road to wander for the month of June; then back to Merton and down to work.

I'll mail this on landing and write again soon as I've breathed English air. Write me c/o Merton; they'll know my stopping points and will forward news, I trust. The fact that I'm gone doesn't mean I'm gone. Soon please.

Love,
Hutch

June 3, 1955

Dearest Ann,

We passed Land's End—my landfall on England, on anything but home—at sunrise this morning. I was up to see it in surprising clear light with only a handful of old British stalwarts on deck beside me. They drank up the sight with ravenous reserve. It scared me a little, the low brown rocks seeing me as plainly as I saw them and stating their case—Why the hell are you here? I'll postpone my answer a year at least. You'd have had one ready, right?—He's running. Not at all sure you'd have been wrong either.

The coastline has gentled at least since then, the celebrated green hills and occasional chalk. We'll be called to our last vast meal shortly now, then wait off the Isle of Wight for a good tide to lift us in. Once landed and rested I'll write in detail (with two roommates rest has been pretty scarce—not sleep but rest; with two strangers near I don't dream much, and dreams equal rest for me).

I did want to say I dreamt of you once—in a deck chair, chilly, two afternoons back. I went to a party and you were there, happily talking to a ring of other people. I walked straight up and gave a little bow. You flat didn't know me. I thought you were kidding. I told the strange man on your right your name; you looked at me blank as a square of tile and said,

"I'm sorry but I know I've never seen you." I said, "You've hardly seen anybody else for some years now." The stranger took your elbow and said to me "Prove it." So I told you a joke—"A young nun died and arrived at Heaven's gate. St. Peter stopped her there, examined her record, and saw she'd had little time to do good. But he liked her looks, so he set her a test —if she passed she was in. He'd ask her three questions; she must get all three. 'Name the first man.' —'Adam.' —'The first woman?' —'Eve' —'All right, now tell me Eve's first words to Adam.' The little nun broke out in beads of ice. She racked her memory and found not a trace; so she bowed her head and said, 'Oh that's a hard one.' Three hundred gongs sounded, the gates swung open, young angels ran to greet her." The strange man dropped you; your other friends vanished. I burst out laughing and you knew me at once. We were both still laughing when the deck steward came round and offered me tea. If I'd had any place to be alone (better than a two-foot-square saltwater shower), I'd have taken the dream on forward—conscious—and studied again my best memory of you: ten days ago, Richmond, late afternoon light, you astride and posting solemn as a saint toward the last gates of grace, me half-dead with thanks to be the road you traveled and to have my own reward poured through me in my own good time. With any luck at all, I'll have a place tonight—a room and just me—and if I have six kilowatts of strength left, I'll study you.

More after that then. And till then remember the best you've seen; keep it clear till Christmas. And write.

Love,
Hutch

An hour later. If you hate anything in this, please tell me. I count on you to keep me told when I change for the worse—though the way I've felt in recent weeks, I suspect any change will be for the better. Even jackasses get a little dignity with age.

June 3, 1955

My dear Hutch,

I had meant to get a letter off to meet you on your landing, but the old summer slow-down crept up on me, and the days have gone by. I can't even think of three things I have done since leaving you, and neither one of them is worth writing down and shipping cross the second-biggest ocean on the planet Earth. I remember lots of naps and that we have been blessed so far by the weather—not a day above 75, evening showers, and cool nights for catching up on my thinking time. Everybody else is fine and await first news that the Family Hope is safe on his pins and dry and not treading water off the Greenland coast. If you are, keep treading and send word soon. I'll be there somehow or Grainger will at least.

I didn't mean to sound sarcastic just then by mentioning Hope. I was being honest. I was never really much of a hope to anyone but Rena (who hoped I was God) and your mother (the same), so I've felt no jealousy and know what it means. It means three people now alive—Eva, Grainger, me, and maybe some dead—would be grateful if anyone looked back on us (not down) and saw that we'd made anything like a diagram in these fifty years, anything more than harum-scarum tracks in the dirt as a handful of scared souls scuttled for cover. My dictionary tells me a diagram is "a writing in lines." I can't recall seeing an ugly diagram; so that's the hope, Son—that we make some figure. If we do you'd be the one to know (though it may take awhile to know you know).

Why should I think that? No doubt you're the smartest since my father at least or have read the most books. But the real reason's this— somehow you're the one named Kendal-Hutchins-Mayfield that escaped having whatever worm gnawed us. I have spent some time lately guessing what its name was or what it was after as it ate through us all; and I think what it wanted was happiness—from other humans, here and now. Of course it never got it. Oh minutes here and there. I have had in my life a total of maybe forty-five minutes when I rose up to clear air and felt satisfied; the rest was various stages of want. You escaped that, didn't you? Something spared you that. Even as a young child (three or four), you were safe to yourself. I can't recall you crying for anyone or anything but pain, real physical pain. Maybe you hid more from me than I knew; but until that bad last time I was drunk at Polly's and you left me, I sometimes wondered if your nerves were normal or if you were slightly numb. You had good reason. The thing, passed on to you through me and Rachel, may have just been exhausted or somehow fed. Or all of us may have earned a kind of peace in you, earned it for you. I hope so. Please enjoy it. And if all that is crazy, if you've been in torment of your own from the start and were keeping it from me, better not tell me now. I doubt I could handle the news this late!

At least have fun if not happiness. I wish one person had told me that when I was your age or a few years younger (but remember that your father didn't use bottled *fun very admirably). And once you get your car, don't let any Limey corrupt your good habits. You drive to the right whatever they say. Damned fools—no wonder they lost the world.*

Let me hear.

Love,
Rob

June 4, 1955

Dear Mr. Mayfield,

    You said to let you know when I had plans and now I do. My brother and I will be getting to London on July 10th. I should take a week or ten days to be with him. Then he will go to Paris, and I could come to you wherever you say for maybe a week till I join up with him again and head east. He wants to see Germany which—since he is more like Hitler than anybody else I know—is fitting. I'll go to hold him down.

Anything though will be an improvement on Edom, Virginia in June. I have been drunk in a few bat caves. I have done some painting on the house for my father. I have come pretty close to screwing a doctor's wife who shall be nameless—and may report total success when I see you. I have read every book in the house and county. But now I've had it and am hitching down to Wilmington in your trash state to visit Morse Mitchell and snake hunt with him. He has already made more than two hundred dollars catching cottonmouth moccasins to sell for the venom. I'll help him out till time to fly.

Write to me soon at my home address. I may be dead or a triple amputee by then and need someone to open the letter for me. Wouldn't want to miss your news or seeing you in your new better life.

Till I do,
Strawson Stuart

June 6, 1955

Dear Alice,
Your letter got to me in time. It was waiting on my narrow chaste cot in my cabin in the—yes—Queen Mary, and thank you for it. But you didn't need to worry after our visit. You never need to worry, not about anything I may ever feel when I'm with you or later. After all you've given me (and you gave the main pattern), it would take much more than an hour's high spirits—it would take bleeding real wounds to reach the deep veins of thanks that run in me and have run since we met.

—And surely long before, as you've now helped me see. You'll understand, I trust, that I was so full of my trip when I saw you as to be a poor listener or a slow responder. I stored what you said though and thought through it often in the slow days at sea. Nothing in it surprised me *is the first thing to say. I'd known, from Rob and old things you told me, that you'd helped Mother in her really bad time; and since the only kind of help I ever want comes through actual touch, I guess I should have known how you reached her then. And in light of my instant attraction to you, I should also have known the chief way I was yours—not just through shared needs. I want to think about that a good deal more (what, if anything, it means for me to have you as a parent); and I may be asking you some questions later. For now though just thanks and some recent news.*

The voyage wasn't much but food and sleep and dodging old doctors from Cleveland or Nyack and their monologous wives. If the Mary's any omen, the Empire is finished, though may take awhile to die. Still the crew (who were callused and grinningly roguish) gave a fair exhibition in sunset glow of the broad backs that bore the Union Jack round the world.

The first impression of England was of course rain. Owing to some delay in the tide—!—we docked two hours late; and by the time I cleared immigration, it was dark as Egypt. Rain began about an hour from Oxford; so I reached that alarmingly famous station (the size of your apartment— used by Ruskin, Newman, Arnold, Wilde, Dodgson, Hopkins, Verlaine, Housman, Eliot, Graham Greene, Auden, Spender, et al.) in an earnest downpour and was drenched when the taxi abandoned me at Merton in a seersucker suit at 9:15 with trunk and grip. I stumbled through the low black wooden gate and was in a short arcade with a clutch of young men, all furiously talking, none noticing me. An open door on my left so I entered; in a glassed-off space in a dark suit and tie, a plump bald man about fifty was eating what seemed to be salad in thick white dressing on a broad white plate. The sight of raw greens, after five days of Mary's stewed sprouts and cabbage, gave me courage to knock. He was Victor the porter; and though he sized me up as stringently as if I were volunteering atom bombs at bargain rates, he said "Yes you're expected." Then he took a ring of keys straight from Les Misérables, *a huge umbrella from* Robinson Crusoe; *and led me out, saying "Simpson will bring your bags along, sir." We walked thirty yards through a big quad, an arch, another arcade, and were in a small quad—through a door, up a flight of worn wood stairs, to a room maybe twenty by fifteen feet: a big bay window facing the dark, stuffed sofa and chairs, a desk, long table, an oak bookcase. Off that was a cubicle twelve by seven—a swaybacked bed, a wardrobe, a brand-new basin with running hot water. The surprise was, it's mine. I'd understood they'd put me up for a few days in a guestroom, then expect me to leave till the students clear out in two or three weeks. But Victor departed and Simpson arrived, my grip in hand, with the news that "The chap who had these rooms came down with dreadful jaundice a few days ago and was sent to High Wycombe" (his home, I hope). Simpson—a wiry man who seems fifty, may be thirty, and bears not one whole atom of fat—proves to be my "scout." He will wake me for breakfast, make my bed, clean up, and wash my teacups. He had saved me some supper in a tin warming-lid and made my bed with college linen while I ate the regulation two pounds of starch. Anyhow it was nice not to lay my tired head on hepatitic sheets, and lay it I did. In spite of a short round of bibulous song from somewhere below, I was out of my soaked clothes and dead by ten. With my last conscious breath, I thought, "Rise! Dress! Your first night in Oxford!—you should be prowling lonesome through the dark haunts of Sidney, Raleigh, Donne, the Scholar Gypsy! Thomas Wolfe would be up embracing the rain, licking the holy scurf from the stones." Then I slept nine hours till Jack Simpson came in at 7:30, threw back my curtains, and said "Morning, sir."*

It was, actually—a square of deep turquoise sky at the window. When I stood and looked out, I knew (from my reading) where I'd spent my first night—in Mob, the oldest quad in Oxford, built 1306, a small near-square of two-story buildings in ruinous stone, with a mat of healthy grass the size of your new rug and the Chapel tower rising just to the north. That seemed more than even I bargained for—celebrated by a great throat-lump that's recurred more than once in the past two days as I've wandered the surprisingly busy town, the central meadows by the Thames where silence is deep as a well and the town as distant-seeming as home (the windows in my sitting room look south over the same meadows toward the river, hidden in trees).

But lest I melt too soon in careless ecstasy, I'll list a few drawbacks noted already. The nearest toilet is downstairs, outdoors, fifty feet away leaned up against the Chapel; and toilet-paper holders, containing tiny sheets of what is apparently waxed paper, were just installed a week ago after nearly seven hundred years (a note today in the student complaint-book takes account of them and adds, "Let it not be forgot that the French Revolution was precipitated by a slight alleviation in the plight of the Third Estate. . . ."). The baths—tubs only, circa 1880 (very tall, very deep, and so far very scummy with the last man's leavings)—are outside, fifty feet in the other direction, in a peaked dark hovel. Proximity to locals in confined spaces does not yet suggest that bathing ranks high on the young gentlemen's priorities—we're having warm days, mid70s now. They are all still in green tweeds and oatmeal trousers that would adequately clothe a polar expedition; the effect is quite memorable (horses in a closet? brown bears in a car?—not fetid but, well, piquant). I went to the corner chemist's today and asked for deodorant. The clerk produced one small spray bottle of Odor-O-No, wreathed in spring flowers. I said, "Don't you have any roll-on for men?" She said, "But it's not for men, now is it?" Apparently not.

It's not the effluvium though that's kept me from meeting any students. And it's not the fabled English chilliness—no one has been unkind, no trace of the plentiful harshness of the American northeast, just the sense till now that I'm invisible. I've been here the best part of three days now and have been addressed only when I was the man seated nearest some bowl of food that was needed—by members of the Middle Class, that is; lower orders have been warm and helpful from the start. I don't much mind. In fact I welcome the chance to watch from a distance just now— learn the rules from the shoulder of the road before driving (I only hope they are watching me too; if so, they're perfect spies).

Speaking of driving—at the end of this week, I'm to pick up my new black Volkswagen, straight off the boat from Germany. I had some qualms about commerce-with-the-enemy, but the cars are so plainly superior to similarly priced English efforts (as were their torture and death machines too—well, Americans worship competence, right?). Then I'll strike out to see as much as I can hold—maybe Scotland, Wales, Cornwall—before coming back in a month or six weeks to sit. Or to turn on myself—in this room, at this desk—and hunt for tangible evidence that I'm here as more than an aging drifter, a light-weight skater on ponds and backwaters, safely alone. I'll forward any evidence I manage to find.

Till then, just some postcards from the heaths and hedges. Please write me a letter at least this long and with no single word of apology in it. Unless you stop me, I would like to think of you as the willing receptor of as near to a journal as I can bear to keep. I've always avoided the rapt mirror-gazing that diaries invite; but if I talk on to you through this, then there'll be some sort of archive at least—a drawer full of time that I could ask to search when these present sights, clear as water, have clouded or sunk.

The best love from,
Hutch

June 7, 1955

Dear Hutch,

Well I told you what I looked for here, to be bored shit blind in under a week. I has been four days and I can't see daylight, just a uniform brown haze on everything. My mother has fed me every half-hour sharp and all her old girlfriends have come round to see me like the lad with the two-pronged cock in the fair. I'll have to check that in point of fact. Maybe mine has split up to search for ways out of this box it's in. Otherwise I haven't really seen it since Canada. Youngest girl anywhere near is well over fifty. That may not be any obstacle soon.

Hope you are doing better, not so good however that you cancel your plan to rescue me. I told my muvver an American poet would be paying me to give him a tour round Cornwall. She said "You wouldn't know Cornwall from Spain and if he's a poet you'll be wanting to paint a scarey face on your arse." So I have done that with iodine and am ready when you are. For the trip I mean. I checked and found I can use my Canadian license to help you along with the driving. Let me know when. You could come here and spend a night just to see how the working class live, then we could start. I have always meant to see the Scilly Isles. How does that sound to you? If I don't hear in another few days I shall strike off alone. Hoping then,

Your cabin mate,
Lew

June 9, 1955

Dear Lew,

Sorry you've had such a bleak homecoming. I won't say that my home-leaving has threatened me with high blood-pressure yet. But I have had several nice moments in the past week, all alone and looking though. Your countrymen—upper middle-class division—still haven't thrown any welcoming parties, and in any case I'm planning to wander a little before work begins. So sure let's merge our forces for that. If it's O.K. with you, I'll leave here three days from now—Sunday morning—take my time driving down through Burford and Gloucester, and spend the night somewhere near Tintern Abbey (maybe flat on the ground in the ruins themselves). Expect a possibly rheumatic old groaner then sometime Monday, by noon I should guess. I'd like to see as much of your native spot as you can bear to show, and I feel some need to assure your mother of the relative safety of unproved poets, so you decide when we push off for Cornwall. I mainly want to see the King Arthur country round Tintagel and Fowey; otherwise I'm game for the Scillies or whatever, provided they're cheap and not cold or hostile.

You may not have time to answer by mail. If not you can either send a telegram or phone and leave me a message at the Lodge. If I haven't heard No by Sunday morning, I'll strike out after the dazzling breakfast I'm sure to get and see you Monday noon.

Yours,
Hutch

P.S. I'm to pick up my car after lunch today, a German bargain with American drive. The above assumes that it works and that I do (under local conditions, I mean of course).

JUNE 10 1955   11.30AM

WILL WAIT BESIDE TURNING FOR OXWICH CASTLE NOON MONDAY. HURRY.

LEW DAVIS

June 11, 1955

Dear Hutch,

This is my first day off since I got your letter. I had to stay late last night typing stuff since, on Monday morning, Mr. Tidd goes to court to defend Lily Quarles, the fifty-five-year-old lilac-haired lady I told you about who stabbed her husband in fourteen places above the waist, bathed the body, put fourteen separate bandaids on the holes, got him into clean pajamas, then phoned Mr. Tidd at 1 a.m., and said she had something curious to show him. Now he thinks he can save her. I plan to stay in all weekend and pray!

In fact I've just spent the morning washing hair—mine. It was still feeling filthy from old New York, so I scrubbed myself half-bald and am drying my new clean pate in the sun out back. The gent next door has been out to check his birdbath three times in an hour—and no bird for miles— which I hope means I look a lot better than I did. The third time I caught him looking and he smiled. I nodded, serious as the Widow Quarles; but to tell the truth, was glad for confirmation that I'm visible again and no bandersnatch. Think he'll ask me to lunch? He cooks a lot.

Later. Took a little nap there apparently. Now awake and finding myself intact, I read your letter again. Here goes. No I don't hate anything you say. Or anything you're doing, that I know of at least. If I put up any kind of fight before you left—and I see I did—it was not from hate, God knows. Puzzlement, I honestly think. Twelve years of public school and four of college did their damndest to find some ambition in me and warm it to life. Forget it—none there. I'm a woman as old-style as anything painted on the walls of caves. I don't much doubt I could do quite well at a number of jobs outside in the world if I set my sights and tucked my chin (I'm well-stocked with chin). I hope that won't be necessary ever. And the reason is this—the brand of applause you can get from the world means as much to me as a plate of well-warmed vanilla ice cream. Not that the world has hung around clapping at the sight of me, but I've had little bursts here and there for chores done. Forget it, again. What I want is to work inside at home, making life easy (or easier) for two-to-four people in whom I'm involved and who want me to be.

So there. I never thought it right through before and surely never said it all out loud, though you heard pieces of it more times than you liked. I don't know why—why would anybody want any sort of homelife after what my parents displayed as a sample?—but from age eleven it was my idea. At first I slouched around, trying to hang it on boys in books or in the movies —I've had more to do in my mind with Toby Tyler and Johnny Sheffield than with anybody since. Then the Great Spring Hormone Freshet swept through me; and soon I was choosing a boy a week, sometimes several a day—real boys in school. Not that they ever knew it, not that one ever touched me much below the neck. But though you never asked me, you surely know since, along with that ancestral wedding-band, you wear at least one more ring—my pink maidenhood.

Don't get me wrong. I'm glad you have it, even if I never see you again. I picked you for it, I hope you know. The day you were called on in freshman English to come up and read your first theme to us as a model of virtue, and you stood to read five hundred words about a grown woman asking for you in a dark hotel room and you saying Yes—I picked you then. I also thought you were dying, which helped. You were so pale and lean. We could get it over fast; then you would be gone. I would be your relic through several generations, telling tales of you.

I got over that, the sudden-death part. By the time we'd gone to two or three movies and talked till midnight behind the dorm, I knew you were roughly as sick as the Matterhorn in morning light. You were going to make it. So I settled in to last long as you did, beside you. You didn't seem to mind. And once we had managed to make real love, that got your attention! You said your best mental picture of me was recent—me on you last month—and you told me to study my best one of you. Since I don't have an album mind like yours (I recall words better), I had to hunt awhile. But I have it finally and can tell you what it is. After our first time you stayed gone a week. I thought I'd failed you some terrible way. Then you called up and asked me to Myrtle Beach. I accepted before I realized the string of lies I'd have to spin to get permission, but I spun like a jenny, and off we went in Jack Hagen's car. The rest you know, up to my favorite part. You slept through that so you can't have known. It was just before sunrise. I had waked up somehow, thinking you had spoken. But you were breathing slowly and were turned away. I moved in against your back, not touching. Then I touched your shoulder and just said "What?" You waited awhile and I didn't move. You had to be asleep, but you said "Wait here" —as clear as urgent. I wondered "For what?" but decided not to ask. Then when light started working through the rusty blinds—Mrs. Benson's Guest House—you rolled to face me and slept in my sight for three hours more. Except for short snoozes I lay there and looked. You looked very fine. I chose to wait.

That's the best part I've got, of us at least. And if you really want us to meet at Christmas—Rome or wherever—I'll save my pennies while studying that. Not full-time, don't worry, but enough to keep it true. Meanwhile I'll struggle in the cause of mercy for Lily Quarles (justice would chain her to oars in a hulk off the coast of Guatemala) and of keeping my own chin up and pointing east, though prepared to tack if that signal comes. One way or another I hope to have more and longer life than the nun in your nautical dream about me. I was glad to be featured in a dream, understand. I just want to have more fun than most nuns—while working like them for the Love of Another.

It's getting pure hot and my neighbor's approaching with what looks like an axe and a glass of lemonade. I could write a lot of questions about your first days—where, when, what, who? I'll trust you instead to tell me all I need or can use to my profit and personal uplift. Speaking of which, my bosoms are lonesome. Remember them too.

Love,
Ann

June 11, 1955

Dear Polly,

The best thing waiting for me on that boat was your kind letter. I've kicked myself every day since then that I didn't set eyes on you before leaving. You probably guessed I came through Richmond to pick up Ann; but I felt so tired from loading my life's goods one more time in Rob's old truck that I went straight to sleep, then had to get on my way to New York. I'm saving the five-dollar bill you sent, to remember your goodness and to keep me from ever forgetting again a thing you told me when I was fifteen and visiting you. You asked me to walk downtown with you to a nine o'clock show, That Hamilton Woman. *I had been out all afternoon drawing the State Capitol in August sun and said I believed I needed to sleep. You said, "Not me. I plan to make up for all lost sleep the first two days after I'm stone-dead." I've still never seen* That Hamilton Woman, *though I do hope to see both Vivien Leigh and Laurence Olivier soon in the flesh. They're doing three Shakespeare plays at Stratford, forty miles north of here; and once the tourists thin in September, I'll try to get tickets (if it means missing sleep). Till then I mean to hide out on the edges of Wales and Cornwall and in my six-hundred-year-old rooms here.*

I'll write you in more detail about those and a good deal else at the end of the month when I'm back from the first trip and settled in here. Meanwhile let me close by telling you one thing and asking another.

I hadn't realized there were still so many American servicemen in England; but Oxford alone has several big bases within twenty miles, all manned with tall chunky fellows from Ohio (and one base graced with atomic bombs poised to fly just a short leg east to Berlin or farther on). Anyhow last night I was feeling mildly homesick, nothing terminal, so walked the three blocks from this Altar of Learning to the place where I'd seen flocks of airmen heading last weekend—White's Bar, High Street (just so you understand, I had two beers; you needn't tell Rob). I was wearing my best Young American disguise—cotton coat, khaki trousers, white socks, brown loafers—but I guess my hair was three inches too long or I wasn't wearing anything powder-blue: that seems the big color in P.X. men's wear. In an hour nobody volunteered a word my way, though I overheard a lot and was near the center of more than one fight. I was ready to leave, feeling much less homesick, when a woman came over and took the chair beside me—young herself, maybe twenty-one. She was ready to talk, over fairly swift glasses of warm pink gin (no ice in the building— in the town, *I gather). Well, to boil down what took her another hour— she was Marleen Pickett, born in London and raised there except for the years of the Blitz which she spent with an uncle in the country near here. That was when she acquired her love of Oxford—"Lovely chaps, like bats in their gowns; I'm the only girl I've met who likes bats"—and when she had grown up and chosen her career, she decided to spend her weekends in Oxford. Keeps a little apartment in Beaumont Street—"All books. I dream of the day I'll read; have the time, I mean. I barely sit down." No doubt but I'd seen well before she spoke that she spent many waking hours prone (or is it supine?). In short she's a fine individual example of American aid. She brings peace and welcome to lost young Yanks; and they pay her rent, her little food bill ("I eat once a day, a big tea at six"), her mother's expenses, and the storage on her dog (he stays in London, spared the sight of her work). Business didn't seem good last evening, so I asked if she liked my compatriots—or the local sample. She gave me a slow examining look; then said, 'I can tell you want the truth. When they're sober, yes—which is rare as bright days. When they're not, it's 'Look at these snaps of my girl—or Mum or wife'; and then they dig in. No insult, mind you; but your chaps got better food than ours for ten years there— milk, cheese, fat oranges. It all went to one place—they're giants, believe me—and I have to bear it, night after night. What I've always really fancied is students—thin, white, built normal (but their dreadful socks!)." I told her I wore fresh socks every day before I realized that I was a student again or would soon be. She didn't even smile. She said, "These airmen are stuffed with money. I know most students scrape by on grants so I make adjustments. Rhodes or Fulbright—which are you on?" I admired her homework but told her I'd tried for a Rhodes and washed-out twice as not really promising sufficient public service. Before she could ask for my private-service record, I also told her I was something of an heir (concealing that my horde of capital amounts to ten thousand dollars worth of pines crushed to paper). She gave that a whole minute's thought, drained her glass, then stood—"Oh well in that case, go buy a duchess. Their need is far more desperate than mine, these days at least." She walked a chalk line to a tall loud boy from Camden, New Jersey; and they'd made a deal before I could laugh. So I didn't that night—laugh, I mean—and I've wondered today: would you say that incident disqualifies me as a warmer in your view? Think and let me know please. I'm only half-joking.*

And if you're not busy, try to get Rob to pay you a visit soon. I don't mean to say I think my leaving has him drooping on the vine; but I do think he'd got a little stymied lately, no one to do for and Grandmother still strong as Boulder Dam. Please think of some way to say you need to see him; otherwise he'll sit there all summer swatting flies. Haven't seen an insect of any description here yet or a´snake—there are no poisonous snakes, only one viper almost never encountered that causes mild swelling. Other problems will no doubt rise to attention. But I'm here for that.

Answer soon.

Love,
Hutch

P.S. In fact I mean to spend your money tonight. There's a half-good imitation French place round the corner called Café de Paris—low stocky

English waiters in black bow ties (and fingernails to match) mispronouncing French dishes. I'll have steak and eggs to brace me for the road.

20

THE boy came back from inside the garage, leaned into Grainger's window, and spoke across him to Rob. "Says if you mean the old James Shorter place, he thinks niggers took it three or four years ago. It was empty till then. You could drive on up there. Wouldn't nobody mind."

Rob nodded. "Thank you."

Grainger spoke to the windshield but firmly. "Care to join us, brother?"

"What?" The boy stepped back—fifteen, sixteen, black-haired, dark-eyed.

Grainger looked and smiled. "No, sorry, my mistake. Up close I thought I could smell nigger blood. Sorry, captain. Many thanks." He moved Rob's truck slowly into the road.

Rob waited half a mile; then said, "It doesn't much matter to me—might even be a blessing, nice bullet through the eye—but I didn't know you meant to die right yet."

Grainger shook his head. "Don't."

"Then let me drive. You've lost your mind."

"Why?—kidding that child?"

Rob nodded. "—In *Virginia.* They don't have the sweet sense of humor about Negroes you're used to at home."

Grainger laughed. "Maine's my home. You're the one from Virginia."

Rob looked to his right—a long low hill bare of all but grass, with the sweet swell and tuck of a young girl's side; a mule staring toward him as if its whole mission through years of cold nights had been to wait here for this moment as proof that one living thing was loyal and still; a clear stream talking its slow way east, no house, no person. He said, "You lived here longer than I did."

Grainger said, "Don't mean a pig's ass-hole to me. I left this place. You were born here though; *born* is what counts."

"Counts how?" Rob said.

Grainger pointed. "Look yonder." They'd turned the last curve; and up the hill before them was the Shorter place, its charred remains. "Niggers got it and *gone.*" Grainger took the narrow drive, now two deep ditches.

Through the hard jolts Rob sat and wondered if he *felt*—no question they'd found the first destination on their little last tour. The place James Shorter had brought Hattie Mayfield, his young second wife; the place

Hatt's brother Forrest brought his own new wife (Eva Kendal, sixteen and happy in the first days); the place where Eva conceived and made Rob, in growing desperation, and brought him forth—herself nearly killed. They'd found the site at least. Once up the drive and stopped, Grainger's guess was confirmed; whoever had lived here last burned the house. Or hunters, boys, lightning. Gone—just the chimney, front and back steps, tin sheets from the roof. Rob wondered if it mattered. He turned to Grainger. "When was Hutch here last?"

"Ten years ago maybe. He come with us to Miss Hatt's funeral; when was that?"

Rob nodded. "Ten years." Then he faced the pile again, surprisingly large for an eight-room two-story house plain as anything drawn by a child with a ruler. "Shall we get out?" he said.

Grainger said, "This is your trip, Rob. You say."

Rob opened his door.

21

Rob had eaten the big cold supper Polly gave him and helped her stack dishes before he had a real chance to study her. But once she'd refused his help at the sink, he sat at the clear pine table and watched her—her back straight as ever, her left profile in the white bulb-light. He knew she was only a year short of seventy. She'd thrown in her young lot with Rob's dying grandfather and moved with him here—this house in Richmond— the year Rob was born. Still she seemed much younger. Or if you dimmed your eyes enough to soften the two strong cords in her throat, she seemed no age—foolish to calculate. The fine auburn hair was maybe half-white, the eyes slightly veiled when she looked down as now; but her long hands were white and unspotted, quick as ever as they scrubbed at plates and knives they'd scrubbed in that same spot more than fifty years. He thought, "All the women who've mattered to me refuse to age." He meant Eva, Polly, Min, his dead Aunt Rena, Rachel dead in her fresh youth; he himself felt worn as any felled column in his father's old photographs of Rome, still hanging. *Dissolved*—who'd have thought there were scraps enough left to draw cancer on him? Was it why, after all, *all* women had mattered (barring eight or ten mean-mouthed bitches)? More than any other man he'd known or heard of, he'd valued women; really loved them for them-selves—creatures separate from his own wants and needs—and craved their nearness. Other men wanted them for humping, cooking, children; Rob had wanted them simply as the crown of creation, the last best work. That Eve had made the first mistake gave him no cause for grudge, nor that his mother had been unable to love only him when he most wanted that. He steadily forgave them as they'd forgiven him—though any harm he'd done was harm they requested. If his own fifty-one years had ever broken through the lovely sad crust of this present world onto glimpses of permanence, constant reward, they had always come in the company of women (mostly bare but not always). Or was that soft whining from a dying brain? Had there been a single glimpse? If so, why was he now commanded to pass through pain and suffocation to reach full sight?

Polly looked back, shuddered, then burst out laughing. "Old fool!—me, I mean. You scared me, sitting there. So quiet I forgot you were anywhere near. I was thinking great thoughts."

Rob smiled. "What about?"

She paused to consider, then actually blushed. "Not about *sewing*. I'm caught up on work and no more promised; may never make another cent that way, wouldn't mind."

Rob saw she was dodging and wanted to stop her. He smiled again. "Tell me one great thought. I could use inspiration."

By then she'd finished work. She untied her apron, stroked her hair twice with the flats of her hands. "You want to sit on here? Aren't you too warm?"

"No."

She came to the table, held the back of her chair. "Inspiration was what I was thinking about."

"Reach any conclusion?"

Polly's face tightened quickly. She took the salt cellar and packed the grains down. "No I didn't. If I had I'd keep it inside. I'm no missionary."

"Didn't mean to say you were." He sat forward then; she was three feet away, still watching the salt. To win back her eyes seemed the urgent job. "I'm lying," he said.

She looked.

"You *have* brought a lot of help, to me and many others."

She shook her head. "To two—your father, his father."

Rob said "And me."

Polly said, "Not so. You never needed me."

"Sure I did, when Rachel died."

"I cooked you a few meals, kept Hutch awhile. Any kind colored woman could have done that much. You needed somebody all right but not me."

He accepted that. "I may now though."

"You're lonesome for Hutch."

Rob nodded. "Part of it."

"What's the rest?"

He laughed. He couldn't tell her now. "Tell *me*."

"I *know*," Polly said. "It was my great thought just now." She laughed and touched him, one finger briefly on the back of his hand. "A surprising lot of people, not all of them dark, are born to be servants."

Rob said, "Good night!—the children of Ham."

She paused. "I don't know them. I meant you and me."

"Please tell me."

"All we ever wanted was to work day and night for somebody we loved—time off for naps."

"Naps *with* them," Rob said.

Polly smiled but said "You speak for you."

He waited a little to let that pass; then said, "Why are you sitting here out of work?"

"Everybody died or left."

"We could find other jobs."

"Too old," she said. "People looking for help want young agile smilers."

Rob said, "My turn to say 'You speak for *you*'—I don't feel old."

Polly took that with sudden surprising force, shaking her grand head in fierce affirmation. "Whole days, even now, I don't feel ten minutes older than the girl who stepped through this door fifty-two years ago with your grandfather—my duds in a bundle the size of a lapdog and happy as one, a strong spotted feist. I'd been requested. I knew Rob Mayfield was old and sick—nothing to it; I could cure him."

"You almost did."

"You were not even born. No I eased him some—let him talk, fed him well, bumped against him enough to let him know I stood here and planned to last him out."

Rob said, "What did he talk about?"

"*Plans.* What was coming. See, he believed too that I'd get him right again. Since he left your grandmother many years before, he'd had no permanent woman near him but his own old mother; and she had just died. I know there had been some temporary people—he had been big on roaming—and I know he'd been hunting just what I seemed to offer: steady service, no running, lot of jokes and smiles. He'd believed in women the way most people believe in money; so when Margaret Jane Drewry packed her grip in Washington and followed him here—I was seventeen years old, pretty as a green leaf and far longer-lasting—he thought his prayer was answered at last. He would drag round all day by the stove—coughing, losing blood—then at night get his strength back and lie there and tell me the future by the hour, our future. Different plans every night but with two steady parts—he was moving; I was with him. He had never been west of Louisville, Kentucky; so mostly we would be pushing on past there toward San Francisco. That was always his aim, however we journeyed; and since he died a good year before the quake, the aim was never spoiled. He had all the details in black and white. If he woke up strong, he'd be down at the station searching every timetable from here to California, all the rules, exact fares. Then he'd come back and, that night, lay it out for me—lower berths from here to Denver, a week of rest there (the Brown Palace Hotel; is there really such a place?), then on through mountains and deserts to the ocean. *Hills by water*—they were big in his plans. I'd say, 'There are hills by the James River, Rob, that cost less to see.' He wouldn't even hear me, just take my hand and go on reading his lists. Made more lists than anybody alive; for him to make a list was good as doing something. Funny thing was, they were realistic—the money part at least. His mother had left him a little nest-egg that would see us there, and back if necessary. But he generally planned on us staying gone for good—never said what he'd do about the house here." She paused and looked up, half-surprised to find it round her.

Rob said, "Maybe he meant to contact his children and give it to them."

Polly smiled but shook her head. "They were never mentioned, no more than God's name, even after your father tracked him down that last Christmas and offered to tend him."

"I thought he asked you to notify Father once he died."

"No never. He died in his sleep; and all he ever said after your father's visit was, 'Forrest will be needing help long after me.' "

"He knew he was dying?"

Polly nodded. "One night that February I was doing my last little chore—I used to rub his chest with camphorated balm and pin flannel round him before he went to sleep—when he took my wrists and held them tight a minute. Then he said, 'Lay your hands please flat on my nipples and ask God to save me.' As I mentioned, he hadn't ever spoken of God. I said, 'It may be a little late for Him. If God is any kind of churchgoing Christian, we're both in bad trouble.' I think he grinned—the lamp was down low—but he stayed quiet awhile and I rubbed on. Then he said, 'Please do it anyhow on your own.' So I pressed my palms down hard on his chest—there was no more fat than this table's got—and looked him in the eyes (what I could see of them) and said, 'If any power wants to help you and will use me to do it, let that happen now. Or if me being by you is a harmful sin, let me be sent somewhere I can hurt nobody.' I hadn't really known I felt that way till I'd said it out loud; and once I had, I hoped Rob would say he wanted me by him—whatever the harm, whoever it offended. I waited but somehow he slipped off without me seeing. To sleep, I mean. In a week he had slipped off for good, dead beside me in that same bed, still bound in my flannel—all the help that did him." She'd said her say for now.

And Rob let the quiet spread round them while he thought of what he could offer or beg from her now. He took the salt cellar she'd smoothed and the pepper; and with them and the two clean unused knives, he made a little foursided house—no roof. Then not looking up he said "You still know how?"

Polly laughed. "To do what?"

"Little healing jobs."

She tried to wait till he looked up; he didn't. "No meanness," she said, "—too late for that."

Rob nodded. "No meanness." Then he met her eyes and attempted to smile.

She saw what till now he'd hid so well, what she'd seen in two men's faces before (his grandfather, father)—the worst sight of all: surrender to death. Rob was ready to die. His eyes were glad. She pressed back slightly in her chair. "What is it?"

"What terms are you on with the powers you mentioned?"

"Better now than before."

Rob said, "Then why do they want us all so early?"

"*I'm* old."

He shook his head. "The Mayfield men—not one of us got his three-score-and-ten."

Polly said "You're young" and regretted it at once. He was old as the others. Or as oddly nimble on the lip of extinction.

Rob said, "I have done almost all I can think to do." He hadn't planned to say it, hadn't known he knew it; the plain fact stopped him.

Polly thought he was speaking of desperation. She said, "I know you've got your mother and Grainger, but I'll help any way you ask me to."

He could only think to thank her.

But far in the night as he slept upstairs in his dead father's room, Rob lived through this—pleasure and news. He was traveling in his car, alone and strong. A hot June day but dry as fall, longest day of the year. He had started at dawn; by one he was hungry and stopped at a low white house by the road to buy a meal. There was no sign saying *Cafe* or *Food*, but he thought he was right; he'd be welcome here (and for very little money). The wood door was shut, but he opened and entered—a normal front-room: sofa, chairs, pictures, one small table spread with a white cloth and on it a bowl of broad red poppies. He tried to remember when he'd seen poppies last and wondered if it really was safe to be shut indoors with a living odor as strong as theirs. While he was thinking a woman walked in —or moved in so quietly he heard no sound till she said "Can I help you?" But he was not startled. He turned and looked. At once he knew that—in every particular of face, color, size—she was what his own whole body had wanted since becoming a man. She seemed a woman made from the line of vacant space that hugged his own profile, head to foot; a creature made to be set up against him, to stay there forever in place, not abrading, and who'd waited here till he found and claimed her. Yet she also seemed a feasible woman, as credible as perfect. So he answered her question by moving straight to her and taking her hand. She accepted that, though she didn't meet his eyes. He led her from the room down a short dim hall till an open door showed him one room with a bed—another entirely possible room: throw-rugs, a dresser, an aging mirror. When they stopped in the center of the room, he turned and carefully but quickly began to undress her. She still didn't face him, but she let him work with no resistance; and when he had her entirely bare in unflawed beauty, she set her own small hands on his wrists and drew him to the bed, neatly opening the covers. Rob opened her. Once bare himself against her—she did fill all his adjacent emptiness—he found that he wanted to open and eat her. He left her face and arms and slowly made way down the length of her body, honoring the skin itself with the only tribute he could offer—silent kisses on her firm pooled breasts, the trough between, her flat belly plush with fine blond hair that took the light from a single window, the patient powerful bone of her left hip. He kneaded that with his stubbled chin, her legs moved apart, he thought he could hear her say "Rob. Now." He wondered how she could know his name, but he wouldn't speak to ask. He obeyed both her voice and his own delight in a hunger on the verge of perfect food. He rose to his knees and slid to the small space she'd offered in her fork. His hands went under her knees, her legs lifted, he bent to the gift. In long laps he spread the tiers of leaves that covered his goal, led by the clean salt stench of her blood and her welcoming oils. Then he devoured her. Or thought he devoured. He licked down easily through layers of happiness, each of which seemed a further dream in the longer dream and each one better (he knew he was dreaming). Yet his eyes were shut, and strong in the midst of all was this knowledge—*She dries and shrinks below me as I eat; all the others have.* He consumed her youth unavoidably, speeded her death. She never said "Stop" and he never relented till at last she gripped at his hair like reins, endured the short by-product of his meal, and could speak again—"Good." Still blind he laid his head where he'd worked, knowing he must open his eyes in a moment and see his chief fear—one more woman ruined, who had offered help. She gripped again, rocked him, and he looked up. The same girl faced him, damp but changed only by the smile she gave. She had not smiled till then. He had only made her happy. He would never have to leave.

At the end of the dream—still asleep—Rob began to speak to the girl but also aloud in the room, the door open in hope of a breeze. Muffled sounds but audible.

Polly heard them and woke. At first she thought he was in some distress, and she sat up to go. But while she felt in the dark for her robe, she noticed the sounds were peaceful—little greetings. By the time she was up and had tied the belt, Rob was quiet again. Her eyes however had opened to the seepage of light from the one burning bulb downstairs; the news of his illness gathered weight in her head as she stood there alone. In a minute it seemed intolerable. She'd borne the consecutive years of assaults—her own mother's death, death of the two men who'd valued her, long isolation—with the calm and resilience that had been natural to her as thick hair, a free tongue. No longer. That Rob Mayfield should be asked to strangle in broad mid-life, his beauty still on him, was the thing she'd refuse. She'd earned a choice. So she sat again on the edge of her bed and said one sentence to a God she knew of but seldom consulted—"Not him, not now" (the codicil to which was implied not spoken: *If there's crying need for a sacrifice, I volunteer*). She sat on awhile to catch any answer. There was no rejection; no acceptance either but rejection was what she'd listened for. A decision on the codicil was of no interest to her. She was still here alive, for now at least. And while she lasted she would try to tell Rob. In the warm dark she fully believed herself. So she walked barefoot on clean boards to his door. The light didn't reach there. She waited to hear any sign of his waking.

Easy sighs, deep sleep.

She extended her hands and made her way toward him, landing at the foot of the bed—an island. She pulled herself round, felt carefully, and established that he lay on the far side from her. Gently she sat on the vacant edge. His breath didn't alter.

She reached out again—it seemed as far as England—and found his chest, bare, cooler than she'd planned. Her palm was narrow but the fingers were long. She found she was able to cover one breast with the heel of her hand, the other with her fingers.

He'd grown entirely silent.

She said, "You are going to be all right."

He covered her hand. "Thank you," he said. "I won't doubt that."

Polly sat in place another whole minute, glad to be by him and glad of the thick dark—that Rob couldn't see her. Then the spell weakened slightly; she wondered if he thought she'd broken with age. She moved to leave.

But Rob held her firmly by the hand. "Stay on. It'll be day soon."

It would. Polly stayed—at first upright, Rob's hand strong on hers. Then when he turned away and gave signs of sleep, she carefully lay outside the covers. Her left hand rested in the small of his back, sheet and spread between them; and her eyes stayed shut, but she didn't sleep again. She knew the length of every moment till dawn when she rose.

THE first light woke Grainger. When he'd left Rob at Polly's the previous evening, he'd driven a mile to a house he remembered on a Negro street where an old lady rented occasional rooms. A young woman answered. He asked for Mrs. Adams.

She said, "Mrs. Adams been dead ten years, night Roosevelt died." He'd turned to go but she said, "If you needing somewhere to stay, I could find room, I guess."

Grainger waited; then said, "A whole room?—private? For just one night."

She nodded. "With a hook on the door. Course, children might wake you up before day."

He'd paid her two dollars, and she'd led him to a small swept room at the back. The only other thing she required was his name, which she wrote in his presence with plain difficulty. Then she'd given him hers— Lela—and left him alone. He'd locked the truck carefully, walked till he found a clean place to eat fish; then gone to the Booker T. and watched *East of Eden*, remarking how much the young boy favored Rob—Rob thirty-one years ago when Grainger first saw him. He'd walked slowly back, not looking for friends but thinking he might encounter one or two from the years he lived in Richmond. Not a single face in hundreds, so he got back to Lela's at a little past nine. On her porch there were two men and two other women to whom she introduced him—"Sit down and drink beer; I'll send for you one." He excused himself on grounds of fatigue, wondering as he left who she'd send for beer (the children she mentioned had still not appeared).

In the room he latched the door, took off his new shoes, lay down with his head at the end of the cot to catch the center light, read two chapters in *Robinson Crusoe*—"I am Very Ill and Frighted" and "I Take a Survey of the Island"—then was tired and stood to undress for sleep. He heard something crying, put his ear to the door—a child, almost surely, and close to his room. He waited for the sound of Lela to ease it; but no sound came and when he was stripped to his underwear and the crying went on, he switched off the light and cracked the door open. The crying wasn't frantic, just a steady thread of pleading; no other children spoke to help it or join it. Grainger took two steps out into the dark hall—no sounds from the porch. He was here with the child or whatever was here; they'd left him the guard. He went back, put his trousers on, and—in the dark—went toward the noise. The next room was open; it came from there. He stood in the door, waited for a pause, and said "Who is this howling?"

The pause drew out; then the child said "Tossy."

"You by yourself?"

"Yes."

"Where your brothers and sisters?"

No answer to that.

"Where your mama?"

No answer.

Grainger said, "You got you a light in here?"

"In the air, in the middle. Too high for me."

He felt his way forward and found the hanging bulb. "Here it comes," he said. "Shut your eyes a minute."

The child had obeyed. She lay in a big iron bed—a girl maybe five in white underpants, on top of patched sheets, both eyes shut but calm.

Grainger walked over to her. "Let em come open slow now and see who's with you."

She obeyed again, screening her raw eyes till they opened; then she studied him gravely.

"I'm the man paid your mama to sleep next door." He pointed to his room.

Tossy nodded twice, took her left thumb, and sucked it.

Grainger said, "I'll be nearby. You sleep."

She shook her head No.

He smiled. "You cry, you'll keep me wake. I'll want my money back."

The thumb popped out. "Lie down here, else I'll dream again and holler."

"You dream a lot?"

Tossy said "When they leave me."

Grainger said "They coming back."

She thought that through. "If they don't, you staying?"

The answer surprised him. *Yes* rose in his head like a cork on a pond. All the things that had left him (and most things had but his health and strength) seemed small by this—he'd never had a child. Even in the days before Gracie left, when she'd welcomed him in most nights of the week, she had begged for no child. He'd respected her, thinking there was time ahead. Now there was nothing his body had made or nothing more responsive than the shrubs he'd planted, the roofs he'd mended, the three white men (Forrest, Rob, Hutch) he'd stayed near and watched. He kept the Yes silent though. He said, "Let's turn this hot light off. I'll wait here with you."

She'd never smiled. She slid to her right to give him space and took her thumb again.

Grainger reached for the light, then took the three steps, and lay straight beside her.

Tossy lay where she'd landed, not moving to touch him. When he'd settled she said "You kin to me?"

"May be."

"Hope so." She was out in an instant.

Grainger followed her easily, exploring as he sank unbroken spreads of rolling field ankle-deep in grass—his unchallenged new home, empty as summer air. In an hour of sleep, he still found nothing. Then he woke and felt a quiet path to his own room through the silent house. Lela had left him a pitcher of water by a clean washbowl and a clean slop-jar.

23

WHEN the first light woke him, he could hear other people—three voices, he thought: man, woman, child. It was quarter to six; Rob expected him by nine ("Don't let me down please; Polly may have talked me out"). He rose, washed himself; dressed in clean underwear, the same shirt and trousers. He hoped he could leave unseen, find some breakfast, and maybe drive past Gracie's old cousin's house, give her his thanks. She had sent him a sympathy card when Gracie died nearly two years ago, the first word he had. He'd forgot her street but could poke round and find it; it was not far from here. When he opened his door, the voices were louder and came from a room at the back of the house.

He had taken three steps to go when Tossy ran forward and said "Breakfast ready." She was in a blue dress.

He said, "Got to run. Somebody waiting for me."

"You'll die," she said.

He laughed. "Who'll kill me?"

"Not eating no breakfast."

Lela called from the kitchen, "Getting cold, Mr. Walters."

He followed the child to the good-smelling kitchen.

Lela stood at the stove. At a big center table, a young man was eating fried bread and bacon—maybe seventeen, eighteen. He looked up, unsmiling. Lela turned and grinned, fresh as if she'd slept ten hours underground. "How many eggs you want?"

"Thank you, none, Miss Lela. My man's looking for me."

She reached for a pot. "Drink some coffee anyway. Tossy say she kept you wake."

"I enjoyed it," Grainger said.

"She been begging to go in your room all morning."

Tossy sat by the young man but still watched Grainger.

He told her, "You could have. I'm too old to sleep."

Tossy pointed to a chair. "That's yours. I wiped it."

So he sat two feet from the young man's left; and before he'd drawn his chair up, Lela set down a plate of neat eggs and bacon. "Mr. Walters, this boy say he known you forever." She touched the boy's left ear with the towel she carried.

The boy looked down.

Grainger studied him a moment—never seen him surely. But there was a band of deep ease across his eyes and nose, a memory of someone.

"Name Eric," Lela said.

Grainger offered his hand across the full table.

Tossy leaned out and took it.

The boy looked up and said, "Your wife was my cousin. My name's Eric Fishel." His bright eyes were Gracie's.

"You live here?" Grainger said.

"No sir, Mama sent me. Somebody come by the house last night, told Mama you were here. She down in the back, so she told me to step here this morning on my way to work."

Lela said, "You were sleep. I made him eat and wait."

It seemed to Grainger he'd been slowly led here to stand this trial, that this strange house had worked all night behind a screen of welcome to charge him at daybreak with unanswerable wrong. Again he thought of standing, trying to leave. He looked over dishes and salt to Tossy.

She said, "I don't have no more dreams."

So he saw no way but to sit on and meet whatever was waiting. He chewed and swallowed a mouthful of eggs. Then he said straight to Eric, "Where was Gracie when she died?"

"Mama's kitchen."

"Who was with her?"

"Eric Fishel." With their ease his eyes also had Gracie's speed; they were cold now with offense. "I was all she knew, all she wanted to see."

"What killed her?"

Eric ate again, carefully swabbing his plate.

Lela said "Dollar-wine." She'd never sat down but stood by Tossy, drinking coffee from a glass.

Eric said, "Wanted to—died wanting to die."

Lela said, "Her mind been eat up for years."

Tossy said, "I don't like no kind of wine."

Eric said, "She was crazy but she knew my face. She cooked my supper every night and watched me eat it. Any money she had, she give me half. Thought Mama meant to hurt her."

Grainger said, "I hadn't seen her since early in the war."

"She knew you too. Talked about you anyhow."

"Don't guess it was very sweet music," Grainger said.

Eric shook his head. "She was giving you things, all the time walking round giving you things. She wouldn't sit down except to sleep. She would touch little things that were Mama's or mine and make up a wild tale of where she got them. Then she'd tell me, 'Eric, you see this gets back to Grainger Walters, Fontaine, N.C., care of Rob Mayfield.' "

Grainger smiled. "You never reached me."

But Eric insisted. "Wasn't nothing to send—old clothes, empty bottles. She did keep one old suitcase locked. When she passed, Mama told me to bust it open—two hundred paperbags all folded like fans and one little box. Mama said that was yours. She saved it till you came." He reached to the floor and brought up a narrow box, three inches deep and shut with rubber bands.

Tossy said "Can I have it?"

Lela thumped her on the head.

Eric set it by Grainger's right hand on the table.

Grainger said "What is it?"

"Swear to God I don't know. Didn't want to know. Mama kept it. I'd forgot it. Then she heard you were here."

Tossy said "Whose is it?"

Grainger still hadn't touched it. He told her gently. "Belonged to my wife."

"Where she?"

"Long gone."

24

HE drove up the dirt street from Lela's four blocks to the main paved road. He turned left there toward Miss Polly's and Rob but, in two more blocks, remembered it was early—twenty minutes to seven. There was no traffic yet—some old men walking. He pulled to the curb by a dry-cleaning plant and listened to the news. Then when he'd heard that the weather promised well, he took up the box from the warm seat beside him and slid off the bands; they were oozing with age. The first sight was cotton, a strip of batting old as the bands. He lifted that. Lying on its back, gazing up and all but smiling, was a five-inch-long Negro doll—a girl dressed in what seemed to be a handmade nightgown, drawstring at the neck. He raised the hem and touched the stiff leg, still cooler than the morning round them. If she'd had this when he knew her, she'd kept it hid. Well, he'd seen it now. He covered it carefully, wished he could go back and leave it with Tossy; but he cranked the car again, and went on for Rob—a last rescue.

25

BY nine that evening Ann Gatlin had finished an hour's nap and a solitary supper and was reading Moravia, *The Fancy Dress Party*. She was waiting for a visit from Linda Tripp, the new girl at her office who was hunting a room. Ann had offered to share, which she hadn't done in all the years Hutch was near. She'd read for forty-five minutes on her porch in dry slant light when the telephone rang—Linda, postponing? But when she stood to answer, she surprised herself by thinking, "I haven't thought of Hutch Mayfield in two hours."

Polly Drewry said, "Ann, I'm ashamed to call you this late in the evening; but I've worried all day, and I have to speak."

Ann assured her she was welcome to phone anytime.

Polly thanked her, promised she would not abuse the privilege; then said, "I don't know an easy way to tell it—Rob Mayfield was just here visiting me. He's sick to death."

Ann at first felt relief. Hutch was safe anyway. Mr. Mayfield had never really liked her from the start. When she'd heard what was wrong and the expectations, she said, "You just found out today?"

"Last night. Grainger drove Rob up here to see me; they left this morning. I've worried ever since. He'd have called you, I know; but you were at work. He had to get home."

"When did Hutch find out?"

"That's the thing," Polly said. "Rob still hasn't told him and says he never will. He's sworn me and everybody else to keep quiet."

"Why on earth?"

"You know."

Ann said "I'm not sure."

"Hutch would come straight back."

Ann said "He might."

"No *might* about it. He'd be on the first plane."

"Hutch has changed, Miss Drewry."

Polly paused for that. "You've seen him more than me, in recent years at least. You may've seen something I've failed to see. I've known him since the day he was born though, Ann; and the main thing I seem to have noticed in life is that people change about as much as children change rocks by hopping across them. When Hutch Mayfield hears Rob is going, he'll be back with him. If I'm wrong I'm crazy and have lived in vain."

Ann thought *She has and she's bats too at last.* But she said, "Mr. Mayfield doesn't want that, it seems."

"Of course he does." Then silence extended, humming like a kite-string.

So Ann spoke to end it, having seen her own chance. "Can I be any help?"

"None at all. No none."

"Then Miss Drewry, let me ask you politely why you're calling."

Polly paused again, then loosened. "I'm asking if you think I should do anything?"

"Such as what, please ma'm?"

"Such as take it on myself to write Hutch now. Or ask you to do it."

"And bring him back?"

"I've said that, yes."

The chance was a sudden door opened in what had been a seamless wall. Ann sat in the ladderback chair; the hall was dark now. "What reason could he give?"

"The reason of being all Rob's ever had."

Ann said, "Hutch couldn't say that. He may know it's true, but it's half of what he's left."

"Is the other half you?"

Ann laughed once. "Oh I'm fifteen percent, maybe twenty-one or two."

Then Polly could laugh. "That runs in the family. They've been fairly fast off the mark through the years, when it came to bolting for their own nerves' sake—all but Rob; Rob would *stay*."

Ann said, "Does Mr. Mayfield's mother know?"

"We never speak of her; Rob spares me that."

Ann said, "If she does, she may have written Hutch."

"Never," Polly said.

"Why? She wants Hutch too."

Polly said, "Ann, Eva Mayfield is a stranger to me; but I've known at close quarters three men she changed. I lived with Rob's father, as you may well have heard, from the year she left him till the year he died —all but forty years. I've known Rob himself since he turned twenty-one and tracked down his father; known him good and bad, thick and thin— and frankly a long strip of it was *thin:* drinking and women and other useless misery. Hutch I held in my arms the day he was born and his mother died; and he's come to me for what Eva couldn't give, though she's loved him like a limpet. What I've guessed from those men is, she'll want this to herself; want the whole of Rob's death, not even Hutch to share it. When Rob left here at ten this morning, I knew I'd never see him above ground again."

The fervor of that had left Ann calmer. It had shown her, in a way Hutch himself had never managed, why he'd left and must stay—till he'd cleared his legs at least from the webs spun at him by housefuls of faces, her own among them. Fairness was no more natural to her than to anyone with needs; but she said, "Miss Drewry, you say Mr. Mayfield left—going where?"

"Back home, Grainger driving."

"Then since you've asked me, let's let him just *go*. Let his mother have it all; she hasn't had much."

Polly said quietly, "She's had a fine life. From where I sit—and I've mostly *stood*—I haven't heard her do any one thing she hated."

Ann said, "Oh she has—her marriage, her mother's suicide, her father's death. She's suffered a lot. Or so Hutch says."

"Don't believe it," Polly said. "Watch her closer than you have, if she'll let you close. Learn happiness from her. She could give good lessons."

Ann said "I like you better."

Polly laughed. "Several have! I'm outliving them." But she also said thanks.

26

LATE in the night Ann was waked by a dream that came as a single sentence not a story. So clear that, as she lay in the dark, she thought she must have spoken it aloud—*Done now*. She first thought it meant Mr. Mayfield's fate, that she'd helped him in his wish to leave Hutch free. But she rose and walked with no light to the toilet; as the cold seat ringed her warm butt and thighs, she saw she'd meant Hutch. She had cut Hutch loose as she hadn't before, even thrust him away when a chance had been offered to hold him again. Hard regret and fear of solitude seized her then and shook her. She bent to her own bare knees and embraced them, crying quite silently.

27

June 15, 1955

Dear Ann,

Polly Drewry called me late last night to say she'd talked to you and said more than I asked her to. I thought about calling you but, in view of the hour and my new inclination to cast myself on the Mercy of Fate, I decided to hold off till morning and a letter.

Polly says she pledged you to keep her trust—of course I'd pledged her. I don't mind you knowing; there's nothing unusually precious to me in having this new twist all to myself. But I have two reasons for the choice I made. First, I want Hutch to have this distance for now. It's the main thing he's lacked; and he'll be better for it, maybe better for you. He's suffered, as I did till well past his age, from thinking our people were more than normally hard on each other—hard in what they expect or who they ignore (we aren't, I'm sure; just run of the draw, though scarey as hell). Second, this next strip of my own road is of uncertain length. I really don't think I want or could stand him back here watching. He couldn't not watch and there's already days when I'm not up to giving my old imitations of joy and peace.

If you've already told him, don't dive off a wall. If you haven't, please think of my reasons and don't. He's had more of my life than anyone else. We can spare him this.

I've always liked you. I hope you'll be a Mayfield (a mingled boon!). You seem to have the grit.

Till whenever,
Rob Mayfield

June 15, 1955

Dear Hutchins,

It's a cool evening here, and the radio promises cool through the weekend. So I'll take the omen and sit down and start a letter to you. It may be long and I won't mail it soon, maybe not for some months. Or it may just wait here for you in your room. I'll go on sending little separate dispatches to keep you up on the little events; this will be about a bigger one, big for me anyhow. When and if you ever read it, you will already know its first piece of news—I will be out of sight—so I'll give the few details I have on that, then pass to what I've been thinking of lately and want you to have.

Grainger and I got back last night from a two-day circle up to Bracey and Richmond. I hadn't seen Polly since New Year's, as you know; and I had an unaccustomed curiosity to see what was left of Hatt's house in Bracey, my birthplace after all. Polly was fine, absolutely herself (which means that, with Rena, she's been one of the two most selfless people I've happened to know). Bracey was worse—or the inexplicably still-unmarked Historic Site of Rob Mayfield's birth is a pile of ashes, a small pile at that. Burned down after Negroes took it four years ago. I don't say they did it, but my point is it happened and in gorgeous Virginia. Wouldn't you have thought that a state which puts up a two-ton silver sign to mark every dead spot left in the weeds where General Lee peed would have taken protective measures round the cradle of Robinson May-field, the Last Rose of Bracey? Well, they somehow didn't. God-Above hasn't either—or if what's underway is protective, then He's got me buffaloed again.

See, two days before I came up to get your stuff from Edom, I got the results of two weeks of tests. In April when I really believed you were going, I figured it was time to change my insurance—revalue my life at a little higher rate and leave you enough to bury me at least with the usual modest ten-thousand-dollar rites. In a man my age, the company insisted on a physical check; so I went to Sam Simkin, and everything slid along fine till I stepped behind the fluoroscope—he seemed to see a shadow the size of a quarter on one of my lungs.

To simplify the next two weeks of the tale, he made valiant efforts to prove it was anything but what it is—had me spitting from caverns I never knew were down there. We couldn't get a sign of trouble that way, just the normal jillion flora and fauna. So three days before I came up to you, he made a last try—highly diverting little episode in which a tube the size of a European sausage with lights and mirrors was slowly inserted down my throat to my lungs for the luxury tour. What was seen was a sizable lesion, as they call it in their euphemistic code, and little lesionettes (or lesionnaires) all up in the bronchials and on into darkness. Sarcoma, which is cancer. They could operate, haul the whole lung out; but Sam says at best that would give me two years. So I've chosen to preserve my beauty intact, my uncut hide. It has maybe six months of its seamless pride left, eight if I'm unlucky.

I'm here at my home. Grainger, Mother, and Sylvie are taking good care. There is no sufficient cause—I searched—to call you back from a trip you need. We said a good farewell. There've been very few points, now I think about it, in all our time together when a sudden final parting would have left either one of us with much unsaid. In recent years at least we've done pretty well at acting our feelings. I feel that I've watched a whole show, start to finish. I wouldn't want to claim it was Buster Keaton, but it surely had speed and curves and hills, and it rolled to a good warm destination.

If there's memory after death (I suspect there is, though the local Christians doubt I remember Jesus' last name or his winter-hat size), I'll hope to remember the view I had of you in the mirror of my truck as I left you in Edom. You watched me out of sight—highest marks in my book. Almost no human friend will stand to watch you go or turn back one last time when they leave you. They are too expectant, too ready for change. I liked you not waving, just standing still—but standing. Of course I'd like to see you. I'd like to see you every other day left in history, but that would be for me. There's nothing here now for you that you can't learn from reading this letter, and it may be long. I'll try to work on it a little every few days—another family author, a tad late as ever. My Life and What It Showed Me or What I Think I Saw.

June 16

Looking for a way to start this that will keep it going. I know you don't need an autobiography of me, long or short. I know I don't plan to preserve my Great Thoughts on Time and Space for babes yet unborn who'll have the punk luck not to hear me in person. I suspect an account of my circumscribed movements would be barbituate. I could write out all the jokes I remember, but I don't remember many (why would somebody loving to laugh as much as me live a life and not make up one joke or remember three?). I could finally entrust my famous recipes—hoecake and popcorn. But I read last week in a good biography of Count Tolstoy that he said any fool could write a novel if he'd put down all one person did and thought in one whole day. He ought to know.

My present days are mostly pretty calm however. I'm still sleeping out here alone with Thal. Grainger wants to move out. Mother wants me to move in. I plan to stay put as long as I can. Far as symptoms go, that could nearly be forever—I cough a few times a day, a dry feather down beneath my breast bone; and my joints are stiffer than usual in the morning (but as the old lady said, "It's good to have something stiff around the house"). So I live my usual summer days—up early for a walk, a big hot breakfast, a piddling morning with the paper and books, then a drive into town for the mail, lunch with Mother, a long afternoon-nap in my old room there, then back out here for the evening and night. Mother thinks I'm taking too much time alone, but I seem to like it. There were years when I wanted somebody nearby every minute of the day—Mother, Min, Rachel, you—but now this solitude seems like a wonderful food I've ignored at serious peril. It well might have saved me if I'd found it in time, even short strips of it. Till now I can't remember ten happy minutes alone, but I'm working to have one whole happy day with nobody but Thal before I quit. I'll let you know.

June 17

That kept me thinking a good deal of last night. I was trying to remember happy time alone—before now, I mean. All I could come up with was the hours spent jacking off. Nobody ever told me it was dangerous or wrong, so I took to that with serious application at about age four. I know that because I recall going over behind a big laundry basket that Rena had painted green and giving myself that neat reward. Then Rena decided she didn't like the color—goose-turd—and gave the basket to old Mag. Mag died well before I started school, which is how I date my first lonely pleasures. I was wrong yesterday—I've had some very nice lonely minutes but all before the age of twelve. After that, however alone I was, I was always working to the close accompaniment of one or another of the many mental pictures from my gallery of hopes, little packs of girls like baseball cards. Or Con DeBerry when I was fourteen (he and I stayed steamed up about each other through that whole summer, all fumbling hands in hot barns and sheds). Nice minutes, as I said, but pretty sad memories—love thrown to the wind.

To cheer myself up for discovering that, I lay on awake and tried to select much longer good stretches. I decided to hunt for the three best days of my fifty-one years. Ever tried that, with your twenty-five? You're a trained hand at memory, and you probably have the best at your finger-tips; but I've never kept any diaries or records, so I just lay still in the dark and asked for my three best days to come back as visions. Nothing came at first. To help myself I divided the available years by three; I've lived exactly three times seventeen years. So I dwelt on age one to seventeen and then this came—

The August I was six—1910—my Aunt Rena said at the table one morning, "You'll be starting school soon, and that ends freedom for good and all. I'm going to take us to Raleigh for a last fling." I of course hol-lered. Mother was sitting there but spoke not a word. Grandfather said, "No such of a thing—never see either of you alive again." But three mornings later Rena spoke up again, "Rob and I are leaving on the first train tomorrow. We'll be spending two nights at the Yarborough Hotel. I've never been anywhere and neither has he; we've earned the right." Grandfather said, "Then Sylvie's going with you." Sylvie stood there with pancakes, nodding agreement. Rena said, "Thank you, no. Rob and I have worked for this. You mustn't keep it from us." I was speechless with joy and flat with amazement, never having heard anybody go against him. He finished his breakfast in silence thick as custard; and I never heard another word of discussion, though there may have been some.

Next morning at seven he walked us to the station, holding Rena's grip (I carried my own, that midget doctor's-satchel you used to play with). The only thing he told us was "Don't speak to anybody younger than fifty; and if you get lost, find a Methodist Church and ask for the preacher." From there on I barely remember the first day—so near a dream that I've lost all of it but the fact that our room had two big beds with white summer counterpanes and one tall wardrobe that we took turns hiding in to scare each other (Rena was still a child herself, not quite twenty-one). The second day is what I remember entirely.

We both woke up a little while before light and could hear each other breathing normally. There was some good distance between our beds. I turned to try to see her, but she was still dark and still hadn't moved, so finally I said "You ready for company?" She thought about that and, for her own reasons, eventually said, "Let's keep our own places, so dry and cool." Then she said "Say your prayers." I did that in a hurry. Rena took a little longer, having more time behind her; and we had a long breakfast in the bright dining-room—beefsteak and gravy, corn muffins and butter in hard ribbed curls. I asked for coffee. The old Negro

*waiter shook his head—"Stunt your growth." Rena said, "That's the idea.
Bring him black coffee." I drank three cups, was pied as Ben Turpin the
rest of the morning, and happier for it—my fatal first hint that ease came
in liquid state, readily procured. Then we walked downtown. I remember
dim hours in the old museum—mastodon leg-bones the size of Negro
houses, some Indian teeth from Roanoke Island, a live snapping-turtle
that had taken two joints of a little boy's finger in Perquimans County,
and a male diamondback rattler thick as my leg that had been on a fast
ever since they caught it five months before. That morning in our presence
they tried again—set a month-old squirrel in beside his bronze eye. I
wanted to leave; Rena said "Pay attention." In under thirty seconds he
drew back and struck, and we stayed to watch him swallow all but the tail.
I remember eating two banana sandwiches (where did we get them?) in
the shadow of the statue to Confederate women (whose idea was that?
anyhow Rena liked it). I remember she took me to Briggs Hardware and
said, "Buy anything that costs a dollar." I bought a full-sized ball peen
hammer; still have it—you can hang pictures with it when it comes
your way.*

*Then in late afternoon when even I was tired of the blistering day,
Rena found a church standing open—First Baptist, unfortunately. She
said "Let's rest." We were near the hotel. I said, "You've paid for those
two cool beds." Even then I could see there was something she'd expected and not found yet. I thought it was hiding somewhere in the town.
She pulled me behind her, and we went in and sat way over on the side
in half-dark. The Kendals, as you know, were not big churchgoers, though
Rena read St. Paul more than was healthy. Still I knew when to sit quiet
and draw in my horns. Right off, she shut her eyes. I figured she was praying, so I watched her and tried to guess what she wanted. Pretty soon I
decided she wanted this to last—us alone off together. I still loved Mother
so much there was small room left for Rena even, so I couldn't share the
wish, but I did keep watching till I thought she was beautiful. You well
know she wasn't, not to see at least—plain as any rake handle. But I saw
otherwise that one afternoon. I thought she was something like Pharaoh's
daughter in* Tales From the Bible. *And maybe I was right. Children are
dead-right about so many things they later get wrong or mislay completely; maybe looks is one. I tried to imagine getting back to the hotel
and finding a wire saying Mother was dead. It ruined me of course, and
my eyes watered some. But I do recall thinking, "There will be Rena
left, who is pretty too." I went on thinking that from then on out and
leaning on it—didn't every one of us?—till you found her that morning,
cold by the steps. At least she missed this. By then she'd finished praying
or stopped. She faced me. I said, "Do you really hear Him talk back?"
She shook her head, solemn—"Not always, no."*

By the time we had had our naps and supper, it was well on to dark. She asked if I wanted another short walk. I was tired to the bone but couldn't say that. I said I would rather she read to me. So after we talked to a gentleman well past fifty in the lobby, we went up and lay in our clothes on the beds; and she read a chapter of My Poor Dick—*I swear to God, a novel she'd brought; all we had but the Bible. It was set in England, and it put me under—a hero named Dick that everybody loved.*

But before I had gone completely, Rena said, "Let me rub those tired legs with cold witch-hazel." It had happened before, more than once for chiggers and growing pains. I knew the procedure. I stripped to my under-britches, lay on my belly, and she rubbed me nicely. What was new was she finally said "Slip down your drawers." I did and she said, "Now lie on your back." I knew we were wading into deeper water but liked the prospect. I don't think I'd ever felt naked before, not for anyone but mirrors. I remember hoping my thing wouldn't stand; it had already started playing me tricks. Well, she kept to my legs as she had before— not much above the knee—and I kept my eyes shut. I was thinking any minute I would be afraid or have to answer questions I didn't understand. But witch-hazel is one of life's cheaper blessings, and its clean odor just steadily soothed any worry that rose. They were all that rose and finally they stopped; and then—somewhere on the near side of sleep—I found myself praying what I'd guessed was Rena's prayer, that this not end. She and I here for good.

As she'd foretold earlier, I heard no answer. But by then I was deeper down into sleep. She woke me with a thump on the navel, laughing. I looked. She was corking the bottle and standing. She said, "Now I've seen one. Thought I might never. Not much to live for!" I didn't understand the words themselves. But gone as I was, I knew we'd come through some narrow alley back into free space; and I knew she'd led me. So before I slept again—eight or ten seconds—I tasted, pure tasted, the thought I will not be happier than this. *I may have thought* safer, *the same thing really.*

Let that be recalled then, by you if no one else, as one of your father's best stretches of time. Notice too—in that tale, like all the rest, he is not the hero and didn't try to be. He waits for a woman to lead him to daylight. You may think he's wrong and will pay ever after but sometimes they can. So can rocks though maybe, ponds in the shade or one standing pine. My wisdom, you've noticed, tends to vanish when fingered.

I'll keep to stories then, as I vowed at the start. Next time I'm horizontal and calm as last night, I'll try to discover the next good day— seventeen to thirty-four. You were born in there. Cross your fingers and hope.

Where are you this minute?—five hours on past me, at the very least.

You were always ahead. Anyhow, whatever I said right above, I trust your fingers are better employed than crossed and waiting. That was my poor line.

28

As promised Lew had met Hutch at Oxwich Castle. They'd spent twenty minutes in its modest ruins—Lew inventing sagas of Roman attack, Hutch looking down to fields and parallel hedges and a clutch of white houses all stroked with damp sun, "in country sleep." Less than two years before, Dylan Thomas had died in a New York November too far from here, his native place. Hutch had thought they'd go on to Lew's for lunch, meet his mother at least, and maybe spend a night. But Lew had called out from a turret "Flee! Flee!" and, when he'd run down, had actually meant it—they must push on at once; he'd had home for now. So they spent three days in the west of Wales—Milford Haven, St. David's, Cardigan, Aberystwyth; then down through the Brecon Beacons and the coal towns to Bristol, Bath, Wells, Glastonbury. They stayed in Glastonbury through a fine afternoon, exploring the probably spurious but powerful traces of Joseph of Arimathea's English visit—the haven of the Grail, the thorn that had grown from his planted staff; the site of the grave of Arthur himself, entombed in a hollow oak, Guinevere at his feet (whose gold hair had powdered at a greedy monk's touch when the bones were discovered). They'd been flushed from the grounds at sunset by a guard, and treated themselves to a long dinner at the Copper Beech; then decided, on wine, to drive through the night into Cornwall—Tintagel.

And till then they had traveled easily together. Lew's appetite was mainly for the road, onward motion; but he'd seemed quite ready to hear Hutch lay out the various stories of Arthur and his woes. He'd even read aloud as Hutch drove, the entire text of Bédier's *Romance of Tristan and Iseult*; it took him two days with his interpolation of oddly convincing passages of photographic *eros*, mostly centered on Iseult's resourcefulness in bed or bower. So when they arrived in early morning mist at Trevena, the dismal village behind Tintagel Head, Hutch pulled up beside the Round Table Cafe and said, "Shall we have a little cold grease and mead before we take the next castle?"

Lew consulted a furry mouth with his tongue, then turned and smiled. "Tell you what—I'm beat and my arse thinks it's dead. Let's find a nice widow with a bed for rent. I'll doss down while you eat. Take all day to look; come wake me when you're done."

Hutch said, "I can drive to Castle Dore now. I'll wait till you're up to see Tintagel."

Lew nodded. "Drive anywhere. Enjoy the day, nice Cornish day"—it was still dim and dense. "Then if you want to take me to see anything, find a whacking color-picture with Marilyn Monroe. Or any kind of show starring anybody naked."

Hutch laughed and agreed.

Lew opened his door and stepped to the street. An old man was passing with a slow camel gait. "Beg your pardon," Lew said. "Do you know a nice widow with a lovely daughter rents rooms by the day?"

The man said "Please?" and stopped with difficulty, still rolling his knees.

"Two gents need rest. Know a cheap dry place?"

The man pointed through the Lancelot News Agency as if it were air. "Next road. Mrs. Mason. Little card in her window. Daughter's fat but blind."

Mrs. Mason was fat—two hundred pounds of red-haired cheer, exactly the color of her asthmatic spaniel. The daughter Jill was half a head taller, pleasant-looking brunette with excellent eyes. They were washing breakfast dishes when Hutch and Lew knocked; and yes they had one room, ten shillings. It faced a yard of hens, all mired in black mud; but the wide oak bed seemed dry and clean. Lew insisted on paying and changed his mind far enough to eat the big breakfast the women offered. Then he did turn in and Hutch set off.

29

The wet gray walls of Arthur's Tintagel struck Hutch as the first perfect site he'd seen. He knew that the visible ruins of the castle were some six centuries younger than any historical Arthur. Still its unroofed walls coiled tense as a snake on the high sea-crag, precisely as advertised by poets, sufficiently grand to have witnessed all the legends bestowed—the deceitful conception of Arthur and his birth by Uther on Ygrain through the arts of Merlin. But though Hutch had been the morning's first visitor and had the whole thing to himself half an hour with mist and gulls and cold salt gusts, he had not responded to more than the sights. Why?—Arthur had been his childhood favorite, with Pocahontas and Alexander. He poked round an hour taking photographs, staring out to sea and back at the Saxon church set alone on the next cliff, as open to gales. By then he'd decided—the place, with all its grandeur, was a *set*; the show was long over. He was wrong of course, knowing nothing of the two millennia of men who'd held this rock before any Arthur (if Arthur ever was) and their sturdy successors. What still bound him in like skin on his eyes was the distance from home, the newness of his break. Even grass here was unlike any grass he'd known; in its rank health it caught at his ankles, soaked and slowed him.

But two hours later, twenty-five miles south, he began to feel freed—or opening slowly. He'd driven the width of the county and come to his next planned stop. A little above Fowey on the spine of its peninsula at a country junction with no human being or animal in sight, he came on two things. A seven-foot stone plinth of obvious age stood in weeds and flowers. Hutch pulled to the shoulder of the narrow road, stepped across, and waited for the sun to take cover. Then he traced with his finger the much-disputed Latin. To him it seemed clearly to say what he'd hoped— DRUSTANUS HIC IACIT CUNOMORI FILIUS. "Here lies Drustan son of Cunomorus." *Drustan* was the Celtic spelling of *Tristan*. *Cunomorus* was another of King Mark's names. In all the stories Tristan was Mark's nephew. Did the inscription signify "son of his loins" or "adopted son"? Had the poets made a hard tale softer?—incest, real or legal, smoothed to household adultery?

Hutch walked through tall dry grass and more flowers (he seldom noticed flowers) toward a huge earthwork maybe ten feet high and easy to climb. At the top he was standing on the mound of Castle Dore—the undoubted hill-fort and palace of Mark, local king of the fields here surveyed, dated early sixth century by recent excavation. He could still see no one and nothing man-made but the green ridge he stood on. Within its small ring the most famous love of the modern world, since Antony and Cleopatra at least, had blossomed and spread—there was real chance of that. The sun cleared again. Hutch squatted to the ground and probed its softness.

He remembered—not Iseult from his *Boy's King Arthur*, slender, low-belted—but Kirsten Flagstad four years before, her last Isolde at the Metropolitan. He'd watched her from the side of the Family Circle, a fifty-four-year-old Norwegian matron whose two hundred pounds were not concealed by the white negligée of Act Two (*the night*) till she rose to the first great crest and poured—

> Have you not known. . .
> The mighty Queen
> Of boldest hearts,
> Mistress of Earth's ways?
> Life and Death
> Are under Her.
> Them she weaves of joy and pain.

He'd taken the question personally then and later in his single room at the Taft. *Had he known Her at all? And was the claim true?* What came with birth and trebled at puberty, he'd known right along. He'd always suspected himself of enjoying his body more than anyone else he'd known. Alone or with others it had simply never failed him, and he'd used it daily at least for twelve years. But had he ever known a constant need only one could fill?—from all reports, that seemed to be love. He believed he hadn't. He thought that such a need must be taught, almost surely by a mother. His mother had died the day of his birth. He'd been set the example by Rob, Polly, Grainger, Eva, Alice, now Ann. At various times one or more of those had aimed at his eyes an offer of love, a plea for love, that had now proved blinding. Dazzling at least. He'd run from that—and first stopped here. This hour seemed the first still hour he'd had in months, maybe years. And it came at Castle Dore, surely one of the earth's main ganglia of love and its famished cry.

What he felt though was ease, a simple light pleasure to be loose in a warm day, splotched by sun, hunched down in sweet grass and digging idly. *Home,* he thought; then knew that home had never meant ease. His nail scraped a rock. He gouged it up and rubbed it clean—a palm-sized parallelogram of gray shale with streaks of sea-green and, on its long edge, jagged stains brown as old blood. With the sun hid again, the rock had its own sheen, lunar but steady. He was not a skilled judge, but it didn't seem shaped by human work. Still it might have been walked on by Iseult or Mark. There were no signs forbidding the theft of a rock; he'd take this one then.

He stood and was instantly hit by the rise. His sight swam; he laughed once aloud and half-spun. Then he waited to calm. His natural compass told him he was facing southwest; that one sense never failed him. A true line grounded here, extended four thousand-four hundred miles, would touch—what? Rob anyhow—Ann, Eva, all the others nested there. *Looking homeward* then, angel or not. Milton's angel had stood on the hill in Penzance harbor forty miles from here, staring out toward Spain in protection and defiance. Hutch said the lines, richer in loss than any other—

> Look homeward Angel now, and melt with ruth.
> And, O ye Dolphins, waft the hapless youth.

Well, he'd work that out—who was who, where was *homeward*. That was why he was here. Rob had asked for a diagram. If one was there he'd find it—from here, sufficient distance. Sufficient *time*—this year, maybe more, stretched before him clear as Roman road. He'd bought himself time.

Then why, at that, did a shudder seize him and cold tears start? They held him another whole minute there high on the green midden raised over Europe's great love and foul deceit.

30

THAT evening they'd bought a can of corned beef, tomatoes, cheese, a Hovis loaf, cider, and plums and driven five miles to lie in a pasture by a small stone bridge that crossed a river barely wider than a creek. They'd asked—nearest cinema with anything bearable was an hour away; so they'd eat here, find a pub, and turn in fairly early. Hutch was tired from his day, Lew still groggy from his nap; and they mostly ate in silence, watching six cows slowly graze toward the river. The smallest would stop every minute or so and throw a long soulful look their way. Finally she moved out boldly from the others and sauntered forward, stopping only at the water, her feet in muck. Hutch and Lew were sprawled ten feet apart. She turned her muzzle distinctly to Hutch and gave a slow bellow.

Lew said, "Are you wearing your bull scent again?"

Hutch said, "I haven't bathed if that's what you mean."

"Oh lovely. That's one thing wrong with your country—people wash too much. You can barely tell they're people when you rub up against them. I like a good whiff when I'm in the mood."

Hutch nodded and smiled. "Me too, to a point."

Lew still faced the heifer; she was drinking now. "Can't recall ever having anything so pongy I couldn't lick it clean enough." He'd spoken as earnestly as if it were a finding of some importance, and he seemed to weigh it. Then he turned to Hutch, grinning. "I had this mate in the army—from Oxford; you should look him up: little low-built chap with deep-set black eyes. He was just eighteen and pure as new cream; but soon as I saw him, I said, 'Stand clear. That one's wound tight as wire. Whoever cuts *his* string had better be seated and gripping iron rails!' He was straight from square-bashing. Anyhow first weekend I took him into Salisbury—me and two others—and this old girl that I'd known some time gave us each ten minutes in a shed. Him first, as the baby— name was Gary; still is, I daresay and hope. He said it went nicely and so did the girl, though she prided herself on professional ethics—didn't blab on her trade, but she thanked me for Gary. Well, *ethics*—poor dear, she'd slipped that week. There were Irish Guards in town; I blame them —worst dogs of all. On schedule my knob popped a nice red blister. I went in for tests and a pint of penicillin. So did one of the others. And I warned young Gary, but he said he was clear—shy as foxes, he was; always washed in a corner with his arse to us. Still in three more days, he woke with this sore at the side of his mouth; he had full lips, another good sign. I asked him who'd chewed on his lip in the night. He flushed red as Christmas and said 'Nobody.' But next day the thing had spread and looked hot. I said he should have it seen to at once before his looks were marred for good. That night I found him, stood over in the dark, rubbing salve on his sore. It really hadn't crossed my mind what he had. I said, 'Got you back on the road to fame, have they?' (we always told him he was made for pictures). He turned to the light and was redder than ever, struggling with whether to knock me flat. I said 'No harm,' meaning I was his mate. He said, 'Bloody right. I'll be fit in a month. Then I'll taste it again—sweet as sherbet, it was.' He'd managed it upright in that stinking shed. Well, peace to his wounds!—a hero of love, through filth and flame."

During that the heifer had returned to her grazing. The sky was suddenly three shades dimmer; it was nearly nine. The mist that had burned off by noon was returning, lying in the middle distance beyond them and extending gradual arms their way, two feet from the ground. The light had gone violet and gave a low hum as far as Hutch could hear. He rolled to his belly facing Lew and pointed to the half-dark bridge. "Guess what happened here."

"Your eighth-great-grandmother passed a kidney stone at age ninety-nine."

"No the Mayfields were from Sussex."

Lew said, "I'm sure you'd know, Master Hutch." But he still watched the bridge. "George Washington crossed it as a lad of ten on his way west to steal Paradise from the Limeys."

Hutch laughed. "George Washington never touched England."

"Lucky sod."

"Or Wales."

"Lucky sod."

Hutch said, "It's called Slaughter Bridge. King Arthur's bastard son Modred met him here, hand to hand, and stabbed him in the head. They took him upstream—there's a rock marks the spot—and he died there at sundown."

Lew said "Lucky sod," still watching the bridge. Then he suddenly turned and faced Hutch fully, his small fine-boned skull clear in the dusk. "Might have known," he said harshly.

"What?"

"—You'd pull this on me." He was plainly not joking.

Hutch swallowed his mouthful of bread. "I'm lost."

"You're *not*. That's just it. You're hauling me round these spots dead as Egypt. I hate all this." He thumbed toward the bridge. "I told you this morning I'd had it with this."

"You said you were sleepy."

Lew laughed, which drained a little of his steam. "So sleepy I'd like to go dead right here, be nailed in a box, and not resurrected till the box reaches New York—Miami at least. Never Canada again."

"Why?"

"You've not seen it, right?"

"Right," Hutch said.

"Don't waste dollars then. It's good for a laugh in the first few weeks —grown men standing round, heads bowed in prayer that they'll turn into Yanks; but all drinking tea and debating if they'll get a nice visit this year from the Queen and her docked-cock husband. After that it's Hell."

"Go to New York then."

"You proposing marriage? That would be my one hope with your bloody immigration."

Hutch said "Sure."

They both laughed and lay back in place on the thick grass. Light was all but gone. The cows had melted off. The mist was nearly on them. Lew said, "Ever had piles or rheumatism?"

"No. Why?"

"You do now."

"Why?"

"Lying out here. Any fool who lies on British soil at night gets piles and rheumatism, dead or crippled in a week."

"How did ancient Britons fuck?"

"In trees. On stones. That's the well-kept secret of Stonehenge, mate —no temple at all, just a great knocking-shop, lovely stones big as beds. All from Wales, by the way."

Hutch laughed. "I know."

They waited another minute. Lew said, "Anything you *don't* know, Nostradamus?"

Hutch laughed but saw Lew had struck something hard. He did know the future, had always known it—what others would do. What stopped him was the past—what had been done and why, where it pressed on him. He said, "I don't know what's happened to me—in my life, I mean."

"Lucky sod," Lew said; "*I* do" and stood to go.

They walked, in faith, through total dark past the slaughter of Arthur —a bridge as fitting for a Mother Goose jingle:

> As I was going to St. Ives,
> I met a man with seven wives. . . .

They were halfway back to their lodging, driving slow in earnest fog, when Hutch said, "You claimed you knew what had happened—to me or you?"

Lew took a little time, then spoke to the road. "Oh both. You've had it very easy, all you wanted—iced lollies in the sun and more on the way. I was one of six children to a drunk stonemason in a four-room cottage on the Gower Peninsula of poor old Wales. Postcard views of Heaven. To me it meant a shit-hole out in the yard with sick chickens staring in the cold and mud while I sat breathing poison from my family's bowels with my blue knees knocking. I had the misfortune to be my mum's pet and to have a schoolmaster who thought I was special—maybe had a brain cell or two to bear me away: Richard Burton at the Vic; Emlyn Williams, you know. What I had was a smile that would melt Pembroke bluestone. That and words; I could talk. Or *sing*—the Welsh chant: *Pardon-would-you-kindly-suck-my-knob?*" He intoned it, high and sweet.

Hutch said "A lovely sound."

Lew said, "Try to *spend* it. Try to start your life with two strong arms, a straight white smile, and fulltime opera streaming out of your teeth—how far would you get?"

"Covent Garden, the Met."

"Very likely. They got me two marvelous years in Her Majesty's forces, all the birds I could shag; then six months in rural Ontario with my dad's sister, sweeping warehouse floors and minding her kids; then two whole seasons with that sorry show."

"Feeding elephants?"

"One elephant, a lion, four bears, three seals—they loved the smile; they had to."

"What was wrong with that? Every boy wants a circus."

"Nothing actually but the owner's wife. See, he was a Jew and died near the end of my first season—worn to the quick; he'd come from Poland after the war. His wife was French-Canadian, a good bit younger. She kept the show going and summoned me on—to her lonely arse. You ever try touring the wilds of Saskatchewan and Manitoba with a one-ring show, you'd find yourself climbing on the baboons if they paused long enough. I liked it at first—she was strong and funny (the seals were hers) —and she ran everything so smoothly I thought I was set for a while. Thought I was seated by a nice warm grate with my feet on the hob. I was really lost on the autumn sea near the rim of a bloody great storm wheeling at me. Every storm is hollow at the core, you know—Yvonne Taborski was sucking me in as fast as I'd come. Which is why I'm here. I ran, I mean."

"—And landed with a Yank fleeing opposite ways on a historic tour of unhistoric sites."

"Suits me, for now. Sorry I spouted back there. I hate cows."

"We'll just rest tomorrow. You set the pace."

Lew thought and shook his head. "I was whacked this morning, but I can't bear rest—reminds me of Wales."

Hutch grinned. "You decide."

Lew still faced the glass; they'd reached Trevena. It seemed to exist in midair, frail, founded on vapor. He nodded. "All right."

For Hutch, by the low green light from the dash, Lew's profile seemed strong as an Attic head—the Kritios boy on Alice's wall: a still survivor of time, acid fate, marauding hungers, triumphant though scarred and gravely generous, ready to share its patient secret if properly asked, its diamond endurance—simple as coal. He was only half-wrong.

31

Mrs. Mason was taking saffron cake from the oven when they knocked at ten. Jill was out with her young man—"wall-eyed but honest"—so she urged them to sit in the kitchen with her for Ovaltine and slices of the warm splendid cake. They were full and tired but agreed and sat. In a moment she joined them and, with no question asked, commenced a monologue on her husband Les's recent long-drawn death. "They told me his kidneys were solid as puddings when they tried to cut. I'd known his *heart* was solid for years—six months after I married him too—but I didn't have the stomach to ask what they found *there*—they cut him, fork to tit, a two-foot seam. I know; I washed it."

Lew stood at that, begged exhaustion, and left.

Hutch stayed for the tale of funeral and bills and another slice of cake. When he managed to extract himself half an hour later, he said, "I'm praying for very deep sleep."

Mrs. Mason said, "You've got the bed for that, all right. It was our old bed—mine and Les's; *he* could sleep. Slept through most of *my* life at least."

Hutch said, "Sleep has never been my problem either."

"Well, I hope Mr. Davis hasn't taken your half."

"I'll move him if he has."

Mrs. Mason thought a moment; she was rinsing their cups. Then she looked back and grinned. "I had two chaps here early last spring—from Cambridge, doing very much the same as you: nosing round old stones, asking me what I'd heard as a child of King Arthur. I told them nobody I knew had ever known him; he came with the cars, you know—trippers, once the good old war shut down. Can't disappoint trippers. Seemed to ruin their day—my chaps, I mean. I reckon they thought I had private news they could take back with them and win big prizes. Never mind; they recovered." She pointed to the wall that hid Lew from them. "I heard em playing leapfrog for three nights straight!"

Hutch laughed and left.

32

Lew had turned out the light and sounded asleep. Hutch quietly washed at the bowl in the corner. Some moonlight had reached through the one high window; it seemed the source of cold in the room. As he stripped to his shorts, Hutch shook and gripped his shoulders. Then he felt his way to the empty side of Les's bed—the usual English millstone of covers, welcome now. Still he dreaded the first touch of clammy sheets. In just a half-hour Lew had warmed them though. Hutch lay back, grateful, and condensed his body to its most economical bulk for the night. They had not shared a bed till now; good luck. He said a short prayer, then saw Castle Dore again—the shape of a great crab extending claws from a green carapace, to capture what? *Safety* surely. Safety from what? Other men. It had failed. Within the shell itself lay Tristan, a hollow heart.

His knee itched. He carefully reached down to rub it. Something cold struck his calf. He waited, then probed on down to find it. His blind fingers finally were forced to admit they'd found a knife, a dull table-knife. He drew it out quietly and held it to the moon. In its homely bluntness it managed a gleam.

Lew whispered. " 'She lay down and Tristan put his naked sword between them. To their good fortune they'd kept on their clothes. So they slept divided in the heart of the wood and were found there, pure by the wretched Mark.' "

Hutch laughed—"A-plus. A fine demonstration of the famous Celtic memory"—and set the knife on the floor by his head.

Neither of them slept at ease all night.

33

But three mornings later they sailed from Penzance in an old island steamer, past St. Michael's Mount (the angel's home) and west thirty-five miles on high seas four hours to the low granite Scillies. Lew spent the time sick in the chilly "lounge," a dim cabin ten feet square with wood benches; Hutch stayed on deck, incapable apparently of that one malaise. They docked on St. Mary's, wandered an hour in gray Hugh Town while Lew's head settled, then caught the mail-launch two miles north to Tresco. It literally beached them in a red shingle cove where an old man waited to take the mail. By then Lew was fit to resume his duties as quartermaster. Mrs. Mason had told them of a cousin of hers, married to a fisherman somewhere on the island, who would take them in; they only knew his name. "Can you tell us where to find Albert Gibbons please?"

The man's face was split—half innocent-islander, half lifelong-seaman. His eyes never met them but consulted the beach or the low hill behind. "You've got a long journey to find Bert Gibbons."

Lew smiled. "I heard Tresco was two miles long."

The man nodded. "Some less—one and three-quarter on a good bright day" (it was suddenly that, all clouds blown clear). Then he shifted the one bag and stepped toward the hill. "Bert ain't on Tresco nor in the world. Drowned maybe two months back; you won't find him."

"But he's got a wife, right?"

The man's back was to them, cresting the rise. From there he turned and looked out to the launch, barely audible, leaving. He gave it a wave. "And two bad children. Walk straight through the Garden, lean right to Lizard Point, ask the first face you see for Kay Gibbons' cottage. If she opens the door, you'll be the first that's seen her."

34

THE first face was monstrous. When they'd skirted the weird Abbey Garden—thick with palms and cactus—and followed a rolling path northeast five hundred yards, a boy stood up from a rock on their right. His body seemed eight or nine years old; his face was huge and his eyes blared wildly, but he made no noise. They stopped in their tracks. Then Lew laughed. "How much will you take for that?"

The boy came forward, still holding to his face a big round glass framed stoutly with metal—eight inches broad, some curious nautical magnifier. He held it out to them. "You can have it," he said. "Just found it by the bay."

Lew took it, held it to his own dark face, and turned to Hutch—a fish-eyed smile and hoggish grunts.

But Hutch was watching the pale thin boy, surprised by his readiness to give up so soon a genuine find any child would have prized. Five minutes before as they'd come through the garden, he'd thought the word *Eden*. He thought it again.

So did Lew, in his way. He gave back the glass. "You'll need this," he said. "It would just scare me mate."

The boy took it slowly, suspecting some part of his life had been abused. He thumbed the brass binding, then looked to Hutch. "You frightened?" he said.

Hutch smiled. "Not of you."

"*You* keep it," he said. "My mother wouldn't like it."

Hutch accepted it with thanks. "I'll remember you behind it."

The boy nodded—"Please"—and gathered to run.

Lew said, "Could you show us where Bert Gibbons lived?"

He nodded. "Why?"

"Mrs. Gibbons' cousin in Trevena said they might put us up."

The boy said "All right" and walked on ahead.

By then their bags were heavy in the sun. The boy was moving at a healthy clip, never looking back. Hutch wondered, "Does he think this is all less than perfect?" To Hutch, with his own life, it seemed perfect so far—sun, a lush garden, no cars, no town, rocks and sea as a permanent guard.

But Lew said "Oy!" to the child and stopped. "I'm an old man. Have mercy."

The boy looked back, said "Sorry," and waited.

Hutch said, "My name is Hutchins. What's yours?"—a very American question, he knew. The British he'd met till now lived happily in ignorance of names; Lew had never said *Hutch* to his face.

The boy said "Archie."

Lew said, "You want to make a shilling?—take this." He set down his bag.

Hutch said, "He's not big enough for that, Lew."

Archie nodded. "I'm not."

Lew said, "At your age I was lifting stones for my dad, twice the weight all day."

Hutch said "—And hated it."

Lew said "*Life*, me boy."

Hutch said "I'll take it." It was heavier than his, Lew's total possessions.

Lew said, "I've been breathing in hope of that." Then he smiled. "Save your strength."

Archie said, "We could all help. We're nearly there."

So Hutch and Lew shared the handle of the heavy bag; Archie took Hutch's. At the top of the next low rise, Archie pointed. Fifty yards ahead at the end of the path in a copse of low trees (some of which were palms) stood a two-story stone cottage, fenced close on all sides.

At the gate Archie said, "I'll tell her you've come."

Hutch said "She's not expecting us."

But the child ran forward, set the bag by the door, and entered shouting. "Mam, there's two big chaps here've come to sleep."

Hutch said "Archie *Gibbons*."

Lew said "I knew that."

"How?"

"Fellow Celt. Celts are magic." He narrowed his eyes at Hutch and bared his teeth as though transmitting power.

"Good. You may have to cast a spell on one crazy widow."

A young woman suddenly stood in the door, twelve feet beyond them. She was medium-sized with strong arms and legs and maybe fifteen extra pounds on her hips; but her face was blond and open as the door, though she hadn't smiled.

Lew said "Mrs. Gibbons?"

She nodded—"Kay"—and pointed behind her. "He says Mary Mason sent you here to me."

Hutch said "She did."

"I really don't know her."

"She said she was kin."

"She is, I believe. I just never saw her."

Lew laughed. "Your eyes have missed a treat. She's four feet tall, weighs fourteen stone, red hair from a bottle, and cooks like a saint."

The woman smiled; her face took it well, fresh gentle light. The boy was clearly hers. "Does that mean she's good? Don't know as I'd care to eat a real saint's cooking; don't they grudge their bodies?"

Lew said "More than me, true."

A small silence then. Lew looked back to Hutch; but before either spoke, Archie reappeared with bread and butter. "Your room will be across from mine," he said.

His mother said, "And you'll have to pipe-down at last."

He grinned and piped three piercing notes, a fine fake whistle.

35

KAY—she invited them to call her that—had given them a scraped-together lunch of eggs, cheese, and creamy milk. She'd spread it in the small sitting-room on the front, which she said would be theirs to read in or warm. Despite the bright sky a low fire had burned in the grate against damp. Once they'd sat they were left entirely alone, though sounds of Archie and maybe two women came in snatches from the kitchen—little questions and cautions. The few things Hutch or Lew said were whispered.

Lew said, "She's done pretty well, I'd say, considering we're the first men she's seen for months." He also said, "Where's the famous bad daughter the old fool mentioned?"

Hutch said, "I think I may just stay here, have my trunk sent from Oxford. I suspect this is Heaven."

Lew said, "It is. I'm the Archangel Maud." Then he said, "Cool your wick. Give it twenty-four hours. I suspect it's *England*." Then he went to their upstairs bedroom for his nap.

Hutch followed him long enough to unpack Bédier's *Tristan* again.

While he was stripping—he took naps seriously—Lew said, "I've read that to you. Branch out. Your face is long as a wet week already. Read something funny now" (he had *Three Men in a Boat* in his bag).

Hutch said, "I think this is funny as they come."

"Suit yourself," Lew said and stepped to the one round window—naked, cupping his balls. He pointed. "Go lie in that boat in the sun with your book. By three you'll be brown as a bus conductor from east Barbados—I quite like them—and I'll come join you. We can bathe before tea."

"Water's cold."

"So are hearts but I've warmed a few."

Hutch stepped up behind him and leaned to see out—a white sand cove like the perfect letter C, no human in sight, the silvered ribs of a fifteen-foot fishing boat abandoned down near the water. "See you there," he said. "I may sleep too."

Lew didn't look back but he nodded. "You need it. Been racing your brain."

"Not at all."

"You have."

"What about?"

Lew turned (they were two feet apart) and searched Hutch's face. At last he covered it with his broad left hand. "We wizards keep a great part of our knowledge hidden. You mortals couldn't bear it."

Hutch stepped back from hiding, grinned, and left. He stopped in the kitchen where Kay was scrubbing the rough stone floor—no sign of Archie and still no daughter. She offered tea; he declined and asked if there was any reason why he shouldn't lie in that beached wreck and read.

She didn't look up. "It won't float if that's what you mean," she said.

"I meant is it private property? Will anyone object?"

"Oh no," she said. "This is Tresco, Mr. Mayfield. People are really quite generous here; nothing else to be. You've heard what they say—nothing else to do in the Scillies, so people take in each other's laundry."

"*Hutchins*," he said. "I answer to Hutch."

She faced him, still kneeling. "As in *rabbit*?"

He laughed.

"You've come home then. We're the rabbit center of the universe. They take everything. Nothing seems to help." She seemed to be ready for a lecture on rabbits, no trace of a smile.

So Hutch turned to go in the momentary pause. At the door he said "Could I bring anything?"

"From where?"

"The shops."

"You haven't seen the shops!" She did smile then, reached up to the table and hoisted herself, held her head with both hands to stop the whirl. "There's a very great deal you could bring but not from here."

36

LYING in the dry boat, Hutch read again the chapter in *Tristan* called "The Wood of Morois"—Tristan and Iseult (fleeing when Mark surrenders Iseult to the lust of a band of mendicant lepers) wander three-quarters of a year in the savage wood, accompanied only by Tristan's man Gorvenal, eating fresh game and missing only "the taste of salt"; for "They loved each other and they did not know that they suffered." It was the part Lew had quoted, with the knife in Tintagel; and like any part of a truthful whole, it seemed to Hutch a sufficient picture of the world in itself—wild hunger generating its own food, rich and nutritious and finally lethal. Then in the sun which had still not clouded, he took off his shirt, lay flat in the hull, spread his arms, and slept.

In his dream he, Ann, and Lew were together on this island in the Garden. They seemed the only people, and they didn't seem in flight from any other place. At least they had managed a calm unquestioned division of labor to fill the days—summer days but they worked against the coming of cold. Hutch wandered the paths and fields and beaches, gathering stones to build a hut. Lew chased down rabbits, choked them with his bare hands, skinned and cured them over smoky fires. Ann softened the dried skins and sewed them neatly, like states on a map, into one growing cover—a broad deep quilt of tan and blue fur under which, with winter, they would sleep together. Till then they slept on pallets of palm leaves, separate but near. Hutch wondered if the others longed for winter like him; but they never spoke of it since *patience* was the element in which they moved, not *time* or *hope*. They were trying silently to teach him patience; he was trying to learn, though his body (strengthening daily with the work) steadily requested other bodies and was steadily balked.

The bow of the boat was long since stove-in, a hole the size of a pony-cart. Toward the end of the dream, Archie Gibbons approached, thrust his head and shoulders in, and stared at Hutch. He could see Hutch was chilly in the rising breeze but fast asleep. He could see in the fork of his legs that his thing was standing hard. He stayed still and silent, wondering if there were any chance in the world this man might stay here and never go. He'd wanted that since morning on the path when the man accepted his gift of the glass. He crawled forward, never shaking the boat, till he knelt compactly between the man's legs; then he touched them, laid both hands on the large knees.

Just before he woke, Hutch thought, "—The first hands to touch me since when?" The answer was "In three weeks, since Ann on the pier"; but he didn't think that. He opened his eyes on the same blue sky; then slowly looked down at Archie, who was solemn as an acolyte. Hutch said "Good morning."

Archie shook his head No.

"Good night?"

Another shake.

"Merry Christmas?"

Archie nodded. "Will you give me what I ask?"

"Is it something I can give?"

"Yes."

"You're sure?"

"It's easy." Archie still hadn't smiled, an earnest transaction.

Hutch said "Better tell me first."

Archie shook his head. "Answer Yes or No—that simple."

Hutch said "I might lie."

"Never lie."

"O.K. No."

Archie waited, then put his hands between his own knees. "You made an awful mistake," he said.

Hutch said "Let me hear."

"I asked you to stay."

"In this boat?—it's chilly." The breeze had stiffened.

Archie said "On the island."

Hutch waited. "I'm sorry. Do I get another chance?"

Archie shook his head.

Hutch said again "I'm sorry," then sat up, put on his shirt, slipped sternward, and lay back down. He said, "Could we talk a little while anyhow?"

"What about?"

"Well, your age—say you're ten?" (Though he'd never had a brother, Hutch knew you must always overestimate age.)

"I didn't tell you, no. I'm eight-and-a-half, nine in January."

"What day?"

"Nineteenth."

"That's also General Lee's."

"Who's he?" Archie said.

"The best American soldier—very handsome, lost all his wars, born on Archie Gibbons' birthday."

"You're American, are you?"

"Till today," Hutch said.

"You changing?"

"I may."

"Why?"

"I've seen Tresco."

Archie shook his head again. "Missed your go at staying here." But he pulled his body through the hole and propped up at right angles to Hutch—below his feet, no longer in contact.

Hutch lay still awhile, then asked what he'd always asked his students for their first short essay. "What's the absolutely first thing you remember in your life?" The students often took several days to decide.

Archie knew at once. "Being in my mother's belly."

"Was it nice?"

"Not half."

"What part was best?"

Archie said, "I liked the way the light looked in there."

"How was that?"

That slowed him and he faced Hutch frankly for the first time since Hutch refused. Then he said, "Do you know what torches are in America?"

"Sticks of wood on fire."

"No, electric with batteries."

Hutch nodded.

"And you press it to your fingers at night, see blood and bones?"

Hutch nodded.

"That was it. Sun shined through my mother and me all day. I could see all her bones."

"And your own?"

"Don't remember. I was looking at her."

"At night?" Hutch said. "It was dark; you were sleeping."

"No I slept afternoons. Nights I touched my dad."

"How was that?"

"In bed. We would lie on our sides. He would press up to Mam. I would feel through her skin; I could feel him all night, till he turned away."

Hutch said, "My mother died the day I was born.

Archie took the connection. "You miss her?"

"Not really. I never had memories as good as yours. I used to dream about her but now I've stopped."

Archie pressed the sole of his shoe to Hutch's ankle.

Hutch said "Miss your father?"

"Most days. Today."

"It'll slowly get better."

"No it won't," Archie said.

They paused on that. Hutch thought it was time for Lew to appear and change the air. He covered his eyes with an arm as a screen.

But Archie said, "There's one I never have missed."

"Who?"

"My sister."

"Where's she?"

"Drowned with Dad."

"Same time?" Hutch said.

"Together." Archie waited; then reached behind and above, seized the boat's rim, hauled himself up, and faced the water. Through the long silence he rapidly aged, revealing the face he would earn years from now —a steady witness of what the world gives, declining to smile. Then he pointed precisely and held the point till Hutch rose to see—blank beach, presumably marked for Archie. "I watched it from there."

Hutch said, "The man just told us about your father."

"He's daft," Archie said. "He hates my mother."

"Why?" (meaning *why hate?*).

Archie said, "Don't know. She stood in the boat, slapped her ear, and fell over. Dad jumped right behind her. They may have come up, but I never saw them. Clear day too like this."

"Was she older than you?"

"She was six, really small but always loud. Never made a sound though the time she fell. Dad neither."

"What was her name?"

"Win."

"What happened?"

"I told you."

Hutch said, "Want to ask me your question again?"

Archie said "Forget that."

When Lew hadn't showed in another silent minute, Hutch checked his watch for the first time since morning—twenty past five. Above them dark gray poured in from the darker west. The Gibbons cottage was still as plain as a model under glass but unreachable from here before the path itself would flood with impassable gray, the air go solid. Hutch said, "Could we walk past the church going home?"

Archie stood, looked down, and nodded. "All right but it's not your´ home."

The church was nineteenth-century, low and ordinary except for a plaque to the First-War Fallen in the island contingent—

> Lovely and pleasant in their lives,
> And in their death they were not divided.

Archie watched Hutch read it. "Know where that comes from?"

"The stone?"

"The writing."

"From the vicar?" Hutch said.

"The Bible. Guess where."

"Book of Acts?—the disciples?"

"Nothing lovely in Acts," Archie said. "Guess again."

"Nothing lovely in the Bible."

Archie shook his head firmly. "Just this. David's sorry for Saul and Jonathan."

Hutch remembered and agreed. " 'The gazelle of Israel is slain on the heights.' " He took Archie's shoulder from behind, tense and bony. "How'd you know?"

"Dad read it every morning at table, one chapter. I hated to hear it."

With no warning creak the logy organ attempted two bars of César Franck. Hutch was game to sit and absorb a basting.

Archie said, "I'm not staying here through music."

Hutch said, "Can I just say one short prayer?"

"I'll wait in the yard."

Hutch stood at the choir steps and asked that his father die soon, no pain. The force of the wish surprised and shocked him. He had no notion of its source or purpose, but he didn't retract it or ask for pardon. When he got to the yard, the boy had vanished—partial punishment in cold wind that rushed his mouth, coarse as dog hair. He strode as if hunted, for the cottage and fire.

37

IN the last broad field, well ahead in high grass, three figures stood in a knot, maybe joined. Despite the clouds and wind, it was daylight—would be light three hours—but partly because they were hid to the thighs by a hump of ground, Hutch assumed they were strangers. They stood near the path; there was no way to skirt them, short of striking through low ground that seemed half-marsh. So he told himself it was England not Ireland—Tresco, the navel of the British florist-trade—and went on toward them. He was ten yards away, the rise still between them, when the tallest turned.

It was Lew with Archie and an older boy. They were all in dark heavy sweaters like a team. Lew said "Did he answer?"

"Who?"

"The Lord. Young Archie says you've been on your knees at prayer."

Hutch stopped where he was, six steps away. "I was. No, no answer."

Lew said, "Never mind. Francis here has provided." He took a side step and showed the strange boy.

Fourteen, tall, with cheeks that threatened hemorrhage, Francis cradled something live in the crook of his arm. It jerked once, then fixed on Hutch and watched him closely.

He went to join them.

The boy held what seemed an albino weasel, ivory-haired with pink eyes hard as enamel and hot. Round its thin strong neck was a noose of common twine; the boy held the coiled remainder, many yards. At his feet by the path lay four dead rabbits, all good-sized and still iridescent—dove-gray, streaks of violet, all the browns, white. No sign of a gun.

Hutch said "What happened?"

Archie said, "This is Oliver, Francis's ferret. He runs through the burrows, Francis stands at the other end, rabbits run out, Francis bashes em down."

Lew said, "I told him you'd buy these here for our dinner—lovely stew. I've left my money in the room."

Hutch squatted and probed the hind paw of the biggest—the pads still warm, the claws ice-cold. He worked the leg in its complex socket, fluid as oil. No blood anywhere. Then he stood and said to the boy "You're Francis?"

"Yes."

"How much?"

Archie said "Four bob."

Hutch said "I asked Francis."

Francis said, "Take em all. They're nothing to us."

"You and Oliver?"

Francis said, "He only likes baby chickens. Still a baby himself." He stroked the fine head, fierce and pointed as a bomb.

Hutch said "May I touch him?"

Archie said "He bites."

But Francis said "Yes."

So Hutch took the last two steps, reached out, and stroked the head.

It accepted the touch as a species of food, the skull rising strongly in counterstrokes, the dry nose guessing voraciously at new prey barely seen by the weak eyes. The rough tongue licked Hutch till satisfied.

Francis said "He likes you."

Lew said "They all do."

Hutch bent and took two rabbits by the ears. He said to Archie, "Can Francis eat with us?"

Archie said "No."

Francis nodded agreement.

Lew said "Sorry, mate" and roughed Francis's hair, then tried to touch the ferret.

Oliver drew back and showed his long foreteeth.

Lew saved his hand and for once was silent, but he took up the other pair of rabbits and looked to Hutch.

Hutch said "We're long overdue" and walked on. "Thank you, Francis. Till tomorrow."

Francis watched him go.

Lew fell in behind, Archie well behind Lew.

Through the four hundred steps, wind steadily stronger, Hutch longed to see his father—not the Rob he had left three weeks ago but the grand lost boy who had lain beside him in infancy, seeking in a child (not yet a year old) full answer to questions the size of rock quarries—*Can I stand up from here, work one more day? Will you only smile? Will you never leave?* Hutch wanted to answer Yes to the last and, in that wish, saw nothing beyond him—the big wild garden raked by wind, the deadly sea; the cottage, safe as an iron spike rusting in stone.

38

WHEN they'd finished supper Lew and Archie went into the front room and played card games, each inventing his rules.

Hutch stayed to help Kay wash up, though she protested. As she worked he watched her. After whatever day she'd had, she seemed fully rested and self-possessed as a healthy tree. He might have thought of Ann; there were likenesses. But his mind stayed here, imagining for once the person at hand. How had she weathered the recent loss (two-thirds of her family) and kept this strength? Or was it some skin over desperation, stretched to tear at one wrong word? Or—given the various stories of the day—was there one final story, truer than all? Had anyone died and, if so, how and why? He started carefully. "Will you be staying here?"

Kay said "I hardly know."

"Any family here?"

"Not really—Bert's father; he met you."

"With the post?"

She nodded but had still not faced him, working intently as if against morning (it was just after nine).

"*Can* you live here?"

"Can we eat, you mean?"

Again he felt caught in idle curiosity and willful benevolence, peculiarly American. "I mean I don't see much heavy industry on Tresco."

Kay smiled. "Not much. There was talk of an anchovy plant but they vanished."

"Who?"

"The anchovies."

Hutch laughed.

"No really, used to catch them by the tubful. We'd have them for tea, mashed in good sweet butter. And crabs—Bert would kill them with a needle through the eye, couldn't bear to boil them live."

Hutch felt she'd drawn a line, a clean stopping-place; so he said no more and dried two bowls.

Then Kay pushed on. "Who told you about it? Did the Masons know?"

"If they did they didn't say—no, the man this morning and Archie on the beach."

"He's the one who knows."

So Hutch said, "It seemed mysterious to me."

"What?"

"The way they went, in Archie's story at least."

She nodded. "It does. No one else saw it though, just their bodies when they came in." Then she'd finished and walked to the door with her pail. She went to the back wall—hens prancing round her—and slowly poured the water on a thick row of tall flowers, redder in the last light than they'd been all day. Then she came on back, dark falling as she walked.

Hutch had sat at the table.

She shut the door silently, threw the black bolt, and said, "What's not mysterious is one small thing—that we've got to find some way to live like this."

"You and Archie?"

"Who'd join us?" She was maybe twenty-eight, facing fifty more years —clearly made to last.

Hutch said, "Any man in his right mind, I guess."

Kay said, "Well, thanks. No there's no one. This is Tresco."

In the front room Lew and Archie cheated and laughed like any human brothers.

39

WHEN the others turned in at half-past ten, Hutch took Archie's torch and walked back out to the beach and the boat. The wind had blown through, and the sky was clear. As a boy he'd wanted to be an astronomer and searched all the books he could find on the subject, making lists of the private terms of a science which he'd thought more poetic than the poems he'd been offered in school (John McCrae, Longfellow, James Russell Lowell)—*Sidereal Day, Universal Attraction, The Principle of Perturbations, The Equation of Time, The Weight of Light*. Still he remembered whole strings of the terms, when his failures at math had long since ended his hopes of understanding and he'd even forgot the names of stars and their seasonal places. He found the Great Bear though and held on her while he thought "*Filamentous Nebula, Zodiacal Light, Stars of Dif-*

ferent Magnitudes, The Rotation of Venus ('which remains unknown')."
They slid him into sleep, and there he invented or maybe uncovered a fact
from *Tristan.* At the end, after decades of adhesion and tearing, when
Mark stands in blessing over Tristan and Iseult—joined, dead as soused
herring—the tragic glow falls not on Mark (who fought after all for his
grim share) or on Brangien (who served the successful potion) or even on
the internationally-famed spent couple but on Gorvenal, Tristan's empty-
handed handyman, unworn as a baby after all his long witness. Hutch
watched through Gorvenal's eyes awhile and felt the same sense of abandonment that had blown in on him this afternoon. A single figure—young
enough and able—who'd thought he was ready for a life of his own, left
suddenly with nothing to show but memory. The fact that Memory was
mother to the Muses hadn't sunk deep enough in his mind for dreaming.
Or had sunk and been refused as harmful or untrue. He saw himself stand
by the glamorous dead till all others left, bearing Iseult above them. Then
he took up Tristan, surprisingly light, and walked toward the sea.

He woke, cold and damp, recalling what he'd seen and pressed hard
by it. The sky was clearer and closer than before; but its lucid figures gave
no relief, barely held his eyes. He sat up stiffly, climbed on his knees
through Archie's hole, and went toward the cottage—impelled by the
dream, still stronger than any wind he'd felt. The torch struck three
grown rabbits as it swung; each froze for his passing, then quickly forgot
him and leapt into darkness.

40

THE ground floor was silent, and no light was on, so Hutch kept the torch
and climbed the steps quickly as old boards allowed (only the downstairs
was wired for power). When he opened the bedroom door, a smell of kerosene stopped him on the sill. A lamp by the bed burned low and hot. Lew
was on the near side, back turned, surely asleep. The window was shut.
Hutch went there first and opened it wide. The lamp fumes streamed out,
crossed by clean salt breeze. There still was no moon, but he guessed
there was starshine enough to undress by. He went to the flame and blew
it out with one breath.

Lew said, "I was hoping you'd leave it be."

"The light?"

"Yes."

"Why?"

"I wanted to see you."

Hutch laughed in a whisper, pulled off the sweater, and began his
shirt buttons. "Why?" By then his eyes had opened to the shine again.

Lew rolled to his back and looked straight up, an ancient recumbent. "I really feel bad."

"Rabbit fever?"

Lew said "Please."

Hutch sat on the chair to untie his shoes. "Then what?"

"This trap, whole bloody sad trap." Lew covered his face with the crook of his arm.

Hutch thought he understood. "You're out of it though. You're *Canadian*—just a tourist here." He stood, dropped his trousers, and folded them.

Lew said "—In *your* life."

Hutch drew back the cover and entered his half, stretched flat on his back. In a minute he said, "Want to talk about that?"

Lew said "Why bother?" Then after a while he said, "You've been very nice, very Yank about it all. But notice you brought me to the end of the earth. We won't be slogging round Oxford together."

"You'd be welcome any time."

"As a tripper," Lew said, "—hot winkles and chips."

"The Scillies were your idea. I'd never heard of them."

Lew said "Fair enough." Then he said "Know why?"

Hutch knew now he did. Their outward flights could cross only here, in unwatched solitude. He wanted them to and, in the next minute, that chance of intersection became all he'd wanted—or at least a seam worth gambling on to close the tear through which he felt his whole life wasting. He rolled to his left side, facing Lew, and laid his hand on the cool lean belly.

Lew lay still awhile, then turned toward Hutch till the hand rode his hip. "You sure?" he said.

"I'm sure."

"Since when?"

"Since New York, when I saw you."

"You're a great one for *eyes*."

Hutch said "They're my job."

"How new will it be?"

Hutch said "Fairly new."

Lew laughed. "Fairly, eh? There's only one me."

Hutch said "Lucky sod."

"Me?"

"No, me," Hutch said.

So Lew reached out in one accurate line and took him where he was thoroughly ready.

For more than an hour, they met one another in all the ways two bodies can meet—released from time at the west edge of Europe, suspended sweating over Kay and Archie, generous and gentle, happy and used.

41

June 21, 1955

Dear Min,

    You and I have talked plainly in the past, so you won't be surprised if I wade right in without waltzing around. I know Rob had supper with you three weeks ago. I know he enjoyed it; but I asked him last night, and he says he hasn't spoken to you since then. So I have good reason to think you don't know his principle news. No one does till now but me, Sylvie, and Grainger. That has been his wish. I am going to fail him one last time though and tell you now, for reasons I'll explain.

    Min, he can't be expected to live many months—lung cancer, widespread. Dr. Simkin did not advise surgery, and Rob has refused any radiation. He's known for a month and kept it to himself till Hutch was gone. Then he told us here, after which it has not been mentioned till last night.

    Meanwhile he has had a normal summer, staying out there reading and working his garden, making a visit to Bracey and Richmond, dropping in on me every day or two.

    Last evening we had a light supper here—he turned up unexpected; Sylvie had left. At first he seemed unchanged from three days before, and he told me about your funny trip to Mount Airy—you ought to have taken that doll; it would have lightened the poor soul's burden—but when we were finished and he tried to stand, he half-fell back. His legs are failing. He sat there, pale, so I sat too and raised a few questions. He didn't want to answer. I had to remind him that a drawn-out death wasn't his sole affair unless he planned to drive west and vanish and be shipped home from some tourist court in Utah, prepaid and ready. I've assisted at two long deaths—Father and Kennerly—and I know. The dead are as selfish as babies.

    He told me then that oddly he has no breathing problems but that his legs are steadily weaker, which is the normal course. One thing he has always been is a splendid walker; you know that. I told him again he should move in here. Grainger has offered to move out there. He's kindly told us both to leave him alone.

    I've known him too long to disobey. What he wants to have is these little visits and the part at the end when he strangles beside me. I'll take it. What I've wondered all morning though—and why I'm writing—is, short of calling Hutch (which he'd kill me if I did, I honestly believe), can I give him anything in the way of ease?

    You come to mind there. I know he meant a good deal to you once, and I think you did to him. If it hadn't been for Hutch, I think he'd have asked you to stay close by; and I've always regretted he didn't see a way to give Hutch his due and still have a man's life. Well, he didn't. He has never known but one thing at a time; that's the Mayfield in him (not that any Kendals known to me were flibbertygibbets).

So what I'm coming to is, you could ease him. Min, I don't know what has passed between you lately. I don't know much about your own life in Raleigh; but something has told me that if you could turn up and say you'd come for a visit, it would do more for him than all but Hutch could. You know I'm not asking out of any wish to shirk my own clear duties—as I've said, the day will come for those—or out of a wish to burden or hurt you (I know you'd be hurt worse by stumbling on the truth when he's gone past seeing). I simply say what I believe to be true. Rob would welcome you now as never before. If you can bear that, and have any time, come and do what you can.

No one knows I've written this. No one ever will—from me. If you choose not to answer for any earthly reason, you'll never hear a sign of reproach from me. I think I can gauge what I've asked, a solid question. Life offers very few, I seem to have noticed (despite what all the easy groaners contend).

Ever yours affectionately,
Eva Kendal Mayfield

June 21
Hutch, you'll notice I haven't touched this for four days. We had a short set of perfect weather, clear as outer space, steady 80° with perpetual breezes. The birds nearly died of singing, and the leaves are posing for that one great long-awaited Southern landscape painter you used to want to be. Did you ever figure why he's never existed? Has it been too hot to work outside? too humid for the paint to dry? too many bugs landing? Why did you switch to poems? Write me one that explains; I'll probably see it. I say that with something like semi-confidence after this weather. I didn't do much but sit on the steps and feel it and take a few walks back into the woods and try to clear the Kendal graves before the new growth over-whelmed my powers—the legs are still unreliable—but it did give me some-thing I hadn't had for a good many years. That is, a certainty that I matter and don't matter at the same time. I seem to have needed that and hope nothing takes it from me now. I think I can do two things at once—say what I mean about how I feel and tell you the next best day of my life, seventeen to thirty-four. Since it also involves sex, I wonder if I ought to say in advance that your father has not been hipped on the subject. But that would be a lie. The truth is, I doubt I have lived through a single hour since, say, age eleven without either wanting to use my body for that brand of comfort or regretting I'd done so or playing back some favorite mental home-movie. Same goes for everybody I ever knew with normal

good sense, some women excepted. So here is the day. Sorry but you're not in it.

I left home in March 1925, twenty-one years old—on my birthday, in fact, to hurt Mother's feelings or see if I could. Niles Fitzhugh and I rattled round a week or so in my old Chevy, taking in a few views. You know I have never been much on sightseeing if the sights involve dead folks, which Virginia mostly does. What I mainly remember is Traveller's skeleton at Washington and Lee. Every square inch of bone had some damned piss-ant student's name on it; they signed him for luck. There was General Lee laid out in white marble like Jesus in heaven, battle-flags in a ring and all his dead children (Jesus was what they intended anyhow; I thought he looked more like a dry-goods jobber dead of gastric ulcers and carved in tallow); and down in the basement were the beautiful bones of the noble dumb horse used for self-advertisement by rich adolescents. You know I think the Civil War is the sorriest occasion in history to remember, and I thought those bones put the tin lid on it. So when we left there, I was ready for something live as I could find.

We asked an old Negro to aim us at some girls. He said "White or colored?" We said "Either one." He said, "Tell me they got some in Buena Vista at the Roller's Retreat, but I ain't touched that stuff for twenty years." I asked him why and he said, "My ears. My ears break out every time I get it and itch for a month, so I give it up. My ears doing fine." We drove right on to Buena Vista. The vista then was better than now, though still no peril to sanity. It was Friday evening and the streets were strung with identical rat-faced mountaineers—all each other's half-brothers at least and ready to kill anybody not kin—but we found our own slow way to the Retreat. It was right up near the Ladies' Seminary, young girls patroling in long white dresses and gloves under oak trees. Niles begged to stop there. I told him we'd be lynched. He said "So be it," but I dragged him on.

Roller's Retreat—still wonder what it means—was a decent old house with a Room and Board sign. You could get a big meal for twenty-five cents, mostly biscuits and gravy with white-girl waiters. When she saw you'd finished, the girl would say, "You're welcome to use our upstairs to rest." And up you went—if you were me. Nothing fancy upstairs, just a wide front-room with sofas and tables and a world of magazines. The first time we went, we were there alone; so we sat down and read. I had finished two issues of The Literary Digest before anybody else showed a face.

Then a woman stepped in, maybe sixty years old and clearly sister to the men on the street. She looked so rough that Niles stood up and said we'd been told we could rest up here. She waited what seemed like a week in December, then said "No you can't." Niles started begging pardon but I stayed still; I was that intent. I said, "Can we spend any more money then?" She said "On what?" —"What you selling?" I said. Plain as any salesman for lightning rods, she said, "Safe liquor, clean pussy. Say which." I said "Both, for me." Niles sat down and nodded. You had to drink first, by yourself in the parlor; girls not allowed to drink or watch you drink. In fact you were not allowed to watch the girls. When we'd had two big snorts, the woman came in again and said "Now follow me." We went down a long hall. She opened one door on dark thick as walnut and waved Niles in; he looked back at me like the Children's Crusade in the hands of pirates but he went ahead. Then she led me right to the end and stopped. She searched me again with her eyes like picks and said, "I'm throwing you a real challenge, son." Thank God I didn't have Niles there to see me. She opened the door. There was dim lamplight and I stepped to my fate. It was not my first time. I started on a cousin of Sylvie's named Flora when I was seventeen and, after that, found several girls in the county. There was one made me take her in her pa's tobacco barn, and the barn was fired. I mean they were killing tobacco in there, late August to boot. I thought I was dying but saw it through, proved at least my heart was good for the race; and so it's been—never missed a beat. I'd never thought of screwing as a challenge though, more like sliding off the slipperiest log on earth into warm clear water that bore me up. At first it seemed the room was empty. Even with the lamp I couldn't see a soul. So I stood very still while my eyes adjusted, thinking every second some six-foot female ape from the hills would fall in on me from the ceiling, all arms. Finally I saw there was this little tuck in the room, a little alcove; I took a step toward it. There by a window was a tall woman in a long blue bathrobe with her back to me. I cleared my throat; she never moved. I said "Good evening." She held still awhile, then half-turned around. She was holding a thick book, open in her hands. There was just a trace of daylight, not enough for me to read. I said, "You must be some kind of cat." She said, "No I'm a very big reader. Let me finish this please. Make yourself at home." I took that to mean Get naked so I did; and she stood there in all but deep night and read four pages of her book, then shut it.

By then I was bare as a willow wand, standing on a throw rug, shivering slightly—mountain air. When she turned I said "Was it good?" She nodded—"Always is. I've read it a lot." I said "What was it?" She said, " 'The Gift of the Magi'—O. Henry." I told her I'd read it, and she set me a test—"Then what's it about?" I said as best I recalled it was about how most gifts people give are unusable but should be given still. She said "That's it" and took her first step, toward the lamp by the bed. I saw for the first time how old she was—maybe forty-five, not ruined or repulsive but thoroughly seasoned. A big head of brown hair and powerful eyes.

Then she took off her robe and laid it on the chair. A strong country body as old as her face but very dignified; she didn't touch herself. She *held out her hand for me to stay put. Then she studied me slowly, not smiling or frowning. She said to my eyes, "You starting here?" I had to say "Ma'm?" She said, "You starting your love life tonight?" In those days I looked about seventeen. A truthful answer would have been "No ma'm. I've had four girls twelve times, maybe eleven" (I'd tried to keep count). But I grinned and said "Starting." She said, "In that case can I just take over?" I said, "Fine by me. I like everything I ever came across except liver with onions and any kind of pain." She still didn't smile but she said, "Nothing I did ever caused pain." I said "Congratulations." She said "Many thanks."*

I don't know that you'll want a detailed account of the rest of the night—might muddy your memories of dear old Dad—but I want to write it for my own sake now. If it doesn't serve you, there's fire in the world; just burn it up.

She didn't say another word till six a.m., and to this day I don't know her name. She stepped over to me, took me by the elbow, and laid me on the bed. It was clean and turned-down. She stretched out beside me, both flat of our backs. In a minute I tried to roll left toward her. She stopped me with her hand. So we lay still the best part of maybe five minutes. I think I took a nap. Anyhow I was brought to by her rising slowly and parting my legs. She took it from there as she'd asked to do, and I lay and watched. I don't mean to say I only watched. There were two of me present—the one that could see and barely believe, the one that was served in ways he'd only half-dreamed existed.

I said she was dignified; she stayed so right through. She worked at me slowly with hands, mouth, and eyes—she never shut her eyes; most women work blind or did in my day. I'd been used to leading and to leading fast. But she gave me pleasure that was so deep and steady I had time to find what the cause of it was. She was worshiping me. I'd never asked for that from anyone alive (though Rena volunteered it in a different way and I mostly refused). The one that was watching could lie there propped on two goose pillows and see a grown woman honor my one body as if it was all and would always suffice, using nothing but clean-smelling spit as her ointment. I'd tried to worship Mother for twenty-one years; now I saw this was better if it only would last.

It lasted till morning as I already said. The strong part ended in maybe an hour when she straddled me finally and took me in and, slow as before, rode us both to a rest like sleep after good work. I slept at least, not thinking of Niles or home or safety or of how much time two dollars had bought. At dawn she was there beside me, looking calm; so I guess she had stayed. She said, "Son, you're started. Better get you some eggs." That woke me.

I washed and found Niles downstairs, eating eggs. He'd slept on the sofa in the magazine room. I was started all right. I just never finished. *That was the challenge. What she hadn't told or shown me was a way to finish, to feed once for all the taste she'd planted—or found; it was there.*

Why does that last in my mind then as happy? Because of the worship surely. Looking back I can see I was lovable, and right from the first— a genial baby (once I'd lasted through whooping cough), a thoughtful boy. By the time I washed up at Roller's Retreat, I was something rare as an albino stag with purple rack—a tall healthy man with handsome face, clean wavy hair, strong arms and hands, and a straight round dick with a low brown mole near the end of the shank. I didn't know that or didn't believe it. Nobody but mirrors had told me so, nobody I trusted. I was fool enough not to trust Rena and Min. But I trusted that woman in Buena Vista. I knew she had ample range to compare (college boys came to her, not just mountaineers); but mainly I leaned on the way she had stood there and studied that story to the end once more, then asked me the meaning.

Could I use her gift? Well, could and did. In a month I'd met your mother and believed her. In nine I'd married her and set you in motion. You didn't arrive of course for nearly five years, but you were the main result of the night I've set down above—that your father was licensed to live a whole life, having earned the right.

Have I had it? Let me know.

June 24, 1955

Dear Rob,

I've stood it as long as I want to. June, I mean. Long years out of school, I still think June is when you crawl home, get your clothes clean, sleep late, and stock up on bedrock boredom to see you through the thrilling future. And business conspires—I need to come search through some courthouse records for a swarthy woman from Lansing, Michigan who's praying she's white.

Will you be at all visible, say the midst of next week? I wouldn't be averse to driving up Wednesday morning, doing my work, and seeing you afterward with suitable chaperone—is Grainger there? If not don't call him on my account. The damage is done.

But if you get this tomorrow, please phone sometime this weekend and say. I'll do the work anyway, but it would seem wasteful at our age not to glimpse each other. Especially since glimpses have been our specialty since before man invented the wheel or steam.

Very truly,
Min

June 25, 1955

Dear Min,

Your letter came an hour ago. If I sit down right now, you'll have an answer on Monday—and an original manuscript by Robinson Mayfield, one of the few—and I won't have had to resort to the phone, which I hate worse by the day. At least in letters you could tell people the truth or what you thought was true without the imminent possibility of them bursting into sobs or apoplexy in your hearing. The phone breeds lies.

So here—it's no lie when I say I feel two ways about a meeting next week. Since Hutch left and you gave me that good supper, I've been by myself so much that I'm suspected by Mother and Grainger of taking the veil. They may be right. If so it's because I'm surprised to like it after years of thinking it was man's great curse—loneliness, I mean, or being alone. On the other hand the long days of quiet have given me space to remember a lot (I've been writing down past things that Hutch may need); and what I remember is company, the good and bad. Mostly the good.

You were obviously good. I haven't forgotten our mistake in Richmond. To have cheated on Rachel that once with you is still the main regret in a life which has several real ones. She never guessed at all though, and who did it harm but you and me and the feelings of whatever supernatural traffic happened to fly through the close air of that room that afternoon? The supernaturals are in business to forgive, right?, so they're doing fine. We let it do us in from then on. Or was it just me who loved the load?

Sure, come up Wednesday. I'll wait for you here in the late afternoon with whatever Baptist deacons I can muster as vice patrol.

Your oldest friend above ground (is that correct?),
Rob

June 25, 1955

Dear Hutch,

Your cards from Wales and Cornwall arrived. You sound a little mildewed. Is the weather that depressing or is it your single state? I haven't gone far but solitary travel in a wet land of strangers seems to me a hard way to win Wisdom and Virtue.

There're no easy ways, I at once recall. For instance I have my first roommate since leaving school, and let me record that the cave of companionship is still as risky as the red sands of hermitage. At least when the two sport the same brand of plumbing or need the same plumbing. I've hardly had one chance to pee at home since Linda Tripp moved in. Have I mentioned her? She was hired at the office two weeks ago and needed a room. She's from up in the mountains—Agricola, Virginia—and at first I thought she was our age or younger. Turns out she is twenty-nine at least, had withered on the vine at a lawyer's office in Lynchburg, and only broke loose to follow her first boyfriend to Richmond—a tall thin lineman for the power company. She met him in Lynchburg; one stroke of the wand and she was set free. Withered in fact is not the word. She is perfectly preserved in rural childhood or was till last week. The peeing is caused by the lineman, it seems—a clear case of honeymoon bladder or is it Virgin's Complaint (Recent-Virgin's Complaint)? But whenever she's visible she's company at least. Much as I've tried to enjoy heroic oneness, I find that I after all prefer to bump fannies with some other creature in the kitchen or hall if nowhere else. And the creature has to be human, no dogs or hamsters—even when her tales of backseat passion recall my own lamented past (I lament that it's past, I mean, or suspended).

Are you happy as you are, or can you say yet? I'm not but you know that. What neither one of us knows, I guess, is how much you're involved in what I feel and how much of it is just me—the barometric pressure, my bloodsugar level, my whole normal (normally gloomy) past.

In brief then—do I sound enough like a legal secretary?—that's another attempt to say how, much as I want to, I'm not holding you responsible for anything. Whether you chose me or not, I chose you and could learn to withdraw whenever I'm given the back-out flag.

Later—Linda interrupted me there with the lineman. I'd seen him through the window but never met him; he'd told her he thought he'd better look me over. So I sat them down with potato chips and we talked. Well, Linda and I talked. He (his name is Bailey) didn't say three words for the first half-hour but ate every last chip and studied me close enough to see if I was also consumable once the snacks were gone. He has black eyes and I'll have to say I liked it. I was giggling like a girl at her first slumber-party when he finally broke in and, apropos of nothing I could understand, told me the one big story of his life. He was electrocuted last winter, the bad sleet-storm in February. Had to go out with one other man at four in the morning to patch wires broken by ice and trees. The other man was new and stayed on the ground to manage the searchlight. The man dozed off or couldn't aim the light. Bailey by then was icy himself and reached out dark, brushed a bare hot wire, and took (he swears) two thousand pure volts. He fell thirty feet to the ground; the wire lashed him. The other man took his time with rescue. At that point he suddenly pulled up his shirt—in the story, I mean (at that point in the story)—and proved it all. He's as brown and lean as a broad leather belt; but from neck to navel, and points south apparently, he has a white burn-scar straight as a die. Said it fried to the bone. I admired it sufficiently. He said it had taught him all he needed to know. I said, "Not to trust anybody on the ground?" He said, "No ma'm—that from now on I'm free." I asked how was that. He said, "I've died, paid for all my sins, and am now in Heaven." I said,

"For an angel, you sure love potato chips"; but he still hasn't smiled. If he's dead though what does that make Linda? What does that make me? And why do I only meet men in love with freedom? I may investigate.

Still later—I've just read the first part of this. Don't it sound noble? Do you think I'll be played by Joan Crawford or Joan Fontaine in the movie of your life? What I'd really prefer is Martha Raye, though her mouth's too small. Let me know your choice in a long letter soon.

Love,

Ann

P.S. I forgot to give you the outcome on Mrs. Quarles, the lady who stabbed her husband fourteen times and bandaged each hole. We got her off, I want you to know. She's walking the streets of Richmond right now, free as you or Bailey. Be sure to contact us in event of your arrest—no crime too awful. Phone collect to Ann Gatlin. She's the mastermind, disguised as secretary.

July 6, 1955

Dear Hutch,

I've already fallen behind, haven't I? Your second letter got here yesterday in the wake of the Fourth (I stayed in at my window all day and watched nearly nonstop parades of Negro Elks and Saints—if they were mad about Virginia White Folks' reaction to the civil-rights challenge, they gave no sign beyond smiles and strong teeth; but oh if they do, there'll be cut throats and burnings). Since it contained the first of those questions you threatened to ask, and I seem to have volunteered for, I feel I must gird up posthaste and answer.

One warning before I do, though I'm sure you know it already—I am not an ideal advisor on matters of the heart, not on the heart-in-the-world at least. What I know (and I do know some things) is spectator's knowledge, acquired from years of fairly steady watching in which I have tried to keep my eyes clean. I may well have failed. I may have seen things the players didn't notice or at least didn't feel or that weren't even there. I may well just be the Dixie Miss Dickinson—but wouldn't you rather ask your questions of Emily than of, say, Hawthorne or Emerson with their wives and babes? Apparently you would.

And in any case I wasn't quite accurate above. I have, as you know, played a few games myself; and if the innings were short or unfinished or finished by the other players drifting away, they certainly went flat-out while they lasted, giving me much cud for lonely rumination (Lord, the scenes my metaphors summon!—a cow at bat: even Disney would quail).

*So now to reply. The answer is Yes. Immediate love—"at first sight,"
I assume you mean—is not only possible, it's the only kind I've known;
only kind likely to last* as love *(slower kinds warm gently, cool back gently
into friendship or fairly oblivious matehood). The Bible, all the good
poetry—and most of the bad—says nothing but that. What it doesn't often
say is the next thing to know and as urgent as the first—find out* why *the
first sight stormed your gates. I don't mean that real love is not mysterious;
it is but at the edges not the center. False love—infatuation, the immediate
need to rub and be rubbed—is what always comes as high and inscrutable
with a clamor of wings. The genuine event however will clarify if you just
watch it long enough. And when it does the mystery will mostly turn out
to be a name. You've loved the person who either is there for present
grasping or the person they promise to be, the one you've perpetually
needed. When I was sixteen I loved Marion Thomas because I've always
taken beauty pretty seriously and wanted to serve it. Later I loved your
mother because, being a healthy woman, I saw I wanted a daughter; and
she was ready to be that awhile. Nothing wrong with either case from my
side—not that I can make out and, believe me, I've tried. Problem came
when Marion and Rachel decided they didn't want to be what they were
(not that Marion ever knew).*

*But aren't you too old to be asking that? Isn't that something most
people get settled in the sixth or seventh grade? I seem to remember dis-
cussing it with Rachel once; then I took the other side and was wrong.
Never mind—I'm right now and there's your answer, however insane. Do
you want to say why you tested me with it?—literary curiosity or present
concern? Anybody as interested in tales of King Arthur as you seem to be
will need clear views on all such questions, no doubt. Glad to help.*

*Did you cut your trip short? In your first you said you'd tour for six
weeks. I was stretched out waiting for a soft rain of postcards from Land's
End to Orkney, and here you're back in Oxford. You've sat still before,
Hutch. Don't stop and think too soon. Both your parents were lightning
leapers-to-conclusions (not merely in love); maybe you should be slower.
Let a lot happen first. Don't take quick answers, even mine—least of all!*

*—Which doesn't mean I won't be eager to see the first installments of
your Tristan poem. Like you I've always suspected the servants had the
true news on all that unpleasantness; why weren't they interviewed? If I
had good sense, I'd write Brangien's version while you write Gorvenal's.
Since I don't I'll await revelation from you.*

*Lord knows, there's very little here to report. As I said, colored people
are keeping present silence in the teeth of Virginia's jackass display of
"massive resistance" to school integration. Have you ever wondered—as I
do hourly—at what precise moment the state that mainly invented America (on paper anyway) was struck deaf, dumb, blind, and halt as an old*

dog sprawled in the manger and gnawing at itself? You picked a good time to seek fresh air. I for one hope you find it. Breathe slow deep breaths and keep me posted.

> Barely breathing (it's hot) but still your loving,
> Alice

July 12, 1955

Dear Mr. Mayfield,

I didn't hear from you before I left home, and there was nothing at American Express when I went there yesterday except a wire from the doctor's wife I told you about. I figure she'll live but she seems to doubt it. Anyhow I'm in London, sleeping at a Polish hotel in Bayswater—cabbage for breakfast—and checking out a few famous ruins with my brother. I thought England won the war, but they don't seem to know it. Can't somebody get them to clean up the place and turn the sun on? Is money all they need? Don't they still own most of Africa and Asia?

I told you my brother is going to Paris, a week from today. I can't get up any enthusiasm for France, not after our trek through Madame Bovary. So I'm still wondering if you want to join forces for a while. You mentioned Cornwall. Sounds good to me. Only limits on me are ten dollars a day, and I'm finding it hard to spend more than $7.50 plus tax. By the time I see you, I could be rich and we could fly to Pompeii. I always wanted to see that whorehouse they dug up with the peculiar murals.

> Say the word c/o American Express, and I'll meet you anywhere.
> Strawson

P.S. Speaking of Africa, which I was in the first paragraph, you might not want to wait till you see me to hear that Waverly Conover from home (you remember, the organ salesman with the withered hand) is starting a fund to export black volunteers back to the Dark Continent. When I left he claimed to have eight hundred dollars and is planning to go nationwide with his plea if Life magazine will contribute advertising with mail-in coupons. Do you think we should warn the English on this or let them be surprised by big boatloads? It might wake them up. German rockets didn't seem to.

July 14, 1955

Dear Hutch,

Relieved to know you're safely back from the Cornish excursion. My reading assures me Britain has an unnaturally low crime-rate (more murders in Houston in a month than in Britain all year, Ireland included); so I don't worry much about your meeting with human violence, but there're always the famous Acts of God, and I continue to suspect that motor vehicles are not really understood outside the American three-mile limit and are therefore even more perilous than here. You can probably use the rest time anyhow. If eleven years of teaching taught me anything, it's that teaching is roughly as exhausting as coal mining or perfect attendance at all Southern Baptist conventions of the past thirty years. Second worst is being a pupil—you've got this pause between the two; sleep a lot.

I'm still worrying, you see. I was hoping, and I suspect you were, that once you vanished I'd get some peace—not yet. I still think the world is dangerous and has a special tendency to try my loved ones. I've even had evidence, you might say. It's one of the two things that kept me from being the model father I intended. The other was your mother's vanishing when she did. I'd planned to be one parent not two. When and if you have a son or children, I hope you will have the strength—and mercy— to consign them to the world once they can walk and defend themselves against human threats (by which I mean an unarmed human of similar size; anything worse is probably Fate). Don't teach fear as I did to you. No use in it. They won't escape.

But I started this to answer the question about your Welsh friend. I'd like to help him but see no way. As I understand immigration law, I would have to provide guaranteed employment and boat-fare home if he's dissatisfied. You remember the Pole Mrs. Picot took right after the war. He came here elegant as Lord Halifax, had the place looking like Versailles in a month; then took up with that trash Pulliam girl, gave her fat blond twins when the Pulliams hadn't made a blond since Cain set them rolling and vanished north by night, leaving three empty mouths Mrs. Picot still feeds. Vanished seems to be my big word this evening, doesn't it? Still as I said, I'd help if I could; but from what you tell me of his past experience and needs, he doesn't seem custom-built for these parts. I doubt he'd be happy, and I know for certain that it's past my power to help him. In any case I gave up—long years back—the attempt to help people by changing their direction. I only caused wrecks except with you, and you always knew where you were headed and only needed to have your windshield buffed occasionally. Proud to have had my chamois rag handy.

One local thing has changed, and I want to tell you before anybody else. Min Tharrington drove up here to search some courthouse records two weeks ago, ate supper, and has been with me ever since. She can do her genealogies here as well as anywhere with quick trips to Raleigh, and I asked her to stay. The reason is I wanted to and so did she. We figured we were big enough to act on that basis. She has no kin to be startled by the fact, and I hope I don't. You'll have guessed Mother likes it, though *she has invented a tale or two as the visit lengthens to explain to friends. My favorite is the one that says Rob has hired Min to track down the Mayfield family for Hutch. Come to think of it, that may be an idea. Shall I set her on the trail? God knows where it ends—in an English jail maybe, some ditch-born baby—but you might like to know, long hence if not now.*

Further things you might like to know at once—I'm aware you and I have not discussed Min for ten years at least and that, when we did, you were strongly opposed. I understood why and honored your reasons the best I could while you were nearby. Now you've gone your way, I will go back to mine—or forward to mine. You were my way for years as I trust you recall. So view this rightly wherever it leads. It may not last long. What I want is not your blessing but your patience. You're old enough for patience. I'll keep you informed on all you need to know.

What else? Weather's hot but dry as Sahara. Grainger drives out every day and helps Min cook (she is no great chef). Your grandmother, as I implied, is fine. I have to visit her though; she won't come here. I asked her why yesterday. She just smiled and said, "I don't want to be there when Sheriff Wilkes pulls up and hauls you two off in chains for fornication." She's studied the statutes and may well be worried. I'm not. I went to school with Delbert Wilkes and have cause, ten times over and he knows it, to slap a citizen's arrest on him and make it stick.

Keep me in your prayers then but hire no lawyers.

The same loving,
Rob

July 16, 1955

Dear Ann,

My silence is mainly owing to work. I got back here three weeks ago and sat right down to start a poem suggested by the trip. West Britain is all King Arthur country; and though most of the sites are spurious, they look and feel right—if they weren't the scenes, they could have been. One of them anyhow stands at least an even chance of being a witness to real events—the fort of King Mark in the country near Fowey may well be the spot where Tristan and Iseult took the great plunge. So I'm working on them, a maybe long poem. Every morning I wake at seven o'clock, eat a big breakfast in the college Hall (served by friendly dwarfs—grown men who have served teen-agers all their lives, with faces like the archers at Agincourt), then come to my desk and write till noon. Then I walk round town for a couple of hours—the book and junk shops are amazing; today I only just prevented myself from buying a mothy tigerskin complete with snarling teeth and a wastebasket made from an elephant's foot. Then I buy cheese and bread, eat lunch in my rooms, take a nap, read, take a walk in Christ Church Meadow which is right outside my window. In the evening I eat curry at one of the many Indian restaurants (one was closed last week for serving cat) and, if it's fair, drive awhile. You can be in the country in fifteen minutes, any direction you head from here. I mostly go to the north or northwest—almost no one in sight, nobody to mind if you stop by the road and step through a field toward what they call rivers (peaceful creeks) or the few stones left of an abbey or an Iron Age family camp. The light lasts well past nine o'clock. I moon some, then drive on back here to sleep. Sometimes I say whole phrases out loud just to hear a voice, to see if mine works. I've had few chances to talk to anybody.

It seems to suit me so far at least—being on my own like this, a trusted stranger—so I'll follow where it leads. Our first night in New York, I tried to answer your questions honestly. I think I need this now. I may not always. You ask it again and the answer hasn't changed. I don't say it harshly, and my hope to see you at Christmas in Rome is strong as ever. You didn't mention that. Do you still plan to come? If so let's set a date—December 24th. I'll be free till at least January 10th. How much time can you get? Let me know right away, and I'll get us a room. Or do you want two rooms? Since your passport will plainly say Gatlin, we may need two. Do Italians care? I'll ask round and see. I've got the ring. Would you wear it there?

Otherwise—glad to hear you've got Linda and Bailey nearby. He especially sounds like "good value for money," as they say here; so keep him in potato chips. All the evidence on his love life seems to suggest he could use the carbohydrates. When I read about your evening with them, I wished I'd been there. The English have taken me at my word, pretty literally in Oxford at least, and left me alone. I could use a little evening company, but for now I'll hold out and try to wean myself—the trouble being that I want company but only when I want it. I still feel over-stocked on being wanted. Part of my plan here is emptying the warehouse, using up the surplus. What's left, if anything, at the end of the clearance is scarey to consider—will anyone want such an empty warehouse? But I've always liked a little scare in my days; stops me sleeping too much, and you know I nap a lot.

Speaking of sleep, in a letter last month you mentioned our first trip to Myrtle Beach—me saying "Wait here" when I seemed asleep and you still waiting. I was asleep and don't recall speaking (aloud at least), but I don't doubt your word. So I wrote this for you by way of thanks. Please keep it if it suits.

No sleeping man is safe. Each volunteers
With baby-calm for any watcher's need.
Most any household implement at hand
Will send him deeper down than he'll have sunk.

Bread-knife, ice-pick, your useless cheap corkscrew
Briefly applied to temple, throat, thigh, groin
Will call his bluff successfully as bombs.
He trusts you won't—trusts kindliness, indifference;
Knows sleeping murder's mainly kept for kings,
Geriatric guests of the Macbeths.

A realer threat bears mentioning however.
The proffered victim may well victimize,
Although unconsciously—spare the dreamer,
Spare the dreamer's dream. This boy for instance—
Age nineteen, no eyesore—sprawls on hotel
Sheets in ocean dawn. Words wake you
(You are curled against his back). You hope
For more, then think you hear "Wait here." You do.
He says the two words clearly, meaning both.
You know he sleeps but take the words one way—

Your way. The other one to know was his.
If you had worked beneath the chilled tan rind,
Ascended knob by knob the fragile spine,
Lain silent in the white dough of his brain,
You would have seen—an orphan, six years old,
Threads underbrush till, standing by a creek,
He sights a girl, tall on the far green bank,
A little older, lovely, turning, leaving.
He knows her in one look and calls "Wait here"—
The girl who bled to death in bearing him.
He wakes and finds you there, prepared to stay,
And joins you long as he can stand your eyes.
Forgive him then for his own distant wait
On his green bank, inevitable hunt—
The chance you take, obeying half a dream.

It's now nine-ten. The college gates are locked, and I'm pretty well the only human under forty defended by these twelve-foot walls. There is one low wall, facing the meadow. I'll climb over that, walk a dark quarter-mile toward police headquarters, grab a rickety post wrapped with earnest barbed wire, swing myself out and over a deep stagnant ditch, and be free in the nocturnal world of adults. Sounds glamorous, right? Well, no—just Oxford in the Long Vacation. I'll drink a pint of cider called Merrydown in a pub called The Eagle and Child, then reverse my escape route and sleep a long night in my own straw bed (my mattress is actually stuffed with straw; how's that for Olde Worlde?).

So your own life there with Linda and Bailey—the Living Dead—and the liberated murderess is thrilling next to mine.

But I've had thrills a-plenty for twenty-five years. Now I need to sit and watch them, years and thrills.

Love again from,
Hutch

42

WHEN he'd swung himself free of the last barbed wire round Christ Church Meadow, he walked up a thoroughly deserted St. Aldate's past Tom Tower, Pembroke, and the small huddled church where Lawrence of Arabia had taught Sunday school. He stopped in the light by the main post office and carefully checked the letter to Ann, address and postage. Then he made a quick sign of the cross on its face as he always did on important mail; then dropped it in the slot and wished he could fish it back, read it once more to dull harsh edges, blur promises. No chance of course short of dynamite. So he walked up the low hill and crossed Carfax, also curiously empty for Saturday night—were the airmen on maneuvers or sent home at last? Even at the doors of the public dance-hall (opposite The Crown, Shakespeare's customary stop on the London-Stratford route), there were only three would-be Teddy Boys, none over fifteen, and one frizzed girl. On through the Cornmarket, past Beaumont Street where the whores kept flats, past the dark Ashmolean with its Michelangelos hung in back hallways, through half of St. Giles to the Eagle and Child. By the time he saw its sign, Hutch was low as a toad, tasting the thin diet he'd struggled for—abandonment. *This place would ignore you; needn't bother to ask.* He stopped in place and thought of hunting down the whore he'd met in White's Bar in June. She was almost surely in her room not a hundred yards from here (she'd mentioned her address and said she stayed in watching telly till ten on weekend nights). Though the evening was mild, his body seemed hung in a cold vacuum-shaft which no human hand would ever invade. He walked back far as the next street light and opened his wallet—six pounds, enough; she'd said she "made adjustments." But he'd lost her name. Charleen? Doreen? He couldn't ask the landlord for a black-haired girl he'd met a month ago. Why not? Any landlord would know her trade. Still he set it as a test. He'd walk toward the pub till he got the name; if it didn't come a pint of hard cider might find it.

43

BUT twenty minutes later in the dim warm pub, the presence of a half-dozen talking strangers had eased the search; Hutch sat calmly in a corner, merely listening. The loudest were a pair of men at the bar—one a parody of the old RAF ace (purple cheeks, fierce mustache, emblematic blazer); the other almost certainly American, though he'd got English clothes and an all-but-perfect accent (his joints were the give-away, the oiled loose-limbs of a people used to space and reared with Negroes). The ace was challenging the camouflaged Yank to explain how racial integration would not in fact bring America down as it clearly had Rome, Gaul, the whole of Asia (the ace had served in Burma and Malaya). The answer involved rich cultural infusions from the Bantu, Kikuyu, Nubian, etc.—jazz, tap dancing, jokes, sexual sanity—and as it proceeded, unearthed a complete set of Ohio vowels in the helpless mouth.

Hutch had heard the conversation before from better antagonists. With the last of his cider, the name came finally—Marleen, Marleen Pickens—so he shut his eyes awhile to find her face and body: would she really help at all or would it amount to expensive chatter with a quick hot clot flung out at the end? First he saw Lew Davis in the pasture on Tresco, the ferret refusing to take Lew's touch; then Ann in the dark Taft below his own fingers; then Marleen Pickens. He'd only seen her dressed, but she came bare easily and stood clear before him. Like almost every English war-child, she seemed to have two separate bodies. The healthy body she would have got, with sufficient fruit and milk in the years of the Blitz, enveloped her actual body like an aura. The actual body was still a little starved, the skin a little taut. Between her nice high breasts with coral nipples, an ugly sternum pressed forward like a face. Above the good calves her knees had knobbed, and webs of purple strung along her thighs and flanks. But a banked unquestionable strength burned in her; she'd warmed herself. She'd help at least.

Hutch had stiffened through that. He smiled to himself. When he'd shrunk enough to stand, he'd go to Marleen. He opened his eyes to quicken the cooling and saw two people at the moment they entered—a girl maybe six or seven, a man maybe twenty. Hutch thought at once that children were not allowed in pubs and awaited an expulsion, but no one behind the bar seemed to mind. And with no discussion the two parted neatly—the man approached the bar; the child approached Hutch, not meeting his eyes, and sat a table away on his right. At once she began to draw small circles on the green linoleum of the table-top, her profile as bent on perfection as Apollo's. She wore a red pullover, nubby at the elbows, with a cross-eyed owl stamped on the front. Hutch said, "Can your owl see to fly with crossed eyes?"

She continued her circles, not looking up. "He never leaves me."

"Why not?"

"I never let him."

"Too young?" Hutch said.

She laid her head on the table, facing him, but didn't answer. She shut her eyes briefly, then looked again straight at him, still silent. At the bar the man was paying for his drinks.

Hutch said "Is he your father?"

She nodded once.

"He's got you out late. Are *you* an owl?"

By then the man was walking carefully toward them with a pint of dark beer and an orange squash. Standing short of the child, he said, "Hop to. We've got hours yet." Then he put the drinks down and sat on her left between her and Hutch, all on the same long window-bench. For three or four minutes, they drank in deep silence; the child was plainly thirsty. Then the man pushed the glasses back and started drawing circles as the child had done. She watched awhile; then joined him, gestures larger than his—circles intersecting delicately, hands never touching.

A game they'd invented? A local child's game? A first means of speech for creatures struck dumb? (they had still not spoken since the man sat) —Hutch listed the questions but kept his own silence, content now to wait. The child had seemed to say the man was her father; could he be? If so she'd been born when he was fourteen, fifteen. Maybe her brother? —he shared the pure line of her features: small, flawless, yet promising somehow to ripen and exceed. Her hair though was light brown, his nearly black. Her skin was ruddy with blood, his pale. Their hands had slowed now, the circles tightened. At last she touched him and both laughed loudly.

"You won!" the man said.

She nodded. "Caught *you*." They returned to their drinks.

Hutch felt them beside him like heaped red coals—a core of energy, harmful but attractive. The man had never looked his way, though their shoulders were only a yard apart. Slowed by a sense that they guarded a secret he'd easily scatter if he did more than watch, he still said, "Could I ask the name of your game?"

The man looked round, slid a little toward the child, then smiled. "Circle-catch. We just made it up." His teeth were the best Hutch had seen since landing—two rows of straight white, rare here as two steady hours of sun.

"She's lovely," Hutch said.

"She's *tired* but she can't sleep yet awhile."

Hutch said "You traveling?"

He thought that over, then turned to the child. "We traveling, Nan?"

She nodded, not smiling.

So the man looked back to Hutch and grinned. "Reckon so."

"She your baby sister?"

"I'm her dad."

Hutch said, "You must have been a child-groom then."

"I was," he said quickly; then grinned again. "A child, all right. I was never a groom. I look much older than I am, even now."

Hutch said, "You must be twelve years old."

"Twenty-two," he said. "Been rough just lately."

"How's that?"

He thought again. "How does prison sound?"

Hutch said "Unexpected."

The man laughed. "Me too! The last thing I wanted." He took a long swallow of beer, facing forward and pulling at the sleeves of his jacket—short and worn. His hands were enormous, well-shaped but yellow with callus in the palms.

Hutch thought, "I should leave. He's finished. I'll press him too hard." He raised his own glass and drained the last inch.

But the man said, "It really wasn't all that bad. Played a lot of football."

So Hutch felt permitted. "Where were you?"

"Lewes Prison."

"How long?"

"Eighteen months."

"Then I guess it wasn't murder?"

Nan had listened that far—her head on the table again, eyes open. Now the man, not looking, reached gently to her hair and gathered her in. She came like a sack of down-feathers to his lap, glanced back once at Hutch, then shut her eyes and buried her face. The man stroked her twice; then said, "Not quite—just assault with a dangerous weapon, a bottle. Put the bugger in infirmary for nineteen days, best rest he ever had."

"A friend of yours?"

"—Her mother's," he said. He stroked Nan again; she was sound asleep.

Hutch extended his own hand. "I'm Hutchins Mayfield."

The man blushed hard and held back a moment. Then he gave his hand. "James," he said quietly.

In the touch, Hutch remembered Grainger's hand—that smooth and dense, warm worn stone, impermeable. When they parted he said, "Could I ask your work?"

James said, "Mason's helper. Just started that."

"Guess Oxford could offer you plenty of work."

He nodded. "It does. All the colleges are rotten—bloody Headington stone. They're all great sugar cubes melting in rain."

"So you'll stay here awhile?"

James drank the last of his beer, wiped the deep blue cleft of his chin with one finger. "Never been anywhere else but Lewes and Reading."

"Reading Gaol?"

"No, for Nan. Her mother lives there. Or did till last week."

"Where's she now?"

"Search me—well, don't. She's not *here*, is she?"

"You want her to be?"

James quickly said "No," then paused a good while. "You want to hear it out?—it's a sordid lot. I'm hoping to sell it to *News of the World.*" He looked up smiling; and as Hutch nodded Yes, James slid out from Nan, stood and took the glasses. "What's your drink?"

"Cider—Merrydown—but let me buy."

James was already moving. "Sit and guard young Nan."

Hutch did. He slipped along the smooth bench till his thighs touched her head. She was now on her back with both hands loosely clenched on her chest. He covered them both with his own right palm. She was cooler than he but warmed in his grip; so he watched her steadily through the wait, calmer than he'd been since when?—Tresco maybe, in the beached boat with Archie or bound to Lew.

James said "You're not Canadian, right?" He stood two steps away with new drinks.

Hutch kept his hand on Nan. "Right—American."

James stayed in place.

"Americans not allowed to drink two pints?" Hutch extended a trembling hand, the comic drunk.

James stepped forward then and set down the mugs. "Most of them shouldn't—the ones I've seen—but you seem safe enough."

Hutch moved to slide back.

But James came round to Nan's feet. "Stay there if you like being there."

"Her hands were cold. I was warming her."

"She's all right," James said. "She's been worse than cold." Then he sat.

So they drank long swallows, Nan between them—now huddled on her side, a short hyphen.

When James had found no way to recommence, Hutch finally said "She seems healthy now."

James ringed her ankle—thin white cotton socks—and studied her.

"She looks it, right. So do I; I just saw my own healthy face." He pointed to the distant etched bar-mirror. "We've sort of had it though."

"From what?"

"Her mother."

"That's the sordid part?"

James faced him, grave and searching. "You do want it, don't you?"

Hutch nodded again. "The story at least."

"You aiming to sell it?"

"How?"

"You look like you might be some sort of correspondent."

Hutch laughed. "I'm a poet—apprentice-grade. You can't sell poems, not for money at least."

James waited, then smiled. "I'll give you my address at the end—remind me—and if you make a shilling on any of it, you send her six-pence." He was still holding Nan.

Hutch said "A deal" and touched her forehead with one finger, cool from the cider glass. She was warmer now. They both had warmed her.

James said, "It's not much but it's what we were handed. I said we were traveling—to here, I meant. Oxford's my home all my life till prison. I was born in Jericho a quarter-mile from here, and we'll be living there now with my mother. She's serving some whacking great party of dons at New College tonight, so we're waiting for her—won't give me a key till I prove I'm cured of my evil ways!"

"She locks Nan out?"

"She doesn't know Nan's here yet," James said. "I just now took her this afternoon."

"From Reading?"

James nodded. "Her mother's sister's. See, I work with this bloke named Rod. He dances all night. Well, Friday morning—yesterday—he lurched up to me at my first tea and said he'd seen my bird last night. I said, 'My bird is the English robin, sign of spring.' He laughed—'Your Helen. She was down at Carfax dancing last night. I asked was she planning to glimpse your face, and she said she reckoned she'd spare her nerves and was heading to Yorkshire today at dawn.' He also knew about Nan and asked. She said Nan wasn't with her, no, and shut up. So I thought all Friday—buggered up three nice cuts of stone—then thought all night. Then this morning I worked my full half-day, rode my bike home and washed, caught the next train to Reading, went straight to her sister's house, and took Nan."

"The sister didn't stop you?"

"They're scared of me. Anyhow she has asthma and runs from a fight."

Hutch leaned slightly forward—no bags with them: only the clothes on their backs, their circle game. "No question she's yours?"

"Nan?"—James still held her but studied her a moment. "No question at all. I know the night I made her." He looked to Hutch and flushed bright again, not smiling now. "See, Helen was dead-keen on me in French letters. She swept up for this mens' hairdresser in Walton Street and every Friday whipped off a few French letters. We'd be on the tow path after the films—some bleeding Anna Neagle tripe; she wolfed that down—and when we'd got steaming, she'd fish out her rubber goods and hand them over in the dark like they were too mean to mention. For months I obeyed and rolled them on, but this one night it was cold as Cape Wrath; and all I could think of was touching her bare, striking real blood-heat. So into the water went three stinking rubbers and me into Helen—just me, first time. She never felt the change, not for weeks. *I* did —made me like her better; and when she came up, wailing *Baby! baby!*, I said 'Cool your chips. I'll marry you.' I thought she said Yes and I made plans; but she went down to Reading to see her scummy sister (her mum was dead; she stayed up here with her dad, an old drunk) and after a fortnight sent me a letter, saying, 'Dear Mr. Nichols'—I swear to God!— 'I have thought a lot and got advice here, and I don't think I want you to be dad to any girl of mine!' (she knew it was a girl; she felt that much). I couldn't understand. She'd bloody sure wanted my cock long enough; started to send it to her in a box with a note saying, 'Feel free to use anytime you need, and show to your girl when she's twelve years old—a warning from Dad.' After that it didn't really bother me much; if she'd ever had a child, I hadn't seen it. I hadn't seen *her* for nearly three years and was going my way very nicely, thank you, packing cases of Cooper's orange marmalade when blimey if she didn't turn back up here with Nan already walking."

"Begging money?" Hutch said.

"Helen?—not her. I'll grant her she never begged a tanner from me. Proud as Lady Docker and just about as kind. I mean, her idea of facing me after two years away—and my daughter half-grown—was to prance up behind me at Carfax one Saturday, cover my eyes, and whisper 'Hullo, James, from a happy mum!' I was hot from dancing, but I went really cold. Couldn't think of anything to say but 'A girl?' and she said 'Named Nan.' Well, you could have floored me with a spoon of cold porridge—Nan's my mother's name. I couldn't speak again. I only thought of bashing her mouth—she seemed alone—but I just stood there like the vicar at a fête. Then she said, 'You can see her at Dad's anytime.' She'd come back to stay with her dad, who was sick. I said 'I may do' and walked away—Christ, walked all night all through Port Meadow. But two days later I washed and went round. I liked her straight off—young Nan, I mean—and she came to me, no gates between us. She could talk very well, and she looked a bit like me. The talking was stranger than the looking though. You step through a door; there's a fast little animal, standing thigh-high with your hair and eyes; and once Helen says 'Nan, come speak to James,' she comes up and holds your knee and says 'What's your name?'—looking up like she hadn't heard Helen. Helen left it to me, so I said it was James. I'm still not clear she knows I'm her father; someone may have told her but never me."

Hutch said, "She knows. She told me first thing."

He nodded. "She calls me James anyway." And by then he seemed exhausted. He asked Hutch the time (the pub clock as always being some minutes fast). It was nearly ten-thirty, closing-time at eleven. He pulled at one stretched cuff of Nan's sweater.

Hutch said, "Will your mother be home by eleven?"

"Quite likely."

"But if not?"

"We'll sit on the step or take a little walk."

Hutch said, "She's surely dead-out now."

James nodded. "She is. She's used to being waked."

"You could come back with me, but we'd have to climb a wall."

"You a don?"

"A student. Or will be in October if I last that long. I'm living in Merton."

James said, "I been there. We're due to work Merton sometime this autumn, lot of patchwork to do. I'll wait till then. Thanks all the same." He drank long swallows and gave no signs of continuing his story. At last though he looked up, entirely earnest. "I'm sorry really. You never asked for that."

"I did," Hutch said.

"Before you knew half."

"I liked it," Hutch said.

James thought through that, then looked up smiling. "Didn't mind it myself, kept thinking I would."

The publican said "Last call please, gentlemen." The RAFer and the transformed Yank were still at the bar, quieter now. Hutch, James, and Nan were the only other patrons. Hutch said, "My go to buy the last round." The winey cider had him high and eased.

James said, "I better not—got to face my mother yet, with an extra mouth to boot."

"She knows Nan surely?"

"A little. But she's sort of had it with kids—bad luck with all hers."

"How many more are there?"

James looked to the clock again. "You want the rest of *me*, there's just time for that."

Hutch said "Good enough."

"They stayed on here. Helen's dad got well enough to work again, so she and Nan lived there and kept up for him the best Helen could;

she's an awful mess. She had no objections to me seeing Nan, and I'd come in and see her maybe twice a week, take her out for a walk or to do something new—even took her to St. Giles's Fair, her first fair. Helen came along that day. We were friendly by then, though nothing too close —I was seeing any other girl I fancied; I hadn't touched Helen, didn't need to try; and while Nan and I went to ride the ponies, Helen went to the gypsy and had her palm read. Came back with her face all down round her tits, saying she would be the cause of blood in others. I laughed. Two years before the same ruddy witch had told me and her we'd be happily married in a semidetached house in under six months with a fridge and hot water! But it ruined the fair for her. She left me and Nan to go her way, and that was the day we fell in love—hours together, spending shillings like water. I took her back at dark. There was Helen still moaning while she made her dad's tea, so it came in my head to say 'I'll keep Nan tonight' and Helen said Yes. Nan slept in my bed, right up against me. She sleeps very *still*, no moving at all and dry as my hand. I kept the room dark; but whenever I woke I'd find her face and stroke it awhile, pretending I was blind. I liked it; I'd slept alone since my brother left eight years before and never with a girl. I got a taste for it. Nan did as well. Helen didn't seem to mind, so from then on for six months she stayed every Sunday night with me."

The publican approached them. "Any last orders please?"

They both said No and James looked again to the present Nan between them. He didn't touch her—her shoe touched his thigh—but he watched her calmly as he might have watched a place, an inhuman field in evening light.

Hutch brushed her hair once with the back of his hand but watched her father. He didn't think then of pictures that lay behind this here—Rob and himself twenty years ago, trailing through two states Rob's desperation and his own plain contentment to be with a father who could make old rocks in the road die laughing. But he felt strong pulses of a similar peace, flickering signals which affirmed again that there were real fires outside himself—welcoming, benevolent, worth anyone's tending. Father and child. The longer he watched, the younger James seemed—unguarded, hunted. Even the fixed eyes, older than the skin, were blind to threat. Hutch strained to find one useful word of warning.

But James said, "I still had my Saturday nights. I was seeing a girl from Stanton Harcourt; and this one Saturday I had her at Carfax, dancing again—clean country girl. There was not a big crowd, just a miserable four-piece band from Witney and a few of your countrymen, sucking down vodka by the quart—very generous. There was this black one I'd talked to before—Alfonso-something from Michigan, quite friendly, big high arse and a lot of teeth missing. Always after me to get him 'some white meat free,' not whores. Said he'd never spent a penny for pussy till then and didn't plan to start just because he was homesick. I laughed him off but thought it was awful, wouldn't ever tell him my own girl's name. This night he'd managed to hook one at least—great palefaced redhead from the pressed-steel works who seemed not to talk—so he was celebrating. I had my own cause to join him too. My girl had just whispered she'd changed her mind; till then it had been set against me working below her ears! It was bloody cold—February—and since what seemed to lie ahead of me was a late trip to Stanton Harcourt on my motorbike and a chance at a frosty shag in the graveyard, I thought I'd better drink as much as he'd give—Alfonso *Masters*. He gave unstinting like I said, and I was pissed when the next bomb landed. There was Helen with a slimy little Welsh tich I also knew, dancing close in a corner. I didn't think I'd care. But since she hated to see me drunk, I went to Alfonso for one more taste; and he gave me the dregs of his bottle, quite a lot. So when I looked round and found my girl gone—she had active kidneys—I sloped up to Helen and her singing midget. Tried to be pleasant enough; and he was willing—gave him the last swallow—but Helen wouldn't hear it, froze over completely and didn't say a word beyond 'Never mind coming for my daughter tomorrow.' That cut really deep, a lot deeper than I'd planned to be cut by her again. First I just walked away four or five steps; then I knew I wouldn't take it. I turned and went back and said all I'd kept up to say for three years. That's the sordid part I warned about; I'll spare you that—guess away, if you like! But it went fast at least. I shoved Helen once; her friend hit me good on the chin (quite strong for such a little newt); I bashed him down with Alfonso's bottle—two times; then it broke and I stopped, not to maul him. Well, of course the first blow had laid his scalp open clean as an orange and earned him weeks of rest like I said." James stopped, touched his glass, decided not to drink. Then he faced Hutch at last. "That enough, you think?" His grin, sudden and white as a flare, surprised them both.

Hutch smiled. "Much obliged." A sweep-up boy was working their way, pausing every few steps to wipe his nose. Hutch lifted the last of his cider toward James. "To a calmer future, you and Nan."

James nodded, took her wrist, and shook it firmly. "But I've liked it, see. I really haven't minded."

Nan was looking straight up, awake as quickly as her father had promised. She looked back to Hutch and studied him a moment, then gave two clear imitations of an owl's lone cry. "Who-ah-oo, who-ah-oo."

Hutch laughed. "Where'd you ever hear an owl, Nan?"

"I didn't," she said.

James stood and lifted her. "Maybe I'll see you this autumn in Merton. Keep your eyes skinned—upward. I'll be on the scaffold."

"Being hanged?" Hutch said.

James laughed. "Just replacing dead stones this time."

44

THERE was no landlord to face after all. The name on a dignified calling-card was pinned up inside the open door, *Miss Marleen Pickett* with directions in a pale script to *First floor back*. Hutch climbed the long stairs, plunged back through a dark hall, and found only one door with noise behind it—Lehar, the Vilja song, a wiry soprano—so he knocked.

A good wait. The Lehar continued; then its volume throttled down, and a woman's voice said "Yes?" through the wood.

"Miss Pickett please."

"Who's calling?"

He was still not sure it was she, but the cider allowed him to say "Clean Socks."

Another wait; the song died midair. The voice said, "I don't think I heard the name."

"Hutchins Mayfield," he said, "—rich American boy, built normal-size."

A laugh. "What's he want?"

"Oh a chance to be better acquainted," he said.

He might have been Orestes with the hungry axe, but she opened then—on a small bed-sitter filled with books as she'd promised and her small self wrapped in a green housecoat, her hair newly washed and lightened like steam from a brief spring snow in the waving gleam of three green candles and a mute television: Anneliese Rothenberger in a grainy bow, troops of violins behind her.

An hour later they'd worked to the closest acquaintance they'd have, though for Hutch it didn't seem negligible. He'd sat while she made them a cup of Horlick's on her new hot-plate (the books by his chair were all war histories—Churchill, Eisenhower, a history of the Greater London Fire Service). They'd watched the still-silent television and drunk the foamy milk, mostly silent themselves—little guesses at the plot of the comedy before them, fat schoolboys apparently drowning an old head-master in a barrel. When it ended in a muddy cricket match, she'd leaned to switch it off and said, "Now I may have to push off to work—"

Hutch had said, "You're a little late tonight."

"I'm a great opera fan," she'd said. "Never miss it. Anyway it's early by American clocks."

Hutch had said "Not really" and stood to meet her on the small rag-mat she said she'd made.

So they stayed upright in the midst of the candles, their palms pressed together like children in a slow game of push-and-shove. Hutch knew he was still high, knew she was clear, but trusted her to let him choose their speed. She consented and finally he rested on her shoulder, close enough to smell her cleanliness—honest soap, no scent. Then he said "Work here?"

She seemed to nod.

He undressed her carefully as a tired baby who might yet yell.

But she bore all his gentleness—his words of encouragement and praise, the serious unhitching and folding of clothes till she stood mother-naked and hugged herself once in a short chill of thanks. Then he paused, rocking slightly; and she said "Right" and returned the favor.

When he stood bare also, he took a step back and stroked her once from neck to belly, then drew her hand down the same stretch on him. He said, "We're the same age. We look like kin." They did, in dim light—matched in health and frank fineness of workmanship.

But she said, "Mind your manners. I was brought up clean."

Hutch said "You smell it" and knelt before her to graze his fill. A tenor bell in the heart of town began on midnight.

She counted its last three strokes aloud. Then in the same pitch and rhythm and distance, she said "Thanking you" and raised him by his hair.

He searched her eyes, smiling. "Shall we read a good book now and go to sleep?"

She laughed two notes, still mocking the bell; raised a palm to hold him in place, then doused two candles with her fingers. "Yes," she said. "Read me *Poor Old London in Flames Again*. I'm a cold-natured child." She went to the bed and lay flat and neat.

He said, "Once upon a time there was a city child named Marleen Pickett."

"Don't say the name please."

"Why?"

"I don't really feel like her just now."

"Who then?"

A little wait. "You training for police inspector, are you?"

Hutch laughed. "In a way."

"Take a night off then."

So he did—or a long unmeasured space in which they worked with the perfect skill their bodies had promised toward perfect reward, for Hutch at least in the few conscious minutes till she drew a quilt over them and let him sink asleep stretched against her right side. Even sleeping he felt no further need or question, though he dreamed this story. He was in his own bed in his room in Rob's house. He had waked after calm sleep and lay in warm fall light, straining the stillness for some sound of Rob in the kitchen, on the porch. But the stillness was pure and ran through his mind with no residue to stop his own rest and start the day. He sat up naked—he was full grown, his present age—and looked out the window that ran to the floor beside his bed. The yard, clear down to the road, was empty of all but Thalia loping stiffly toward the woods like a black footstool that had managed escape. *From what?* he wondered and stood and called Rob. Still nothing so, naked, he roamed the porch and kitchen, slowly fearful. No Rob—the cookstove cold, table clean. But the truck stood safe in the back by the well. He stopped short of Rob's bedroom door and said "Father." He could hear the hum of something alive but nothing spoke. He went on toward it, feeling only dread. The room was lighter than his own had been. On the bureau Rob's gold watch burned like a lamp. In Rob's broad bed covered only by a sheet lay James and Nan. Nan was facing the door, awake and watchful. When she saw Hutch she smiled. He knew he had not seen her smile till then. His worry dissolved. James slept beyond them; the sound was from him, strong steady breaths.

Marleen laid a hand on his hip and pressed. When he woke she said, "You good for the night?"

"—For sleep if you are."

"I just meant that. I'm tired as you but the rent's due Monday."

"What would my share be?"

She thought awhile, kneading his hip like a nurse. "How would three guineas sound?"

"About right," he said.

She turned toward him then, drew small·to his side, touching at every possible point. "Good night, Old Socks."

He thought "Good night" but was not sure he said it before sleep reclaimed him.

45

HUTCH and Strawson had a big tea at a cheerful shop near the theatre (a diabetic at the nearest table had insulin trouble, and the manageress uncomplainingly poured sugar-water down him till his pallor cleared). Then they wandered through surprisingly empty streets past the local swans, Shakespeare's timbered birthplace, the garden of his last home, his tomb in the parish church with its bust which Straw said resembled an inflatable Edgar Allan Poe, ten pounds over-filled. Near that a small flowerseller was open. Hutch stopped—"Inspiration."

Straw said "Oh God."

"*Secular* inspiration—Miss Leigh." They went in and found only stalky field flowers, something like carnations, but bought an armload and had them sent backstage at once to Vivien Leigh.

Act One, Scene Five. In the brown wake of Olivier's first meeting with the hags, she strode onstage, the sudden boiled essence of what had till then hung misty and subtle—essence of the blind need of power, the will to seize it, both pure in a small red-haired gorgeous woman in a sea-green dress with barbarous jewels and a phallic belt slung from her crotch. Once she'd invoked in fevered chant the nursing of demons at her round high breasts, she moved straight forward through the midst of the play like a thin asp, far more potent than its length. She forced Macbeth to Duncan's murder, not by volume or stare but by lust—flicking kisses at his neck and ears, quick stings on a soldier deprived many days of bed and wife. The demons clung to her as she took the daggers from him, smeared the drugged grooms with Duncan's gore; then reappeared in a new incandescence, ready at last to yield her body, hot with triumph and salty with blood. Then the strength left her slowly. In the banquet scene she entered as the smiling hostess whose composure barely conceals a knowledge that her husband is steadily passing her in power and secrecy; then as he panicked at Banquo's ghost, she rose with the natural loyalty of a dog, dismissed the guests, and worked to calm him with wifely tenderness. But increasingly certain that he'd now exceeded her in crime and hunger—having used her body as his vaulting horse and cracked her spine—she left, abandoned by all her strengths, desolate and baffled. Thereafter she was only the grizzle-haired child of the sleepwalking scene—singing her dreamy confessions of blood, her last concerns for the peace of a man who'd found her useful to a point awhile back.

Her pale secretary met them downstairs, led them through dim halls to a door, said "Please wait here," and vanished inside. They stood, not speaking, still held by the end—corrosive black glare that streamed from Macbeth in his fight to live—and a little cowed by what now seemed a pointless request: to stare close-up at a beauty who must be drained and shaken. Five yards beyond them another door opened. Olivier stepped out, bare-chested, with a towel—beard and wig off but his eyes still painted. He saw them and smiled and stepped back in.

Straw said "He's smaller than me"—he was.

Hutch laughed and was on the verge of leaving when the nearer door opened on a woman in a tan robe with brown hair pressed down tight round her skull.

She said, "Poor boys. You're frozen. I'm sorry." Then she waved them in. Only inside by better light did they know for certain she was who they'd come for—the famous smile, the green eyes tilted, the voice now raised to its normal cool pitch. She went to a dressing table where their ragged flowers looked fresher in a clear vase beside a framed picture of Olivier, younger, as Romeo. "Mr. Mayfield, Mr. Stuart—thank you *very* much." She made a deep curtsy. "Which is which?" she said.

Hutch looked to Straw.

"I'm the Stuart," Straw said.

"Are you royal?" she said and took a step toward him, her large hand rising.

"Yes ma'm," Straw said, not moving from place. But he took the hand neatly and bent to kiss it, natural as a bird at a still bowl of water.

She accepted, still smiling, then turned to Hutch. "What a lovely name—Mayfield. And you're Southern, your note said. I'm more than an honorary Southerner myself." For a moment her voice took on the plaintive sweetness of Scarlett and Blanche. "The South was kind to me."

Straw said "Then come back."

Her eyes searched him quickly; she laughed. "You don't think I flourished in Scotland tonight?"

"No ma'm," Straw said; then blushed. "*You* were fine. The other Scots didn't seem ready for you though."

She was serious. "Too true." Then the smile again—"Shall we thank God for that?"

Hutch said "Yes alas."

She said, "Carolina—I've seen it from trains: dark green, all pines. Will you go back there?"

Hutch said "I hope I can."

"Together?" she said.

Hutch wondered how she meant it—Lady Macbeth, now a calm matchmaker?

But Straw said, "I'm a Virginian—no ma'm."

They could all laugh at that. Her face scrubbed clean, the lines of mid-age spreading from her eyes, she had never seemed more beautiful to Hutch—more desperately offered from her frail foothold on the near side of poise. He thought, quick and wild, "I could lead her out of here. She wants to go" (her spells of madness were public knowledge—howlings, clawings). "I could give what she lacks."

But she settled on Straw again. "How long will you stay?"

Straw looked to Hutch.

"You must come for *Twelfth Night*. We do that next. I could save you my seats. I make a nice boy. And *Titus Andronicus*—I lose both hands, my tongue, and my maidenhood but I persevere."

Straw said, "I imagine you do. Thank you, ma'm."

"Kind sir," she said. " 'My Rosenkavalier!' " and dipped to the floor in controlled obeisance, not laughing now.

46

Two hours later they'd scaled Merton wall, picked their way over turning iron-spikes, and walked through the black chilly garden to Hutch's. The sitting room was dank, so Hutch burned both coils of the heater—if this was July, woe betide for winter—and hurried to warm milk for cocoa.

When Straw saw the drift, he said, "I've got a fifth of Scotch. It'd do you more good, ward off T.B."

Hutch laughed. "*You* kissed her. You're the one in danger."

"How's that?"

"She's the world's most noted consumptive."

"I heard she was crazy."

"That too, in spurts." They hadn't talked of her on the drive back to Oxford; Straw had slept the whole way.

"I liked her a lot, offstage more than on."

Hutch said "She liked you."

"Those older women do. I'm the spirit of youth."

Hutch said, "—For ten minutes at the rate you're going."

Straw went to his small bag and fished out the bottle, came back to the sofa, bent over the white cup, and poured a big drink.

Hutch said, "Not for me. Not yet at least."

Straw looked up, solemn as a child on a stele. He thought for a long moment. "So be it," he said, "—plenty others in line." Then he smiled, still standing; drained the cup, and lay back full-length on the sofa.

"This is England. Drink slower."

"Why?"

"You're safe here, aren't you?—no menopausal doctor's wives tracking you down."

"Maybe so, maybe not." He'd shut his eyes again.

Hutch didn't want him to sleep just yet. He himself was awake and gladder than he'd planned—to have Straw here, transplanted intact out of range of home. "You promised to bring me up to date," he said.

"Tomorrow if I live."

"Night's the time to talk trash."

Straw looked out again and studied Hutch. "You're a little low, aren't you?"

"No." His milk was bubbling; he leaned to mix the cocoa.

"—On trash. You look pretty low on trash."

"This *is* a hermit's cell, six hundred years old."

Straw raised up and scanned the long dark room. "Shit," he said. "Bet you young hermits were groveling on each other's butts before the plaster was dry on the walls."

Hutch laughed. "Could be."

Straw was still looking round. "I'm *certain*," he said. "Had to warm up somehow."

Hutch had sat back to drink. "It's July," he said.

"I'm freezing."

"No you're not. Tell the news; that'll toast your toes."

Straw said "Pour me a shot."

Hutch poured two ounces.

"Keep going."

"That's a shot."

"Then make it a torpedo."

Hutch doubled the portion and handed it over.

Straw set it on his breastbone, cradled in his hands. "I lie here before you as a father," he said.

"Of what exactly?"

Again Straw drained the cup in one swallow—no flinch or shudder, though he scrubbed at his mouth. "—Of a pink goldfish about two inches long. I named it for you."

Hutch said, "Many thanks. Do I get him now or later?"

"I said *it*; pay attention. No it's swimming down sewer mains fast as it can toward the Gulf of Mexico. You'd never catch it now."

Hutch said, "You may need to speak plain English. I'm not too good at these dark allegories."

Straw said, "I'm trying to spare you pain."

"Nobody else does. Don't bother; I'm grown."

Straw looked out a moment with utter clarity, the eyes of an instrument collecting evidence for some vast indictment. Then he shut them and set the cup on the floor at Hutch's foot. "I've been fucking Estelle Llewellyn since March, eight times exactly—she's counting not me."

"You wrote me in June that it hadn't happened yet."

"I was lying, to spare you again. You want to hear this or you want to give demerits?"

Against his better judgment Hutch said "Tell on."

"By the time I wrote you, she was already pregnant. She didn't know, didn't tell me anyway—it's not my favorite idea of fun, to poke up a growing baby's ass. But I did, two or three more times; I wouldn't go so far as to say I felt the difference. Then she called me up one evening at home and said I had to meet her at school, nine o'clock—all our meetings had been at school from the start. I wasn't in the mood and told her so as plain as I could with my mother standing four feet away. I'll give her this much—Mrs. Llewellyn, I mean. She never cried a drop or raised her voice. She just said, 'I don't want to lay a hand on you. I want you to know one piece of news.' I knew from that minute, but I went on and met her. She never tried to touch me. I wouldn't have minded; it was *her* idea that she was too old and was cradle-robbing, having dealings with me. I liked how she did most everything she did. We sat in her car, and she told it straight out—she knew it was mine; she was six weeks gone. She'd been down to Staunton to have the test done, false name and all. I knew we were acting in a fairly old movie, but I knew she was hurting under all the big dignity. I said, 'Any doubt that the father's me?' She said there was not; she'd claimed right along she and Dr. Llewellyn had lived like cousins for more than a year, his choice not hers. So I said, 'If you'll have it I'll raise it right.' I meant every word. I could have got a job, found a woman to keep it—my mother would have cut backflips at the chance. Then she told her real news. It was already done. She'd gone to her husband that same afternoon and told him the problem, leaving out my name. He'd solved it right there in his office, twenty minutes. She had cooked their supper and was driving the car. I sat still, glad it was dark at least. I wanted to say some wonderful sentence to end her scene, some noble memory for her to suck on for years. I even ran through all the poems I'd learned. But nothing seemed right. After maybe two minutes I opened the door and stepped out to breathe and here I am." Still blind, he reached down accurately and took the empty cup; licked slowly round the rim.

"You never said a word?"

Straw looked out again, less certainly now. "No I saved it for you. I thought you'd like it."

Hutch felt a yellow surge of nausea in his throat. What he'd honored in this boy for nearly two years was the clear sight of life, a flood of cheerful animal life that had pressed Straw's body and face from within into one more mask of the thing Hutch hunted and worshiped in the world—the same strong grace that still moved the pictures of Rob through his memory. Now supine on ragged cushions in a room that had seen worse surely in six hundred years, Straw seemed nonetheless filthy past cleaning. Hutch licked down deep at the dregs of his cocoa, then bent and poured whiskey in the half-clean cup, then drank a long swallow.

Straw said "I was wrong."

"How?"

"You plain didn't like it."

"What makes you think that?"

Straw propped his head on one hand. "I've done some bad stuff in my time, I agree; but I never to my knowledge made anybody mix good Scotch and cold cocoa."

"It was all right."

"The story?"

"The drink." Hutch drank the rest, walked to his bedroom, pissed in the sink, and ran a little hot water.

As he came slowly back, Straw said, "Anybody that'll piss where he washes his mouth shouldn't blame other people for what they do."

"The john's too far."

"So was love in Virginia."

Hutch sat again. "I was there till June."

Straw watched him steadily. "You were scared."

"Not of you."

"Of what then?"

"Nothing."

"*You're* lying. Don't spare me." Straw sat up finally, gave himself and Hutch drinks, then leaned back upright.

Hutch found no immediate reason to spread out his relics here where they well might be disvalued or abused. "Strawson, I was leaving. What we did was *goodbye*. There was no future for it."

"Did you want there to be?"

"No."

"A lie."

Hutch laughed. "Your lie detector is overheated, son."

Straw shook his head. "I'm a father, remember?"

"Half the world can be that, any man with a minimum of one working ball."

Straw said "Why not you?"

"Give me time."

"We have. World's *waiting* for your heir; you're aging fast."

Hutch nodded. "That's why I've washed up here. That's the scarey thing."

"—In a hermit museum? With your woman in Richmond, four thousand miles off? You mailing her bottles of your warm white seed?"

"Not yet anyhow. I mailed her a poem."

Straw said, "I know that eased her pain."

Hutch said, "I've retired from the pain-easing business."

"Never knew you had such a long list of patients."

Hutch grinned and drank a little. One or two gates opened. "I don't claim to be Father Damien of the Lepers; but I have been the target, since the day I was born, of a high wall of *hope*. I have more than normal sympathy for instance with poor Baby Jesus and the pre-teen Mozart."

"Nice crowd to run with."

"I'm not claiming kin, just making a point. I was loved as a child; it can be a hard blight."

"You were needed," Straw said. "That's a whole nother story."

"Then tell me the story of love, O mage!"

Straw said, "I just did. It made you piss."

"You and Estelle Llewellyn?—quick bangs in a car?"

Straw nodded. "—Broom closets, wrestling mats in the gym, anywhere I could get her."

"The saints of love are howling," Hutch said. "That was pure goat-need, no offense meant to goats."

"Us goats *are* the saints."

"Please expand," Hutch said.

"I did. For a poet you're pretty damned deaf; never heard of a great deaf poet before."

"First one," Hutch said. "You'll need to speak plain."

Straw said, "How's this? I'm nineteen years old or will be soon. I need to go to college like a mule needs tits. I wanted that baby. Didn't know it at the time. At the time I was getting my wand stroked in company; but from here—lying here in a hermitage, having seen the Oliviers act out a marriage at least as enviable as my own parents', and watching you—I can see I was hoping to really *make* something, the thing that matters."

Hutch laughed well before he saw Straw's tears. "We've had a little too much of this," he said, extending the cup.

"Not enough," Straw said. His eyes indicated there might never be enough, not in all the years.

Soon after that Hutch had brought out a pillow and covers for Strawson to sleep on the sofa. It was past two o'clock; he was worn flat down. Straw had only said he'd sit awhile longer; so Hutch had quickly slept in his own bed, the door between them open. Sometime later he'd waked to hear Straw's feet on the stairs, going down—the john—and he thought he should call him back, give him the flashlight (the chapel johns were blacker than night); but he stayed still for once—let him learn his way— and was out again before Straw reached ground. A sleep so thick and untroubled that he thought in a fragment of dream, *I am being rewarded. For what? For what?* No answer seemed needed and he knew nothing else till a little past four, false dawn at the window.

Straw was standing naked by the sink in the window-end of the bedroom. His head was buried in Hutch's towel; he was mopping at his hair and face, silent and slow.

Hutch tested the chance that the sight was a dream; under the covers he clawed at his own bare thigh and felt the nails. So he whispered, not to startle Straw, "You braved the vile baths?"

Straw looked up but not at Hutch—outward at the first glow.

"You all right?"

"Frozen." The window was open.

"Should have waited till morning. No real hot water till breakfast-time."

"Been swimming," Straw said and went on with his drying.

Hutch said "Good God" and—still half-asleep—imagined the drunk boy climbing out by the low south wall, walking through the otherwise empty meadow to the river, stripping, plunging in over dozing swans, stroking in the cold water, walking back bare with his wadded clothes. All the guesses were right; he knew Straw well. "I've got some flannel pajamas," he said, "in the bottom drawer there beside your feet."

Straw dropped the towel, leaned to fish out the flannels, stood to put on the jacket.

Hutch had slept again by the time he was half-dressed.

So Straw left the pants on the floor, walked forward, and found his own way to the warm narrow trough in Hutch's ruined mattress.

Hutch woke enough to give him a little extra space—the trough they were in had untenable slopes—but he said nothing else. He lay facing Straw and, never quite waking, accepted for what seemed hours the gestures of pure blind service—mouth and hands, anointment and soothing; no word of request, no feeding gaze. The pleasure was strong as any Hutch had known, maybe stronger because of the silence and dark. He climbed through its spaces in a blindness of his own but safe, well-led. No eyes to thank, no debt to pay. Even Lew had begged rescue. He thought of Marleen's kind competence a moment, but gratitude quickly returned him here. He was happy here, one actual room. So, mind and body, he stayed for the rest. At the end he considered asking one thing—"*Have you made something now?*"—but the boy slid straight from his work into sleep. Hutch stayed there facing him till light showed his face, sealed again and young in sobriety. Then he crawled out quietly, went to the sofa, and napped in the shallows till the first morning chime. When Simpson came to wake him, he sat up, pointed to the bedroom; and said, "I've got a guest asleep."

Simpson said "No lady?"

"No *lady*."

Simpson winked.

47

July 24, 1955

Dear Rob,

Your letter came four days ago while I had company here—Strawson Stuart, my student. You remember he helped us load the truck my last day in Virginia. He's touring with his brother but stopped off alone for three days. We got to see Macbeth *in Stratford on Avon with Laurence Olivier and Vivien Leigh, a really big sight. I still can get chilled, remembering him—so calm at the start and so winning in appearance that you found you'd climbed in the palm of the hand before you noticed that the hand was iron and was closing fast round you with no sound louder than the crunch of your bones. Her voice is better for movies than stage—a microphone catches all grades of her best strengths (poisonous sweetness and serious guile) which are lost in the theatre—but nobody's ever looked or moved any better or half so well. We sent her some flowers and went backstage to see her at the end. On top of the beauty, which is literally incredible (despite her few wrinkles—she's forty-one—I found it hard to talk in her presence; too busy reminding myself she was* there*), she's warm and funny. Or was for five minutes; you've probably read of her mental problems.*

Otherwise I'm trying to settle in finally and do three good months of reading and writing before term begins and I'm a schoolboy again. So you can be assured I'm safe as any man in western Europe—western civilization. I live in a stone building heavier and older than the combined structures, private and commercial, of the town of Fontaine. My driving will consist of short slow prowls through gentle countryside; and in any case English roads are so narrow and winding, you can seldom exceed forty miles per hour for more than ten seconds (when you can it's a sure sign you're on a Roman road, some arrow-straight stretch laid two thousand years ago and thinly varnished with asphalt now). I'm even learning to pick my way through the breastworks and minefields of English food— mainly by resorting to the Covered Market here where I buy fresh carrots, tomatoes, oranges, dried figs, cheese and maintain the health of my gums if not my soul.

It's the soul that's in danger—if anything, Rob. The Mayfield Soul. Or is it a Kendal or Hutchins Soul? All of which is to say that the dangers I smell don't originate in sin. I know I'm a Christian, though I don't go to church (I mean I believe that the Gospel of Mark is a thoroughly trustworthy news-account of actual occurrences some years back but relevant still); yet I honestly doubt I've ever committed a sin of any weight. So far as I understand the Ten Commandments, I've never broken one. I've slept round a little, a relative little, but never by force and never with anybody pledged elsewhere (St. Paul might denounce me, but that was his line; ever notice how little Jesus says about sex?—at least it didn't give him the fits it gave Paul). I've coveted in snatches but never stole the thing, the object or person. If I have a prevailing Deadly Sin, it's obviously Pride; but anyone who knows me as well as you knows my pride is external, a transparent glaze. Inside I'm doubting—a Mayfield as I said. Or is it just a human? Since we never really talked about the doubts, maybe I should lay them out briefly here. Don't bother to brace yourself—no surprises, just the fairly standard sinking spells of a twenty-year-old in my social class (only I'm twenty-five). Can I do anything worth doing for, say, the next forty-five years? If so, is there any way to do it alone?

*Well, the lay-out was briefer than even I expected; but those two sentences cover the matter, I'm all but sure. I'm not very sure the second question is as common as I claimed above, not as early in life as this anyhow (I see nearly all my contemporaries walking off in matched pairs and issuing small warm replicas; it's one of the sights I came here to rest from). The first question though is bound to be widespread—*proof: *the number of men my age who are drunks and I understand why. But again no fear—it's one of the last routes I mean to take. I suspect I might be chemically prone to quick dependence.*

So—I *know I can teach. I could come back now and have three or four decent jobs by fall, teaching prep or high school. If I stay here long enough to get a degree—two years' minimum—I'd have a good chance at two or three college jobs: freshman composition and English Lit. from Adam and Eve to Anthony Eden. If I start to* publish *books at a heartwarming rate—anything: poems, stories, a history of feed-and-seed catalogs, so long as they're bound in stiff cloth-boards and come from a press that the author doesn't own—I could transpire to some good private university and stay there till dead or too congealed to talk. The teaching is—is it?—useful in the world. For me it would be the means to eat while I did what I want and need to do. That, I think, would be writing. And what use is that to anyone but me, the four or five people who take everything I do on faith, and God in the skies? Should that be enough? Should I shut up groaning and make my items,* even if they finally turn out to be cottage-industry white-elephants like scale-model copies of the Smithsonian Institute in toothpicks and glue, admired by the builder's mother and minister?

What if the answer to all those is No? *I doubt I could jump out the window just yet; I like too many things. I doubt I could be a bad teacher for long—too many opportunities for permanent 'harm. I doubt I could be a good husband-and-father with no income and time on my hands. Cable instructions, as they say in beleaguered frontier forts. But don't give it too much midnight oil. I'm a self-winding watch, it begins to appear, though I may lose hours. It also begins to come to my notice (something children never see) how very few people ever lie down and quit; how most break the finish-tape some way or other, even creeping or crawling.*

Present business, then. I understand your feelings on the question of Lew Davis's immigration. I'd just thought some ready solution might come to mind there at home to start him on his way. He seems to have gone a way at least; I haven't heard from him since we parted in Dorchester a month ago at the home of Thomas Hardy—he was hitching back to Wales or so he said. He has a lot of life which I hope he gets to use.

Understand too your feeling that I might have qualms about Min turning up in your life. I do and don't. Eleven years ago I objected to her strongly on the grounds that I'd missed you so much myself in the years you lived in Raleigh. I wanted you with me, sharing you with no one. Looking back from here, I don't feel shame. Not having a mother and raised by old women, I genuinely craved you—dogs crave grass. I've thanked you more than once for coming to me then, and thank you still. What I guess I haven't done is find a good way to make up to you the sacrifice I caused—leaving you with an adolescent boy through years when you must have been famished as me, for a different food. A big part of what I hope to do here and always is pay that debt in coin you can spend; a further doubt is, what coin would prove good and useful to you. Maybe that would simply be to do what you ask—raise prematurely patriarchal arms and shed warm blessing over you and your choice. But even I balk at some brands of pretension. I used to bless you when I was a boy—in my prayer every night, the years you were gone, and a lot of times silently when you were nearby—but then, like a lot of children, I felt safer than you and responsible for you. The child can be "father to the man" in more senses than Wordsworth meant, and you asked me to be. Or so I thought. It may be one reason I'm a little tired now. I've played more parts—lived them as duties—than a good many men or women age sixty. Thus a short rest now.

So sure, from my rest stop here by the Thames, the strongest blessing I have to send—on you and anyone you want it to land on.

I feel pounds lighter, having passed that miracle; so I'll stop now and take a long walk. It's a fine cool day. Three miles southeast lies apparently the country church where John Milton married his first disastrous wife, Mary Powell. I'll try to get there and back before dark, then work all evening. Let me hear some news on Grandmother, Grainger, and the whole home squad. They are keeping their counsel, but I think of them often— never meant to forget.

Love then from
Hutch

Midnight. *Safe back from the trek to Forest Hill (found the church empty, no Miltonic chords to shake the peace). I reread this, then reread your letter and noticed finally that you asked for patience not benediction. And here I've poured out grams of tortured ethereal ink in the effort to bless! I don't have the heart to copy it over. Also I feel like owning up. Don't hesitate to laugh.*

Blessings anyhow.

August 1, 1955

Hutch, your benediction came this morning and reminded me of several things. The one I can still act on is this letter I laid aside six weeks ago. Min arrived after the last installment; and while we haven't been on any wild scramble, the kind of evening conducive to lengthy retrospect has been a little scarce. Thank God, I guess. The presence of company has also made my hunt for the third good day of my life seem less urgent and a little ridiculous. I mean to finish though. Since you'll be the only one to see it, I'm as ready to have you laugh at me as I was to grin at your letter this morning.

I've had the day pretty much to myself—Min had to go to Raleigh after breakfast for some work—so I sat down to find that last day for you, age thirty-five till now. I was fairly certain it would center on you; you're right in thinking you've been the hub of this wheel at least for twenty-five years. I even got out my shoebox of pictures. In an hour I'd worked through a lot more memory than I knew I had of you and me—except for my own fears and failures, good memory. I won't say the hour was peaceful though. I seem not to mind the first half of my past—Mother, Father, my jackass behavior for so many years. It's pictures, on paper and in my mind, of Rachel and you that seize me. Not painfully exactly but deeper even now than I like to be seized, in my final quick. Proves there's quick meat in there still—a strip about the size of a laborer's hand to the right of my heart, alive as a year-old bird dog at first frost. Here's the day it pointed, out of all our days.

It must have been in early June 1944—you took a lot of pictures but neglected to date them. Our famous eventful Virginia trip when we burnt up so much war-rationed gas chasing each other down from seashore to mountains. I'd just been relieved of my job in Raleigh and was facing one more of the blank walls I faced fairly often back then. You must have been fourteen, already enough of a man to throw additional high walls across my path (though not at all blank and generally gated). But you still had the fascination with Jamestown, Pocahontas, and Captain John Smith which Grainger had given you before you could read with all the tales he had manufactured round two normal people.

By the time we got there, you must have been one of the world's experts on the actual story. On the drive from Virginia Beach, you'd briefed me pretty thoroughly—thoroughly enough for me to know how patiently you listened to the flood of romance that met us in Jamestown, the decrepit couple selling souvenirs who gave us the White-Virgin-Christian-Lady word on Pocahontas, so dear to native Virginia hearts. I left it to you; and your only resistance was to tell the old man that No, we wouldn't need his guidance round the site. He felt the rebuff—can you still see his face?—but stood his ground there beside his junk feathers and tomahawks and let us go.

Am I right in seeing us there alone from that point on? I believe I am, few people sharing our luck in having an uncle on the local Ration Board. Perfect weather so we wandered on the green slope there above the James, on the actual dirt that had borne all the story and still held the bones of starved and killed colonists, the Indians they killed. I gather they've done some reconstruction since and built a museum for Pocahontas' earrings; but then I remember nothing but the hill itself, a lot of old trees, the ruins of a brick church standing near the site of Pocahontas' marriage, and separate statues of John Smith and her. I liked the one of her in a buckskin dress that fell to her knees, stepping forward with her palms out and looking slightly up. We sat at her feet to eat our lunch. I remember the lunch as something you fixed, but can that be right? We'd stayed in a hotel the night before; where would you have got celery and pimento cheese? Well, however, we ate and picked up our mess; and I told you I had to lie back a minute now and rest my eyes. So you wandered off again. I leaned back under Pocahontas' moccasins and snoozed.

How long was I out?—fifteen, twenty minutes? Long enough at least to have a few dreams of the punishing variety I specialized in. Then a low thumping on the ground woke me up. The sun had moved down and was bright in my eyes. What I saw twenty yards downhill toward the river was a naked child turning cartwheels slower than a normal child could manage. It came to me peacefully that you had just told me two hours before how Pocahontas used to come here as a child, naked as a jay, and turn cartwheels with the white cabinboys round the first English fort. (I just looked it up in your room before I wrote this to confirm I was sane—William Strachey writing in 1612: "Pocahontas, a well-featured but wanton young girl, Powhatan's daughter, sometimes resorting to our fort, of the age then of eleven or twelve years, would get the boys with her forth into the marketplace and make them wheel, falling on their hands, turning their heels upwards, whom she would follow and wheel so—herself naked as she was— all the fort over.") I hoped at first I was still asleep and dreaming, not drunk—you recall I was also in drinking trouble then. It went on another ten seconds or so till I knew I was conscious; then the hope was that I wasn't being entrusted with some revelation from the Womb of Time. I thought something might be calling me on, requiring me to give when I felt about as bankrupt as I'd ever been—of answers to give to God at least or the magic ground.

The child had turned out of sight by then. I shut my eyes and took the sun and put my hands down to feel the grass beside me—the grass had been shivering—and I felt your shirt, a blue summer shirt warm with your sweat. So I looked again and even in the glare I could see you walking up the rise toward me, barechested in your tan shorts, not really a child. But a real revelation that would need acts of care for the rest of my life and maybe beyond. I'd have run if I hadn't known you could outrun me. I pre-

tended I was out still and you walked up. You watched me awhile (I strained you through my lashes), then slid your shirt from my fingers and put it on. You said, "This statue is making me mad. She never wore any dress half as long as that, and her titties should show." That set me free to laugh. I looked up and said what I wanted to say, "Let's make a run for it." You didn't say "To where?" but laughed back and nodded.

I didn't realize we were happy then. I still thought the world was a custom-built millstone with ROB MAYFIELD sewed neat in its neck like a college boy's sweater. You'll recall also that I acted on my misunder-standing posthaste—the drunk I pulled at Polly's in Richmond, ruining the trip. Well, we got through that and what came after, eleven years. Some of it's been all right, and 85% of the worthwhile enjoyment was owing to you. But it could have been better, which is why I can now see our James-town day as the last high point—the last big tree they let me climb. What I saw from there was right. We should somehow have run. Don't ask me to where? There must have been one place left back then where we could have hid out and had a plain life and learned to ignore all the want-lists posted from cradle to grave to train every human into baying at the stars (which do not bay back) till finally we could face each other and say, "I don't want anything alive or dead but you."

Maybe that makes our Jamestown day the worst day of all. Maybe my mind is affected already, though they don't mention that on my schedule of symptoms. I don't think so. We were happy and knew it. Shame on us for the rest.

T W O

THE ROTATION OF VENUS

DECEMBER 1955–JANUARY 1956

A PACKED autobus from the airport left her in Piazza Esedra with her sensible baggage. Three in the afternoon of Christmas eve, warm sun, clean air; and Hutch's map (he was fogbound in London, maybe here by six) showed their rooms only three or four blocks away. So she draped her raincoat over one shoulder, hoisted the bags, and set off briskly southwest toward the light down Via Nazionale. Every five yards one of an unnumbered squad of lounge lizards in pearl-gray suits would glide up and offer lavish assistance, all gallingly in English—"You need a nice room?" "You need a strong boy?" "I get you big room and two Parker fountain pens for three thousand lire." She smiled at each one, firmly refused, and was weak with relief to see the brass plaque for Pensione Pacifica.

When the birdcage elevator bumped down to get her, it unloaded three American boys—soldiers by their haircuts. The safety she felt in their guileless faces and prairie voices was cut by chagrin; like all serious tourists she wished to be unique, the only stranger. They ignored her in beery oblivion. On the fourth floor she stepped through a half-open door with a duplicate plaque—a long dim hall, low music at the far end (Peggy Lee?), not a soul in sight, no sign of a check-in window or desk. She set her bags down and walked slowly forward. Closed doors, a strong presence of international hotel-smell. Finally on the right there was one room open with windows on the sky. A lobby maybe—wicker furniture with worn flowered pillows; one man in U.S. Air Force trousers and a T-shirt, drinking what seemed water from a heavy glass and reading *Paris Match*. When he didn't look up, Ann said "You work here?"

He debated awhile—"No ma'm, in Germany"—then went back to reading.

"*Anybody* work here?"

He didn't look up but halfway smiled. "They're all working *now*."

"How would I check-in?"

He looked up, serious. "Pick a door. Listen good. If nobody's laughing just step on in and make yourself at home." The Appalachians were still in his voice.

"West Virginia?" Ann said.

"Yes ma'm, near Monongah."

"Good luck then." She turned.

A woman stood behind her—tall, a chemical blond, in rose-colored smock and matching scuffs. "*Prego?*" she said in a startling high voice.

Ann spoke very slowly. "I have a reservation, two reservations—Miss Gatlin, Mr. Mayfield."

The high pitch plunged to contralto. "Sure. Where is the man?"

"In England in a fog. He'll be here by night."

"You sure?"

"I'm sure." She was not of course.

"I got fifty chances to rent his room. This is Christmas, understand."

Ann nodded. "I heard. But it's Rome not Bethlehem. Or am I wrong? If he doesn't show up, I'll pay for his room and sleep in two beds."

The woman's mouth accepted the promise with a letterbox click. "You his sister?"

"No."

The woman bent to whisper; but the pitch rose helplessly, winging each word to the farther hills. "I can give you a bargain on one big room."

Ann stepped back and smiled—"No *grazie*; we're rich"—then regretted the joke: overcharges? room-thefts?

The woman thought a moment. "You change your mind, tell me. I'm a sport."

Ann thanked her. "You'll be the very first sport to know."

2

By five o'clock she had walked the length of Via Nazionale in sun that kept its warmth as it sank. She'd paused unavoidably to register her first encounter with the Victor Emmanuel Monument. Then she'd circled the Forum, Colosseum, Circus Maximus, the Palatine Hill—gingerly, not sure of what she passed, not wanting to know before Hutch could join her. The tender gold light and the scarce other walkers made a skimming easy. No one asked for the time, no one winked or pinched her; and only one more Parker fountain-pen salesman had approached with his wares, sallying politely from the Arch of Constantine, retreating politely with a "*Buon Natale*" when she shook her head. It had been the first sign of Christmas since her landing. There were no decorations in sight anywhere; but how decorate Rome, in all its layers of effortful time spread drying in light that seemed little older than the walls themselves? She thought of going back, haggling for a pen. They were probably stolen or Japanese forgeries, but Hutch could use one, and she wanted to speak. A circle of fullness had grown in her chest. She mistook it for joy and thought she could share it— the uncomprehended splendor of the place, her own strong youth, Hutch's slow approach. When she turned though the seller was back by the Arch, a thin brown boy dressed poorer than she'd noticed with his bare arm propped on another boy's shoulder, laughing hard. She'd keep it for Hutch then and pray not to swamp him.

But half an hour later, having skirted the Temple of Virile Fortune and survived the test of thrusting her hand in the frowning lips of the Mouth of Truth, she climbed a long stairs and stood on the crest of the Capitoline Hill in brown old Santa Maria d'Aracoeli at the feet of the famous Santissimo Bambino in his plain birth-crib. She didn't know the church's claim to stand on the spot where the Tiburtine sibyl had foretold to Augustus the imminent birth of God's first son. She didn't know that this small olive-wood Child, crusted with votive jewels like a beetle, was one of Catholic Christendom's main targets of devotion. But waiting in his presence with other happy lookers—fixed by his frozen eyes, his promise to smile or scream in an instant—the globe of her own hope grew and spread to her mouth and arms. Beside her a middle-aged man in business clothes was streaming quiet tears. He faced her and grinned; she hurried out the door.

On the stairs in near-dark, she was stopped by a swarm of living children in white, pressing up toward the Child. She stood and let them brush her like lambs, dazed with their own anticipation and herded by nuns. One girl, maybe six, was singing as she came by; Ann touched her fine hair, but she gave no sign of notice. So the fullness remained and was not desire. When the children had passed her, Ann held on awhile at the summit, looking down on the city—alive now, lighting in its stacked high windows and along the snaky Tiber—and finally asked the question that had poured elation through her: *What do I hope?* There was no quick answer. She'd walk down slowly and know by the time she reached the street. But before she'd descended six steps, music reached her—keen and grievous. She could only hear that through the new cold wind.

On the street three figures were grouped at a lamp—a man, a boy, an older boy. They were dressed alike in black country-clothes and hats, frayed and dusty. The man wore leggings to his knees, sheepskin with the gray wool exposed. The music came from him, a bagpipe made from what seemed like a bladder. The boys stood by him with their hands out mildly, not begging so much as offering; at their feet a good-sized lamb slept, its feet hobbled. Actual shepherds. Well, she'd hoped for them at least without really knowing. One wish was granted. When she laid a hundred lire in the older boy's hand, her joy only grew.

3

YET back at the Pacifica, unpacked and bathed, she managed to sleep through dinner and a laughing skirmish between a boy from Missouri and a girl from Sorrento. Her dream insisted that she still wasn't here. For nearly three hours she continued east in an open boat that apparently soared without wings through dark. Then she woke in dark or was waked by the sign her dream had awaited. Beneath the tall connecting door to Hutch's room, a slot of light showed—firm footsteps. She was dressed. She sat up and listened for words. A man said "Thank you," not certainly Hutch. She went to the thick door and listened—nothing. Then the sound of running water and footsteps again. The steps came toward the door and stopped. The door seemed to rustle. She pressed her face against it. A hand was scraping at the other side, gently but steadily two inches away. She joined with her own nails, following its path. She felt very calm.

After maybe twenty seconds Hutch said, "Is this a symbol of the tragic plight of modern man?"

Ann laughed. "No it's just a really good French movie. Don't stop. We can wear this away by Easter."

He threw the bolt on his side.

She hesitated, still digging at the wood.

He said, "It's Christmas or will be soon. Take the easy way."

"We never did before."

"We're in Rome," he said. "They invented ease."

Her bolt was stuck but she managed at last.

Hutch opened the door. He looked exhausted but was smiling broadly. "Do you get the feeling we're living in a whorehouse?"

"Positive," she said.

"Shall we leave?"

"Not yet. Might get a few invaluable pointers."

"We didn't used to need them."

"We were *babies*," Ann said. "Wait till you see Rome."

They said the first half of their welcome on the threshold—two clear minutes of unblocked meeting, their eyes open wide. Then Hutch said, "I'm dying. Not a bite to eat since dawn."

Ann suddenly thought that was her problem too. She slumped in his arms. "I'm *dead*. Please administer intravenous glucose."

He lifted her well off the tile by her butt. "I doubt hot pasta will pass through needles. The madam says she'll feed us here gladly."

"They do everything here gladly, you'll notice."

"Then we're where we should always have been," Hutch said.

4

THE dining room of the Pacifica was strongly lit by overhead fixtures from the Mussolini years, swollen and featureless. The glare off the apple-green walls threw an undersea haze into every corner; and though Hutch led them to a distant table, they both looked startlingly drowned at first. Ann gurgled loudly like the sinking Ophelia, and the few other eaters turned in astonishment—two large old ladies in perpetual mourning; five more American soldiers together, a young waitress laughing as she cleared their mess. Ann gurgled once more, then laid her head among the knives and napkins.

Hutch touched her scalp. "On guard—girls that doze off here wake in Turkish harems."

She stayed down—"Good"—then slowly rose. "Not good. I'm glad to be right here."

Hutch assented, no conditions.

With that commitment they'd silently agreed to raise no serious issue now. The place conspired. The only waitress ignored them entirely, bending all her force on their countrymen who'd now called for more wine and were eating what was plainly a cake baked in Omaha, shipped to Naples or Frankfurt, and hauled here intact.

Hutch said, "If you ask them nicely, they'll give you two pieces—our only chance of a touch of home."

Ann was ready to ask when the blond woman showed in the kitchen door, dressed now. Ann beckoned to her.

She came, smiling broadly on wartime teeth, but spoke to Hutch. "You tell her yet?"

Hutch blushed (Ann had never seen him blush). "Not yet. Could we eat a quick dinner now? We're headed to church."

"San Pietro?—big crowd."

"Santa Maria Maggiore."

The woman said "Better," then stroked Ann's hair. "*Guarda, cara.*"

Ann had studied a Berlitz book for months. She ventured "*Perchè?*"

"Because they show you the bed of Christ. *Molto potente. Guarda* for sure."

Hutch said, "Any power would kill us now. We've got to have food."

The woman said, "*Pronto.* You leave it to me" and went to the kitchen.

Ann reached for the salt, poured some in her hand, and licked it up. "What's the secret you share with our Mother Superior?"

"Nothing. Her American verbs are fuzzy. She wants me to ask you to merge our rooms."

Ann laughed. "Me too. She met me with that. I said we were rich."
Hutch nodded. "True."

5

BUT at three in the morning—when they'd let themselves in with separate
keys, brushed their teeth at separate sinks, and Ann had entered her own
broad bed—Hutch came to her side in the chilly dark and said, "Are you
sure you were right about *rich?*"

Ann was at least as tired as he. "Oh no I was lying—for me anyway."
She stayed where she'd fallen in the midst of the bed.

Hutch shuddered with cold.

She moved to her left. "You're welcome to join your assets to mine.
It's too late to count on a discount though."

"They're awake," Hutch said. "They're all awake. I can feel them
pulsing in every room from here to the street, international relations—
Arkansans, Calabrians, Bantus, nuns."

"No nuns," Ann said. "They're all on their knees."

"—And frozen," Hutch said.

"Then tell em Merry Christmas and avoid pneumonia." She opened
the covers.

He told them and joined her, and at once they embraced—quiet,
except for the short laughs and groans of perfect depletion, and inevitably
chaste (though they made a try). Neither of them minded. They knew
they were well past the limits of even their young reserves; they thought
there were long restful days ahead. What they hadn't mentioned or acknowledged yet was the actual weight of the mass they'd watched—the
actual power announced at dinner, when as they stood in the bronzed
smoky dark of the church, four sturdy men had borne straight at them
through packed fervent bodies a long gold palanquin with angels and rays
whose heart was a crystal box containing the promised fragments of the
only Manger: undoubtedly splinters of ancient wood as credible then for
Hutch and Ann (for separate reasons) as the laws that suspended a ceiling
above them or anchored a floor. It had pressed from each of them their
unknown will to start a child, here now in Rome, from the simple juncture
of bodies adequate as any alive.

That will endured their natural fatigue, and through the night the
silent stories they told themselves both nursed its force and explained its
reasons. Ann dreamt scattered scenes from a life in which a trustworthy
woman, who seemed to be Ann, sat on a straight wood chair in a field and
watched steady relays of people walk toward her slightly uphill and in
single file. None of them wore recognizable faces, but all seemed as peace-

fully glad to come as she to receive them, and none of them left. The field filled slowly, though space remained for each newcomer to sit or lie. Hutch mainly saw more scenes from the day when he'd find James Nichols and Nan at the Mayfield house in warm fall light. James never spoke but worked with a trowel as bright as a sword to repoint the stones of the kitchen chimney. Nan stayed by Hutch as he walked wide circles around the yard, also quiet till at last she said "We've made a ditch." They had, with their feet—a shallow trough like the plan for a moat or a dry breast-work against road and trees and eventual passers.

6

NEITHER of them thought of the dreams when they woke. They woke together at a scratching on Ann's door. Hutch sat up. The scratch became tapping. Ann said "Yes?"

A bass voice half-whispered "Ho-ho-ho!"

Ann mocked it. "Ho yourself."

"Santy Claus is out here. Wake on up." A girl's voice giggled.

Ann said, "Blessings on you, old Santy. Go to bed."

A wait, then the bass again. "We're having Christmas breakfast. Want to join us?—real bacon." It was West Virginia clearly and the all-night waitress.

Ann looked to Hutch.

He smiled but shook his head.

So she said, "Thanks but No. We've had our Christmas." They hadn't, not entirely, but the visitors left them to finish where they'd paused.

Hutch began that (Ann had rolled back to sleep). The room had been hot since well before dawn. He threw back all the covers but a sheet, then stepped to the window and opened one curtain—a narrow courtyard below in shadow; a facing wall of identical windows in yellow sun, no faces or noise, no cars or bells. For a moment the city itself pulled at him—he'd still seen only the church by night and two sets of shepherds—and seven months of Britain had taught him to seize any patch of sun. But turning he saw how the light had reached Ann. He went to her. They woke to-gether slowly—first to one another's faces, smoothed and ready; then the plentiful remainder. For more than an hour, the only sounds were the shiftings of cloth and hair and skin. All questions between them dissolved in what Hutch gradually saw as perfect work. When they finally lay en-tirely bare and joined in all their length like one whole person—even feet and hands—Hutch thought how his other loves (including Ann till now) had been forms of play, cheerful misunderstandings. Here now he and

Ann seemed finally poised to work at the single job they'd ignored, a job they could gladly manage forever (or till the shared body had worn away). The rubbers he'd brought were in his own room; he remembered them and felt no need or fear. Neither did Ann. A child was among the last few things they thought they wanted. They didn't start it then for all their quiet eventual laughter, and again they didn't mind.

7

BUT later in the day, they each had a full clear sight of the other, which kept their new will alive and patient. After breakfast they'd exchanged gifts in Hutch's room (a wool scarf for Hutch, a silk scarf for Ann—the source of more laughter). Then a little after noon, they'd walked out finally into sun that gave no threat of ending. Ann had still not mentioned her previous ramble, so Hutch navigated by his Touring Club Italiano guide. And at first they followed in Ann's footsteps—straight down to the Victor Emmanuel Monument, almost invisible in dead-white glare. So they circled to view it head-on from Piazza Venezia. Hutch said, "It's undoubtedly the World-Cup winner in the Carve-Your-Own-Ivory-Soap contest." Ann said, "It's the world's biggest stone typewriter." Hutch said "You win." Then almost alone—few cars, few walkers—they climbed the broad ramp of the Capitoline and saw the bronze she-wolf with sucking boy-twins; Marcus Aurelius in curls on his horse, fending off vandals and all other foes of mental health with a stiff right arm. Ann didn't point out the church still above them with the jeweled Child (on its steps now a single man sat in white shirtsleeves, no shepherds or nuns). Hutch led them back down. They took off their coats—it was sixty in the light—and entered three hours of happy silence, broken only by Ann's occasional questions at the next pile of rubble and Hutch's replies verbatim from the guide.

They'd poked through the eastern slope of the Palatine—megalomanic walls and arches on ground that had borne more reason and madness for longer than any other place, on earth at least. By four o'clock they'd worked to the west slope, and Hutch was drowsy (Oxford had trained him for daily naps). He sat on a stump of travertine by what he didn't know was the probable floor of the House of Romulus. He leaned back and watched Ann retreat a few yards to a thicket of tall green ilex trees round a high platform with narrow steps. She climbed and went forward till she halfway vanished. She was facing the sun, which was two-thirds sunk; and its light sought the line of her head and shoulders. Hutch leaned, took a stick from the ground, and copied the line invisibly on the stone beneath him. She held in place while he traced the line again and again as if to gouge one more memorial in this memory dump. *Useless*—the bare line was not the sight, could never produce the sight for anyone more than himself. If the boy he'd been ten years ago were here now with paints and the skills of solitude and adolescent patience—if Ann and the sun would hold their pose—then the sight would survive and repeat itself for any willing watcher. The fact that he'd set those old skills behind him, or watched them depart, still seemed a big loss. No collection of words by anyone could summon this visible instant with its meanings. Words could do anything but make a reader *see*. Try naming this picture—*Young woman in ruins of the Palatine, late afternoon, Christmas Day 1955, as seen by the eyes of a young man who's known her seven years now and begins to love her here.* The picture was better—so much so that when he suspected she'd turn, he almost called "Stay!"

She turned, came back to the top of the steps, and said "Where am I?"

"Lost."

"I know that," she said. "What's the mess underfoot?"

"The Lupercal," he said. He was guessing.

"What's the book say about it?"

"—Site of the cave where the wolf nursed the twins."

"You're guessing; look it up."

Hutch said "Aren't you tired?"

"Not a bit. Look it up please. I like it up here."

He looked up *Lupercal* and read it to her. " 'Sacred grotto where Romulus and Remus were suckled by the wolf. Later site of an altar where was celebrated on February 15th the *Lupercalia*. Priests of the goat-god Lupercus sacrificed goats, daubed two naked youths with blood, bathed them with wool soaked in milk. The youths cut the skins of the victims into whips and ran through the streets, lashing all passers. Women especially sought the encounter, believing it strengthened fertility.' "

Ann looked back a moment, then faced Hutch again. "Wrong," she said.

"Ma'm?"

"There's no cave here, just the statue of a woman—no head but her bosoms resemble my mother."

Hutch said "She's a *goat*" but consulted the map. "Amazing—first mistake of my life! The Lupercal is down the hill there. You're standing in the Temple of the Magna Mater."

"Meaning what?" Ann said.

"Great Mother."

"What else?"

" 'The Sibylline books foretold to the Romans that they should prevail in the Second Punic War if they obtained from Asia Minor and honored a certain silver statue of Cybele, Great Mother of the Gods, giver of life to gods, men, and beasts. The statue, whose head was apparently a black meteorite, secured the promised victory and was installed in a temple here *circa* 191 B.C. Her priests emasculated themselves in imitation of her dead lover Attis; and annually on March 24th, her "Day of Blood," they danced to percussive music at her altar, gashing themselves anew and splashing her with blood.' "

Ann had stayed at the top of the steps to listen. When the last word flew past her toward the Tiber, she said "Good *night!*", then started down. Halfway she stopped, reached out to the wall, and pulled something loose. When she got to Hutch, she handed him a marble shard the size of a biscuit, perfectly white. Then she gave her best imitation of Mae West— "Keep this in your shaving kit, big boy, and remember me when your razor slips." She was already walking, with bumps and grinds, due north toward the Forum.

"They close this an hour before sunset, it says."

"Good," Ann said. "We could sleep in that wolf-cave. Find it and call me."

But he'd followed her down past the generally dormant Farnese Gardens to the House of the Vestals. They'd passed one middle-aged Italian couple taking their time and a uniformed guard who had not mentioned closing (how to close a space that lacked a whole wall?—release wild dogs or famished cutpurses?), so Ann paced off the length of the atrium, and Hutch sat again on the rim of the pool. The guard had vanished. He took out his stolen shard of Cybele and dipped it in water, shockingly colder than the day itself. Submerged, the marble that had seemed pure white showed numerous spots, the brown of old skin. As a boy he'd have got a lot of mileage from the sight—the signs of old blood, loyal stains, actual atoms of a wild priest's life. He rescued it, laid it beside him to dry. If the guard reappeared, it would look quite normal—the millionth scrap.

Ann called from thirty yards behind him, "Read me this please but check the map first."

He'd known it all his life from pictures at his Grandfather Mayfield's in Richmond; but he checked anyway, then faced her and read. "—'Residence of the virgin priestesses of Vesta, who never numbered more than six and were chosen between the ages of six and ten for a term of thirty years at the end of which they were free to marry. Their duties were the maintenance of Vesta's sacred fire and their own virginity. Failure in the former resulted in scourging; in the latter, live burial in the Campus Sceleratus (her lover being flogged to death in the Forum).' "

Ann shook her head, waited, then said a short sentence which didn't reach Hutch.

"Should I hear that?" he said.

"Yes."

He stayed in place, smiling.

"I'll deliver it then." Again she came toward him. He faced her the whole way; and that was how she saw him, the cooler light in her own eyes now, already half-evening. She'd always been a retentive reader, or hearer of anyone else's reading (she still knew the plots and minor players of every story read to her in grade school); so she naturally saw him through what he'd just said. Who would risk live burial—dry dirt in the mouth—for that boy there? Who would risk having his flesh cut from him as he clung to one of these standing columns till the white gristle showed, then the lungs and heart? In five steps she answered herself—"*Ann Gatlin.*" Why not? What else? *Why?* Because he'd seemed to ask her at times. How crazy was that? No crazier than all this tonnage round them, this all but endlessly durable wreckage that would easily outwear the race itself to be prowled over by whatever spacelings or angels survived for soul-restoring visits. She reached him silently and stood, looking down at the drying shard.

"I'm waiting," he said.

"Good." She laughed.

"—Your message," he said.

She'd forgot it in the walk. "Is this what I gave you?" She pointed at the shard.

"I gave him a bath."

"It stained him though."

Hutch nodded. "Old blood. From the loins of dead priests."

She laughed again. "I was trusting you to say that."

"Seldom fail," he said.

She remembered her message. "They took it very seriously—the Romans, I mean."

"What's *it?*" Hutch said.

She looked out briefly. "Their poor bodies. Sex."

"They patented the orgy. They loved every minute."

"No they didn't, Dumbo. Your brain's in Oxford." She touched his forehead; he reached for her hand. "This is all sex-magic," Ann said, "every cobble. They were scared to death."

"And they're all dead, notice." Hutch waved wide about them. "Don't see them multiplying." Far as they could see, they were perfectly alone. Behind the last high ruins, the city was silent. He picked up the shard, nearly white again.

"Better leave it," Ann said.

"It's my Christmas gift." He put it in his pocket and stood. It was heavy. He gave a mock stumble as if sinking with the load.

The guard was beside them, having come from nowhere—a tall blond man in a tight uniform. An Ostrogoth?

Hutch assumed there were penalties for palming the antiques—fines or years? He stood and said "Evening."

Ann took a step toward the man, not hinting a smile. "Do you know a good Parker-pen salesman nearby?"

The guard said "*Prego?*"

"My crippled friend here's a poet, overwhelmed by the tides of inspiration."

The guard said, "*Scusi ma adesso è chiuso*" and grimly pointed them out the east gate—Arch of Titus, Arch of Constantine, the Colosseum looking very much like itself. The first motor scooter was the sound of safety. Hutch stopped limping then. They stalled in the midst of the broad hub of streets on the buried base of Nero's colossal statue of himself.

Ann said "This is getting unmanageable."

"What?"

"The layers round here."

He touched her shoulder. "The lay-ees too."

"I mean the *time*, Dumbo—the stacks of time. Any D.A.R. from the Old Dominion would give her best corset for an acre of this, and there's hundreds of acres."

"Five hundred-eighty square *miles*, the book says."

"Burn the book," Ann said, "Let's invent it from here." She took him by the wrist and led him toward the Via degli Annibaldi; and though they passed the church with Michelangelo's Moses (and St. Peter's prison-chains), they ignored it, discovering their own better spots in the fast-falling night—Cleopatra's colonic irrigation studio, Michelangelo's model agency and escort service, the site of Roderigo Borgia's Wasserman test, Mussolini's French-tickler purveyor (by appointment). Ann said, "Can't you see him in it now, at attention? It had rabbit ears, translucent and veiny, and pink straps that looped up over his arms like an old tank suit; and at critical moments it would play dance tunes from his mother's native village, up-tempo but softly."

By the time they reached the Pacifica, it seemed a real home. The whole city did, though by then it was cold.

8

AFTER dinner they'd found the one English-language movie and sat through *Doctor at Sea* with Dirk Bogarde, accompanied by only six other scattered bodies—one of whom turned out, when the lights were raised, to be the blond *ingénue* of the plot, a small-boned girl in a tan duffle coat that made her unadorned coarse skin look ill: swamp fever or jaundice. Ann said to Hutch, "I thought they'd drained the Pontine Marshes"; the girl's escort heard, grinned, and nodded. Outside the wind was strong and they took their first taxi. Hutch tried to converse as they roared through empty streets—"Where are the tourists?" —"Just you," the driver said in unaccented English but appeared to smile also.

So they entered the Pacifica again, tired but easy, thinking of nothing but clean teeth and bed (the notion of merging rooms had been shelved with no further discussion). Hutch passed the lobby without looking in, but Ann saw the same West Virginia boy still there as if he'd sat through Christmas. He was not even turning the worn magazines but staring at space with an awful patience. She caught up with Hutch as he opened his door. "Can we go back and cheer up Monongah awhile? He's looking blue."

He said "You go."

She could see he meant it. "What will you do then?"

"Bathe my tired back and read till I sleep."

"What if I wake you?"

He made a loose fist and rapped her belly. "I'll be mad if you don't."

"I'll stay," she said and took a step in.

"Ann, let me read you the first rule of travel"—he lined it on the air—"*Cabin mates will require an absolute minimum of one hour alone for each day together.*"

"We're alone all night."

"Not really," Hutch said.

His grin reassured her (and the rule sounded right). She said, "This may not last ten minutes. He may be drunk."

"Or deader than us—he's Santy Claus, remember?"

But she took off her raincoat, gave it to Hutch; and not even stopping to comb her hair, went back to the lobby and stood in the door.

The boy took a minute to sense her and look.

"Merry Christmas," she said.

"You said it was over, way back this morning."

"I'm sorry," she said. "I was fast asleep."

He accepted that. He was neatly dressed now in a purple short-sleeved shirt and gray trousers. He looked under twenty; they'd never swapped names.

"My name is Ann Gatlin."

He stood slowly. "You could sit down, I guess."

"You waiting for somebody?"

"No ma'm," he said.

She sat on a small couch across from his chair; the dry wicker creaked outrageously. She laughed. "This place!"

"It's all right," he said, "—good eats."

"Good company?"

He blushed, then cracked the knuckle of his long middle finger so loudly Ann looked to the ceiling for damage. That was all his answer.

"Where'd you go today?"

"Cross the street," he said, "—that American Bar. It's about as American as Mount-damn-Everest. I ordered a grilled cheese sandwich; ought to *seen* it."

"Just the name makes me hungry."

"The sandwich wouldn't."

"That's all you did?"

"Yes ma'm. I'm not a traveler."

"What you doing here then?"

"I come with two buddies from Germany. They had to see Naples, know a girl near there. I told them, 'Just leave me here to sleep.' They'll pick me up Wednesday; said so anyway."

"If they don't?"

"I'll wait."

"Aren't you in the Army?"

"Air Force—better food."

"And you won't be AWOL?"

"I might, yes ma'm."

"Would you go to jail?"

"Not for long," he said. "They don't call it jail."

"Call me *Ann* please," she said.

He nodded.

"Who are you?"

"Rowlet," he said.

"First name?"

"Rowlet Swanson."

"Why did you leave Monongah?"

For the first time he laughed. His new beauty tore through the space like a ghost and struck her whole face. "You ain't seen Monongah."

Ann knew she should smile, but the sight still held her. "Just pictures," she said. "You plan to go back?"

"When I'm about a hundred years old, in a box."

"It's really that bad?"

He looked off blankly to consider the question, then answered toward the door. "The *place* has got this town beat to hell, but I've got a bunch of brothers." He faced her and laughed again. "You a missionary?"

This time she could join him. "—For *leaving*, yes."

"You got a bad sister?"

"A normal mother."

"Who's your brown-headed friend?" He pointed through the wall.

What to call him? She could only offer "Hutchins Mayfield."

"No kin?"

"Not yet, maybe later."

"Married people aren't kin. That's the point, I thought."

"Then why have babies?"

"I'm a private, lady. You're asking a lot."

"Sorry," Ann said. "I work for a lawyer."

Rowlet said "You could quit," then looked up quickly.

A girl in a green dress stood in the door—black hair, a dense glamor. It took Ann awhile to see it was the waitress, finished in the kitchen (at eleven, Christmas night). She moved to stand.

But Rowlet said, "Rest. I'll be here tomorrow." Then he went to the girl. He could say her difficult name, and did—*Smeralda*, Emerald.

9

ANN didn't switch on the light in her room; but the curtains were open, there was some streetlight, and soon as she entered she saw the bed was empty—carefully made. The door between the two rooms was ajar. She went to the sill and, not looking in, listened quietly. No sure sound of life. So she didn't look in and didn't think why. She undressed, found her nightgown, brushed her teeth; then turned back the covers of her bed and slid on her back to the middle. She oared her arms slowly full-length in the coolness of linen still smelling of iron-scorch. She thought she liked that. She touched her pooled breasts through cloth, smiled, and told them "Just *rest*, doll-babies." She said a short prayer, which was not customary —thanks for the day, that still seemed good; blessings on her mother, who had not tried to phone. Before she had managed to ask for the future, her eyes filled with tears. Even then she thought they were excess pleasure (though she'd always noticed how men wept for pleasure, women for pain). And though they continued for the three or four minutes till she'd sunk to sleep, she didn't suspect they were signs of failure—hers or Hutch's. That came when he joined her.

At five he'd waked to find himself alone. In the dark he couldn't know how long he'd slept—he felt fully rested—and he'd lain still to hear the hall outside. At first there was nothing, then eventually the slow wet slap of a mop—end of night or start of day? He strained for more sound of Ann and the boy—hopeless of course; that was yards away. He didn't once think she was nearby, unconscious. It came on him then, in the crazy accuracy of night, that she'd left with the boy. To where? For how long? He'd heard the table of soldiers last night planning a visit to

Bricktop's nightclub. Would that be it? He knew he was still dazed and untrustworthy; but he stood up naked in the cold air, opened the hall door, and looked out gingerly. An old man he'd never seen before was wringing the mop ten feet beyond him. Hutch asked was it morning.

The man said "No."

"*Ma che ora è?*"

"*Cinque ore forse.*"

Hutch didn't know enough words to ask for Ann, but his mind had cleared sufficiently to think of her room. He went there slowly. She'd left the curtains open; and he saw her at once, sprawled neat and alone. The relief he felt seemed out of proportion even as he stood there (he'd already lost the dream that waked him, another prediction of Rob's disappearance). But he went straight forward and entered the bed. Though she'd stayed in the middle, Ann had warmed the whole surface; and at first he lay flat on the edge, still shivering. The relief had settled into gratitude; so once he was warm, he was ready to thank her. She was on her right side, away from him. He turned toward her gently and fitted his front down her warmer back—his hard cock downward in the crack of her legs. He knew she was awake (any falling feather woke her), but she gave no sign of welcome. He tugged at the muscle that thumped his cock like a dog-snout against her—*Attention! Love me!* He'd forgot the Morse code; but he thumped out a spurious stretch of dot-dash meant to greet, thank, beg with his amiable universal greeter-thanker-beggar. Her lean upper leg lifted slightly at last, and he slid into harbor or offshore anchorage. He rubbed his rough chin on the crest of her spine and said "Happy Boxing Day."

She said "What's that?"

"The day after Christmas in Merrie-Olde, when you give gift boxes to servants and tradesmen."

"Which am I?" she said.

She only sounded sleepy; Hutch thought she was volleying. "—The giver," he said. "Lady Bountiful." His left hand moved round her thigh to the slit. She was dry as a child. He worked against that, not harshly but fast.

They'd been in sophomore English together. She said in her street voice, "Patient Griselda."

But he laughed and persisted in the tuning skills which their years had perfected; and in two more minutes (still spooned to her back, licking her neck), he entered the performance he'd never failed at. Through it he constantly watched what he'd seen in the afternoon. *Young woman in ruins of the Palatine*, a nimbus of late light, the clear news he'd waited for longer than he'd known—that he'd go home to her. When he'd calmed again he found Ann's right hand and, after long fumbling, slid his

Great-grandmother Mayfield's wedding ring from his own hand and closed it in her palm.

She lay still a long time, discarding many questions. Then she said "What does this say?"

" 'Robinson Mayfield to Anna Goodwin.' "

"No, *now*. It says something."

He took her middle finger and put the ring on it, still too large.

"You're supposed to use words."

He seized a damp hank of her hair in his teeth and pulled back gently. "—In the morning," he said.

"We talk better at night."

Hutch had gone by then—into sleep like a trapdoor, though still close against her.

Ann wore the ring but never shut her eyes. She lay for an hour, not moving away, in the hope of freeing her body from the net of failure that had fallen across it the moment she woke, the warning that she and Hutch were suddenly parted after one perfect day and would not meet again—not meet, not join. In all her racing through grievances and fears, she never touched the reason.

At ten to seven someone knocked on her door, serious and loud. Ann rose at once, found her robe, and answered.

Rowlet Swanson, still wearing his late-night clothes, stood three feet back. "Is Hutchins Mayfield the name of your friend?"

"Yes."

"I think he's got a call from the States. I'm not sure."

Then she found the reason; the net clung tighter. "Are they waiting?"

"—In the lobby. Smeralda answered it finally. She doesn't know much."

Ann said "He's coming." She shut the door, no mention of thanks.

Hutch was watching by then.

She came halfway. "You're wanted on the phone, they think—in the lobby."

He didn't show fear or bafflement but lay still an instant, then loped to his room and rushed to dress. As he left he called back "Yule greetings from home."

Ann knew he was wrong. When she felt she could move, she washed herself carefully, pinned her hair back, dressed warmly, and sat in her one chair to wait.

10

An Italian operator—sounding worlds away, barely speaking English—established his name and vanished so thoroughly he thought the line was cut.

Then "Hutch? You hear me?"

"Yes"—Grainger as plain as the sun on his bare feet. "Where are you?"

"Sylvie's house. You well?"

"What time is it there?" He could hear Grainger turn and ask Sylvie, hear her answer "One o'clock—black night." They seemed entirely tangible. He might have reached out an actual hand if Rowlet hadn't stood in the door behind him and if cold nodes of fright hadn't formed all through him.

Grainger said "You feeling good?"

"Doing good. Merry Christmas. Did you get my package?"

"Not yet. Thank you though."

The sound of Sylvie coughing.

Hutch saw he'd have to start it, bring it on himself. "Everybody all right?"

"Sylvie's got a bad cold. Miss Eva's pretty good."

"How's Rob?"

"Bad, Hutch. I'm calling to tell you."

"What?"

"They put him in the clinic here two days ago."

"What's the trouble?"

"Can't breathe. They got him in the tent."

"What's the trouble?"

"A cancer."

Sylvie said "Going fast."

"Who's with him?" Hutch said.

"Miss Eva. Miss Min—Miss Min's there now. I left to call you."

"Can I call him?"

"He don't want you to know. Me and Sylvie doing this."

"Then what must I do?"

"Depends," Grainger said.

"What on?"

"You want to see him?"

Sylvie said "Tell him 'Hurry.'"

11

IN Ann's room he said, "That was Grainger. Rob's dying."

She said "Where was Grainger?" She'd stood by the chair.

"At Sylvie's, one o'clock in the morning."

"What else did he say?"

Hutch was dry as pressed cloth. He went to her basin, ran water, drank a handful. Then he went to the bed and sat at the foot to face the window. "Please sit there," he said. "It's cancer—his lungs. They can't operate. They've moved him to the clinic in Fontaine for oxygen. Nobody knows how long it'll take. He told them not to tell me."

"Why?" She sat again.

Hutch was watching the bright sky. "—To leave me here."

"Why?"

"He thought I'd asked for it."

"Did Grainger say that?"

Hutch shook his head. "I knew."

Ann said "So did I."

Hutch lay back on his elbows, inspected the ceiling, then faced Ann finally. "Knew what please?"

"I've known about your father since June fourteenth."

"How?"

"Polly—he told her on his trip to Richmond. Swore her to silence but she called me."

"You didn't see Rob then?"

"He never called me, no."

The space between them—eight feet—seemed a moving shaft, lengthening, narrowing. The light in his eyes had almost blanked Ann. "Polly swore you not to tell me?"

"Your father did, Hutch. Polly called him that night to confess what she'd done. He wrote me a letter next morning; *he* swore me."

"Have you got the letter now?"

"Not here. I'm not lying."

"But you have, for six months."

She nodded. "All right." When she breathed after that, she thought she might not breathe again—air was thin and scarce.

Hutch stood. "Let me put on my shoes and wash. We have to eat now."

Between them they ate all the rolls set out, the curls of butter and apricot jam, and drank big basins of cool strong coffee. They said very little and neither asked questions. They knew they were gliding low on declivities neither could see; any glance down might break the frail balance. They could only look forward. Hutch refused more coffee; then said, "Will you let me take a long walk now?"

"Long as you want." Ann nodded, half-smiling.

"It's not what I want."

She nodded again. "I'll wash my hair."

He put his hands forward to the rim of her plate and spoke to its blankness (she'd eaten every crumb). "All I can say now is 'Pardon us please'—Rob and me."

She touched the nail of the finger he'd stripped the ring from at dawn. "I don't have the right but, sure, full pardon."

He looked to the window; the sun was steady. "Don't stay inside. If you want to, walk. I'll be back for lunch."

She nodded. "So will I."

12

HE stopped by the room for his money and guidebook, then set out southwest again down the broad street—no destination for the first ten minutes. But when he pulled up at the Victor Emmanuel, he saw it had grown since yesterday; and he took a hard right through Piazza Venezia and on up the Corso. It was choked with cars, blue with exhaust at barely nine; so he took the first street west in blind hope of steering for the Tiber and air and came out shortly in a small car-park with a marble elephant bearing an obelisk, and a few yards ahead, the rear of what was plainly the Pantheon swathed in cats. He sat on the steps of the nearest church and opened his guide.

He'd landed at one of his few planned targets—or had he been led? (he suspected that). The midget elephant was an early Bernini. The obelisk was left from a temple of Isis that had stood nearby; the church was built on the ruins of a temple to Minerva and contained the tomb of Beato Angelico and Michelangelo's only statue of the grown live Christ, Risen with bronze underpants ("a later addition").

He entered brown dark and went straight forward past chapels and tombs through a haze of incense to the steps of the choir where Risen Christ stood bare, the pants gone. An inch was broken from the end of the penis, but the balls were intact, and their thin-skinned availability measured more terribly than wounds the day of agony He'd borne to stand here, unquestionably risen, His thick hips and haunches an adequate promise He'd suffered for all and would not fail again. Hutch moved up to meet His sideways glance and planned for the first time this morning to ask that his own choice be made, not painless but right. The eyes wouldn't meet him. They wanted no prayers; they knew all outcomes. Nothing was possible but prone adoration—to fall face-down on the steps in thanks. It had surely happened here thousands of times. But thanks were as needless as begging or praise. Hutch looked back once; the nave was still empty. He went through it quietly toward the street and sun and straight through the fierce watchful cats to the doors of the Pantheon.

He knew it also had always been a temple, built to All the Gods by Hadrian, reconsecrated by Boniface IV to Mary the Virgin and twenty-eight wagonloads of martyred bones hauled up from the catacombs to wait here in light. For all its external gloomy mass, the vast inner globe of its heart seemed afloat—a transparent heart loose now in sunlight, slowly ascending; the open eye in its apex peering calm and unblinking at a sure destination: a patient socket in the breast of a sky even clearer, calmer. He walked to the absolute center of the floor, stood on the marble disc still wet from the night (he'd heard no rain) and looked above. Unbroken sky of a blue no painter had matched, never would—no camera, no dream. He spoke to that silently. *Show me now please.* A distant crack reached him. He knew it was knees and looked for the source. An old woman knelt on the stone by a niche containing the Virgin with obese Child. He didn't know that the box beneath contained the dust of Raphael. Unnecessary news. He had the one answer required today—infused through his whole skin as if he were bare as the neighborhood Christ, though with no pain or scar.

He consulted his map, found American Express, found it open and ready, and booked the earliest seat he could get—tomorrow noon: New York, then home. It took all his money but sixty-five dollars.

13

THE blond woman helped him place the call to Virginia; then left him alone in the lobby with the old phone, traces of gilt arabesque on its cradle.

Alice was awake as he'd known she'd be, at five in the morning. Neither one mentioned Christmas; and though she seemed farther off than Grainger, she went for the throat. "Who's in trouble?"

"Don't you know?"

"Sure, everybody my age. Which one you mean?"

"Rob. You haven't heard from Rob?"

"Not for years, Hutch. Years. Rob thinks I took you."

She had; he saw now. But he pushed through that. "Grainger just called from home. Rob's going fast—cancer. They knew when I left; he made them keep it from me."

"They were right," Alice said. "Is he conscious still?"

He hadn't asked; he stalled and weighed the omission.

But she said, "Can I meet you? What plane? What time?"

"New York in the morning, then the first plane to Raleigh."

"It's rush-time," she said.

"I'll tell them it's death. They keep space for deaths. Let me call you once I'm home. It may be crowded—Grandmother, Min Tharrington."

"Is she back on?"

"Somehow," Hutch said.

"I'll be here. Always am."

"You can help today."

"I'm dressed," Alice said.

"Find some way to cable me five hundred dollars, care American Express."

"That enough?"

"Should be."

"Is Ann coming with you?"

"Not yet," Hutch said.

When Hutch had finished and stood, there was Rowlet (Ann had told him the name over breakfast). At some point in the call, he'd managed to enter and sit by the door on the deafening wicker couch. Hutch passed him and nodded.

"You got a plane yet?"

Hutch stopped. "Noon tomorrow."

"Want a ride to the field?"

"Thank you. I can take the bus."

"I'll meet you here at ten. Rich buddy left his car when he went to Naples. I got the keys."

Thanks were plainly unwanted. For a moment Hutch thought "Everybody claims a part"; but he did say, "Thanks. Maybe half-past nine? I need to get some money that's being wired to me."

"I could lend you fifty easy."

"It's coming from home. I'll leave some with Ann to pay my bills here."

"You leaving her here?"

Hutch said, "I guess so. She's got two weeks. I can't haul her back to what's waiting for me."

"She'd go," Rowlet said.

Hutch extended his hand. "Hutch Mayfield," he said.

Rowlet gave his long brown hand over like a dog, some young animal in need of slow care. It was solid horn-callus though. He said "I know your name."

"Is Ann back yet?"

Rowlet nodded. "In her room."

Hutch took a step toward him.

"I saw her new ring."

Hutch smiled. "You see all."

"They pay me too. I'm in tower-control."

The voice—dead-flat in its West Virginia vowels—held Hutch in place but with nothing to say. Also the narrow face, steadily offered as any wrecked column in the city. He watched it. After ten seconds it still seemed blank but increasingly strong, for mercy or harm.

Rowlet said "You eat?"

"Not yet."

"Want to eat?"

"I'll check on Ann."

"She's ready. Go call her."

Hutch nodded and took a step.

"After that I'm driving the waitress home. She's got a day off, lives out in the country. Plenty room in the car."

Hutch said "I'll ask Ann."

Rowlet said "She'll come."

14

SHE did. They piled into the rich buddy's Plymouth; and Smeralda pointed them silently north, Rowlet nosing through streets that were filling again as Christmas ebbed. Up the Via Flaminia, past the Villa Borghese (green core of the city with its weird Caravaggios, which Hutch would not see), cross the Milvian Bridge where Constantine triumphed as promised in his vision; then the traffic thinned suddenly, and after a few miles of gimcrack housing, they were in open country. Hilly pasture with small cows, clumps of gray olives and the huge bolls of cork trees, occasional scraps of ancient wall. Smeralda stayed silent, Rowlet only spoke to clarify directions, Ann said "Look" a half-dozen times at fine prospects, Hutch would look and nod.

Otherwise he practiced for thirty minutes his oldest skill—calm witness, all eyes. He saw the beauty of woods and farms. He sensed the unthinkable strata of effort, unbroken relays of human labor, that had gentled the land to this sun-struck peace. But he felt no regret to be leaving tomorrow, and the fact of Rob dying was a sight he'd postponed.

It would come in its time late tomorrow—a sight as incalculable as what he now passed through, the land that fed Rome and all her predecessors.

Smeralda said "Stop" at last, and Rowlet stopped hard in the midst of the road. A dwarf tractor crossed fifty yards ahead, led by a black dog. She turned to the back seat and smiled at Hutch. "I'm very sad for your father," she said.

It was many more English words than Hutch had thought she knew. He thanked her.

Then she pointed to Rowlet. "Make him take you to see the old *castello*, Santa Maria di Galéria. Just a few more minutes." She touched Rowlet's shoulder once and was gone, jumping a shallow ditch neatly in her best dress and climbing on strong legs toward a tan house set back in pines with a staring goat. She never looked back.

Hutch almost called to her, thanks again; she seemed that lonely.

Rowlet said "You want to see it?"

Hutch said "Why not?"

"It's not a coal mine, is it?"

Hutch laughed. "No a castle."

"Then aim me. I'm running."

Hutch climbed into the front seat and opened his guide.

Before they moved on, Ann lay back to rest.

15

By the time they'd found the eight-foot-deep track that led like a tunnel to a green river-valley, she was fast asleep. Rowlet stopped at a barbed-wire fence at the foot of a high plateau and faced Hutch for word.

Hutch read out, " 'The ruins of the castle of Galéria stand on the site of Etruscan Careiae. Commanding the wooded valley of the Galera, it served from the ninth to the nineteenth century but was finally abandoned for reasons of health.' "

"Another ghost town," Rowlet said. "You guess it's healthy yet?"

"It's fertile anyhow." Hutch pointed to the thicket of vines on the gateway, the massed bay trees. It seemed an illustration from every child's dream of the gate into strangeness, all laws reversed.

"Want to limber your legs?" Rowlet killed the engine.

Hutch said "Sure" and looked to Ann. Her dry lips had parted, and her teeth were clenched. He turned, put his hand to her mouth, felt her breath—normal heat. Then he touched her forehead, exhaustion not fever. "Shall we wake her?"

"Let her be." Rowlet opened his door.

Hutch wrote her a note on the back of a map of Bavaria—*We are up in those ruins, 4 p.m.* Then he locked Rowlet's door, locked his own; and followed Rowlet up a weedy path toward a fine belltower, no hands on its clock. Sun was strong but a light wind pushed at their backs with a fresh river smell. Hutch turned to face it and take the light for a long quiet minute. Then Rowlet was gone. When he looked up the path again, he saw only shards of tile, naked brambles, and the ash-blond huddles of broken stone walls—roofless warrens hacked open to the sky. No sound at all. Even river and wind moved silently. He pulled on upward, trusting Rowlet would show—maybe jump from hiding in some ghost act. But he reached the arched gate, still alone and silent. The climb had been easy, but his breath came fast; so he stopped by a hole of standing brown water and waited to calm, looking only down. In another long minute a hard rush flooded his mouth and eyes, a fresh sense of having what he'd asked to have—absolute space, the empty world, and time to watch it. For what?—its picture, the figure Rob had missed. For whom?—who but Rob? to reward, win, hold him, protect him from his life. Which had won him now, dissolved him in pain. Leaving Hutch again with memory and no one to hear, an unworn witness in an empty court—an unused fool. He saw no way to laugh, though laughter seemed required.

Rowlet said "Come here." He was hid to the left.

"Where's here?"

Rowlet said "Just follow the voice" and started singing. His speaking voice was deep, but he sang in a strong pure tenor—no words—the tune of "Sweet William."

Hutch found him at the top of a broad staircase in full light; he stopped. "No, finish your song."

"Not mine," Rowlet said. "Don't know it to the end. My sister used to like it."

"Where's she?"

"Jesus knows."

"What killed her?"

"Maybe nothing. She may be alive."

"You don't want to find her?"

"She'll holler if she's hungry."

"Who you looking for now?" Hutch said.

Rowlet faced him, came down a step, and smiled (Hutch had not seen him smile till now). "Your girl," he said.

"Is she still in the car?"

Rowlet came down. "I guess so. I couldn't see more than the roof. Maybe you ought to check."

"You worried about her?"

Rowlet sat on the huge bottom step but spoke to Hutch; concealment seemed as foreign to his nature as lace. "I'm thinking I may ought to worry over you."

Hutch went to him, passed him, climbed three steps above, sat, and touched both his shoulders—he was warmer than the light. "I'll make it," he said.

Rowlet said "Don't doubt it."

"Stop worrying then." His hands stayed in place.

Rowlet bore them like buckets; but he said, "Not till you tell me how I got to act once you're back home and her and me are left together."

Hutch finally laughed. "How old are you?"

"Twenty soon," Rowlet said.

"Age fast then, son. She likes experts."

Rowlet said "Are you one?"

Hutch took back his hands. "She's come here to see me."

"Where do you live?"

"England."

"Why?"

"I'm studying there."

"To be what?" Rowlet said.

"A writer."

"She your subject?"

"Not yet. Too soon."

"How long have you known her?"

"Seven years."

"You engaged?"

"Very likely."

"And you're leaving her here." It was not a question.

But Hutch said "No choice."

"If she asked would you take her?"

"She won't."

Rowlet bent to the ground and took up a scrap of rose-colored brick, dug at it with the nail of his index finger till he'd scored a short line. "That's what you're an expert in?" he said. Not turning, he handed the clay back to Hutch.

Hutch took it—common scrap, the color of brick everywhere on earth. "I haven't given much thought to brick," he said and gouged at the line.

"—*People*," Rowlet said. "You know what people will do in advance, knowing she won't ask to go home with you."

Hutch grinned. "Maybe so."

Rowlet turned just his profile, clear against the dark ground as coastline on maps. "Then foretell me this—what will you do if her and me take up together, two orphans in Rome?" He smiled again downhill toward the car.

That simple line from forehead to chin seemed now to Hutch all he'd ever meant to understand, praise, and save—its brave seal thrust toward the patient fruitful matrix of the world. He leaned, pressed his own mouth against dry hair on the ridge of Rowlet's neck. "I'm the orphan," he said. "Good luck anyhow."

Rowlet stayed a moment, then laughed and stood.

Ann said, "Keep laughing. I'm tracking you down."

Hutch laughed in earnest and threw the scored shard. It cleared a high wall, banked higher on wind, and sailed toward the river.

16

AFTER dinner Ann read in the lobby while he packed (Rowlet had vanished again with the car). At ten he finished and came in to get her. "You tired?"

"Pure dead." She regretted the word.

Hutch was too tired to notice.

They undressed in her room, set her travel-clock to alarm at seven (not counting on Rowlet), and doused the light. After two quiet minutes on his back, Hutch turned and slowly consulted her shoulders, neck, face with a hand as gentle and baffled as a child's. He found no message, though he even pressed a finger through her lips to the teeth and rubbed their warm blankness.

She accepted the prowling long as she could, then spoke to stop him. "Any signs of pyorrhea?"

"No'm, perfect," he said.

"Well damn. I was counting on a full set of dentures, every other tooth gold." She still lay flat.

He tapped her nose, laughed once, ringed her warm throat. Then tears overcame him.

Ann felt them and knew there was cause, but she didn't move or speak.

In a while Hutch said, "Do you want to ask questions?" They had still not discussed his going, her staying.

"Not really," she said. "But I know what you mean."

"That's more than I do."

So she rolled to face him, not seeing but taking his clean breath for presence. "You mean do I understand what's happened here?"

"Do you?"

"How's this? We had a good three days in Rome. You gave me this ring again, and this time I took it."

"Will you keep it?"

"—Till you ask me to stop," she said.

"I haven't."

"I know."

"But I've asked you to stay here."

"I know why," she said.

He waited and then said "You better tell *me*."

"You love your father more than anything else."

"How much do you mind that?"

"I might not at all if I understood why."

Hutch said, "He was what I had from the start. He was lovable."

She laid her right hand on his breastbone and pressed; then spread her fingers and tried to span his nipples, missing by an inch. "Please tell me everything you know about your mother." She'd never asked for that.

"You know what I know. Her name was Rachel; you've seen the few pictures."

"I know she'd had some kind of breakdown before she met your father."

"—Thought she was pregnant; she'd never touched a boy."

"Then she met your father. They had a few years, and she died bearing you."

Hutch covered her hand. "That's the story I know."

"Think harder," Ann said. "You lived in her body—Great God!— nine months."

He laughed once. "I used to remember that. Till the time I was five or six years old, it was all I remembered—all the past I had."

"How was it?"

"Very still. I had time to look."

"At what?"

"Oh light. I'd wake up and hang there for hours, warm in a bath of mild light—the sun through her belly, I guess: rose with blood."

"Maybe you dreamt it."

"Maybe not," he said. "I'd forgot till now." (He'd forgot Archie Gibbons's memory on Tresco.)

She kissed his throat. "Then I'm glad I asked."

"I killed her though."

"Never mind," Ann said. "She volunteered."

"There *is* one dream I've had more than once. I'm a half-grown boy. I find her in the woods and know her on sight. She's the image of me and nearly as young. I ask her to wait while I go for Rob. She's gone when we come. I wrote you that."

"She wanted just you. She'd have stayed for you."

He'd never thought it. "Why?"

"She wanted you before she'd ever seen your father."

"Say why."

"She still wants you."

"Say why though." He kissed her at the edge of her mouth.

"I couldn't. She couldn't. But I'm right; so was she."

Hutch chose to believe her. He lay still, seeing old versions of the dream—Rachel's face, his absent mother. She stood to be watched, gave no sign of flight. She was his present age, a feasible woman.

Ann waited through that, then said "Now me."

Dark as it was, he also saw her—no dream, plain memory, her face in the Forum as she'd brought him her finding: "They were *serious*." He reached out, freed her left ear from hair, and traced its rim. "Dear Dumbo," he said. He was ready by then.

They worked toward it slowly, there on their sides, and slowly arrived—reward for both. When they'd thanked each other, they lay on joined. Ann said, "I'll be in Richmond on the first." She felt him nod but he didn't speak again. Before his head was still, he'd started his sleep. She was calmly awake an hour later when the child began.

17

ROB studied Hutch a moment; then said, "She's gone out to get me a shot."

Hutch smiled. "I leave and here you start drinking."

Rob nodded. "Morphine. White Lightning worked better." When he smiled the teeth that had showed through his translucent lip were the only unchanged things—perfect and white. The hand that lifted the oxygen tent was a long bone rake.

Hutch leaned in, kissed him on the forehead, leaned back. The tent fell between them, fanning out its cool gas and the burnt smell of cancer.

"You're meant to be in Rome."

"I'm not. Here, feel."

Rob took the right hand. "Appears to be you." His voice was familiar but shrunk like the rest, a condensation.

Hutch said, "That sign on your door seems to work—*Absolutely No Visitors*. Grandmother post that?"

"Had to. We were running a menagerie, me the ape in the tent." He pointed to a chair. "Pull that over here."

Hutch sat a yard from him, tasting the oddness of his joy to be back (he'd phoned nobody, come by bus from Raleigh, a taxi to the clinic).

"I sent Min home with Grainger to supper. He'll be back after dark." Rob took three silent shallow breaths. "They have little arm-wrestling contests to see who gets to sit here through the night and watch me."

Hutch nodded in hopes of slowing the talk.

But Rob turned toward him—"Am I that pretty still?"—and smiled again.

Hutch reached out and covered the hand. "Rest a little. I'll be here now."

The smile survived. Rob looked to the ceiling. "You talk. Tell all."

"Let's rest a few minutes."

"They'll be back by then." Rob shut his eyes and waited.

So Hutch said, "Grainger and Sylvie called me two days ago. I called Alice Matthews; she wired the money. I took the first plane and came straight here. Nobody knows but you."

"Did that woman see you?"

"Mrs. Hayes, at the desk."

"It'll be on the radio by now," Rob said. "There'll be swarms to see you. Ne' mind, ne' mind." He breathed again. "You got any questions?"

Hutch said "Not yet."

"Now is your chance."

"I'm staying, remember?"

Rob nodded.

The door opened wide on a nurse with a small nickel tray and a needle. She stopped on the threshold. "It's *you*. I've lost. I bet Emily Hayes a dollar it was any other human but you. What blew you in?"

Hutch stood—Alta Allen; she'd nursed him through pneumonia nine years ago. "East wind," he said. "Happy New Year."

"Hold your horses," she said, "—four days of this old year left to get through." She walked on to Rob and touched his bare forearm. "You feel like it's time?"

Rob said "Yes ma'm."

She brushed him with alcohol, gave him the drug, and rubbed the arm. Then she looked back to Hutch. "You remember this—Rob Mayfield is four months older than me. He calls me *ma'm* but I know him of old. The tales I could tell!"

Rob tapped on the tent. When she faced him he shook a warning finger slowly, then sank straight to sleep.

Alta smoothed the sheets, checked the oxygen valve, stepped to Hutch, and laid her wide hand on his head. "Nothing bad," she said, "—my tales, I mean. They were mostly funny. He was nobody's enemy but his sweet self's. You got here in time."

Hutch said "Yes ma'm."

She opened the door. "I'll be at the desk."

Hutch stood and whispered, "Did he ask for me?"

Alta faced him plainly. "Not to me, not anywhere in my hearing." She searched his eyes, smiling. "You're past-due to eat. Come eat with me."

"I can't leave yet."

She nodded toward Rob. "He'll rest half an hour, maybe more if God loves him. I'll fix you anything you want in the pantry—provided it's biscuits, bullet-peas, and boiled chicken."

Hutch was suddenly empty and deeply tired. He looked at his watch and knew it was two in the morning in Rome. He could feel Ann awake. Then he followed Alta.

18

THEY'D finished the tepid food in the pantry under white light when Alta said "You've lost your ring."

Hutch's hand was on the table; he extended the fingers. "This Christmas," he said. "I gave it away."

"Anybody I know?" She lit a cigarette with the calm intensity of addiction.

"Ann Gatlin," he said. "I doubt you've ever seen her."

"Heard her name, heard about her." Alta ate another mouthful of smoke. "Is she worth it?"

"I think so."

"Where is she?"

Hutch checked his watch again. "In Italy asleep, I hope."

"She had to stay on?"

"I asked her to."

Alta stood and took his plate. "You need some lime jello?"

"Not today, no ma'm."

She went to the sink, ran a burst of cold water, then turned in place. "Will you listen to a little unsolicited advice?"

Hutch smiled, cupped an ear.

"Call her up, get her here, this'll get a lot worse." She pointed through a pink wall toward Rob.

"He doesn't seem in pain. Is that the morphine?"

"He just calls it morphine. It's Demerol. Pain won't be the problem. He'll drown in himself. They used to say drowning was a peaceful death, found smiles on their faces when the bodies washed up. But you'll have to watch."

Hutch said "How long?"

Alta walked to the back of her chair and held it. "I'd say two or three more days like this, then a long day to drown. That'll come in late evening. You'd better sleep tonight."

Hutch chose to believe her. He gauged his strength and thought he could walk the mile to his grandmother's. "Tell a tale first."

She thought a long moment. "I was kidding him. They're just child's play, his jokes."

"Remember the best one though, save it till tomorrow."

Alta laughed. "I'll try. My brain's gone to seed."

Grainger said "Well Lord—" He'd seen Hutch's bag by Rob's bed and found them.

Alta said "Is he asleep?"

Grainger nodded.

"Come in then and talk to this refugee a minute. He's sinking too; got to put him to bed if you mean to use him later." She left them quickly.

Hutch saw at once that Grainger had aged, first time since he'd known him. The wide black eyes were skinned over now with a bluish caul. He said, "You could use a month of nights yourself."

Grainger covered the distance and offered his hand. "Who brought you?"

"Bus from Raleigh, Genie's taxi from the station."

"I'd have met you anywhere."

Hutch said, "I know. I was just moving fast." He sat again and motioned Grainger down.

Grainger came to the back of the other chair and stood. "He seen you yet?"

"We talked a few minutes; then he got his shot."

"He understands more when he's sleep than wake."

Hutch said, "Who talked to the doctor last?"

"Miss Min, this morning. He won't estimate."

"Alta Allen says three or four more days."

Grainger nodded. "—Why I called you. Anybody known him long, know he's running now."

"But he didn't ask for me?"

"You well know why."

"What did Min have to say?"

Grainger spread his long fingers on the oak of the chair-back, then leaned forward suddenly and scrubbed Hutch's forehead with his palm. "Quit that. She don't mean much. You the one he was dwelling on, whatever he asked."

Hutch stood. "You well?"

"Don't matter," Grainger said.

"Your rabbits multiplying?"

"Everyone of em gone."

"What happened?"

"The buck. The doe got pregnant. I was busy and missed it. She dropped six babies in the night. He killed em, bit clean through their throats. Just him and the doe were there in the morning. I killed em both. Couldn't give em my time."

19

COLD as it was, Hutch stepped off the walk and stood by the maple, still studded with nailheads that measured his height on each birthday. From there he could see his grandmother's face. She sat in her chair and looked out at what was apparently nothing, clearly unchanged. The dim lamp beside her only stated again what he'd known as his earliest certainty—that time was her element as air is an eagle's, that it fed and sustained her while lashing all others. It still seemed a fact he could stand on safely. He went to the porch, climbed the steps silently, and tapped at the door.

Eva switched on the porch light, then opened fully. She looked for three seconds, indulged half a smile; but said, "You can't have seen everything in Rome."

"It'll wait," he said.

"Rome's a *she*," Eva said. "She's waited all right. Here, step in the warm."

He entered the room where he'd spent his boyhood, directly under the room he was conceived in, and set down his bag. Eva's eyes were dry —kindest sight of the day. He folded her slim body in and held her, his lips on her forehead.

When she stepped back she said, "I knew you'd get here."

He smiled but said, "Who was going to tell me?"

"Anybody—the trees! We were all sworn shut. But I knew you'd know."

He said, "I didn't. I was happy where I was."

"Who told you?—Polly Drewry or Min Tharrington?"

He'd never heard her say Polly's name before. "No, Grainger. He phoned me the day after Christmas."

"That's one cause for thanks," Eva said. "You hungry?"

"Exhausted," Hutch said. "I'm asleep right now."

But an hour later he lay in his old room, dark and awake. He'd run through the possible causes of worry—Rob, Ann, Min, his interrupted work—but now in this house he could face them calmly. He even made a schedule—a week more with Rob, maybe ten days of business, a chance to see Ann and Polly and Alice, then back to Oxford barely late for spring term. The calm was not coldness. He knew it was only a temporary strength. Other strengths would be needed when the eye of this present storm had passed. He tried to plan what he'd need to know and do, how to move on upright in a world swept clean of its prior engine and goal—

how to move on at all (he saw now he'd *circled* but felt no regret). Say he'd live a full span; then a third of it spent in circling a center as tall as Rob was surely no waste. He heard his grandmother start upstairs; she'd stayed down to finish *Life* magazine. He counted her steps—sixteen: somehow she'd inserted an extra. She stopped at his shut door and opened it quietly. He'd forgot her hatred of secret space. He saw her stand a moment, then step toward her room. He said "I'm awake."

Eva stopped on the sill and said "You're still in midocean."

"Bring me in then please."

She came to his bed and sat on the edge—old outcry of springs. After a silence she reached for his head and scratched in the coarse hair, slow but earnest. "Shut your eyes; see this—there's a wind from the east. You're a grown corsair with dove-gray wings. Spread them and glide."

Hutch laughed. "The wind's blowing up my tail."

"But it's warm off the Gulf Stream; count your few blessings." She'd found as always the chicken-pox scar in his scalp and picked at it.

For more than a minute, he took her suggestion and skimmed westward fast over mild green water.

But she said, "How much do you know about this?"

"Rob, you mean?—that he'd known he was dying since before I left, that he wanted me to go, that Min's here with him; that he'll stay three or four days more, then drown."

"Who told you that last?"

"Alta Allen, over supper."

Eva said, "Don't depend on any Allen news. She's been wrong all her life."

"She's known him all her life."

Eva said, "I'm the person who's known him all his life, nobody but me."

Hutch gave her her rights. "How long has he got?"

She sat straight to answer. "He told me yesterday he doubted he'd die. Grainger took me over when Min wasn't there; and I was just trying to lift his spirits (Min keeps him *low*), telling things I'd seen, things Sylvie said. I guess I was chattering. He held up his hand and beckoned me over and said, 'No rush. I don't plan to leave.'"

"Is he in his right mind?"

"Clear as you," Eva said, "but he didn't know one thing. Till you walked in that room tonight, he didn't know every good cell in his body was holding out hard for you to get word. He'll go soon now."

Hutch said, "Would you have called me?"

Eva thought a moment; in the shuttered streetlight, he could see her head shake. "I'd given my word. I harmed him at the start by breaking my pledge to live with his father; I'd have kept it this time."

"Are you angry at Grainger?"

"Too sad to be," she said. "Every hair of my head aches with sadness every minute. You wait till you watch a child waste and die. Pray God you die first."

"He doubted you loved him."

"Ne' mind *love*," she said. "I'm speaking of *made*. I made Rob Mayfield sure as Sylvie makes bread. You think that through." She sat a long moment; then said "No, sleep."

20

W HEN he got to the clinic at a little past seven, Grainger was washing Rob's hands with a rag. Rob's eyes stayed shut when Grainger spoke. "Wake early."

Hutch came up beside them. "It's past lunchtime where I was yesterday."

Grainger folded the rag and touched Rob's chin. "I'll shave you tonight."

Rob still didn't look. His whiskers were white, a web round his face, though half his hair was brown.

Grainger said "You walk?"

Hutch nodded. "It's warmer."

"I'll leave the truck here. You might need it later."

Hutch said, "No take it. I'll just be here."

Rob looked then, to Grainger. "Leave the truck. Hutch'll need it."

Grainger took out the keys and set them by the rag on the table. "I'm going—Miss Eva's day to shop. See you after while."

Rob nodded from what seemed enormous distance, unbridgeable, and Grainger left.

Hutch touched the hand again where it lay, the fingers spread.

"You don't have to do that. I may be catching," Rob said but he smiled.

Hutch stayed in place. "I may be. And that would be worse."

"I'll risk it," Rob said and ringed Hutch's wrist; then took his own hand and hid it in the sheets. "You didn't sleep enough."

"I did. I'm fine."

"At Mother's?"

"Yes. She's all right. She'll see you later."

"You haven't talked to Min?"

"I thought I'd see her here."

"I had Alta call her in the night. She's at home."

Hutch said "Whose home?"

Rob faced him harshly. "Mine, where she's welcome."

Hutch nodded, not smiling. "You need anything?"

Rob breathed three long breaths, open-mouthed. Even on the low hiss of oxygen, they grated. Then he grinned. "I'm debating a serious point—would I give all the good screws of thirty-four years for one deep breath?"

Hutch said, "Better not. Where would that leave me?"

Rob said, "That's the next point. I'm coming to that."

Hutch moved toward the chair.

"Stand still," Rob said.

Hutch stood. Pure early light was behind him.

Rob pointed a finger and traced the full shape of his son's right side, a likeness as visible as any while it lasted. Then he said, "I need this—drive out to the house and speak to Min."

"Right now?"

"She's there now."

Hutch sat. "Is there anything I need to know first?"

"Turn the key, put the engine in gear, and ride. Nice views all the way—not Rome, to be sure."

Hutch stood and took the keys.

"—Nothing new since I wrote you. She's not my wife. I just asked her to stay."

Hutch said "I'll be back."

Rob said, "Remember—*right* side of the road. Don't kill anybody you can possibly miss."

Hutch laughed and went.

21

By the time he'd cleared the outskirts of town, he began to wonder how he'd ever left—the place at least, bare of people. The clinging sun threw a white shine as different from its English gray or Italian rose as the tall pines here from the low umbrellas that sheltered Rome. In its truthful light the road, not flattered or pitied by the sky, narrowed to a dirt lane and curved on gently through woods—rolling fields of dry brown stalks with only the odd suspended buzzard to watch his progress. Empty as they were of human life, the woods seemed full of a single waiting presence—some actual messenger in raiment and wings or khaki trousers and faded shirt who would step out into the road at any instant and extend a paper with legible guidance, forward and inward, to the place Hutch craved. What place?—surely here. What had told him otherwise? Where else could he find the stillness and space to hunt out the diagram Rob had requested?—some usable answer to the question set by Rob's balked life and now his gasping grin.

The house on its rise had begun to fade. Hutch hadn't really noticed before he left. The paint he and Rob and Grainger applied ten years ago was all but gone; the timbers were silver and dry again. No rot though; the heartpine was good for longer than anyone alive. It had sheltered four generations of Kendals, two of black tenants, and now Min Tharrington. Her blue Chevrolet was baking in the yard; the kitchen chimney smoked.

He knocked three times and waited a good while.

She spoke through the door first. "Grainger?"

"No, Hutch."

She said "Hutch—" but the door stayed shut.

"Open up, Min. I'm not even armed." He laughed.

She was fully dressed, a pencil in hand; and she smiled at once but searched him with her eyes through the screen a long moment before she could say "I had no idea."

"Rob said Alta called you last night."

"She did—just to say not to come in today before noon, they'd be testing."

Hutch said, "We're the test, I guess—you and me, Min."

She knew she couldn't ask him to enter his own house; she unhooked the screen and stepped well back.

He came in, shut the big door, and glanced round. "You part-Eskimo?" (it was cold in the hall).

"Two-thirds," she said. "But the kitchen's warm."

He followed her there through space that showed few signs of her stay—a knitted cap on a peg in the hall, a brown sweater draped on a dining-room chair, her working papers on the kitchen table.

She gathered them aside.

"Rob said you were climbing the Mayfield family tree. Found any serpents?"

"Not really—a wormy apple or two." She went to the stove and touched the graniteware pot. "Coffee's hotter than the room at least. Get your special cup."

He did have a choice and found it on the top shelf, one lost silverfish squirming in its depths. He drowned it at the sink, rinsed the cup, and held it toward her. When she'd topped it he moved to the table and sat.

Min leaned on the counter and blew at her cup. "Grainger said Christmas Day he might have to call you."

"Did you tell him Yes?"

"He didn't ask for sanction, just wanted your Roman address. I found it."

"You didn't tell Rob?"

"Not a word."

"Why?" Hutch reached for the near chair, pulled it out for Min.

She came but took a different seat, on the other side and down. "You might not have come."

"Why would anybody doubt that?"

"I may have wanted to." She tried then to face him and found that she could.

So he smiled briefly; then thought of a question he needed to ask. Asking it, any way, would grant Min's knowledge of portions of Rob beyond his own reach. Rob had sent him here though; he should walk the whole path. He said, "What reasons did Rob ever give for not telling me?"

Min took the pepper shaker and screwed its lid tight. "I wondered several times but I never could ask; he never brought it up."

"Never swore you to silence?"

She looked off then—the sink window, bare willow. "Before we go one step farther, listen well and believe every word—your name wasn't spoken aloud in this house, unless to a blank wall when I had gone out, from the day I came here in June till this morning."

Hutch heard it and knew he must wait to weigh it. He drank a first swallow. "Where's Thal?" He'd missed her wheezing welcome.

Min smiled. "He and Thal may have had talks about you." Then she sobered her face. "He put Thal to rest, day after Thanksgiving."

"To sleep?"

"—To death. He did it himself."

They'd bought Thal the summer they moved out here. Rob claimed she was needed to collect destitute fleas from Jarrel's hounds (the Negro they'd evicted), but Hutch understood from the first sight of her—her stove-in shimmy—that she came as a mute but attentive witness of their promise to serve one another four years. She'd done that well and neatly, barring flatulence; and once Hutch had left for college, she'd met each vacation visit with an ecstasy no less watchful for its heights, no less retentive (she'd never forgot the first flea she gnawed). Hutch said "Was she sick?"

"Strong as me, just older. No he didn't ask my advice and didn't explain. I saw him take the pistol and walk her out to the nearest woods, and I heard one shot. In a while he walked back with her in his arms and dug a deep grave in the shade by the smokehouse—it took a good hour; he was already weak. When he came in he said 'You understand, don't you?' I had to say Yes."

"Grainger would have kept her."

"She wasn't Grainger's, was she?"

"—Kept her for me."

"Who knew you were coming?"

Hutch said, "Please tell me why you moved in here." He was calm but knew he was hoping to hurt her.

Min knew she could turn the first thrust at least. "The week you left he called me and came down to see me, Sunday supper. He looked tired but well. Then Miss Eva wrote me the news and asked for help. I had to come up here on business and saw him; he still looked well but he asked me to stay."

"How long?"

"He never said. We took it day by day."

"You didn't mind that?"

She wanted to stand but stayed in one place. "Great Jesus, Hutch— I've minded it more than my whole life till now."

"Why please?" he said. The *please* was a truce flag, however small.

Min chose to accept it. "How much do you know about Rob and me?"

"Only what he told me more than ten years ago—that during the time he taught in Raleigh, he was close to you; that you'd thought about marriage but he asked you to wait till he got me started and you said No."

She nodded. "All but true. Two people said No—me and you. Or so Rob told me."

"When?"

"Back then, 1944."

Hutch said, "I did. You must have known why. I'd never known a mother. I'd spent my time with people who loved me and were kind but were women—Polly, Grandmother, Aunt Rena, Sylvie. I was fourteen that summer; I claimed what I needed. It really was mine."

Min said, "I knew that, never tried to deny it. But I knew this too— I had loved Rob Mayfield, not blind but clear-sighted, long before you were born; before he knew your mother existed and well before he had shamed one soul, much less himself. I saw he was large enough to cover us both, a wife *and* a son. Or that you and I were large enough to cover him finally, hide him from himself. I was ready to say you were here and to join you and for all of us to try." As she'd spoken the skin of her face had drawn tight, a memory of the young face Hutch had never known—inexhaustibly ardent. It loosened again in their mutual silence but was still plainly ready for all she'd ever promised.

At last Hutch said, "I couldn't understand that—then, I mean."

Min smiled. "Can you now?"

"I'm trying. Not easy. Rob's dying may help."

Min shook her head once, in surprise not denial. But her smile remained. If his hand had been on the table, she'd have touched it.

He said, "Can I take you to the hospital now?"

22

THAT night at eleven Alta gave Rob his shot. Hutch turned out the light then and stretched in the chair under a blanket; and with all the day on them, they slept simultaneously though differently—Hutch black and help-less, Rob borne on the drug above his quick panting through an unhurried dream that was one more promise of the total rest he also approached. He knew at the start the dream had a name; the name was *Reward*. But in it, right through, he was his young self—Rob Mayfield, twenty-one, the week he'd left home with Niles Fitzhugh to work in Virginia. Niles was with him in the dream but always silent or grinning at the edge. They reached a small town after long mountain driving and stopped at the obvious eat-ing place—a big white boardinghouse with old men in chairs and swings on the porch under dense maple shade. No one spoke as they came up the steps but all watched; and when they reached the open door, a woman stood waiting—maybe forty, black-haired, in a clean white apron. She didn't smile but said, "We were counting on you. I cooked for three extra." Rob said, "Then charge Niles for two; he eats double." Her eyes stayed grave but she led them to a book on the round hall-table, pointed to a clear space, and asked for their names. Rob wrote his true name; Niles wrote *Jasper Mayhew*. When they looked up from that, the woman had gone; and a young girl, plainly her daughter, stood by them. She was so near the size of a perfect armful that Rob reached both arms slowly to take her. She didn't draw back but his reach failed by inches; and deep in the dim rooms, a bell rang for supper. Old men swarmed past them, the girl swept away, Niles pulled Rob to follow. No one spoke at supper. All the sounds were of eating—knives on chipped plates, drinks of water from glasses heavy as fieldstones. The girl and her mother moved silent and quick in opposite circles, replenishing bowls and feeding one man who seemed apoplectic down his whole right side. Then they'd vanished with the brisk convenience of dreams, Niles was off on business of his own, Rob was standing in darkness behind the house by a loud wide creek that hurled through rocks. Yet he heard the girl's steps a good way before she reached him. She still didn't speak but stopped at precisely the length of his arms; and when he had gathered her in and kissed her forehead, he explored her tilted face and found her smiling—her lips were parted up-ward at least; he touched her dry teeth. He thought this was surely why he'd left home and wandered. He finally said "Where now? You lead." Her hand found his and she led him a long way round toward the house— the front side again, though the porch was empty and every window black. The door let them in on a darkness deeper than the sky outside, but the girl knew a path and took him through sofas, umbrella racks, tables with no sound or brush. They climbed a high stairs, walked the length of a narrow hall; she stopped and Rob heard her open a door, deeper dark. She finally spoke—"Stand here." He stood. She went forward easily, struck a match, lit a lamp. They were in a normal bedroom—wardrobe, washstand, a big iron bed. In the bed a single body was stretched flat, covers to the chin, hands open on the pillow. The girl said "Now step here." Again he obeyed, thinking surely this was Niles; that the room was his and Niles's for the night; that he'd misunderstood and the girl was leaving. But he bent to look, and the boy was Hutch. Even in his youth, Rob knew the face, the rate of its breath. He thought, "It is not time for this—years to wait." When he turned to the girl though, she whispered "No, now"; went past him to the door, and closed it firmly. Then she came back, smiling. The three of them would stay in the room maybe always. He asked her her name; but Hutch moved then, ready to wake. The name of the dream, even there at the end, still seemed *Reward*.

In his chair in the room—Rob's room in the clinic—Hutch dreamt at the same time. His was not a story but a still clear picture, set in no special place. There were only two actors, himself and Ann. Ann stood in the center of a well-lit space in normal street-clothes. He stood just opposite ten feet away. Her belly, though covered by a Scotch-plaid skirt, was clear as washed glass. In the pink convolvulus of sinew and organ, he could see a child hanging by a white cord of flesh. It was still translucent with newness at the edges; but even while he watched, it clouded further—solidifying. He thought of no name for the child or the dream, but it seemed a good promise—no shock or fear—and it did not wake him.

23

WHILE Rob and Hutch slept in the early night, Ann slept in Rome in the Pacifica an hour before dawn. She'd spent the whole day on the far side of Tiber—Castel San Angelo, St. Peter's, the Vatican—and had been left alone. No one spoke to her for more than directions except when a short seminarian from Akron approached as she lay on her back on a bench in the Sistine Chapel and said, "I could read you the canon law on napping here but will just count to ten." So she'd slept since nine like an honest field-hand, unconscious of passers; and it took four bursts of knocking to wake her. She sat up, clanging in her mind, and said "Yes?"

A voice, not whispering, said "This is Rowlet."

Ann stood, found her robe, left the door locked, and said "It's night."

"No, morning."

"What's wrong?"

"I can't tell a *door*. Please open," he said.

She opened. He was fully dressed and soaked to the skin (a cold rain had started at sunset and lasted). He held a windbreaker; his shirt was short-sleeved.

"You're drowned. Is Hutch calling?"

Rowlet shook his head slowly, then grinned and extended his dripping arms. "Just me on the line." He might be drunk—his face was white and slack—but he stood still as rafters.

She said, "Go dry off and get straight to bed."

His arms stayed out and his head shook again.

"Is Smeralda back?"

"Don't know. Don't care." He took a step forward.

Ann didn't back away.

"I need to tell you one secret," Rowlet said. He brought his hands forward, took her shoulders, pressed her inward. He shut the door carefully and faced her plainly, a face any sixteenth-century painter would have walked through Flanders in floodtime to see—scooped bones and kid leather, the eyes of a celibate starveling on the edge of stigmatic grace or the massacre of thousands.

She saw it that way; but she said, "Tell your secret. Then rent your own room."

He marked it on the air with a finger, word by word. "This-is-my-last-day. My-buddies-coming-back. So-bye-bye-me." He dropped the sodden jacket to the floor.

"Where've you been? It's raining."

"—Saving my soul. I'm a Footwashing Baptist. Or my mother is; this is her Christmas present." He began undoing the buttons of his shirt.

Ann said, "I doubt any known brand of Baptist could want you to die of Roman pneumonia."

"Hold still," Rowlet said. "I know what I'm doing."

"Take one more minute and tell me then."

"I remembered my mother showing me an old picture of lions gnawing Christians. I remembered it had took place somewhere near here; so I slept till afternoon, then went out looking to tell her I had. At dark I found it—big rundown stadium, the one in her picture. Nothing to see but I went on in and climbed through the mess high up as I could and tried to memorize something to tell her—how big it all was, how poor they kept it."

"You're lucky you're alive. Crooks go there at night."

He said, "One old girl touched my ass when I first walked in. She was all I met, but I heard more moaning." He slid from the shirt and dropped it too. "The rain started then and I thought I'd leave; but before I'd gone six steps, I was wet. So I sat back down and stayed till just now."

"Why on earth, Dumbo?"

Rowlet thought a long moment, then grinned again. "I already told you—saving my soul. More ways to be a martyr than nourishing beasts."

"You sat in the cold rain and stared at old stones?"

"Well, all stones are old. I may have took a nap." By then he was opening the belt of his trousers.

Ann didn't speak again but waited in place.

24

HUTCH woke at four, eased by his dream (which he didn't recall). Then he heard the oxygen, the wide-spaced gasps, and said "Rob" once. No answer so he sat in the warm dark and felt two things—first, a deep relief that Rob was going and yielding him room; then a deeper fear that the room would be vacant, containing no center round which he could move in the confident swings he'd learned from birth. What would stay?—his grandmother, Grainger, Alice, Polly. But much as he honored and thanked them, he knew they'd never been pivots. Ann—he drew up her image and watched it. After the perfect days in Rome, she seemed more than ever his surest friend, the one with whom he'd shared more pleasures than anyone likely to last for years. But the heights of their meeting—Palatine, Forum, the Pacifica's beds—seemed distant in time as in actual space. The critical gravity they'd both felt at Christmas had weakened for Hutch to a clear line of pictures he could watch with thanks but no strong compulsion. Had he ever felt that toward anyone but Rob? He'd accepted most of the bodies offered him—Ann's, Strawson's, Lew's, Marleen's—in unquestioned readiness and felt no remorse, only a grainier sense of the gifts concealed by common faces, the infinite speaking tenderness of gestures surpassing speech. He'd accept them all again here now, if they'd ask again. Would he ever ask them though, require their presence? Here, a step from the father racing to die in his own proliferating flesh, the answer seemed No. Rob had asked for a diagram; was it maybe this?—out of the intricate toils of a knot comes one strand, single filament, not plaited or paralleled? He watched that a moment, as plain as Ann's face. Like the dream, it eased him. He stood quietly, touched Rob's bed, and entered the hall. Alta was seated at the nurses' desk in blue light, working at charts. He went to the long bench opposite and sat.

She wrote on awhile, then looked up. "How is he?"

"Asleep. Hasn't moved since you saw him at eleven."

Alta said, "Wrong. You're the one never moved. He pressed the button for me at two-thirty."

"You must have talked low."

"Didn't need one word, known each other too long. Just gave him a shot. Doctor says he can have it anytime he calls."

Hutch said, "He doesn't sound worse than before."

"He's moving though. What I told you was right."

Hutch nodded as if she'd predicted rain.

"You go back to sleep."

"Couldn't now," Hutch said. "Once you wake me you've got me."

Alta said, "I never woke you and I've got all I need."

Hutch moved to speak.

"No, stay. I'm lying. You don't know, do you?—Tim died last August."

Hutch said, "I didn't. How, Alta? I'm sorry."

"Everybody in Fontaine was sorry, I tell you—not one cookstove has worked right since *or* radio; he could evermore make electricity behave. His heart stopped while I was fixing his lunch. He was already waiting in his chair, just slumped. I went on talking a minute or two."

"Where's Jeanette?"

"High Point—good husband, two babies. I'm a double grandmother."

"You stay in your house?"

"Little as possible and never at night. It's why I'm here on the hoot-owl shift. I pray the day comes I can sleep alone, dark. It hasn't come yet."

Hutch said, "Any Mayfield could help you with that. We seek single beds."

Alta tried to see his face, but the far wall was dim. She nodded anyway. "Rob was the one broke the mold."

Hutch said, "I hope that's the story you found."

"I haven't thought back—try to move mainly *on*."

He didn't insist but stayed on the bench.

Alta took a ruler and drew lines awhile. Then not looking up, she said "He was *kind*." She seemed to be claiming it against strong denial.

Hutch had thought of his father many ways but never as kind. He only said "When?"

She looked to both ends of the hall; they were alone. Still she lowered her voice. "You knew about Tim and the Phillips girl—"

He didn't but said "Maxine?"

"No the young one—Martha, God help me."

Martha was Hutch's age, had been in his class from the first grade on —a pale straw-blond with wide-set eyes like open shafts in the ground. He said, "She's in Florida last I heard."

"Heard right," Alta said. "Did you hear of the boy?"

"I knew she was married—in Tampa, round there."

"That came awhile later. The boy was Tim's. He took her down there."

To say he didn't know might stop her now. He said, "How old is the boy?"

"Don't make me count." But she did. "Six, seven. Martha'd finished high school. I knew she had gone to a typing college in Raleigh. I knew Tim was gone a lot most weekends. I never said a word. He wouldn't answer questions; he'd just vanish longer. Finally one Saturday he left in the truck, didn't even take his razor. I was wild by Wednesday; but I still hadn't told a soul, even Jeanette (she was gone too by then). I stayed home and cooked—I canned beans and peaches to feed half of Asia. Then Thursday night Rob knocked on the door. It was blistering hot and I asked him to sit on the porch; but he said, 'Let me come in first.' He had news he didn't want confided to the breeze—the Cokers were next door, ears like mules. So down we sat. Tim had called Rob from Tampa and asked him to see me; he'd loved Rob ever since they wrecked that carload of bootleg liquor on the way back from Weldon—sixteen years old. The message was, he was living down there and could Rob pack his suitcase and ship it? I said, 'He hasn't *got* a suitcase; it's mine.' Rob had to laugh. But later I gave him a cardboard box and showed him Tim's drawer, and he packed a few shirts and underpants. As he left I said, 'I've known you forty years. I never thought you'd end up a messenger-boy for a grown man chasing baby-ass through orange groves.' He looked a little sheepish but left anyway. One week later, same time, he came back. We sat on the porch and talked about childhood; all of us that age had the same childhood, knew each other's whole lives well as our own. Every Wednesday night for two months, he'd turn up—never let me cook him so much as an egg, just drove up at dusk and sat till bedtime. The Cokers were spinning; Rob didn't give a damn and neither did I. I thought he was tending a miserable soul. Well, it turned out he was but in his own way—he was testing me." She stopped, seeming finished.

"For what?" Hutch said.

"—Was I fit to live with?"

"Did he ever decide?" He laughed once for safety.

"Never told me. But after three months Tim rode in at daybreak and didn't leave again till they carried him out in that tacky coffin I paid a leg for."

"Rob had talked him back though?—from Tampa?"

"Tim finally told me. Rob had mailed him his clothes and not said a thing. Then after two months Rob wrote him and said, 'If you don't want her, she's just my speed. Speak now or never holler'—not a word of blame. It took Tim another month to see he'd grabbed something he couldn't hold, but Rob set him thinking and opened his eyes."

"You welcomed him in?"

"*Let* him in," Alta said. "Couldn't stop him if I'd tried; he still had his key. I was in bed asleep when I heard the door move. Tim was standing on the sill. He said, 'Is there room for me to take a long nap? I been driving fifteen hours.' I said, 'There is everything here there always was, plus a pantry full of peaches; but do me this favor—take a hot tub-bath.' I couldn't stand to think there was any Martha on him."

"You said she had a son."

"After Tim was back home. She had some kin down there and stayed with them to have it. Tim sent her monthly checks till she wrote him she was marrying a radio announcer." Alta stood and took a step. "You're bound to be the only one in Fontaine didn't know."

"I must have been in summer school."

She nodded. "Must have been." Then she smiled. "Plan to finish?"

"Ma'm?"

"How many more books can there be you haven't read?"

"Not many," Hutch said. "Now I'm writing my own."

"You'll have a good place."

"Where?"

"Won't Rob's house be yours?"

"Yes."

She nodded—"Green and quiet"—then went to the desk. But before she sat, she whispered "Bring some *company*."

"Why?"

"To live longer. You want to know the truth? Rob Mayfield has killed himself sure as any suicide—plain loneliness."

"Didn't Tim?" Hutch said.

Alta waited, then faced him and found her saving answer. "Oh no. You haven't heard a word I said."

25

WHEN Rob woke at five and had his shot, he seemed much the same, not visibly lower. He told Hutch to go back to Eva's and shave. So when Grainger came at six, Hutch drove back and shaved and sat in the kitchen while Eva and Sylvie cooked and served in a calm intensity of purpose as ceaseless as the gaze of seraphim (when Eva left the room, Sylvie said, "You praying he die today? You ain't, you praying wrong"). Then the force of his dream, which he'd still not recalled, sent him to the hall phone to try to reach Ann. All circuits were busy; they'd call him soon as possible.

His grandmother spoke from the head of the stairs. "I've turned down your bed. Stretch out awhile."

He knew he was tired, though he felt strong and slightly elated—soaring. "I've placed a call to Ann. I'll wait for that."

Eva came down slowly, never looking to her feet. She brushed his hair back. "Thank God she's not here."

Hutch stepped aside. "Why?"

"I doubt I could stand to share it one more way."

"It's not a cake, Grandmother."

She nodded. "—But I think you'll find it's a *meal*. You'll see people grabbing far sooner than you thought."

"For what? He's been broke since before I was born."

"So he thought," Eva said. "He was one big vault people drew and drew on."

"Not you," Hutch said.

"Maybe not, maybe not. But he stopped wanting me." For the first time in Hutch's presence, she was older—a burr on her words. She would also die soon. Still she said, "Make your plans now to go straight to England."

"There'll be a little business."

"Nothing I can't handle—or Grainger and I."

"I may need to get my bearings here, a week or so."

Eva looked round her slowly as if at new sights. "It's good for that—bearings—but it takes your whole life."

Sylvie cleared her throat behind them. "Miss Eva, I can't fry but two of them chickens."

"I just told you four."

"You counting on needing what you don't need yet. You wait till he gone, I'll cook em all then."

The phone rang; Eva waved Sylvie toward the kitchen and followed her.

Two operators, then Ann very clearly.

"I was afraid you'd be out," Hutch said.

"It's raining hard. You left in time."

"Is it lunchtime there?"

"Any minute," she said. "I'm a little late. I was reading in the room."

"Has Rowlet left yet?"

"This afternoon, I think. They'll drive straight to Germany, not stopping to pee."

"Met anybody else?"

"One priest at the Sistine. Italians don't seem to be falling down to know me. The Sistine was worth it."

Hutch said, "Will you fly home and come straight here?" He had not planned to ask it.

"Has he died?"

"No but soon."

"Is it awful?"

"Not yet. Not for me at least."

Ann said, "Does he know you're calling me now?"

"He's past minding anything. He always liked you. I'm asking you to come."

She took two seconds. "I'll call you tonight and tell you what time."

"I won't be here; tell whoever answers. Somebody'll meet you in Raleigh. Need money?"

"I'm pretty sure not. Rowlet's just walked up; he'd like to speak to you."

Before Hutch could speak again, Rowlet said "Hey."

"How are you?"

"All right. I slept most of last night in the Colosseum."

"Ann said it's raining."

"Was then too."

"You drunk?" Hutch said.

"No, sleepy."

Hutch laughed.

"Is the trouble there over?"

"Not yet. He's failing fast."

Rowlet waited. "You tell him I said 'Good luck.' "

"Thank you."

Rowlet said "Listen, I thank you."

"Can I speak to Ann again?"

"She's already gone."

Hutch said, "Give her your address. I may come to Germany."

"She knows it," Rowlet said.

26

Upstairs in his old room, Hutch tried to rest; but his prior sense of glide over distant ground had lasted with no threat to slow or fall. So he went to the bottom drawer of the chest; and there under wilted caps and sweaters from his early childhood, he found what he'd hoped for—a Blue Horse tablet of lined school-paper, the remains of his first try (at ten or eleven) to write a long story: twin brothers on an ocean liner to Europe. Kneeling he read through the six finished pages, tore them off carefully, lay down again, and wrote to the person who'd now come to mind.

December 29, 1955

Dear Strawson,

I'm home unexpectedly. Ann Gatlin and I spent Christmas in Rome and meant to stay on into January, but I was called back here two days

*ago. My father is dying—lung cancer, which he knew he had before you
met him last May in Virginia but kept from me. I still wouldn't know if
the Negro man who lives with us hadn't phoned me in Rome. He is conscious and knows me but is now dependent on an oxygen tent and
Demerol for pain. The doctor says he could live indefinitely. Grandmother
and Grainger and the night nurse (who's known him all his life) say he'll
go this week. I'm praying for soon and staying through nights in his room
in the clinic. He was what I had for so much of my life—the part that
registers—and now I can only stand and watch him fade off. He talks very
little but that's all right; we said our say.*

*I don't know where you are and that's my fault. I meant to write
often but got plowed under by the unexpected shock of studying again,
plus the Oxford climate which is worse than advertised (and the ads are
gruesome), plus trying to start a long poem in the scraps of free time and
warmth. Did you go to college finally? If so, did you stay? I'm sending this
care of your parents in hopes it will reach you somehow. It says—a good
new year and thanks again for your visit in July. I remember it all and still
feel glad. I might even have a few new things to answer to the questions
you asked me after* Macbeth. *Or maybe I should wait till this quake passes
and check the main guy-wires before marching out onto any long bridges.
I've never left here but I told you that. I'm planning to leave.*

*—To England, I mean, in roughly three weeks. Then on from there.
On* may mean *back, since the scene here is shifting.*

*Still you could drop me a note to Fontaine—I'm known hereabouts—
and give me the news. Despite my silence I do want to hear.*

> *Affectionately,*
> *Hutchins M.*

Then he slept for two hours—not hearing a sound, though his door
was open. When the phone rang at last and Eva called to him, he still
didn't hear.

She climbed the stairs, raised the shades, and shook him.

He surfaced slowly.

She leaned at his side, holding his arm. "Grainger just called here and
said you're needed."

"Rob?"

"Must be. What he said was 'Tell Hutch to come back.' "

He sat up—ten-thirty. The soaring he'd felt since dawn thrust its
wings for a pull in actual air, the strong light that now filled the room
like a substance. He lifted higher.

"Should I go?" Eva said.

He heard her but went to the chest for his keys, not thinking of an answer. Then he folded the letter to Strawson and said "Any envelopes upstairs?"

Eva thought he was weighing her question. She nodded, went quickly out, and came back with stamps and three envelopes.

Hutch addressed one and sealed it. He said, "I'll call you as soon as I know."

She accepted that.

It was only as he came down the post-office steps that he thought, "She's outlived him. She wanted to see." But he went straight to Rob.

27

THE room was half-dark; and his sense of smell, refreshed outside, was stunned by the old stench—a low eager burning. Dr. Simkin and Grainger were standing by the bed; there was no sound of breath. Hutch came up beside them. Rob's eyes were shut. His face had gone blue. His dry lips were gaped wide and sucked in a silent irregular nursing.

Grainger said "Here he is."

Rob seemed not to hear.

Simkin said "Let him be" and took Hutch's arm. In the hall he said, "We're in a new phase now. The right lung is gone."

"He seemed the same when I left at six."

"That caused it. Grainger said he thought you were gone."

"Gone where?—I told him."

"We're not dealing here with a healthy mind. He struggled hard till we got him sedated."

The man's face and voice entered Hutch as a taste more offensive than any decay from Rob, but he said "What now?"

"Do a tracheotomy. That'd give him more air. Stop him trying to talk. Min Tharrington is not his wife, far as you know?"

"No."

"Then you'll be the one to sign the permission."

"Never," Hutch said.

"He'll strangle."

"Won't he anyhow?"

Simkin said "In time."

Hutch said "Then today."

Simkin thought it through. "Stay with him."

"—Never left."

28

Rob still seemed asleep. Grainger sat close by him on a straight wood chair. Hutch brushed the covered shin, then drew up his night chair. "Were you here when it happened?"

Grainger nodded.

"What confused him?"

"Don't know, not a dream; he was wake when he started."

"Did he say anything?"

Grainger nodded. "Your name, every time he could breathe. I told him you had just gone to wash your face. Next thing I knew, he had sat bolt upright, pulled out his tubes, and was clawing this tent down. I had to call for help. They give him a big dose; I held him till he dozed."

"No blood?"

"Dry as sand. I don't think he knew me."

Hutch said "Soon now."

Grainger faced him. "Don't rush. This happened before."

"Since I got back?"

"God, no—thirty years ago in Virginia, first time I ever saw him. He was twenty-one years old; he'd just left home and had tracked down his Aunt Hatt, that I used to help. He was born in the house but hadn't been back since Miss Eva took him off when he was a baby. He seemed to enjoy it, and we both liked him (squirrels in the treetops liked him in those days); but second day he stayed there, he heard from his mother—long letter. I brought it from the post office, sealed; never knew what it said. But you know Miss Eva's tongue can slice cold bricks if she see the need. He was far gone in liquor even then, that young; so he had to get drunk. I helped him on his way—old cousin of mine, Slip Dewey, made corn— and once he was high, he wanted to ride: always a big *mover* when anything failed. I rode with him. I was still a fool then, for cars anyway. He did his best to kill us—himself of course but I was along—and finally he managed a little wreck, involving just us. After that and some more mess, I got him to my house and thought I had him calm. I read him that Pocahontas book I gave you and cooked him some eggs. He seemed cold-sober and laid down on the bed soon as I suggested it. I watched him till it looked like he'd sleep a good while; then I went to chop wood. I'd worked half an hour when I heard his voice—didn't know it was him, but it came from the house: deep bellows like a steer. I took the axe with me and went back in. He was sitting upright on the bed, staring wild and making that noise like it hurt him to do it, like lightning down a tree."

"Calling who?" Hutch said. "I was some years off."

"No name, none I could understand at least. Just *calling*."

"You answered."

Grainger said, "Thank you. I did up till now."

But Hutch saw he'd stopped him too soon. "How'd you calm him?"

"First I was mad. I drove that axe two inches in the floor. Didn't faze him a bit; don't think he even heard it. By then he reminded me of boys in the war—they were going trench-crazy by the hour some days. Nothing you could do but throw em down and press em and moan even louder. He let me do that; he was still in two minutes and slept long hours. Then I drove him to Goshen and never left since." He stood to see Rob—silent, unchanged. "You call Miss Min?"

"She'll be here at one; let her just come then."

"Miss Eva want to come?"

"She asked me," Hutch said. "I told her to wait—no way she can help."

Grainger stood a long moment. "*Help* ain't the question. She ought to be here."

Hutch said, "Go eat your lunch and bring her back then."

Grainger quickly lifted the edge of the tent and touched Rob's chin. "I'll shave him when I can."

Hutch saw him out the door, then sat in the straight chair, found Rob's left wrist under the covers, and felt for the pulse—not beats but an almost steady dim signal. He kept his hand there, only listening.

In five minutes Rob's head turned; the eyes opened.

Hutch said, "I went to breakfast. Now I'm back."

Rob pointed to the door. "Lock that."

Hutch stood. There was no lock. He went though and pressed on the handle. Then he sat again and took his father's wrist.

Rob said, "Is it saying anything you can read?" He managed his smile.

"No it's idling now."

"Good news." Rob waited, still looking. "I've left you a lot of reading matter at the house."

Hutch thought he meant the few books. "Thank you, sir."

"Don't thank me till you've swallowed it."

Hutch smiled to stop him.

"—Some days of my life I wrote down for you. They're locked in my desk."

"I've got your keys with me; I'm using the truck."

"No rush," Rob said. "Give yourself enough time."

"I'm already late."

"To what?"—the smile again, appallingly slow.

"My life, I guess."

Rob waited. "You were grown years before I was. I used you for guide."

Hutch laughed. "—And I lost us."

Rob nodded. "Never mind." Then he fished up his hands, lifted the tent back over his face; and whispered quickly, "I don't have a will. Use your own best judgment. Give Min something nice. You and Grainger take the rest. Don't let any sermon be preached over me, just music."

Hutch nodded, then stood and lowered the tent.

Rob said "Can't something be done?"

"Sir?"

"For *me*." The face, drawn taut as a drumhead, was young.

Hutch said "Not now."

Rob waited a good while, staring up; then shut his eyes.

Hutch found the wrist. "One more thing please. You mentioned Goshen, being buried with Rachel."

Rob said "You choose." He didn't speak again. By then it was noon.

29

HUTCH sat through the afternoon—holding his father, eating nothing, and standing only to bring in chairs when Min and Eva and Grainger came. They talked on quietly about Hutch's travels, avoiding Rob. Rob heard long stretches of all their voices, though he seemed unconscious of them and the staff that came and went, now spectators too.

At five dark was settling. Eva walked to the bed and called Rob gently.

He heard and answered in his mind but slept.

She tried again firmly. "Son, you want me to stay?"

Still nothing, though he thought "All but one of you, go."

So Eva bent slowly, kissed the covered ridge of his thigh; and said, "Min, you come sleep at home tonight."

Min waited. "Yes ma'm." Then she stood, kissed the same spot, and gripped Hutch's shoulder.

Grainger said, "I'll take them and be back soon."

Rob thought "Stay home."

Hutch nodded, not breaking his hold on the wrist; and when the room was still, he took the first chance to say an urgent thing—"I'm sorry if I ruined it." He meant his father's life, the last half at least; and he spoke it out clearly.

Rob heard but was now in his own free flight and thought of no answer. He believed that he opened and shut his right hand (in greeting not reply), but the hand never moved.

Hutch quietly said their prayer. "Your will."

Rob wondered at the need to ask again. He had reached an old house in the side of a hill. He was neither young nor old but his same steady

self, his permanent companion. He was tired but relieved; the house promised harbor, though in late spring evening it showed no lights. On the
porch he could make out one object, a lantern. He lit it, knocked twice.
No answer so he opened. High deep rooms darker than the open windows
warranted. With no sense of trespass, he walked through every cube and
hall downstairs—every human need provided for (chairs, beds, a pantry)
and all waiting orderly but no sound of people, no trail or scent. He felt
no fear, only patient curiosity to see the remainder and peaceful confidence the house had a center which it somehow served in total silence. He
climbed the pine stairs in a bell of warm light and again walked slowly
through empty rooms—many dozen, each smaller and lower in succession.
At last at a closed door, he stopped, doused his light. From the crack at
the sill, another light seeped. He knocked. No answer—a normal wood
door with a cool china knob. He turned it, took a step—narrow room,
high bed, clean lamp on a stand. On the sheets lay a girl (sixteen, seventeen), brown hair flooded round her on huge stacked pillows. Her knees
were up and parted, her gown at her waist. From her fork a new child
eased into sight. She saw Rob and nodded but continued her work. The
child came free—normal crying and flailing, mucus and blood. The girl
rose then in her own fresh blood, took the child by the sides, held it
slowly to her breast—sounds of feeding. His mother, himself, the room
he is born in. Feasible center, discovered in time, revised now and right.

Hutch was blank in the stillness; the pulse stopped then, a flat clean
end. He didn't turn loose but stood to see.

The body groaned once, a long low exhaling. The face, purple now,
clenched furiously. The head shook hard and flushed a wave downward
through chest, arms, legs. The whole shape arched high, shuddered again,
fell slowly back. Then the teeth showed white.

Hutch uncovered the head and leaned to the brow—cool and dry.
The same dense wave that had drowned his father spread up through his
hand and raised him higher than he'd been this whole day of hope, now
granted. He stayed in place calmly till Alta walked in, stopped, and saw
the smooth face.

"You never deserved one instant of this but you're safe now," she
said.

She'd spoken to Rob but Hutch smiled and nodded.

30

At ten Hutch was drinking coffee in the kitchen, Sylvie scrubbing pots
behind him. Grainger hadn't come back from the undertakers where he'd
gone to shave Rob, though the coffin would be sealed. Eva and Min were

in the front room with straggling callers. Sylvie hadn't mentioned Rob, hadn't mentioned going home but had worked on—manufacturing food for far more friends than anyone here possessed or needed, adding to the excess the visitors had brought since before Rob was cold: deviled eggs, a whole ham, three cakes, chicken salad, jello desserts for a wilderness of children. Hutch said to her back, "Let me take you home now."

"Sit still."

"You're tired."

"—What I'm paid to be."

"We've got enough, Sylvie. Great God, call an orphanage to haul off the surplus."

"I know it," Sylvie said but started dicing celery. When she'd done the first handful, she faced him finally. "Time *you* left though."

Hutch laughed. "Where'm I going?"

"Ain't you staying at Rob's?"

"There's still room here; Min can sleep downstairs."

"Ain't talking about room."

"Then you'd better say what."

She watched her black knife, the same carbon blade she'd used at that table for more than fifty years. "You need to sleep where his spirit be tonight."

"Won't it be here too?"

Sylvie thought and shook her head. "People's spirit seek places they were happy in."

"Was he happy out there?"

"*Act* like it. Sure God wasn't happy much here."

It seemed the right thing. He could phone Alice, Polly; maybe read whatever Rob had left while numbness made a confrontation easy. "Will Grandmother mind?"

"She minded things a-plenty; none of em killed her yet. Just tell her and go."

Hutch waited. "Please step in and call her for me then. I can't get kissed once more tonight."

When Eva came she said, "I forgot your phone message. Ann Gatlin called from Rome. She'll be here Saturday, Raleigh airport at ten. I wish you'd let me know."

"What?"

"That you had asked her here."

Hutch said, "I'm sorry. But she'll cause you no trouble. She'll stay out at Rob's."

"No such a thing—*here*. This town has had long months to fan its gums over Rob and Min; let it rest till he's buried."

Hutch stood, went to her, rubbed the crown of her head with a stubble chin. "Will you be all right if I sleep out there?"

"Tonight?"

"I really ought to."

"Take Grainger with you then."

"No ma'm," Hutch said.

Sylvie said "Go on."

As he moved toward the back stairs to get his suitcase, Eva said, "Polly Drewry—will you be calling her?"

Hutch nodded.

"You know I have never seen her face, but she helped Rob more than once when I couldn't reach him. I'd welcome her here if she thinks she should come."

"I doubt she will."

Sylvie faced him. "*Thank* Miss Eva."

He came all the way back, thanked her, then went.

31

MIN had left lights on, upstairs and down; so the house seemed possible at least from the yard. Still he paused by the truck, thought of Sylvie's claim; and silently said, "Come now if you can." Nothing changed in the air, which was bitterly cold; and once inside, he hurried to light all three oilstoves. They boomed with flame as he went to the hall phone, so loudly the operator said "You being shot at?"

Alice said "Alice Matthews."

"—Hutchins Mayfield."

"Where?"

"Rob's house, in the cold."

"I've been standing by," she said.

"So have we. He died this evening."

Alice waited. "Too soon. Are you all right?"

"Tired."

"Is anybody with you?"

"I'm here alone now. Ann's coming for the funeral."

"You got the money then?"

"On time. Please forgive me; things have been moving fast."

"Now they slow," Alice said. "Do you need me—any way? I can leave in ten minutes, be there by one."

Hutch said, "Please wait. I'll need you next week. Let me come up there."

"Any hour you say."

"Do you mind?" Hutch said.

"What?"

"—Not seeing Rob now."

Alice said, "I saw him when he meant to be seen."

Polly seemed hoarse at first but denied she'd been sleeping. Hutch tried to start gently and ask about her Christmas, but she forced his hand. "Are you saying Rob is gone?"

"Yes ma'm, right at dark."

She waited a good while. "I knew it all day. Oh Hutch, be strong. Was he in much pain?"

"Not pain, I don't think."

"When did you get home?"

"Two or three days ago; I'm so tired I lost count."

"And he knew you?"

"Yes ma'm."

"That's something," she said. "Who told you?—Ann Gatlin?"

"No, Grainger."

"Bless his soul. Hutch, I've *choked* since June, being sworn not to tell you."

"I understand that. Will you come to the funeral, Saturday at three?"

"Who wants me?"

"I do. I can send Grainger for you."

"Buses still run," she said. Another firm pause. "Hutch, I've never been there. I can't come now if there's anyone to hurt."

"Grandmother told me you'd be welcome if you could."

"I could *walk*," Polly said. "I miss him that much."

The stoves had quieted; the hall was warmer. Hutch waited by the phone—no one else to tell. And no new presence in the air around him. Empty house. So he went to the dining room and sat at Rob's desk—big oak roll-top, neat now as an airfield, pigeonholes emptied, even the three framed pictures gone (Aunt Rena, young Eva, Hutch himself at Jamestown). Had Rob swept it all away, along with Thal, in a final stripping— a simplification for his own sake and Hutch's? He unlocked the long drawer. No they were there, just stowed out of sight, too hard to watch. Hutch left them. But beside them was an envelope bearing his full name and Oxford address. He took that up and, not knowing why, smelled the edges—only paper and glue. That freed him to open it cleanly with his pocketknife. A thick pack folded once, dead-center. He felt some reluctance to face it ever but recalled his impulse to take it quickly, in the strength of shock. He moved to a better chair, lit the bridge lamp, and read straight through Rob's account of the three days and something he'd added a month ago.

November 27, 1955

I thought I'd finished this in August. Maybe so. But it's pretty plain now that this thing in me is gathering to run, so I've spent a week using my sparse energy to sweep certain decks. I've always pictured myself as moving light, just a toothbrush and comb; but Monday I woke up to the fourth day of rain and realized I hadn't moved anywhere for years. Here I was ending in a warehouse of paper that you or somebody would yet have to clear. I lay still an hour, not praying exactly but hoping fairly hard that one of the stoves would act up at last (as I always thought they would) and send the whole pile off in cinders and smoke—me and Thal included, sparing Min somehow. No such luck of course; so from Monday through Thursday (we skipped Thanksgiving), I sorted paper and Grainger hauled out twenty bushels, I guess, and burnt them in the yard. Then Friday on my own I put Thal to rest with a single head-shot and buried her neatly. Min can show you where. I know she came here at first as your dog, but she'd been mine lately—right?—and she and I'd discussed the matter more than once. The paper was old checks, jail-threats from creditors, duplicate class-attendance reports on children who've long since made their own children and noted their absence, plus any letter which didn't seem likely to help you later in whatever questions you choose to ask. What's left—from my father, Eva, Rena, Grainger, Rachel, Min, yourself—is tied up in three shoeboxes in my wardrobe. Yours, with prayers for mercy not judgment.

Not that I really care, which is why I'm writing. The surprise in this, Hutch—this funnel of months, now tapering fast—is what I want to tell. I look forward to death. I feel more than ready, not from pain or exhaustion (there is no pain yet, though exhaustion's ever present). I've read enough to know this is not my invention, and I've never been one to understand people who woke up at four a.m. sweating ice at the prospect of turning back to—what is it?—sixty cents of minerals and water, but it seems worth recording: I'm calm as this desk.

Why is it exactly? Maybe something very natural—the thing could be making, as a normal by-product, some substance that acts as a handy narcotic (how handy I'll presumably know soon now). Or maybe I'm bathed in a light rain of grace. That's the strong hint offered by the two local preachers who've paid recent calls. I can join in the hope, though I haven't asked for it. But if God turns out to be Protestant, I may ask for transfer (I speak of course as one who has known few Catholics and fewer Jews).

I know what it isn't. It's not impatience or boredom with my weakness. Nor any bitter spurning of this damaged world. Nor walleyed eagerness to don harp-and-halo, though I won't underestimate my hope to be somewhere—not as a spy, don't worry; I'd refuse (the idea of dead invisible eyes dancing round the picture molding on down through the ages, watching every nose-picker and driven ass-scratcher, is at least as repugnant as total extinction): assuming I can refuse, that is. I won't make the rules no doubt, there as here. If they send me back on guard, however, I'll try to tip my hand. Listen closely for laughs. Finally, it's not any sense of completeness. There are two things left that I'd planned to enjoy—a second calmer marriage, once you were underway, and the sight of your children.

So it must be hope, some brand strong enough to override smaller hopes—the pure hope of rest? or a child's hope of life? Right now I'd take either, though personally I feel I've had enough rest. Anyhow all I ask is for it to be new; and even if it's rest—just thoughtless sleep—I have some confidence the Patent Holder on Time, Space, and Matter can lay me to rest in a manner that differs attractively from the eight-hour struggles with feathers and sheeting I've known here below. If it's life, then (despite the days I've recalled and a decent share of others) I'm in no doubt whatever that it's bound to be—well—more imaginative.

Strange postscript, I guess, but I wanted you to know. No further wisdom on past or future, no outstanding mysteries, and no requests but

Love still from
Rob

It had taken half an hour—no real surprises, no apparent assaults (beyond the existence of this perfect record of the voice and its mind). Hutch sat on awhile and listened to the rooms—normal sounds of an old house gripped by cold and dark. No owl, no squirrels in the attic this year. He hadn't been upstairs; he wouldn't go now. His room would be frozen, the sheets stale at best. He stood, laid the letter in the desk, locked the drawer. Then he went to the tall bay window—Rob's nap-cot—climbed under the blanket, and slept at once: not turning, no dream.

When Rob stood over him an hour later, Hutch was on his left side and sensed no presence—his mind a close black bread of rest.

Rob saw the man below him, heard steady breath, smelled a general air of ease in the room—he was almost surely welcome—but though he looked a minute and touched the man's hair (cooler than expected), no name came to him. By the dim lamp the profile seemed familiar like the room—safe, even well-meant, but in no need of Rob and blurring as he watched. In something like respect he leaned once more and laid two fingers at the gap where the lips had parted in sleep. Three warm breaths stroked him, sufficient meeting. Then he went through every other room as slowly, touching every other object that might need care, and was gone by one.

Hutch had still not moved.

32

GRAINGER woke him at seven—entering with his own key, walking through the dining room lightly toward the kitchen, not noticing the cot. He'd started the coffee and come in to turn out the lamp when Hutch spoke. "If I'd been choosing I'd have asked for you."

Grainger showed no surprise. "Choosing what?"

"One person to see this early today."

"*Late*," Grainger said. "Miss Eva and me been up all night. How many eggs you want?"

"How many I need?"

"Not that many here and they're all Miss Min's. I'll fix what I see." He returned to the kitchen.

Hutch joined him in ten minutes, washed and combed. Lean bacon was already hissing in the pan; sun had reached the window and was taking the floor. He said "I'll make the toast."

"Cooking now," Grainger said, not glancing from the bacon.

So Hutch gathered Min's books and charts to one side, laid two places, and sat at the table—his hands in the light. For two full minutes he watched them as blankly as he'd slept all night. Then he saw they were Rob's. As a boy he'd hoped more than once for just these, his father's long-boned thick-wristed hands. Somehow he'd failed to notice that he had them.

Grainger poured in the eggs. "You lost your ring?"

"You'll see it tomorrow."

"How's that?"

"On Ann."

"You married?" Grainger said.

"Not yet."

"When's your plan?"

Hutch said, "Maybe this summer, maybe next—when I get home from England."

"You heading back there?" Grainger brought the loaded platter now, perfect and plain; the fresh strong coffee. He sat facing Hutch and had still not smiled.

"—When things here are smooth."

Grainger served himself sparsely, then actually laughed.

Hutch bristled but grinned. "What's the joke?"

"No joke. I was thinking you could leave in one minute."

"How?"

"Hutch, things here are smooth as a greased pane of glass—Miss Eva, me, Sylvie all dying with our teeth; plenty money, good car. We're leaving fast and sporty. Don't need you to watch."

"You're all strong as buffaloes. You'll outlast me."

Grainger nodded. "May do." He ate for some while with the disciplined famine Hutch had always admired, like an orphan still only half-convinced of rescue. Then he said, "Stay round long enough for one thing."

"What?"

"Move Rob's grave."

Hutch said, "Where? It's not dug yet."

"Miss Eva said you burying him in town."

Hutch nodded. "That space by Aunt Rena."

"He ask to be there?"

"No he told me to choose, last thing he said. Something wrong with the choice?" He assumed Grainger only meant Goshen, by Rachel.

But Grainger said, "Feels a little off to me."

"Goshen's just too far."

"I'm speaking of here." Grainger pointed to the window—the small Kendal graveyard behind the last shed, not used in decades.

"That's choked out with briars."

"Rob cleaned it this spring right after you left."

"Did he say for what?"

"Not to me. I never asked him."

Hutch said, "I doubt he knew anybody buried there, maybe that last old great-aunt—Carrie."

Grainger said "Don't matter."

"What does?"

"You think. See if this don't matter. He moved here with you when he'd ruined other places. You stayed here with him the whole four years he built back his life."

Hutch said "Then I left."

"Had to. He didn't doubt that."

"You saying he was happy here?—Sylvie said that."

Grainger waited through it carefully and looked up smiling. "Sylvie's wrong about a lot, but he had some good days."

Hutch knew from the letter what Grainger didn't—none of the best days were set on this hill—but he also knew that (for reasons of his own only partly clear) he would stand in a minute now, call the undertaker, and move the grave site. They'd be digging by noon.

33

SATURDAY night to discourage callers, Eva turned out the lamps in the front of the house and herded them all to the dining room where they sat in candle light—honestly hungry—and made inroads on the hill of food still left in the kitchen, urged on quietly by Grainger and Sylvie. Their first time together round this large table, they sat where Eva had placed them briskly (she and Hutch at the ends; Ann and Min to Hutch's right, Polly Drewry to Eva's); and at first they said little, still hushed from the drive out in cold bright sun, the short grave service in the old Kendal plot—Paul's grand vision of resurrection: "Behold, I shew you a mystery. We shall not all sleep, but we shall all be changed"—and the slow drive back.

Finally Ann, who was somehow not exhausted by her flight from Rome, said, "I haven't seen many but that was the best."

The others nodded but Eva said "What?"

"Mr. Mayfield's funeral."

Eva seemed to accept; then said, "I wish it could have just been music."

Hutch said, "You'd have had to dust your vocal cords off. I wasn't going to put him through a big church service with Miss Mamie Roebuck assaulting the organ."

Eva smiled. "He always enjoyed her efforts."

"Too much," Hutch said. "I didn't want him to laugh."

Grainger stood by Polly with a bowl of glazed yams. He said "I did."

Polly said "So did I." Then even in the dim light, she blushed a hot red.

Eva faced her, registered the blush; and said, "He did laugh better than any other human from the time he was born. I used to brush him with a feather when I bathed him just to hear his laugh; people would run upstairs to hear." She pointed overhead.

Hutch said, "I wish he had had more chances."

Polly nodded.

Min said, "He got a fair share" (despite Eva's frown she'd lit a cigarette).

All but Ann, who'd barely known him, were surprised by the claim. Yet they all thought it out and came on memories that partly agreed. Eva said, "Maybe so—I see him that way—but his expectation was much too high."

Hutch said "What was it?"

Polly had nodded so Eva looked to her. "Am I wrong, Miss Drewry?"

Polly said "No ma'm."

Eva said, "He always planned to be happy." She didn't look to Polly again but Polly smiled.

Hutch said, "I think he made it, right at the end."

Min said "I know he did."

Eva said, "I never saw it. Somebody should have showed me."

Min set down her cigarette and met Eva's eyes. "You could have come out to his place any day these past six months; he asked you many times. You'd have seen him calm as water in a glass." She stroked her own glass.

Eva said, "I'll try to trust you."

Loud knocking at the front door.

Grainger moved to answer.

But Eva said, "Hutch, you go. They'll want you. Please say we're grateful but have all keeled over."

Grainger said, "Some stranger. Never heard such a fist."

When Hutch lit the porch light, Strawson Stuart was leaving—already halfway down the walk. Hutch opened the door, came as far as the steps; and said, "However did you find me here?"

Straw stopped in the farthest edge of light and looked at Hutch closely. "I didn't think I had. A grease monkey told me."

"We're eating in the back. Turned the lights off for peace."

"I'm sorry," Straw said.

Hutch laughed, now warmer than he'd been in days—since Rome, Christmas night. "Come in quick. You're welcome."

Straw said, "I was wondering. I left so fast, got your note this morning."

Hutch said, "Father died right after I mailed it. We buried him today. Ann flew in this morning."

Straw said, "I'm sorry. I can leave right now." But he came a step forward. Since summer the planes of his face had lengthened—leaner, maybe two years older that quickly. He was neatly dressed after four hours' driving.

Hutch said what he thought he suddenly knew. "I'm gladder to see you than anybody else."

Straw accepted that, an honorable wage, and came to the steps.

34

At nine Min left for the country house; Strawson followed her. Hutch kissed his grandmother and Polly and asked Ann to walk him to the truck. Only then did Eva say "You won't forget Sylvie."

He had. Sylvie waited in the kitchen for a ride. He asked Ann to join him for the short breath of air. She found her coat and they went to Sylvie, who was dozing in her chair by the sink. Hutch said "Bedtime."

Sylvie looked. "Way past." She was already wrapped in her thick green coat. She leaned to take up the black purse and hat she'd worn at the funeral.

Hutch said, "Put your hat on. I like that hat."

She held it a moment, then refused. "Bad luck."

Hutch laughed. "Why's that?"

"—My mourning hat. This hat killed people since before you were born." But she smiled at Ann.

In the truck Ann said, "Did your family come for Christmas?"

Sylvie waited; then said, "Hutch, you ought to told her my sad old story."

Hutch laughed. "Be ashamed. You're the freest soul I know."

Ann sat in the middle. She turned to Sylvie's profile. "You tell me, Sylvie."

Sylvie looked on ahead but pointed to Hutch. "He told you. I'm all you see; not another living soul want to claim kin with me."

Hutch said "Be glad."

Sylvie first said "Huh." Then she said, "You wait abovt forty-some years—see how glad you be."

Hutch said, "Your fault. You had plenty of chances. Even I can remember long shoals of boyfriends round your door."

She didn't answer but sat in silence for the next half-mile till he climbed the rutted track and reached her yard, the low dark house. Then she groaned. "Forgot my light. You step in with me."

Hutch said "Sit still." He opened his door, came round, and helped her out (she handed him the hat).

Ann said, "Thank you, Sylvie. I hope you rest."

Sylvie said, "Yes ma'm. It's tomorrow already."

Hutch said, "It's nine-fifteen. Plenty time yet."

But Sylvie was already climbing her steps.

He followed her quickly. "Don't leave your hat."

She entered the main room, switched on a light, walked straight to the midget refrigerator, and put in a small paperbag she'd carried—some pre-dawn snack.

Hutch shut the door behind him. The room was stifling; her stove never stopped. "Safe now?" he said.

Sylvie nodded, watching him closely though. "*You* not," she said.

He smiled. "How's that?"

"Acting so happy all day, tonight. You ain't happy yet."

Hutch saw that his tired efforts at cheer had sat badly with her. "I'm sorry," he said. "I'm at least as sad as you. I've just been trying to skate through today."

Sylvie shook her head. "You falling."

Hutch extended his hand; half the room was between them. "Want to balance me then?"

She shook her head again. "Not in my power."

He waited, then laid the hat on her chair. "I'll see you tomorrow."

"Lord willing." Then as he took the first step to leave, she said, "Don't think I'm evil tonight. I'm tired and aching and I hated to see them new friends of yours making you think you hadn't lost the *world* today."

Hutch nodded. "I did."

"Luck to you then." She took two steps as though to touch him but stopped short and waved.

He smiled. "Sleep good."

"I won't," Sylvie said.

35

HUTCH turned the truck, drove them carefully back toward the paved road to Eva's; then pulled to the edge in the last of the woods, and killed the engine. There was heat to last them five minutes maybe. Ann was sitting far enough away to make him move. He slid to touch her, her fine hair first. She faced him and he kissed her—first time since Rome (the airport greeting had been quick and public).

She seemed glad to join, then dissolved it herself and looked straight ahead. "I think I'm scared."

His arm pulled her toward him. "This is Fontaine not Rome. We're safe again."

Ann said, "I think I felt safer in Rome."

"It was fine. I'm sorry I ruined your trip."

"You didn't. I pretty well saw all I wanted."

"You go to the Sistine?"

She nodded on his shoulder. "Better than planned. Only the second thing that ever surprised me, that turned out better than its advertisements."

Hutch laughed. "The first was me?"

"Sorry, Dumbo—the Canyon, the whole Grand Canyon."

"I never knew you saw it."

"I told you; you forgot. The summer my father died we drove out there."

Hutch had never known her father, and she mentioned him so rarely that he'd never been a visible presence in their life. "How did you take that?"

"—Mouth open. It was gorgeous, more reds than Rome."

"His dying, I meant."

Ann waited, then sank her head deeper in his arm. "Just the end of the world."

"You loved him that much?"

"I was fourteen; he was all the men I'd known. He was gone a lot and quiet when there, though he'd talk to me if Mother wasn't near. So *love?* —sure, I guess. But once he was dead, once Mother came in where I was doing homework at six p.m. on a black card-table and said he'd died in the Pitt Hotel in Bristol, Virginia, having just unloaded more Crosley radios than any other salesman in the district and stretched out to nap— well, the end of the world."

"Why?"

"Who was going to keep us? Every Shirley Temple movie told me orphans were bad off, fair game for all."

"You made it," Hutch said.

She waited. "To where?"

He moved his arm and gripped her neck. "Here, now."

"You aren't staying here."

He had not meant the place but his body, its refuge. Yet she'd showed him that his choice of Rob's grave site was at least the first gesture toward a whole life here. "We could," he said.

"Not with your grandmother still here, not *we.*"

"I thought you liked her."

"*Admired* her, I said. I admired the Grand Canyon, but I couldn't live there."

"Where then?"

"You name it, just far from our kin."

Hutch laughed. "Now look who's running for the light."

Ann nodded. "I always was. You never noticed."

"I noticed. I was scared you'd picked me for the light."

"I had. What was scarey?"

Hutch said, "I'd been picked before—my father."

She waited. "That's over."

"So far as I can see."

Ann said, "Estimate how far that is."

"Long as I live."

"Then what happens now?"

He said, "I do a few chores on Rob's estate. I visit you in Richmond, and I'll have to thank Alice. I fly back to England, finish my classes, and start my thesis."

"—Which takes you how far?"

"Through a second year, eighteen months away."

"Where do I wait till then?"

Hutch said, "There's no way we could live in Oxford. I'm on a lean budget—even leaner with this trip—and you'd never get permission to work, except maybe something in the country with the air force; and I wouldn't feel too easy with that, too many Rowlets round. So why not Richmond? You don't mind your job; the time'll melt quickly."

Ann seemed to nod—her head dipped slightly—but she didn't speak again. She was finally tired.

So was Hutch. He sat still, her weight pressing heavier each moment on his arm, and knew that a fierce desire was called for—love against death, in poems at least. And he did lean to kiss her again deeply, slowly.

But she met him on his own grounds—courteous greeting at the end of a long day, no further request—and said at last, "You're dealing with a *sleeper*."

So he said, "You know how grateful I am?"

She took his hand and pressed it.

"Have you got the ring?"

"In my suitcase, buried in talcum powder. Customs never saw it."

"It was legal."

"So I trust."

He stroked the one finger. "Too big to wear?"

She nodded. "Too soon. We can size it when we're ready. I'll dig it out every few days and talk to it."

Hutch drew in his arm and cranked the engine, instant heat. "Give it love from me."

"It knows that," she said.

Half an hour later he was climbing toward Rob's house—the porch light shining—when he knew he'd forgot to wish her happy New Year. It would be New Year in another hour. Well, he'd sleep right through it.

36

BUT Min and Strawson were awake in the kitchen. Straw had provided a fifth of Jim Beam; and when Hutch walked in, they were seated at the table under raw bulb-light with nearly empty glasses. A third glass stood ready. Straw said "Your ice is melting."

Hutch stopped in the door, startled to be angry. Since Rob had quit drinking the year they moved here, the present sight struck him as a desecration—the body covered only seven hours ago. He said, "We don't dilute it in England."

Straw's eyes were slightly glazed; he looked round the room. "I doubt this is England or will ever be."

Min understood the moment and set her glass down; but she said, "We all need a whole night of sleep."

So for something to do till he calmed again, Hutch went to the sink and washed his hands. Then he sat.

Straw poured four ounces of bourbon and slid it toward him. "You have a flat tire?"

"Had to take Sylvie home. She seems very low."

Min said, "She'd known him second-longest of anybody left alive"— a small true discovery.

Hutch drank a long swallow.

Straw said, "Colored people believe in death."

They rolled that over in silence; Hutch laughed. "It seems to be a fairly universal belief."

Straw shook his head. "Wrong. The minute some white person dies— blam!—flowers, Hammond organs pumping tunes Kate Smith wouldn't touch with a forty-foot pole, preachers grinning like cats. Negroes stand up and yell."

Hutch saw the boy was high and nodded to stop him.

But Min said, "There're various ways to yell. I've wailed fifty years, barely pausing to breathe. Very few people noticed." She smiled at Straw.

Straw said "I'm sorry." He filled her glass and his; then said, "I'm not sure who you are—in all this, I mean." He gestured to the room.

Hutch said, "She was one of my father's oldest friends."

Min said "Still am," straight at Hutch. Then she gave the rest to Straw. "I'm one of the several relicts of the man we buried today. Did you ever meet him?"

"Yes ma'm—once, last May."

"He knew he was sick by then; could you tell?"

Straw said, "No ma'm, he mostly laughed."

She waited awhile, then drew two large figure-eights on the table with a firm forefinger, then faced Straw again. "Let me warn you to-night; leave here knowing this—any human being laughing as much as Rob Mayfield is dying in pain."

Hutch said, "Min's Law?—does it always hold?"

She nodded but to Straw.

Hutch sang the first bar of "*Ridi, pagliaccio.*"

She said, "He asked me to love him way back when we were just children—we grew up together, houses fifty yards apart—and I stayed true for forty damned years."

"He didn't?" Straw said.

Min thought, shut her eyes, and shook her head.

Straw moved his hands toward her, flat on the table, but stopped short of touching. "What does that make you?"

Hutch said "Easy, Straw."

But Min laughed. "I *know*," she said. "I've had time to know. It makes me a fool about the size of east Texas. There used to be lots of old women like me at family reunions. We thought they were freaks but also heroes—some boy they'd loved had been killed or died. They were fresh as wax blossoms at sixty years old, ready for anything—trips to Alaska! No one ever said they were laughable fools."

"They weren't," Hutch said.

She faced him at last. "I know they were."

Straw said "You live here?"

She shook her head. "No sir. I've stayed here since June and Fontaine's my home, but I work in Raleigh."

"Doing what?"

"Family trees. I construct family trees in the State Library for elderly white folks to chin themselves on."

Straw said, "They'll be needing them any day now for more than exercise."

Hutch said "Meaning what?"

Straw looked and grinned for the first time tonight. "—The great tide of blood foretold in The Book. The niggers' revenge, black Jesus with a *blade*. Very few family trees'll be tall enough to save all the scramblers."

Hutch said "Not funny."

Straw said, "Damned right—you're the one with good sense; run to England and hide."

Hutch said, "The sad thing is, nothing's going to change—look at Sylvie and Grainger."

Straw laughed. "They're old. You stay in England."

Min said, "Rob agreed. He talked a lot all fall about what would come when Negroes really noticed the door was thrown open."

Hutch said again "Nothing."

Min locked on his eyes. "You keep thinking that but think it at a distance. Rob said one night, 'Grainger Walters would kill me quick as pass me the salt.'"

Hutch smiled, "Rob was *hoping*—a fast clean end. Grainger loved him more than us."

Min said "Speak for you."

"I am," Hutch said.

Straw said "You're a lie."

Min pushed her glass from her. "This is your table, Hutch—your house overhead—but can I speak freely in it one last time?"

Hutch nodded.

Straw made the first move to rise.

Hutch said "No, stay."

Min said, "While you're measuring people's love, I wonder now if Rob loved you at all. The longer I stayed here—the more we talked—the more I think he selected you as his one halfway acceptable excuse for quitting life, a decent man's life. Then when he saw you'd be vanishing, he planned his death—all secret choices, from himself at least."

Hutch smiled. "That's fairly stale news to me."

"And it makes you smile?"

"No I smiled at you, Min—your big discovery."

"But you left him, knowing what that would cause?"

Hutch said, "I left here seven years ago. I want one of those decent lives you mention."

"He came here for you; you begged him to come."

"—When I was a child eleven years ago, a child he'd made. He knew I'd grow. You wanted him always; I turned out not to."

"You've got him though," she said. "You see that now?"

Hutch said, "I'm very much afraid you're right."

Straw lifted his bottle and poured all round. "This'll stunt everybody. We can still be dwarves."

They sat in silence till Min laughed and drank.

Straw raised a finger and shook his head. "This is serious business. Anybody wants to shrink has to stay grim and *try*."

Min looked to the clock, twenty to twelve. Then she nodded and smiled. "Can it happen by midnight?"

"With luck, yes ma'm."

Hutch said, "Happy New Year—in case we can't talk by then."

Straw hushed him too.

37

HUTCH woke at the sound of feet in his room—vague light of dawn. His head stayed down but his eyes opened carefully and looked to the window. Straw had left the other bed and was standing bare at the long east window—his back to Hutch five yards away, sun rising beyond him, no cloud in the sky. The door was shut and the air was cold; but Straw held firm, not shivering, and looked out steadily. So Hutch watched, never having seen him still before. He was taller since July. The boyish fullness had sunk deeper inward, the back and legs were lean and dense, the right hand clasped the broad left shoulder as if two flat breasts were all that needed hiding. Hutch recalled having seen him last May at school, laid back in sun on the hood of the car, as a permanently youthful god of Need—poised to seize and use his least whim. And in Oxford, cold from his crazy swim, as a child endangered by a world too willing to join his wildness. But here now he seemed a satisfactory image of one of the three kinds of beauty Hutch loved—man, woman, nature. He also recalled Ann in May at her sink, scraping potatoes. Why couldn't both stand still here always—sky and trees beyond them—for him to watch and serve, serve *by* watching? Diagrams of objects as near to perfection as objects came. No touch, no friction, no wear or change. The sun was high enough now to flood Straw.

He turned toward Hutch, saw the open eyes, held another long moment (his heavy sex not shrunk by the chill). Then he said, not whispering, "You all right?"

"I was."

"What stopped you?"

Hutch was silent.

Straw took four steps and paused on the rag rug between the two beds.

Hutch still faced the window. He said "Thank you, Straw."

"For what?"

"Driving down."

Straw said "I'm still here."

Hutch nodded but slowly turned away. "It's still night. Sleep."

Separate as brothers, they slept again in the full cold light. Straw dreamt of a field in which a small child stepped backward from him as he strained to reach it, protect and claim it.

By the time they woke—past ten—Min was gone. They didn't check her room, didn't know she'd packed and cleared all her traces; but they found half a pot of coffee on the stove. Hutch warmed that, toasted bread, found peach jam; and they sat and ate quietly as sun swept round the house and struck the kitchen windows.

Straw stood in place and looked toward the graves. "She may be down there."

Hutch said, "Her car's gone. You want more toast?"

Straw sat. "Has she really got a place to live now?"

Hutch nodded. "Sure, in Raleigh."

"Have you?"

Hutch laughed. "Too many—here, Grandmother's, Ann's, Polly's, Oxford."

"You picked one yet?'

Hutch stood and brought coffee. "I've picked here as home; I buried Rob here. I don't see any way to live here though."

"Why?"

"The trees grow leaves, Straw, not dollar bills."

"The ground grows tobacco. You got an allotment?"

"Eight acres, worked by tenants."

"You ought to be living on the damned Riviera in a forty-foot yacht."

"I won't see two thousand dollars a year, from tobacco anyhow."

"Then you're being robbed blind; better get a new tenant."

Hutch said, "I didn't know you were such a big farm economist. The man we've got has been with us forty years. We put him out of this house when Rob and I moved here; I have to trust him now."

Straw said, "Your grandmother—she's doing all right. Won't she help you along till you're world-renowned?"

"She's doing fine—twenty acres of tobacco and miles of pulpwood."

"Won't that come to you?"

"In the year 3000." Hutch laughed again. "You've seen her; she'll *last*."

"Then come here and sit. Write your poems and get thin. Let her see your ribs shine. She'll chip in quick."

"What makes you think that?"

"I saw her like you said. She loves your ass."

Hutch smiled. "Well, my *soul*. No I think you're correct. But I wouldn't come alone, and she wouldn't keep two."

"Who you planning to join?"

Hutch studied the face again, quickly but closely—the new broad planes, wide chin, curled mouth. Even now, awake in daylight, it seemed a sane option. Inexhaustible ikon. But he said "You know."

Straw nodded. "Does she?"

"Yes we settled that in Rome."

"Starting when?"

"After Oxford."

Straw said "She'll wait?"

"No choice. People wait. She's got a decent job, decent roof, a safe roommate."

"I like her," Straw said. "She never says much."

"She was tired last night—she says a good deal, no baby talk though. Don't you be dropping by Richmond to check." Hutch grinned, thrust a slow fist, and bumped Straw's nose.

Straw said "Too old for me."

"I thought you liked ripe ones."

Straw had still not smiled. "I thought so too. They cost too much."

"So you've found a cheap child?"

Straw said, "That's most of what college has to offer."

"I thought they were all gents at Washington and Lee, Christian cavaliers in suede boots and plumes."

Straw nodded. "They are. But they also *smell* and the smell draws Christian maidens in droves from Sweetbriar, Hollins, Buena Vista—maidens for about four minutes once they hit the city limits."

"Then you've had a good fall?"

Straw finally laughed, deep and hoarse. "A *fall* all right. I feel like I fell down a bottomless hole."

"Of girls?"

"No, fools—some of them were girls. I'm not going back."

Hutch said "You flunked out?"

"Hell no—three As, two Bs, and a D. I told them I might come back someday. In my eighties maybe, my *second* childhood. I'm too old now."

"What did your parents say?"

"Not a damned word as always. They're just sitting pale and blank —drinking gin, watching their new rugs, and asking Sweet Jesus what they did to earn me." He turned back and pointed north toward his parents, four hours away; they were palpably stunned.

Hutch said "Where now?"

Straw said "I'm asking you."

"You got any money?"

"Fifteen hundred dollars my great-uncle left me."

Hutch said, "You'll be needing a job pretty fast."

"Want to hire me?"

"For what?"

Straw said, "I was thinking all night while you slept. This house'll be empty. I could caretake it for you—keep the pipes thawed out, paint it up. Houses die if you just lock the door."

Hutch nodded. "They do. I doubt I could afford you."

"I don't cost money."

"You wouldn't burn it down?"

"I don't play with matches," Straw said. "My heart's cool."

"But you drink a lot of bourbon."

"You want me to stop? I can stop this minute. Willpower's my *name*."

Hutch said, "Try to half it—say, two drinks a day."

"—And then I'm hired?"

Hutch said, "You couldn't bring any former maidens from Sweetbriar or Hollins; Grandmother wouldn't stand it."

"That go for locals too?—farm girls now and then?"

Hutch said, "Understand, Straw. This house used to mean the world to me and my father. It may again, to me at least. Anybody who wanted to caretake it now couldn't really change its life."

Straw said, "I know that. I want to stay alone. Any company I need, I can leave and find on quick weekends."

Hutch drained his cup.

Straw said "A deal?"

Hutch looked again slowly. "Is this for me or you?"

Straw smiled. "Don't know. Am I selfish or a saint?"

Hutch said, "Probably neither. The loneliness may kill you; if it doesn't you're a saint."

"I await the outcome with interest then."

Hutch stood and took their plates. "One other thing though—if I ever come back here, I won't come alone." Facing Straw in the sun, it cost more to say than he'd known it would.

Straw nodded. "Yes sir."

Then they walked out silently to see the fresh grave. The night's hard freeze had already thawed, and the red clods were damp. Straw bent and took one and gave it to Hutch, who crushed it in his own palm —dyeing the skin.

38

HUTCH had got to Alice's at six in the evening, five days later. The three-hour drive in steady rain had tired him; so after the greetings and a glass of sherry, he'd kicked off his shoes and stretched on her sofa while she worked in the kitchen—not her favorite place. When she'd nearly finished she called "Hungry yet?" No answer. She finished, came to the door, and whispered, "I've done it. Are you game to risk my cooking?" He was deep asleep on his side, facing out, hands clamped in his knees. Well, the food would keep. She lit the two candles on the dining table, switched off the lamp, and sat across from him—sketching on the firm blue wool of her lap the lines of his body with her dry forefinger. He'd always refused to let her draw him—"Wait till I'm grown. I don't like my head." Did he like what he'd got? Even slack now, resting, it was plainly grown. The brow had roughened, the cheeks hollowed out, the neck thickened strongly. Only the wide shut lips had survived from his first young face. She traced them separately, large, on her leg—three times, invisibly but memorably. She thought of the several Picasso etchings in which a sleeper is closely watched by a big-eyed girl—intent on what? Not protection surely (her own size is frail). Not investigation (her gaze is calm). *Memory* then. But to what earthly use? The girl wouldn't know, not for years if ever. Alice knew, here now; she'd always known—for the years of waking movement and absence, movement which always ends in absence. In her own life at least, all the lives she'd seen. She started the long ridgeline of his legs before she saw his eyes.

He watched her, not blinking.

Alice said "Twelfth Night."

"Ma'm?"

"Happy Twelfth Night—I just remembered."

Hutch stood. "I forgot my frankincense."

"No you didn't. Let's eat. My feast awaits."

39

THEY left next morning at ten and drove west through flat brown fields still soaked from the rain; the sky promised more. The weather and their late night of talk kept them quiet through the first fifty miles, but then near Farmville the sun broke behind them; and thick stands of bare trees took the light as if it were rations, delivered in the nick. Hutch said, "I think I may manage to live" (they'd drunk a lot of wine).

Alice said, "I'm gratified to have that news" and consulted the map. "Ever seen Appomattox?"

"Not in person, just pictures of the house where Lee and Grant met."

"Me either. They rebuilt it not long ago. It's right up the road. Have we got time to stop?"

Hutch said, "You're the guide. I take orders nicely."

"Then turn when I tell you. I think any Southern boy should face up to where the big native doom fell before he goes roaming back through Cornwall and Wales."

Hutch said, "Too late. I've roamed them already."

Alice laughed and folded the map correctly. "The theme of my life, when the sun's out anyway, is 'Never Too Late.' "

"General Lee disagrees."

"General Lee won't be giving us the tour," she said. "He's seated in bliss, playing chess with Hannibal or Antony."

"Or spitted in Hell, barbecued by slave-cooks."

Alice smiled. "Hush and drive."

The surrender house had been rebuilt only five years before on the site of the first house, torn down by speculators after the war and quickly dispersed (though every thirteenth brick in the reconstruction was original). A pleasant middle-sized two-story house perched above a high cellar on the old foundations, it existed now for its left front-room, a small glum parlor packed with bulky chairs and the two small tables where the acts of offer and acceptance had occurred less than ninety years ago (the tables were copies; only the iron-maiden sofa had been present in April '65). That was all told them by a sweet-voiced woman, well-up on her facts and grateful for guests—no one else was in sight. Then they wandered on past the square courthouse, the jail, three old houses, to where the high spine of land dropped away to a wooded valley —the river, no people, no visible building between them and hard cloudless sky. They stood five feet apart and looked out awhile. Hutch said, "Every good place turns out to be empty."

"Who said that?"

"Me."

"We're here."

"We're respectful."

Alice said, "I thought you liked Rome—Rome's full."

"Not of people, not two weeks ago. The places that had seen most were all but deserted."

"Where was your friend Ann?"

"Mostly with me."

Alice said "She's people," then went to a low stone bench and sat. "I knew an old man who had been at Appomattox."

Hutch smiled. "We *are* there now. It's still here."

Alice waited, shook her head. "He was here that day, when it was itself—what it waited through all of history to be. We're just late prowlers in the graveyard, aren't we?"

Hutch laughed. "It was your idea to stop."

Alice said, "He had to line up before dawn—somewhere near here; he said he could hear the river—and then march past a spot and lay down his rifle. He was twenty-one years old; he'd fought the whole war."

Hutch said, "There were none for me to fight. I came between wars."

"Maybe not—I haven't heard of universal peace."

Hutch laughed again. "Right. I'm an old veteran too. Want to see my wound?"

Alice stood and waved a slow hand down his length. "I've seen it, my darling. Let it rest for now."

40

By the time they'd eaten a late lunch in Lexington, bought the flowers, and ascended the narrow pass to Goshen, it was late afternoon. But the sun had lasted on the cliffs and the rapid dangerous stream; and when they reached the cemetery, there was almost a heat above the clustered stones. They were silent again as they found the Hutchins plot. Hutch at once set the yellow high-smelling chrysanthemums at the base of one stone—RACHEL HUTCHINS MAYFIELD, *May 27, 1905–May 12, 1930*: his mother among her parents and kin, dead at twenty-five and buried twenty-five years ago when he'd waited in a Richmond hospital, four days old. He pulled at the tall dead grass, soon harvesting two handsful of hay. Alice bent, joined the work, and dislodged a flap of turf with bare dirt beneath it. She was pressing it back when Hutch crawled closer, took over, and dug. Two inches down he uncovered a coin—a worn fifty-cent piece. Then he recalled Rob here last May, grubbing with his hands by the one flashlight. He held the coin to Alice.

Her glasses were back in the car, but she thrust it to arm's length and said "1948—where on earth?"

"Rob and I stopped here last spring. He must have left it. I saw him dig here."

Alice thumbed at the silver another few times, then set it back in Hutch's palm. "This never was Rachel's."

"Not in '48, no."

She stood with difficulty, dizzy from the squat. "He owed her a lot."

Hutch looked up. "Money? This wouldn't cover much."

But Alice was looking toward the nearest mountain, the one they'd sketched many times years ago. "—Pleasure," she said.

"I didn't think that."

"Why?"

"I thought they hurt each other."

Alice turned back finally. "At the first and the end, there was some pain, yes. Otherwise they were happy; I watched them be." She leaned and touched her chin to the stone, then stepped away.

Hutch buried the coin again, pressed the turf, and stood. His head swam too but he waited to find some message to say. Only "Goodbye" occurred so he said that silently and went, leaving Rob's odd half-dollar gift—as tangible an offering as any Hutch had made in his own life to the unseen girl in whom he'd started.

41

WHEN they'd finished supper—the last two diners—in the Maury Motel, the waitress poured their final coffee; then said, "Excuse me if I'm wrong again, but you've got to be a Hutchins."

Hutch smiled. "Half-right. My mother was a Hutchins."

"Was she Rachel?"

"Yes ma'm. I'm Hutchins Mayfield. This is my friend, Miss Matthews from Petersburg."

The woman—short, stocky, maybe younger than Alice—set the pot on the table and stepped back a little to study his eyes. "I went to the wedding."

Hutch didn't understand.

Alice said "So did I."

The woman glanced toward her but continued to Hutch. "I was Joyce Meadows. I was younger than Rachel, one or two years behind her in school; but I watched her like a hawk from the day I first saw her. I wanted to *be* her; she was that good to see."

Hutch said "Did you tell her?"

The woman thought awhile. "I'm Joyce Neal now. May I sit down a minute? I own this place."

Hutch waved her to a chair.

Only then, when she'd carefully stacked enough dishes to give herself room for her broad elbows, did she really see Alice. "*You're* doing well, aren't you?"

Alice laughed. "For my age."

"No that's what I mean. I knew you first—before I saw his eyes" (she flicked Hutch's brow). "Your name is Alice."

Alice nodded. "Good memory. Did we meet at the wedding?"

Mrs. Neal grinned broadly. "I hated you. Rachel's maid of honor! No I wouldn't come near you! I saved your face though—I knew you right off. You've taken time well."

Alice said, "I can thank you and still think you're wrong. Time has seemed more like a Mack truck, head-on, than anything softer."

"Call me Joyce. Me too, the part about the truck." She turned back to Hutch. "You're the one never saw her."

"I'm sorry to say."

"*Be* sorry; she was fine, for all her troubles. Where's your daddy these days?"

"Dead, last week."

Her face went blank for an instant in respect. Then she grinned. "You people quit early, don't you? You feeling well?"

"Fairly well."

"Don't leave. This mountain air'll save you. Look at me. I thrive." She extended one arm and waved its hanging weight—pink, firm as packed sausage.

Hutch leaned out and stroked her. "My place here is gone."

"The old hotel?—Rachel's daddy's old place? Did you get that?"

"When my grandfather died."

"We were gone in those years; spent the whole war in Norfolk, nailing ships together—my husband anyway. I stayed indoors. Norfolk's wild, all sailors. We got back in '46; the hotel was gone."

Hutch said, "I sold it and they scrapped it for lumber."

Joyce nodded. "Good lumber. We bought a raft of it to finish this place—great heartpine boards; shellacked it myself." She waved to the walls, stained yellow as a jaundice. "You could sleep here tonight, be right back at home. These are Rachel Hutchins' walls."

Alice said, "Her walls were plaster, white as down."

Joyce said, "I never got asked upstairs. The Hutchinses were shy."

"Still are," Hutch said.

She checked him again. "You look bold as bobcats."

Hutch laughed. "Thank you, no—just a sleepy fieldmouse."

"You'll sleep," Joyce said. "This air is a drug. See, I *told* you to stay."

42

THEY both were tired but, as they walked in the cold toward their rooms, Alice said, "Maybe we ought to see it in the dark."

Hutch knew she meant Rachel's home—the wrecked hotel—though till now they'd silently agreed to bypass it. He said, "I was there last March. Nothing left but scrap."

"Can I borrow the car?"

Hutch paused, rubbed his arms to indicate the chill; but he said, "I don't guess anyone would shoot us."

Alice said, "I'm not too old to dodge."

So they drove out slowly through the shut-up town to the dark far edge. Hutch entered the old drive, narrowed by laurel, and stopped well back to avoid nails and glass. The headlights reached the brick foundations—half-hid in broken lathing, plaster, shingles. He said, "In Italy they'd charge to see this."

"They'd be right." She was watching the high cube of blackness where the rooms had stood, the site of memories hung now in air. She reached for the door. "They must have spared the spring."

"They did," Hutch said, "but it may be dirty. I don't have a flashlight."

She climbed out anyhow and walked ahead.

He gave her the lead she seemed to want, then followed. The air was black—no stars—and spikey with what seemed crystals of ice, but he navigated safely by recollection and soon grasped the springhouse rail. He shook it, still firm as when Grainger restored it years ago. "Any water?"

No answer.

"Alice?" He stepped round and found the narrow entrance. Then he circled the springhead with arms extended, sweeping for Alice. She was not here now. He felt brief fear, then recalled she'd known the place longer than he. He reached above to the ceiling for the dipper—the long copper dipper that had always hung there and was there last March. Gone now—thieving children or an antique dealer? He squatted and raised the lid from the spring; then gripping the rim with his left hand, he leaned toward the water. Absolutely dark and empty space. Not even the promising echo of water. Did it sink in winter; had it frozen or dried?

Alice said, at some distance, "They left the servants' quarters, solid as ever."

"Can you see me?"

She waited. "Yes sir. You're on your knees."

"Where are you?"

No answer. Then footsteps behind him. "Is it clean?"

"It's gone."

She laughed once. "No. It was here for dinosaurs; it wouldn't leave now." She touched his right shoulder, felt her way down his arm, then knelt beside him.

He could still not see her, but he heard her reach down—her nails scraped the wall, then the crisp quick dabble of fingers in water. "Warm," she said. She drew in her arm. "*Warm*. Taste and see."

His face found her hand, tightly cupped. He licked at the palm— two short swallows, colder than his own lips and throat.

Alice wiped his forehead slowly, then kissed him precisely at the line of his hair.

The lock had been pried off the door of the quarters, but the door was shut, so the inside held a little warmth from the bright afternoon. They were back in pure dark though. Hutch led the way down the narrow central hall, both arms out again to brush the walls. His left hand found the door to Grainger's room; but the right found Della's, the hotel maid. He turned toward that, drawing Alice behind (she held his coattail). The door opened silently on what might well have been infinite space—no glow, no sound, none of the stench of a shut airless room. Yet he took two more steps (Alice still with him), trusting his childhood memory to lay a firm floor beneath them, no knives or traps. The floor seemed clear. He said "I wish we smoked."

Alice laughed once. "Why?"

"I'd at least have a match."

"Ask me," she said and fumbled in her bag. "I usually have some, in case I meet a bomb with an unlit fuse." She found them, passed them forward.

Hutch lit four in succession while they saw the room. No whole piece of furniture, empty gunshells, sardine cans, paper—all in corners, oddly neat. Where Della's bed had stood was a low pile of newspapers, spared by the auction. Hutch said "Build a fire," a thought not an order.

But Alice said, "Man's work. You burn, I cook."

Hutch said, "It's a deal—tin-cans-*flambé-in-dried-squirrel-droppings*." He went to the fireplace and probed up the flue. The stove had been ripped out and sold, but the flue seemed open to the sky. He wadded paper.

Alice said, "This all may explode on our heads."

"Ne' mind," Hutch said. "Nobody cares but us." Fire raced through the pages, half of World War II. Then he added the rounds of Della's wrecked chair and went to the yard to hunt more wood.

Alice said, "Now tell me all you want me to know" (the previous night they'd talked of Rob and Rachel, very little of Hutch).

The fire had made the air tenable by now, a fierce success. They were seated on the floor at the ends of the hearth, half-facing one another. Hutch smiled. "My news comes in two forms, long or short."

"I already asked—just the news you brought *me*. Your letters thinned out pretty soon, I recall."

"I was swamped."

"By what?"

"Well, at first by getting what I'd asked to have—bald loneliness. The English will definitely leave you alone if you want to be left. You can feel like a ghost in very short order—hanging round, full-size with hair and teeth more than ready to grin, but invisible to everyone unless you stop and tell them you're in desperate straits: then they're helpful in a tidy way, elbows tucked. That was June through September."

"You had the trip to Cornwall."

"Worse still. That left me alone as any skunk."

Alice said, "Skunks are sociable souls, good pets."

"Once they've been de-smelled. I was still spraying musk."

"So you sat down to work?"

"I sat down, right. Work was hard to live with."

"You said you were starting a King Arthur poem."

Hutch nodded. "Tried hard—Tristan and Iseult from the butler's point of view."

"No luck."

He fed the fire and laughed. "Luck in torrents—thirty pages, each line more depressing than the last."

"Why?"

"Oh the butler was me—the gimp spare-leg, the wheyfaced witness."

"Did you finish?"

"Not yet. Term began in October."

"Did they notice you then?"

"Less, if anything. Oxford education is a swift introduction to utter self-help. After days of waiting to be told what to do, I asked a few questions and by teatime had a message—delivered by a troll—saying call on Mr. Fleishman. He'd been mystically chosen to direct my work. Mr. Fleishman received me in his flat in north Oxford—just across the road from where Lawrence of Arabia's mother still lives, over ninety and blind and oblivious to the fact that her private scandals are now world news. He's middle-aged—Fleishman—and looks like a carefully controlled but crazed Victorian lepidopterist: brown hair and eyes, brown tweed plus-fours, brown stockings, brown jacket, brown kerchief in his sleeve, brown paper on the walls (so help me God), and little rat-mazes through the books on the floor. He heard me out, unsmiling as slate, over raisin cake and sherry—I meant to be a writer but would also have to teach and would need some advanced degree to strengthen my wings for the academic glide. That stoked what was later revealed as a big bed of anti-American coals in his breast. 'You *Americans*' is mostly what he calls me, when he calls—they hate like hell having lost the world to us; I try to assure them we won't keep it long. But I decided to hump my back and bear it, not reminding him that I was twenty-five years old— no Eton choirboy. And by the time I left, he'd vented enough condescending smoke to invite me to his Wednesday-night openhouses (he's a bachelor). I went along to those, shoulders still bowed; and before long he quietly agreed to my plan—I could read for the Bachelor of Letters degree with a thesis on the love and nature poems of Andrew Marvell. He even, the afternoon we reached agreement, read me Marvell's 'Definition of Love'—or recited it. We sat by his window, no light but the sun and it was far down; I could see he'd shifted his eyes from the page to a spot on the hearth and was speaking to that."

Alice leaned toward the fire and said the first lines—

> " 'My Love is of a birth as rare
> As 'tis for object strange and high:
> It was begotten by despair
> Upon Impossibility. ' "

She sat back smiling. "None but the Lonely Hearts know *that*." With a finger she wrote on the floor at her feet.

Hutch guessed, from the motion, that she traced her name. He also leaned out and covered her hand.

She paused; then drew it in slowly, not looking. Then she sat back, darker, and said "So you started."

"—Mornings at lectures and in the Bodleian, long afternoon walks, gigantic awful dinners."

Alice waited. "Nights?—they don't have nights?"

"Very long frozen nights."

"You didn't have friends you could see after work?"

"I know a lot of people now; we talk a lot—Oxford's one small chatterbox. But most of the students are younger than me; and even the ones who've spent two years in the army in Suez or Malaya seem boys—broad waxy grins, inattentive as bricks. If the British have truly lost the world, I suspect they've lost it through inattention. They didn't see it leaving, didn't guess it yearned to go."

Alice said "*You* stayed."

"I love it; do I seem to be saying otherwise?"

She laughed. "I couldn't claim you've been singing valentines. You've left out what you love."

He waited. "The place, the green natural place—the way they've let time pile on it like snow, to irrigate. Their big towns are ugly as anybody's—worse: they're awful when they try to be modern—but small as the island is, there's miles of country left. I drive round a lot."

"Will you stay?"

"Long?—no, just to finish the job. Maybe eighteen months more, then back here."

"Where's *here?*"

He laughed. "Wherever in the U.S. wants to pay me to teach."

"You couldn't stay in Fontaine and write for a while?"

"—Not unless my grandmother rings my forehead with crowns of tobacco; Rob left next to nothing except the old house."

"You could stay there surely, a year anyway—grow your food, write your poem."

Hutch nodded. "I could. But it won't be just me."

"Ann?"

"I've asked her to join me soon as I'm home."

"Why?"

He tried to see her face; she was still set back at the dim edge of light. "I can't live alone."

"Sure you can; you haven't tried."

"Do you want that for me?"

"You wanted it, you said."

"When Rob was alive."

"And you think he's not now?" she said.

"I kissed his dead eyes. He was cold as this room."

Alice leaned forward smiling, threw bark on the fire. "We've warmed this room."

43

WHEN they got back to Alice's the next day at two, she offered him lunch; but he said Ann would be expecting him in Richmond and soon drove on. Ann was at her mother's though and would not be in till six. He could stop at Polly's now and clear one more obligation from his list; but before he'd gone a mile, he felt strong need for a lonely stretch—when in the last two weeks had he had a solitary hour, awake and thinking? He stopped in the road and consulted his map. Jamestown was less than an hour away; he could go there and still meet Ann by dark. So for thirty miles he sped through the fields of the James's south bank, then waited at Scotland for the slow old ferry (he'd forgot its slowness).

It was nearly four when he parked at the gates, but the sun was still clear, and the air was only cool. The couple whom Rob had remembered were gone with all their factory-made junk; and the boy who took his money and gave him a pamphlet was plainly an Indian, sealed in calm and saying nothing but "I close up at five."

He skipped the museum, knowing the story; hurried past the recent reconstruction of the first huts (quaint as a Disney elf-village and more vulnerable), and settled at the base of the Pocahontas statue to watch the broad river. He was mostly alone. No more than a half-dozen others poked past, snapped pictures, and vanished. Only one of them spoke.

An old woman came up, studied the statue, then said "You a native?"

He laughed. "Of here?—no ma'm, a paying guest. Do I look that wild?"

She nodded. "Your eyes. You look like you're daring somebody to land."

"Maybe so. I'm tired."

"Well, I'm leaving." She smiled and turned away.

"—Not for me. Take your time. I can rest anywhere."

So she came back and, sighting quickly, took his picture—bronze moccasins above his thick hair. "If it comes out I'll send you a copy," she said but went without asking his name or address.

That left him entirely alone, first time since Rome—the Risen Christ, the Pantheon. He looked from the river to the fading sky, the apex. Now he was the eye, no perfect architect's lens to guide him. He sat a long moment, staring up, to ask the same question—*Show me now*. But he couldn't ask it here. He'd been answered clearly two weeks before in the center of the pavement of Hadrian's temple—*Head home, say an adequate farewell to your father, assume his strength*. He'd obeyed without question, fulfilled the first two; the third would take years. But he'd bent to the task.

His eyes came down on the far brown bank of the James, shadowed now; and his hand reached back to touch the bronze foot. He thought of Pocahontas, her last days in England, her sudden encounter with the man she'd believed dead for nearly eight years—John Smith in her room again, a blond smiling guest. Smith had written, "She turned about, obscured her face, as not seeming well-contented; and in that humor, with divers others, we all left her two or three hours, repenting myself to have writ she could speak English." But then she'd recovered and called Smith "Father." When he'd laughed off the name, she'd insisted gravely, "Were you not afraid to come into my father's country and caused fear in him and all his people (but me) and fear you here I should call you 'Father'? I tell you then I will, and you shall call me 'Child,' and so I will be forever and ever your countryman." She'd died weeks later, bound back here to live with her husband and son.

He knew Rob's absence fully for the first time—the site on the earth round which he'd turned, the single point on which he'd described his own lean figures, father and goal. Could there be another now? Everything his eyes saw, the cold stone behind him, said a firm silent No.

But he stood and found his way on to Richmond.

44

THERE was no car in Ann's drive, no lights at the front, no answer to his knock. He'd got here before her, and his key was in Oxford at the back of a drawer. Too cold to wait long. He could go on to Polly's; but he didn't want that meeting now, after Alice and the hour in Jamestown. He sat on the stoop—he'd wait till he froze, then drive awhile. In another two minutes he was shuddering and no sign of Ann; he'd trot to the corner. The door cracked behind him.

"Was that you, Hutch?"—a strange woman's voice.

"It was. He's frozen now." He stood and turned—a dim white face—and remembered the roommate.

"I'm Linda, Linda Tripp. I'm cooking in the back. Ann should be here soon. Come on in and thaw."

"That may take a Saint Bernard with brandy."

She nodded. "I've got one."

The brandy was beer and its owner was her friend Bailey Ferguson, seated in kitchen glare. He was maybe a year or two older than Hutch, a little younger than Linda; and when Linda said, "Bailey, this is Ann's Hutch," he stayed in his seat but offered a large hand and said "Linda's Bailey"; then made a sour face that ended in a grin. He stood—well over six feet—brought a can of beer, opened it carefully, and set it near his own. "Hutch's beer," he said.

Linda said, "Behave. I'm slaving for us all. This is meant to be good. Watch in silence and respect."

The two men obeyed awhile—drank and watched her back, a strong narrow back. Then Bailey said, "You the author from England?"

Hutch laughed. "No the fool from Fontaine, N.C."

That silenced him briefly and Linda turned. "We're all very sorry about your dad."

Hutch smiled. "I was sorry to break Ann's trip."

"She wouldn't have had it any other way," Linda said. She was stirring a deep pot that smelled like turnips.

Bailey said, "I saw it in the Navy—Spain, Greece, north Africa. It's all the same hole, just different colored rats."

Hutch said, "You didn't enjoy your stint?"

Bailey knew at once. "I enjoyed hell out of it, barely shut an eye. No I just said, 'God save the world from most people east of Hatteras.' "

Hutch agreed. "—And west."

Linda said, "I hope Ann warned you I was cooking."

Hutch said, "No but I've had some dangerous meals. I try to be brave."

She actually flushed but laughed. "Well, help! I'm a *famous* cook. I meant I hope you're starved."

Hutch nodded, mouth open.

Bailey said, "Poets starve a lot. Give him small helpings."

Hutch faced him. "I thought you were long since dead."

Bailey paused, then brought his chair down from its tilt. With both hands he thrust back long coarse hair, black as his eyes. "That your latest poem?"

Hutch shook his head. "Ann said you'd been electrocuted."

Bailey waited, then stood in place, and pulled his shirt up to the tight dark nipples.

Linda said, "Stop showing that thing. I hate it."

"You don't," Bailey said but he only watched Hutch.

Hutch's eyes traced the burn—white and satiny—the length of chest and belly to the navel, the trouser waist. "Does it go to the ground?"

Linda laughed but had still not turned from the stove.

Hutch saw she was prettier than Ann had implied, a wide country face with immense blue eyes.

Bailey said, "It knew where to stop, took pity on Linda." With a finger he stroked its trail to his belt and reached beneath. He looked back to Linda.

She said, "I can show *you* pity, Big Boy. Let me sprinkle this Drano on your pork chops, you'll be out of your misery in a New York jiffy."

Bailey nodded. "Go to it. You'd be out of a life."

Linda said, "Stuck-up. There're more where you came from."

"Wrong. I'm my mama's only boy, custom-made."

"—In the world, I meant."

Bailey looked down to Hutch. "Tell her how wrong she is." He lowered his shirt.

Hutch smiled. "She's not."

Bailey said "Pig shit."

Linda said, "That's *his* latest poem, Hutch—applaud."

Hutch laughed, really happy for the first time in days—plumb at the center of what seemed the world. But he didn't applaud; he put out a flat hand and pressed Bailey's chest, the height of the burn. "We're glad you were spared."

"Speak for *you*," Linda said. She had turned now, grinning.

Bailey said "He is" and leaned into the hand.

For a moment Ann watched them from the door, not speaking. Then she said, "I'm here; let the revel begin."

45

IN the time since Rome, he'd forgot her body—his eye could hold any other sight for years but not the bare bodies he'd wanted or loved, their lines and shades—so he'd left the dim lamp on and moved in its glow to restore a memory as good as any. Ann had joined him naked; and in the warm air, he'd thrown back the covers. For the first slow minutes, she took his greetings like a courteous child, formally grateful—kisses, cool hands, no audible words. Then he pressed her gently to her back, stroked her whole length with one light hand; then lowered his own length slowly above her—lips on hers, the dry insteps of his feet precisely against her soles, his palms on her flanks. He lay there still for another long minute, trusting she'd warm now and give a sign of welcome. Her head turned left away from the lamp. His chin brushed her ear.

She said, "I am one tired girl tonight."

"Of what?"

"—My mother, three days of her woes. The drive back here. Three hours of Bailey."

"I thought you liked Bailey."

"I used to," she said.

"Want to say why you stopped?"

She waited, shook her head.

"He never tried to harm you?"

"Oh no." She faced him, their eyes all but touching. "Is this *harm*, you think?" Her hands brushed his back, clamped in at the rise of his butt, and stayed there.

"Yes ma'm, in the wrong hands."

"Who says '*right*'?"

"Ma'm?"

"Who gets to choose which hands are right?" she said.

Hutch raised on one arm above her and touched her forehead. "The inmost mind." He rolled his eyes wildly.

Ann didn't smile but nodded.

He saw it as a welcome and again worked slowly down her body, crown to foot, with his lips this time—returning to her dry fork, persisting there with his famished tongue till he'd opened her and freed her odor, fuel in the room. Then he moved up to meet her eyes and take their permission to enter her deeply; but her hands held him down, and her eyes were shut. Baffled and urgent, he waited; then said "Too tired?"

Her head shook No; both hands dug once at the crest of his spine. So he chose to obey. Not pausing to guess at the strangeness, he crouched between her knees and bent to continue the licking service she now required—was it punishment, thanks, or adoration? Quick sights of her shut face gave him no clue. Or gave all clues—she seemed both to suffer and accept boundless praise. It lasted a long time (the shapes they made, the new clear language of yip and moan); and near the end when he tasted her climb toward the quick long glide, he finally set his own hand on himself and fiercely stroked out a parallel leap.

Separate on their backs, they calmed in silence. All Hutch's questions survived unanswered—what had she asked for? what had he given? what had she got?—but he knew not to ask and was half-asleep when Linda's door opened and firm steps passed in the hall.

Ann said "Bailey's gone" and turned out the light.

Hutch said, "He won't be here in the morning?"

"He's never slept here, just hovers and goes."

"That why you don't like him?"

She sat to retrieve the covers, spread them neatly; then lay on her side, facing Hutch.

"All well?" He touched her throat.

She seemed to nod.

But as he felt upward to close her eyes, he found tears—the first he'd known her to shed. "Anything I can help?"

She shook her head.

"Anything I should know?"

"Just sleep now please."

"Yes ma'm. Good night."

She slowly lay flat, a handspan away.

He thought he would thank her—she hadn't thanked him—but he sank straight to sleep.

And Ann followed soon, herself not knowing the one vital thing. Beneath her slack fingers their child grew constantly, still a circular disc in its sac of yolk but safe now and avid.

46

POLLY led him down the hall toward her sewing room (the room where she and his great-grandfather had slept when she came here fifty-three years ago). As they passed the sepia pictures of Rome, she waved without looking. "*Please* take these with you. I know them by heart."

Hutch said "When I'm back."

She stopped at the shut door and met his eyes. "You're back now or are my eyes gone at last?" Then she entered, slid the oak rocker into sunlight, and pointed him toward it. Her own straight chair was backed to the window; she took up a pile of white lace and sat.

"If you're making lace your eyes are fine."

Polly smiled. "It was made in Japan, I believe. I'm sewing on six million seed-pearls and sequins so some girl's mother can tack it to her wedding gown and claim full credit." She found a needle and threaded it in one thrust.

"Just swallow your pride," Hutch said.

She swallowed hard and speared up a row of opal sequins from a saucer.

"Excuse me."

"For what?" She didn't look up.

"I didn't mean to sound like a wise old man."

"You don't," she said. "I can swallow on my own--swallowed so hard last week, my throat's sore."

"How was that?"

"You know."

"Rob's funeral? Grandmother?"

Polly took four stitches, straight, without glasses (she'd never worn glasses). Then she nodded. "We very nearly liked each other."

"Grandmother liked you."

"Did she say that much?"

Hutch said, "Not in words but I noticed."

"There were quite a few words. The night of Rob's funeral, when you all had left and Ann was asleep, she and I sat on in the front room and talked. I'd started upstairs; she asked me to stay. I could see she was

wide awake; I knew *I* was—it's the only big blessing in old age, Hutch:
you never get tired." Polly looked up and offered the gradual smile that
had been her most useful gift to friends. Then she speared up ten of the
pearls, mere grains.

"Should I know what was said?"

Polly smiled again, downward. "It was not about you."

"Hallelujah, amen."

"She told me her life, just three or four sentences, and asked me
mine. Mine took a lot longer!"

"The Kendals were all good *arrows*," Hutch said, "—flew straight to
the mark."

Polly nodded and touched her chest with the needle-hand. "I volunteered. I've mostly been the mark."

"It's made you strong."

She thought that out. "Who wants to be strong?"

"Everybody."

"Not me." She shook her head twice, then shrugged in apology.
"Maybe I'm peculiar, some ugly exception. I wanted to live in a warm
cage, tended."

"You never had that?"

"Ten minutes here and there through the years, no more."

"You told that to Grandmother? That's been your life?"

She faced him again, gravely now. "You didn't know that? Rob never
told you that?"

"He told me what I asked. I didn't ask much."

"Tell *me*," Polly said. "Tell me all you know."

"You came here to help my great-grandfather when he was old. You
stayed on when he died, and my grandfather moved here after Eva left
and stayed till *he* died."

"Was that two sentences or three?" she said.

"Two, I believe."

"And you plan to be an author? Won't you need more skin for the
bones than that?"

Hutch laughed. "Yes ma'm, but the skin was what stumped us. Rob
hoped they loved you; he never knew for sure."

"That made two of us"—she was working again. "And Miss Polly
Drewry is the only one left. I still don't know. I sit here and tell myself
the story, hours on end."

"The one you told Grandmother?"

"Longer than that but similar, yes."

Hutch said, "I'm in no hurry at all."

"Sure you are. England's begging you back."

"In four days, four whole days till I leave."

Polly laughed. "It's lasted nearly threescore-and-ten and hasn't ended yet—unless I'm dead and don't know it."

Hutch rose, leaned toward her, and found her pulse. He counted ten strong beats and sat again. "You'll outlast me."

She waited, then said "I truly hope not," then folded the lace.

"Don't ever say that."

She nodded. "I do. I'm meant to be a lesson; you're the last pupil left."

"—And willing," Hutch said.

"I started like you. My own mother died at the time I was born, which wasn't as rare back then as now—Lord no, dead mothers were common as sacks of drowned kittens. So I took that in stride and grew up in Washington beside my dad, who was cracked as a bell but nicer to hear. He'd been in the war as a boy (losing side) and had set up this wondrous Confederate museum, three rooms of wild junk that people paid to watch. You'd have loved it—knives, sabres, a whole box of hair from Rebel boys killed before they were grown, a stuffed dog that walked through the battle of Antietam and was still grinning wide when it died years later. I sold tickets to it and dusted at night and cooked our meals. I thought I was safe. I *was* in a cage. What hadn't dawned on me was, I was the show or a big part of it—for adult men. I was filling out fast. If I had any pictures, I think I could prove I'm telling plain facts not blowing my horn. My eyes and skin were frequently mentioned; I learned to say 'Thank you' and look occupied. I thought I *was*, thought I'd work there for life. The word *unhappiness* had not been invented then. People sat and bore their lives or jumped down the well or left for Oklahoma. Well, to my big surprise—and Dad's, you can guess—I left for Oklahoma. This room, to be exact, but it might as well have been the Sandwich Islands for newness."

"You met old Rob?"

Polly nodded. "Met him, sold him a ticket, heard him start a blood-hemorrhage in the first room of junk—he was full of T.B.—helped him calm down and rest, and accepted his offer: all in one afternoon."

"The offer was what?"

"Come here and share his life."

"You could see he was dying. But you said you wanted safety."

She smiled. "I did. I wanted him too."

"He was older?"

"Much older. Women don't mind that—I didn't. I never really asked other women."

"Is that called love?" Hutch said, "—wanting both: him dying and safety?"

"I seldom say *love* and never tried to name whatever I felt. I guess I figured it would name itself in time."

"And it didn't?" Hutch said.

Polly thought and laughed once. "*Waiting*," she said.

"Ma'm?"

"At your Rob's funeral in that cold sun, I realized the name of what I had was *Waiting*. I waited through nearly a year of old Rob, helping him the best I could. Then his son came—Forrest, when Eva'd left him—and I waited through forty years in this house with him."

"For what? Do you know now?"

"I always did. You said it just now—dying and safety. To protect *and* protection. It's a rare wish maybe, but my mother still wants it."

Hutch said "Where?"

"In my dreams, one dream at least the other night. I've gone long months, maybe years without her—never thinking her name, which was Lillian Drewry. But the night of Rob's funeral (young Rob, your Rob) after your grandmother and I finished talking, I dreamt a whole sensible dream about her. I used to have odd dreams when I was much younger, tracking my mother down through strange awful towns and finding her old or poor or blind, never recognizing me. But that one night at Mrs. Mayfield's, I dreamt she was not much older than me (she wasn't—seventeen the month she died); and we had a smaller house than this with a lot of shade and good friendly noise in the street. We never left that but tended each other in neat succession. Just plain daily care but easy and quiet like a good balanced wheel—spokes in a wheel, just meeting at the hub. I woke up knowing how much I missed her, how much we could do for each other now we're old. My dad always said she could make a snake grin." Polly turned back to face the clean window and laughed. "I sit here waiting for everyone that's gone." She faced Hutch, her eyes bright as when she'd first come here. "They're *gone*. Don't let anybody say they're not." Then she took up the band of lace, rolled it out quickly, draped it round her neck, and stood in place. "They never sent a word back to me anyhow, and I've been quiet enough to hear if they spoke. Let's eat this sweet-potato pie I made." She walked past Hutch and toward the door.

"Won't you ruin your lace?"

Garlanded with all its pearls, Polly turned. "If I do I'll pay."

Hutch said "Is that the lesson?"

"Sir?"

"You said I was the pupil."

She considered that a moment but beckoned with her head. "Eat the pie. I can really make pie." She moved again to go.

He said, "Would you come down and live in Rob's house?"

If she heard she didn't stop.

47

HUTCH entered Eva's door and walked through the front room, hall, and dining room with no one in sight. In the kitchen Sylvie stood at the window, back to him, and seemed not to hear—studying the warm noon in progress outside, sudden midwinter spring. The stove cooked beside her obediently. He came up behind her, not trying for stealth; but she didn't look round. So he stopped near enough to lay his hands on her shoulders—stout and firm, though she'd somehow shrunk.

Sylvie still didn't turn.

He kneaded twice. Then he said, "Who you cooking this great spread for?" (it was his farewell lunch; he'd leave tomorrow).

She waited. "Miss Eva. Miss Eva that pays me. I'm keeping her live."

Hutch said, "She's gone. Nowhere to be found."

Sylvie put out her own arm and touched the window, tapped one spot. "I can find her," she said. "I always could. Even when she left here, I knew where she went."

Hutch looked. Back beyond Grainger's house in full sun, his grandmother sat—not reading or working but facing out. The face was in profile, the eyes seemed open, she seemed to look north—the way she'd gone when she left here, a girl, with Hutch's grandfather and the way she'd retraced when she came back single with Rob in her arms: journeys she'd never mentioned to Hutch. He still held Sylvie. "Was she sorry?"

"For what?"

"Coming home so soon, not leaving again."

Sylvie waited, then sank an inch—out of his hands—and stirred at a pan. "You want Miss Eva's secrets, ask Miss Eva." She wouldn't meet his eyes.

"How long till we eat?"

"Twenty minutes, *I'll* be done. You can eat then or not."

"You mad?"

"Always mad."

"Big sin," Hutch said.

She looked round at last, black and solemn as a gorge. "Everybody I used to like is frying in Hell now. I hope to join em."

Hutch laughed—"Happy landing!"—and went toward Eva.

48

"You warm enough?" he said (she wore a light cardigan).

"Yes thank you, most always." Eva gathered to stand.

"Let's sit awhile. Sylvie says she needs twenty minutes."

"That means forty-five."

Hutch squatted, felt the ground—cool but dry—and sat. He flicked her right shoe, a trail in its dust. "What you watching?" There were starlings in a bare oak beyond her, conversing.

"I hope to see England, see what weather you'll have." She looked down smiling at the shoe.

"Wrong way—north*east*." He pointed to England.

Eva followed his hand. "Cold rain." Then she faced him. "Stay here."

Hutch grinned. "We need rain."

"Stay here." She touched his hair. In all his life she'd never begged before; in all her life—no, her father's death: she'd begged him to wait.

He answered her stroking hand with nudges—strong unpredictable thrusts like a horse fed one good morsel—but he said, "You'll be all right and I'll be back."

"When?" She reclaimed her hand and spread it in the light.

"When I'm a certified academic wage-earner of the second class."

"You won't need a job."

Hutch laughed. "I beg to differ. I've spent two weeks—remember?—adding Rob's slim assets. If I really get the full death-benefit from his school insurance and pay his few bills and give Min something, I'll have very little over three thousand dollars. That'll cover these two unexpected plane tickets, some petty cash for Strawson in case of house repairs, and maybe one more eye-opener for me—Florence or Athens."

Eva said, "You'll have every penny of mine."

She had no share in Rob's estate; she had to mean her own solid holdings. He couldn't say "When?"—she sat here, strong and welcome in her place—so he laughed. "When I'm ninety! They'll come up to me in the Old Gents' Home, hand me this check on a silver tray, and I'll be far too feeble to endorse it."

Eva waited, then joined him (his favorite laugh, any laugh of hers). Then she said, "Trains leave when the platform's empty."

"You diesel or steam?"

A broad smile survived. "Oh *steam*," she said, "—big tanks of white steam."

Hutch said "All aboard!", then regretted his rough cheer.

Sylvie said, "Anybody want to eat, wash they hands." On the bright kitchen stoop, she was glossy as the starlings.

Eva whispered, "Please give her five dollars when you go. She's run this whole thing."

Hutch nodded but said "I did my own part."

49

THE warmth had survived into late afternoon. Hutch had driven back to Rob's house, packed for the trip, and was at Rob's desk writing memos for Strawson (how to keep the place alive) when he heard a car take the last turn of the drive and stop in the yard. He got to the door in time to see Straw unfold himself and stand by the car doing regulation knee-bends and limber toe-touches to start his blood. He hadn't seen Hutch. As he leaned to the back seat to find his small luggage, Hutch said, "How much would you pay a strong redcap?"

Straw looked and waved. "Not one plugged cent. I never bring more than I can tote in one hand."

"Why's that?"

"Got to have one hand free to fight."

Hutch said, "You're in fairly peaceful country here."

Straw said "Maybe so" and when he came forward, both hands were loaded—an old suitcase and a double-barreled shotgun that looked antique.

"You rob a museum?"

Straw came to the foot of the steps; then extended the gun, barrel-first.

Hutch took it, pulled it to him, sighted past the boy's head toward the low sun, and pulled one trigger—harmless click. "Welcome back," he said. He lowered the weight, examined the mellow walnut stock. "Plan to forage for food?"

"Yes sir, squirrel stew—make me quick and trusty."

Hutch laughed. "I never thought of squirrels as trusty."

"Yes sir," Straw said and took the first step. "You can trust them to thrive and multiply."

Hutch said, "I asked for just *one* caretaker."

"You got him," Straw said and moved toward the door. "—one nineteen-year-old former alcoholic who could guard you if you stayed."

Hutch said, "But I'm leaving at six in the morning."

With his hand on the door, Straw said, "You go. I won't tell a soul."

"Tell what?"

"—You're a fool." Then he entered, confident the place would receive him.

*   *   *

An hour later it plainly had. Hutch had shown him to his room, Rob's old room. They'd drunk hot coffee and then Straw had asked to be shown the bounds of the land itself, his hunting preserve. So they walked out at four into slant yellow light and cooling air. Hutch loped ahead, hands empty at his sides; Straw came behind with the loaded gun. They skirted the graves (Hutch had finished there this morning); then crossed a brief thicket and entered the fields, plowed into one broad fallow whorl. On the far edge as woods began, Straw said "Wait." They'd been silent till then. "This is all tobacco?"

"It will be in April."

"And you still claim you're poor?"

Hutch laughed and turned out both empty pockets of the khaki trousers. "I explained that before—you pay overhead on a colored tenant-family, buy seed and supplies, give the tenant his share of eight strict acres of a crop as delicate as Japanese dancers, you'll be so poor you'll beg God for handouts."

"He gives them," Straw said. He nodded toward the trees.

Hutch looked—the deep acres of hardwood and pine. "I'd rather sell slaves than trees, these trees."

Straw waited. "Can I work with your tenant this spring?"

"I told him you were coming. He'll be by to see you. You ask him yourself if you last till spring."

"I'll last," Straw said.

"On what?"

"Sir?"

"On what? I promised you'd be lonesome."

Straw smiled and tapped his forehead with his free hand. "My mind's a stag movie, cast of thousands, never stops." He brought the gun slowly to his shoulder, aimed, fired. A gray squirrel fell from a tall straight poplar. The echo slapped round them in punishing rings.

Hutch said, "That was mine. You didn't need that." Then he entered the woods.

They walked twenty minutes in Indian file—Hutch leading, both silent. At first they advanced in easy space. The hardwoods were old with thick bare boles and undergrowth was sparse, so the light still reached their faces and chests. Then pines began, with dogwoods and cedars; and the soft dry ground was tangled with scrub. They moved darker there in a green glow, wiping limbs from their eyes and digging their heels in against the downgrade that rushed them on toward the crooked west boundary, the rocky creek. Its far bank was cleared, a field of cornstalks belonging to neighbors; so the sunset was visible across the low stream. Hutch went to a big rock and sat. Straw went to the midst of the water, not pausing, on a fallen willow. They both watched the sun long enough to see movement. Then Hutch said, "I guess I'm a little uneasy."

Straw carefully turned; the gun was his balance. "Over me?"

Hutch nodded. "Come sit down a minute."

Straw came to a separate rock and sat, facing out like Hutch. "Ready," he said.

"For what?"

"Bad news."

Hutch laughed. "Not bad, not yet anyhow." He bent for a handful of washed gravel.

"You're scared I'll burn the place down and run."

Hutch laughed again but waited awhile. "That's more or less the first part."

"The second?"

"—That you won't, that you'll be here in a clean painted house when I return."

Straw said, "I may be. I hope that's more likely than me harming anything." He faced Hutch's profile; Hutch didn't meet the turn. "I'll stand up and walk out of here this minute and grab my duds and be back at my parents' in time for their sleeping pills—just tell me 'Go.' "

Hutch still watched the sun. He wanted to say it—"Thanks. Now go."

But Straw said "Look here. Remember this."

There was nothing to see but the boy's own face, changing from child to man each instant at a rate no slower than the sun's descent but surely as permanent as any other living thing visible and offered. Hutch watched it five seconds, still meaning to say some grateful dismissal.

But a sound arrived from far behind them, long high notes like an animal wail.

Straw said "That a bull?"

Hutch shook his head. "Rob's fox horn. Grainger's calling us in. He's come out to cook us a farewell feast."

Straw said, "I was hoping for something like that."

They stood simultaneously and retraced their steps. At the edge of the fields, Straw claimed his squirrel—cold now and locked in the shape of its fall, only one streak of blood.

50

NEAR dawn Hutch dreamt the last dream of the night. He was in a dark house and at first seemed alone. But as he felt a path from room to room, he began to know there was someone else; that the other was behind him at varying distances but following. He moved on steadily by groping out

objects like milestones or gates—the corners of tables, railings of stairs—
and at times he was far ahead in wide empty rooms (his outstretched arms
touching nothing as he went). But then he'd enter passages with walls
at his ears; and there on his neck he'd feel slow breaths from whatever
pursued him, occasional clicks as it swallowed or gaped. He never was
frightened; and he wondered at that, thinking as he dreamt "This is meant
as a nightmare. Why am I calm?" But he didn't turn and stop, never
felt for the lamps that were surely on the frequent tables he passed. He
moved through all the last hours of darkness, forward (to him the path
seemed forward). Then windows began to appear, faint light. He seemed
clear again, no sound behind him; and by the time day had confirmed
itself, he'd come to the last room—an ordinary kitchen. There was no
door onward. He stood, looking out at an endless bare field, and thought
he was no longer safe but trapped. So he went cold with fear and wanted
to hide. There was only a table in the midst of the room—long and broad,
dark wood. He crawled beneath that and condensed his body to its smallest
size, still an awkward mass. Then he waited, trying hard to silence irregular
noises—blood and breath. When he'd finally succeeded and was quiet as
the air, he heard steps coming and faced the entrance. What entered
slowly was a human child, nothing strange or strong. At first it didn't see
him and circled the room, also touching walls and corners as though still
blind. He knew it was his, that he'd seen it before as it hung in Ann. He
thought he would speak any moment to claim it, and he searched for
words. But by then it had stopped at the sink and seen him. It extended
a hand in the clean early light, no longer translucent but firm and free.
On numb cramped legs he began to move toward it. Though the room
enlarged, the child waited in place.

He woke in his room, listening for any move that might have waked
him—only occasional natural creaks. Strawson was thirty feet away in
Rob's room, Grainger downstairs on the dining-room couch. He felt on
the table by his bed for the flashlight—ten till four. He could sleep forty
minutes; he tried to take it. But his body seemed rested, his mind stayed
clear; so he lay and recalled as much of the dream as survived. Just the
movement—the strange calm chase through a house that must have been
this house (he remembered the feel of objects in the dark, familiar local
objects). The end—his discovery on the floor by the child, their silent
greeting—had gone or sunk.

The calm continued. He felt no trace of the parting uncertainty he'd
felt in May as he woke in New York, no sense that anything here required
him more than his postponed work in England. He composed himself flat
in the covers—face up, eyes open toward a ceiling that might have been
sky for all its tangibility—and again said the prayer he'd said since childhood before any trip: the names of his kin and his few urgent friends,
that they'd stay safe in places they chose till he saw them. As he reached

Grainger's name, he heard Grainger stand beneath him downstairs and move toward the toilet, beginning the day. After that there was only *Ann* to say. He said it aloud and rolled to his left side, touching his lips to the cold spare pillow.

51

THEY were twenty minutes from the Raleigh airport with time to spare when Grainger said, "I found out Gracie died too. I didn't tell you that."

They'd said very little but ridden quietly as sun rose reluctant through a mist from the warm night. So Hutch took a moment to think through the sentence—Gracie, Grainger's long-gone wife; he'd never seen her. "I'm sorry. Where was she?"

"Richmond, her cousin's where she'd been since the war."

"Was she sick long?"

"Twenty years. She drank poison wine."

They'd both watched the road through that. Then Hutch faced Grainger. "You see her at the end?"

Grainger was driving; he never glanced over. But he smiled. "I saw her at the end of me."

"When was that?"

"When she left me the last time for good."

Hutch said, "You've done all right, I think."

Grainger said, "I been thinking you're wrong a lot lately." He renewed his smile.

"Want to tell me how? I moved Rob's grave."

Grainger said, "Don't mind me. You know your business."

"Is it Strawson?—you worried about him in the house?"

"Not a bit. Far as I know, he's got good sense."

"Is it me leaving Grandmother?"

Grainger laughed. "If any three other human beings alive were strong as Miss Eva, the world couldn't take it."

Hutch nodded and thought they could leave it at that.

But Grainger said, "I may be leaving soon myself."

"To where?"

"I still got my little piece of house in Virginia, got nieces in Maine."

"What would you do in Maine? You've been warm too long."

"I'd get on the Welfare and rest my tail far as I can go north of this integration mess."

"It won't touch you," Hutch said, "—any place."

Grainger waited. "Too true. Too late to touch me."

"And you haven't got any friends in Virginia."

He faced Hutch quickly—"No friends above ground"—then looked to the road.

"Where does that put me?"

Grainger said, "You're putting yourself; *you* say."

Hutch smiled unseen. "That's the thing I can't do."

"But you're leaving here."

Heard in Grainger's voice, as calm as "Morning," it seemed the decision made and acknowledged. For the length of a mile, Hutch tried to test it against the pine woods that flanked the road, the persistent light that was now winning through and drying the ground. He could see their strong ordinary beauty—had seen it all his life—but they drew at him no more powerfully now than the round Cornish fields, the melting ochre of Roman walls, or the cold heat of Oxford's decay. He turned to Grainger and said, "Nobody will mind for long."

Grainger nodded—"Maybe not"—and seemed to be finished; but once they had both seen the white hut of the airport, he said "Nobody else'll *die* at least."

Hutch had not really known how he'd waited for that, the actual blame. Min's harshness had been easy enough to bear, the fumes from her years of deprivation. But could he accept this verdict from Grainger, who'd shown Rob devotion that was either pure love (unaltered by time) or a force undescribed in the world till now? He said "Thank God."

Grainger laughed. "Thank us. Thank the tough ones, Hutch." Not looking, he put out his wide right hand and blocked Hutch's sight, barely touching the nose. It held there an instant, then returned to the wheel.

When Hutch could see again, he saw clearer light—the air of the landing field swept by engines. He said "Thank you all" and felt its weight as a farewell from which he could hardly return.

52

January 13, 1956

Dear Ann,

I tried hard to spot your chimney as I flew over Richmond two hours ago, but we moved too fast, and you'd already left for work. So the day's one successful accomplishment to now is landing in New York in driving snow and waiting again. I'm at Idlewild with an hour to go till we breast the storm—if we breast it at all—and am stuck in a lounge with a congregation of British nurses bound back from a tour of our native hospitals and still aghast from exposure to U.S. postwar medicine in full bloodless cry. I'd introduce myself and agree if I didn't think they'd all terminate in midAtlantic—each one at this minute is smoking six cigarettes (*bargain Yank tobacco*)—and leave me friendless.

Maybe that's the other accomplishment today—feeling thoroughly alone, half in England already. The past week has been my second orgy of goodbyes in nine months, and I feel fairly sapped. But also light. I've never felt lighter on my feet in my life. When I shook Grainger's hand in Raleigh just now and walked toward the plane, I knew some hobble was gone from my feet. Or not even a hobble but a band of flesh that had joined my ankles like the Siamese twins, joined me to the ground. I suppose it was Rob. And Rob is removed.

I don't say it flippantly—you understand that—but I sit here now in this dismal lobby where no one has names or precedents or futures and feel vast relief. I loved him all my life and for nearly half of his. I did what I wanted and had to do when I knew he was ill. We had a good parting, and I really think he left. Nothing in the house or the grave or the woods seems to warn that he's stayed, expecting me still. I don't expect him, however much I thank him; and I trust that can last.

What I do expect is you. I expect us together in a short while from now. We can sleep through the interim or maybe even meet in England in the fall. If I get any word that I'm rich on tobacco, I could bring you over and we could repair what I had to ruin in Rome (which is used to ruins). Would your job turn you loose for two or three weeks or does Commonwealth justice require your ceaseless presence?

I'll write again as soon as I've slept off the trip—all the trips (I'd have made a poor pilgrim). I thought you were still a little tired yourself. Let me know when you're rested.

> Thanks, thanks forever and love
> from Hutch

January 13, 1956

Dear Min,

I'm held up in New York by snow, hoping to leave for England any minute; but the wait gives me time to say what got neglected or swamped when we were there together at Rob's. I don't look back on those meetings with pride, not on my part of them. Whatever my best is, I wasn't at it then. I'd like to plead surprise and exhaustion but I can't. I should have been better prepared. Please forgive. I don't know that you and I will ever wind up again in such close quarters with such hard parts, but if so I hope to remind you more of Rob than Hutch—Rob in this last year, strong as he got.

What I didn't say was thank you, not a formal thanks on behalf of

Rob (*I'm sure he took care of that himself*) *but my own and real. The
thought of him enduring those final months without your presence is
terrible, and I honestly do not wish I'd shared the burden with you or
had it for myself. My hope now is that you've started to rest and that life
can be level soon again. But I wonder if we're cut much deeper than we
know, by a sharper blade?*

*Grandmother will be writing to you with something Rob wanted you
to have—she's executrix and will always be.*

*Yours tardily,
Hutch*

January 13, 1956

Dear Grainger,

*I got as far as New York in one piece, then snow set in. Can't leave
till it stops, which may be April. Why didn't you tell me it was Friday
the thirteenth? Drop by if you head to Maine before spring and see if
I'm here. Otherwise I'll count on seeing you back at the old stand there
in eighteen months. Till when, and beyond, I won't forget your help. It
meant most of all to me, especially this morning.*

*Ever,
Hutch*

*Dear Rob, I napped twenty minutes just now,
Upright in my vinyl Iron Maiden in a
New York airport blanked by snow
And dreamt you'd made your way underground
From home to here and were butting with what
Was left of your head on the green terrazzo
Like Hamlet Senior ("canst work in the earth
So fast, old mole in the cellarage"?) or Lycidas
Washed to the Hebrides, scouring "the bottom
Of the monstrous world," except that you'd dug
Every inch of your own way with still-sprouting
Nails through mantling rock and that I on
The outer rim of South Queens am stalled
In as monstrous a world as yours
With its dormant grubs and older dead
(Though I grant your last mile, till you nosed out
My shoes, was hardest—the Mafia graves
Of Brooklyn). But the butting was all—
No questions, no orders, just thuds at what*

I recall as the rate of your living heart
When calm.
        So—awake, sentenced to hours
Here before any chance of taking the air,
And trusting you won't breaststroke the Atlantic—
May I now do the talking, the facts and questions
I couldn't advance in the face of your dying
Which lasted the length of my life till now?
(I never believed you meant to stay,
That you wouldn't leave at the sight of one
False move by me. Since no rules were posted,
Which moves were true?)
        I was mostly a child.
Did you ever see that? Through the years
When you came to me for what the Mother
Goddess herself would have been strapped
To furnish—bedrock beneath you, daily
Reward—I was technically a child: technically and
Really. And though I noticed it as seldom as
You, those treks in which I bore your weight
(A widowered semi-reformed alcoholic
With the density of pitchblende) packed me down—
A dwarf in the mines, a huddled porter
When what my bones requested was height,
The usual chance to rise in makeshift
Scaffolding toward the general view—a life
Of my own.
        Don't misunderstand. I welcomed
The job, steady child-labor
In the good old Depression
When others my age could barely feed
Their hookworms. Grumpy, Sneezy, Dopey,
Bashful, Happy, Sleepy, Doc
Never took deeper pride in a day with their picks
Than I in our years—you were healing, smiling
Occasionally; I accepted credit. But I wonder now.
Couldn't I have been offered the chance to volunteer
Or renege and join the Cub Scouts and
Prove my merit by looping knots of
Staggering complexity in plain hemp rope,
Not press-ganged at birth by a charm that had long
Since stripped the trees of birds and leaves
Throughout Carolina and the Valley of Virginia?
I assume your answer, now as then, would be

That is what you were for. *I assume it is what*
Most children are for, but I can't fail to notice
How many decline (and the sky doesn't fall)
Or to ask the next question.
                              What am I for now?
By your terms I seem to be finished, retired—
A twenty-five-year-old pensioner in appallingly
Good health. You left me no answer. All
Your awesome summary letter breathes
No hint, though some months ago you did
Throw a challenge that could last awhile—
Find the figure made by our family's path
(A hundred years of private parabolas,
Beelines, halts, scratched in blood
On the unavoidable public maze!)—
And your actual last words were "You choose."

I've chosen, had chosen before you spoke.
The choice is the answer—I will have your life,
The life you hunted but never caught.
It was not you and I in a house on a low
Hill, a dog, a manservant, your mother
At the moat, all other bridges raised. Whatever I
Planned as a lonely boy or you
As a dying man in that house, we were stopped
By two things—age and body. We were separate
Ages (you were bound to quit before me) but
Identical bodies. What we had was years
Of circling a spot, mules at a mill.
The figure was rings, concentric rings
Round an unseen center (what were we grinding?)
Till I fled and you quit.
                              Don't misunderstand.
We were first-rate mules;
I wouldn't have missed it. It was my war and peace,
My genuine blaze, while Europe and Asia
Burned out of reach. What I hope I learned
Is the single lesson of any war—
The properties of fire: life and death.

—Which lands me squat in my graybeard
Robes again (the boy-Diogenes, tubby
Wisdom), the son who winged you postal
Blessing when you asked for release.

Well, pardon, Rob. Pardon please
For what I gave prematurely or uselessly
Or never knew to give or flatly
Refused.
        What I have now to offer as recompense
Is memory—a file of memory, my childhood
Hobby, squirreled up in lieu of arrowheads
Or the stamps of Chile and Madagascar.
They aren't yet sorted for Best or Worst,
Improvement, Caution, Terror, Laughter.
I'll wait to sort till the final sight
(Your foaming extinction) has shrunk to size
And trust the shrinkage will come more quickly
On foreign ground—a reason to go.

One sight though insists, here now,
Its natural buoyancy sailing it past
More than once in the recent wakes and dreams.
So here in this frozen port, I watch
It again—nine months ago, you and I in
Warm Springs; the circular pool of fuming
Water (female essence of the heart of the
Ground) accepting your hard white limbs and
Head in farewell grip more total than
Any you'd known in air with prior
Partners (a region of willing girls, my
Famished mother). Seeing, I sink to
The depths in a mock-death (mystery! a sleep
And a change); then rise to your best gift
Again, the sight sustained—a man
Embraced by the killing earth, your potent
Grin as you warn "Remember."
        Here's proof
I have, this far at least—the burdened
Last patient American rock
Before the sea.

THREE

THE CENTER OF GRAVITY

FEBRUARY–MARCH 1956

Aꜰᴛᴇʀ two unbroken hours of driving in cold early dark, Ann crossed the state line. The crossing itself, where rough Virginia road met its well-kept Carolina extension, seemed a question solved. There was help in the world; the car had brought her toward it (refusing every chance to turn west toward her mother's). The first lighted town had a hotel sign in green neon—*Good Coffee Shop*—so she pulled in, calmer than she'd been since Richmond. But when she'd gone halfway across the frozen lawn, she was rushed by the fear that had followed her down. It filled her chest with the milk she'd drunk at noon, hot and cheesy. She stopped. This was crazy; any help was in Richmond or—pray God, not—at her mother's. She turned. She'd go back to Linda, ask Bailey to leave till she'd told her news.

A man had opened the door of her car and was scrounging in the back.

Ann said, "Can I help you? This is my car, sir."

"I know it"—an old head looked up, grinning. "I'm the night clerk— Winston. I was coming on duty and saw you get out. Thought I'd bring your bag for you." He set her small bag on the ground and stood. The inside light from the car showed a face as white as his hair.

Ann said, "I'm not staying here but thanks."

"Better had. We've got rooms that never seen a lady."

Ann laughed. "They'll have to wait awhile longer then. I just need coffee."

"Too late," Winston said. "Coffee closed down at seven." He stood by the bag as though she might change her mind.

She did; he'd forced her. "Is the pay phone closed?"

"That's open all hours and I'll make your change."

"I think I've got change."

He shrugged once. "You won't take assistance, will you?"

Ann said, "Oh I think so, eventually."

Winston smiled. "I'm seventy-two years old. I can't stand out on a freezing Friday night, making useless offers."

"Put my bag back please. That'll be a big favor." He obeyed so slowly that Ann almost thought she'd spend a night here and decide in his shadow, as good as any. But once he'd shut the door and headed toward her, she caught the old smell of his skin and teeth—sweet burnt stagnation. She'd make the call and head on to Raleigh, whatever.

Min answered the first ring loudly—"*Tharrington*"—to discourage a heavy breather who'd called the night before.

Ann deposited coins; then the line seemed dead. She said, "Miss Tharrington, it's Ann. Can you hear me?"

Min waited. "Very clearly. Ann who?"

"—Gatlin. I met you at Mr. Mayfield's funeral."

Another wait, longer. "Of course. Where are you?"

"Norlina, N.C. in a telephone booth."

Min said, "I've been there. It's got a good poem on the wall or it did. Look for it when you're through."

"Yes ma'm. I'm coming on to Raleigh right now. Could I see you this evening?"

Min said, "It'll take you two hours—ten o'clock." Her voice was plainly reluctant with fatigue. "What about tomorrow?"

Ann said "Well, I could"; then stopped and swallowed. "But I guess I'm asking hard to see you tonight."

"Bad news?"

"Not yet."

"From Hutchins?" Min said.

"Maybe so."

Min said, "Ann, I finished with Hutchins at the funeral."

"Yes ma'm, I understand."

"You can leave off the *ma'm*. I still walk unaided." The voice tried to laugh but was seized by coughing.

Ann said, "I am asking for me not Hutch." She had not said the name all week; it surprised her.

Min said, "Have you got a hotel or a friend?"

"Not yet."

"You have now, an old davenport at least. I'll be here beside it."

When Ann had thanked her and shut her purse to go, she remembered the poem and searched the booth. On a stained oak shelf, she could trace these lines—

Alexander Graham Bell, a word of
Thanks from Baxter Conway who spent
Eighty cents here in 1950 to insure
Eternal peace for himself and a friend.
All others forget. I will always recall.

2

Min said, "I guessed you were hungry. Was I right?" She had watched Ann eat three scrambled eggs, a sliver of cured ham, a slice of cold bread, a glass of milk.

Ann nodded. "Apparently. I didn't think so."

Min stood from the table, took the plate and glass; and went to the alcove, the rusty sink. "You want me to tell you what else I know now or wait till morning?"

In the forty-five minutes since arriving, Ann had made no mention of her news. "We could wait. It's past eleven."

Min said, "Maybe you could. I wouldn't sleep a wink." Her back was still turned to Ann—a slow job of washing.

Ann laughed. "You said you already knew."

"I meant I'd known Mayfields all my life, the men anyway. You're here about them."

"The young one at least."

"They don't come separate," Min said. "Deal with both. If you can't, walk away."

"Like you?"

Min waited. "I didn't, not away—just over to the sidelines, in sight."

Ann said, "Are you sorry?"

A longer wait while she polished the glass; then she stowed all she'd washed, came up behind Ann, and said, "We had better sit on easier chairs." They moved farther into the small living-room. Ann took the armchair. Min switched off the main light, leaving them dim enough to watch each other with a minimum of pain; then she sat on the davenport. "I'm sorry as hell several times every day—right after I wake up, just before I sleep, more in fall and winter than spring or summer. I'm a living barometer." She raised her right arm, stiffened it, then moved it down slowly like the needle of a gauge—her face clouding over.

Ann said "That's normal."

"The moody part is, sure. The rest is bad, being locked in alone here at my ripe age."

Ann said, "Don't you own the key?"

Min smiled. "I do. I use it all the time. But what they don't tell you
—there comes one minute, quiet as wool, when you open; and there's
nobody standing on the ledge or landing, nobody in the *streets*. Not for
you anyway."

"Then what?" Ann said.

"Then you've got two choices—learn to be a good nun or go nuts
fast, start eating your own dry hair and nails."

Ann said "What's a good nun?"

Min laughed. "I was reared Presbyterian so I speak from private
speculation only." She paused till she knew. "Oh a watchful well-wisher—
equal stress on both. The contemplative life."

"Are you one?"

Min knew at once. "Never. I grudge every *pony* that gets what I lack,
not to mention live humans."

"That what keeps you young?"

Min touched both her eyes. "Am I young?"

"Yes ma'm."

"Since Rob died I have felt—what?—every day: not younger but
lighter. It's far more relief than I guessed it would be, not to hope anymore. Not that I sat here, keeping vigil by my flame (I'd go weeks, months
with no thought of his face); but long as he lived, there were cells deep
in me (actual cells) that kept a blank watch without informing me—their
sole little duty: would he ever want me again? You may know by now that
of course he never did. He needed me though, once Hutchins skipped out.
The cells were ready." Her arm came up again, limber now, and waved
round slowly as if showing the walls.

Ann looked. There was no more than she'd seen when she entered—a
reproduced Winslow Homer of waves, the text of the North Carolina state-
song illuminated with pine bough and flag, a coltish Gainsborough girl in
pink. No sign of Rob Mayfield, picture or word. She said, "Will you stay
on here now?"

Min balked in puzzlement, then said "I live here." Then she grinned.
"Whatever others think, I truly *live* here. I'll live better now."

Ann nodded in collusion with the hope.

Min said, "You aren't here on the spur like this to glean the wisdom
of my harvest years."

Ann smiled. "Why not? I am, more or less."

Min said "You're pregnant, right?"

"Yes. Heard today; doctor phoned me at four." Ann sat still and
cold, holding her knees.

It was Min's eyes that filled. Her whole body shrank to its full age
silently. She picked at her skirt.

Ann said "How bad is that?"

Min shook her head, no answer.

But Ann said, "Please. How bad is the news?"

Min leaned forward suddenly and opened a new magazine on the table—a two-page picture of Mamie Eisenhower, all earbobs and bangs. Then she said "I guess it depends."

"On what?"

"Do you want it? Does Hutch?"

"Hutch has no idea."

Min smiled. "Hutch has no idea of a *lot*. You can call him from here."

Ann looked at her watch. "It's four in the morning over there. No phone in his room."

"They'll get him; say it's urgent."

Ann said, "I'm not sure it's his."

"What?"

"The child." Her hands had stayed on her knees. Now they came to her belly and pressed in lightly, first time since she'd known. She felt nothing more than her meal at work; yet for the first time, and for no clear reason, she felt what was true—that the child was Hutch's, that the will of those days in Rome had worked itself.

But Min said, "How many other candidates are there?"

"One—a lonesome boy in Rome after Hutch left me."

"Was he leaving you or just heading home?"

Ann said, "Both, I thought. I may have been wrong."

Min was struck full-face by a surge of indignation—that a possible continuance of Rob had been fouled, that this girl could come here uninvited and tell it as calmly as yesterday's weather. She wanted to stand now and send Ann out—how could she breathe through a whole long night in this hot cube of space (her own space for years) in sound of a stranger who'd fouled half her own hopes—more than half? But something held her tongue, and her legs locked her down. She spread her palms flat on Mrs. Eisenhower's face. Then she said, "Don't you have any feeling whose it is?"

Ann waited but could still say it straight at Min's eyes. "I'm very much afraid it's Hutch's."

Min sat back, took the balsam-stuffed pillow, and smelled its faint cleanness. "I'm not Hutchins' chief defender—never was—but he may grow into something decent yet; his father did."

Ann nodded. "I meant I'm stopping the child. I'm sorry if it's his."

Min stood. "Either way—any way I can see—it's yours, mainly yours." She took two steps toward the closet (sheets, blankets). "I'm no help at all."

Ann stayed in her chair. "You are. Now it's mine."

3

BY a little past noon, Ann had made her way to the old Hutchins place (Hutch had brought her only twice by daylight, but she found she knew the turns). As she drove up the gouged drive, she only thought of Strawson—how to ask him her question. And she saw his car as she cleared the rise, baking in cold sun, Mr. Mayfield's pickup beside it. Smoke from the chimney. She had bet right again. But when she'd knocked three times and waited long minutes, she felt the old fear and went down the steps. She'd rush back to Richmond—Linda would be there, drying her hair; Bailey wouldn't show up till suppertime. The sight of the empty stalled truck stopped her—chalky blue paint, Mr. Mayfield's only means out of here. She could do one right thing at least—see his grave.

At the rear left corner of the house, a row of paint cans. Ann looked toward the eaves. Straw had painted the whole top half of the back, a flat pure white. She liked him for that; everyone else she knew would have started in front, the side toward the world. And the whole backyard seemed cleaner than when they'd threaded through it slowly with the coffin six weeks ago. Piles of old iron and leaves were gone; firewood was stacked by the kitchen door. She tried again, calling "*Straw*" once at the windows. Nothing still.

The graves were half-turfed. Since the funeral the rough ground had been plowed lightly, and a thick mat of field grass had been laid in neat contiguous rows from the wall toward the graves. The two rows of old stones were already socketed in dim winter greenery; the head of Rob's grave was marked by a stake and was still red dirt—dry, no recent rain. The gate was open but she stopped outside. Maybe twice each year since her own father's death, she'd gone to his grave and tried to talk silently —not always of problems, sometimes just in thanks (she'd felt at least *watched* if not *heard* or *answered*). But now that she'd come here, what could she say to Rob Mayfield still intact in skin and bone?—*You never liked me so I've come to your home to ask a young stranger the simplest way to ease myself of what may be your grandchild?* From all Hutch had said, she knew Rob had ruined enough in his own life to have seas of mercy in his heart by now. *Can you pardon me? Can you see any broader path than I see? Can you aim me toward it?* She thought all the sentences but offered him none. Still her natural courtesy made her step forward, stop at his feet, and bend for a split flint that lay on the surface—oddly warm. When she stood she said *Sorry*, thought it clearly as a speech. If anything watched her, it kept the air adamant. No answer, no pardon, only unruffled light. She replaced the stone carefully and turned to go, then heard a creaking behind the big shed.

A wheelbarrow piled with turf, Grainger behind it. He was twenty feet away before he saw her; and at first he didn't know her but came on and stopped at the gate, unsmiling. He took off his hat, laid it on the turf, then found the name—"Miss Gatlin." More than that, he could only think she brought news of Hutch—sick or dead—so he justified his work. "I'm turfing in here so February doesn't wash it too bad."

"Will it root in the cold?"

"I can do it again. We're well-stocked on grass." ·

"The paint looks good." Ann pointed to the house.

Grainger smiled and reached for his hat. "—Look better if he'd wake up and work."

"Strawson?"

"You see him?"

"I knocked, no answer."

Grainger said, "He's in there. Sleeps like a crowbar."

"Is he happy here alone?"

Grainger said, "He seems all right when he's *wake*. Like I said, he's sleeping till he get his full growth. I stay out here now myself most nights."

"I was driving back from Raleigh and thought I'd stop by."

"Yes ma'm." He rolled the barrow in through the gate. "The back door's open. Step in there and holler."

"You don't think he'll mind?"

"Somebody got to call him or he'll sleep till spring." He crouched and pressed down a thick plaque of turf. "You see Miss Eva?"

"No."

"She's got a bad cold."

"Hutch seems all right." She'd said it to test herself; it still stung hard.

Grainger didn't look up. "Straw heard from him yesterday. He'll be all right."

Ann said "I don't doubt it."

Grainger faced her, studied her, then pointed to the house. "Make him fix you your lunch. If he doesn't, call me."

Every step through the yard, she felt under broad attack from the day—the bald sky itself.

4

STRAW was standing at the range—barefoot on the cold floor, shirt unbuttoned, long hair uncombed. He glanced at her. "Ready for my famous French toast?" He said it to the pan in his slow deep voice.

Ann had seen him only twice before, once when she'd visited Hutch's class at school and once at the funeral. Now she was stopped by his firm air of *residence*; he lived, however he lived, in this house. It had let him in easily. She stood on the sill.

He said, "Come or go. You're wasting my heat" and did a quick shuddering dance in place.

She entered and shut the door. "I thought you were dead. I knocked and yelled."

He looked up. "I heard you. Here I am." Then he took two heated plates from the oven and began to serve the bread, fried neatly.

Ann stepped to the table and sat but said, "I ate eggs for supper and breakfast in Raleigh—any more, I'll sprout tail feathers and a beak."

Straw danced five steps again, cackling now and flapping wings. He brought the two plates, then forks and syrup, then coffee strong as brass. He sat at the far end from her and they ate awhile. Then he said, "You leave something here or what?"

Ann laughed. "I never brought anything here. I've barely been here."

"I like it. I wish to God he'd sell it to me."

Ann said "Make him an offer."

Straw buttoned the top three buttons of his shirt. "I did."

"He trusted you to guard it at least."

Straw thought through that. "*He's* the thing needs guarding."

"Hutch?—from what?" She laughed again. "He's guarded like the Unknown Soldier's Tomb."

"—Used to be. All his guards are dying off." Straw stood, reached for her plate, and went to the stove.

"No more. It was good."

So he put the two final slices on her plate, brought it back, set the plate in his, and chewed a mouthful.

Ann persisted. "From what? What's the danger to Hutch?"

"—Just talking, trying to warm my mouth." He grinned and exercised his lips grotesquely. "He'll grow up now. See, he loved his father."

"Will he come back here?"

Straw said "You a millionaire?"

"No, why?"

"Then you can't live here unless you plan to eat leaves."

Ann said, "I don't think I plan anything for Hutch."

"He plans on you."

"How?"

Straw's large hands spread before him on the table. "I'm not you, you see. You've known him years longer." The sun had swung round and struck his right fingers. He worked them in the warmth like an old man at dawn. When he faced her he saw she was near to breaking, blue-mouthed and taut. He said, "Do you want me to touch you any way?"

Ann shook her head.

Straw said, "Then I don't think I know why you're here."

Low as she was she read that rightly, an unconditioned offer of welcome. So she said, "If I tell you, could it stop here now?"

He nodded. "I keep secrets that *God* wants to know."

She drank a long swallow of the tepid coffee. "You know we went to Rome. I wasn't sure I should. Hutch had left here, singing on about his need for freedom; but his letters kept asking me to meet him in Rome. I dug out pennies from every old sock and turned up on Christmas eve in downtown Rome. He'd been fogged-up in London and was hours late; so I had a whole long afternoon by myself to prowl round the edges, steady warm sun. My mother had said I was crazy to go—crazy and brazen and a blot on the name—and I half-believed her by the time Hutch landed. You ever seen Rome?"

"In *The Sign of the Cross.*"

Ann could smile by then. "It's not quite that fierce or that funny either, last month anyway. But if all you've seen is the South and New York and the Colorado Canyon, it's still a big wind. I was knocked right over—or down or onto Hutch. Don't ever meet anybody you feel two ways about in Rome at Christmas; you'll lose your choices."

Straw said "Yes ma'm," wrote himself an invisible memo on the table, then grinned. "Did Hutch?"

"What?"

"Did Hutch take the place hard as you?—he'd practiced in England."

Ann said, "He seemed happy, his old best self; we laughed a lot. But you saw him in England—"

"He was serious there. I gave him a sermon one night—How to Live —from the depths of my wisdom and long hard life."

"Then maybe you're responsible. In Rome he had all his barbed wire cleared; we met more than once. He asked me to wait."

Straw said "Where?"

"In Richmond, till he finished at Oxford and was home."

"But you're down here today." Straw drew his hands back to his lap, out of sight.

Ann nodded.

"Why?"

"To ask you a question."

"I don't know much."

Ann said, "Hutch told me you got an abortion for a girl you knew."

"Hutch was lying," Straw said.

"Or I misunderstood."

"He was lying," Straw said.

"I'm sorry then."

Straw pushed back his chair and stood. "O.K." He stayed in place, staring out the bright window.

Ann stood. "I'm sorry. I'll go on now."

"Yes ma'm," Straw said—not turning back; not conscious of the splendor of the line his face made, pressed on the sun.

Ann saw it but left by the front door quietly.

5

February 11, 1956

Dear Hutch,

This was Saturday but we worked all day. Well, I worked all afternoon. Grainger was up before light as usual. He finished turfing the graves even though he says February will probably kill it. If so that'll give him a reason to live on and do it again in April, he says. My personal guess is he'll turf us all under whenever we die. Don't worry, I don't plan to die here, not now. I stayed on the ladder from two o'clock till sunset and painted a good deal more of the house. It drinks up paint like a dedicated wino, but it looks strong and healthy.

I guess I do too except for the arches of my feet which are ruined from the ladder. Did you know there was a sealed pint of bourbon in the kitchen when you left me? It must have been your father's insurance. It's still here sealed and I haven't brought any of my own in to join it. No other humans either except Mr. Grainger. I call him Mr. Grainger and he hasn't said Stop. He calls me Straw. We are straining to integrate one house at least. He seems on the verge of trusting me now but goes on watching about as close as radar. I don't mind much. He is pretty fair company. We even started reading to each other after supper. One night I read us a chapter from Lord Jim. *The next night he reads from* The Wandering Jew. *He said that would hold us till you got home.*

You sound pretty good. Send us anything you write that wouldn't disrupt our rural daze or harm our morals. As it is we're rolling back the centuries at a swift clip. By spring we may have forgot how to read and be painting deer and foxes on ceilings by the light of fat from the flesh of wild creatures we kill with bare hands.

At noon today Ann Gatlin came by. She'd been down in Raleigh and detoured here on her way to Richmond. I don't know why. I gave her French toast and one cup of coffee. She looked like she missed you and said you'd told her I'd helped my girlfriend dispose of a baby. That made me mad and she left without excess politeness from me. If she writes you about it, you will understand. See, she caught me off guard with a mixed-up version of something I meant you to take as private. If

she writes you about it, you can try to see my feelings before you an-
swer. I'd have my child here with me right now if I had my way. And
Grainger would like it as much as me. I don't mean to mess in that side
of your business, but I promised you a good caretaking job and want you
to know my view of what's happened in my own small life. It's nothing
I'm proud of—still it happened one way and Ann Gatlin had it wrong.

It's seven o'clock now, pitch-dark outside and cold wind rising.
Grainger's just walked in from checking on your grandmother. She's got
a cold, he says, but otherwise good. I like her too. He'll cook supper now
so I'll stop this and help him. We're having beef hash and waffles, I
can smell.

> *Strawson or what's left of*
> *him tonight*

He folded that and rose to set the table, then noticed Grainger was
in no hurry—greasing the waffle iron with slow precision. He sat back
and said, "Let me read you this one thing I just told Hutch."

Grainger's hands paused a moment but he didn't turn.

So Straw read the sentences about Ann's visit.

Grainger poured the first batter.

Straw said "What you think?"

Grainger still didn't turn. "What you asking?"

"Should I mail it?"

Grainger said "Is it true?"

"Yes."

"She said that about you?"

"Yes."

"And you hadn't hurt her no way at all?"

Straw shook his head firmly, though Grainger hadn't looked.

Grainger's hand had stayed by the waffle iron. He suddenly stepped
toward Straw, reached out, and accepted the letter. Then he tore it four
times, kneaded the scraps, laid them on the counter, and lifted the lid of
the iron—perfect food.

Straw said, "I could just have recopied that page."

Grainger said "She's in trouble" and poured the next batter.

"Can you help her?"

"No sir. She'll find her own help."

"How?"

"I used to live in Richmond," Grainger said. "Richmond's big."

"And we shouldn't tell Hutch?"

"Least of all. Let him rest." His whole right palm lay flat on the
hot iron, no sign of pain.

6

Ann got back to Richmond in late afternoon—the house dark and cold, no sound of Linda. When she'd searched upstairs and returned to the living room, she thought she could not stay a minute here alone. She'd turn up the heat, switch on a few lights, go to a movie. Then if Linda wasn't back, the house would at least be ready to take Ann herself. But after ten seconds she knew she was tired; she hadn't slept a whole night in nearly a month. She didn't want to risk her own room though, not alone. She turned up the thermostat, felt the old furnace lurch into flame below her; then she took off her coat and lay on the narrow cot by her landlady's china closet with its souvenirs of years of world's fairs and expositions—squat mugs, pickle dishes, painted pitchers, knife rests. She drew up the afghan Linda's mother had sent them in August. She said four words aloud—"Help me some way"—then plunged into sleep like any child.

In her dream that came quickly, Strawson Stuart stood barefoot in Rob Mayfield's dining room. He was by the tall window in strong winter light, and his back was to Ann. From the door where she waited, she saw that his hands worked swiftly at a task; but she couldn't see what. She said, "We should be out painting the house in this good weather." Her voice was silent; the air refused to sound her words as she gave them, though it calmly consented to warm her skin and fill her lungs. She tried again, just his name—still nothing. So she thought, "I'm not here. I can go anywhere." She stepped to within a foot of Straw's broad back, then a step to the side. With perfect economy his hands were tending a small tree—recumbent juniper. It was rooted in yard-dirt in a rusty tin can, but it spilled its knots of bluish needles down a watercourse of black limbs shaped by wind—lovely as any pine she'd seen in Rome, lovely as any living thing she'd seen in her life till now. She said "Where'd you find it?"—silence again. So she put out her own hand to touch the highest limb. Not looking, Straw blocked her by ringing her wrist. She stood in his grasp then, watching the tree till beyond it the edge of her sight caught movement. On the couch in the corner, Hutch's father sat, well and strong, signaling to her with a slow wave. She focused on him, nodded. He said, "We thank you and will never forget." Then he rose, walked quickly to Strawson, bent past him, smelled at the needles, and smiled—"Thanks ever." He spoke toward the tree, but Ann knew the offer was aimed at her and bowed her acceptance. She had brought life again to the clean dead house; they would not forget. After that she slept blank.

*   *   *

The front door opened in the Richmond house. Ann didn't hear it. Bailey Ferguson entered from the dusk and stood in the lighted hall, waiting to hear. At first he sensed nothing and moved to stride forward, then paused in the new thought of solitude. He'd never been here alone. But Ann's car was outside. He called her name, normal voice. She'd sunk past hearing. So he stood absolutely still and waited till his body reached its own depth of quiet. Then he cupped his left ear and waited again. Three breaths reached him from the dim room beyond, so slow they seemed inhuman in patience. His own blood slowed. He said again "Gatlin," having always called her that. Then he entered the room and stopped a yard from the cot.

Ann heard him finally, his adjacent stillness. Her eyes didn't know him at first, but she felt no surprise or fear. When his face clarified she said "Linda back?"

Bailey shook his head. "Won't be till Tuesday maybe. I dropped by to tell you."

"Something wrong?"

"Her aunt in Agricola—heart gave out."

"The crazy aunt?"

"No the good one," he said. "You O.K.?"

She waited. She'd been on her back; she turned to her left side now, facing Bailey's knees. "No."

He sat on the cot by her shins, his hands clasped. "I'm sorry."

Ann nodded.

Then he leaned and touched two fingers to her forehead—no fever.

But she laughed. "Ought not to touch live wires; you won't be spared twice."

"I'm a dead man, remember? None of this is really happening. You're in the next world."

"Wonderful." She slowly drew her legs back an inch, not to touch him at all.

Bailey agreed to the distance and sat awhile, watching the china closet—a cut-glass celery dish was handing the absolute last sunlight from facet to facet like a bucket brigade (he saw it that way). At the same time thick blood pooled in his groin; his cock lengthened lazily. He felt no lust but a general magnetized warmth—what he felt when his sister's young daughter would sit in his lap: a will to protect. He said, "Tell me how to help."

Ann shut her eyes and folded both hands beneath her cheek. "Find a place I can stop a baby I've started."

Bailey said, "Got two hundred dollars on hand?"

"In my savings. I can get it Monday at lunch."

"No hurry. I can float you a loan." Bailey stood and went to the china closet; laid his whole hand on the frail arched door, his back to Ann. "You ready right now?"

Ann opened her eyes. "Will I need the cash now?"

"Yes ma'm. I can get it. This town is my friend."

"Can I work Monday morning?"

Bailey said, "Up to you. If you're lucky, I mean."

Ann waited. "I'd hope Linda never has to know."

Bailey still didn't turn. With his dry forefinger he was stroking trails on the glass of the door. But he nodded. "I won't even know, myself."

Ann thanked him. Then she began to sit up.

7

THE woman left her alone with a lamp on a clean narrow bed in a room the size of a steamer trunk. Then the house went silent and the street out-side—ten on Saturday night. On the stand by the lamp was an old dinner-bell; she was meant to ring that for hard pain or bleeding. So she turned her face toward it. "I will watch just this. I will not think a thought." And for minutes she succeeded. The big dose of paregoric still held her; she only saw the dull lunar flare of the bell and its worn wood-handle. Then it slowly shrank. She looked to the walls. The room was receding from her, its center. The single picture was caught in the flight—a foxed mezzotint entitled *Pneumonia*, a bearded white man at the bed of a white girl-child unconscious in the critical hour. Ann thought, "I may be starting to die" and felt at the napkin in her crotch, still cool. Then she slept—that quickly, no panic or prayer. And no trace of dream, no memory of Hutch or her father or the child. She was doing herself a kindness she had lacked all her life; she'd have thought that if she'd thought.

The woman woke her gently, sitting by her knees. "You doing all right?"

"I guess I don't know."

"If you sleeping, you all right."

Ann nodded. "I did. How long?"

"Best part of two hours. He's back to get you now." She pointed to the shut door, her thin arm three shades blacker than her face.

Ann was still half-dazed; the eyes showed puzzlement.

"Your friend that brought you—tall boy, mean eyes." But the woman laughed once.

"He wouldn't hurt a rattler," Ann said.

"—Tried to scotch *you*." The smile continued but the woman drew the quilt down, stood, raised Ann's slip, unpinned the gauze napkin, stepped to a corner, and stood with her back turned for half a minute. Then she rolled the napkin in a sheet of newspaper on a small table there, stepped back, pinned a new napkin quickly in place, and sat again. She took neat pains to smooth the quilt up toward Ann's elbows. Then she looked to the high shaded window. "You all right?"

Ann shut her eyes, then looked to the window herself—mere slot on a world she could not yet imagine, new world she'd made. She faced the woman. "Thank you at least."

The woman nodded. "Most people don't say it."

Ann remembered that she only knew the woman's first name—Bailey had said "Julia." She said, "My name was Ann Gatlin, still is."

The woman looked on at the window awhile, then turned and smiled. "I used to be a Patterson before you were born." She offered no more but picked at a seam.

Ann said "Can I go?"

Julia nodded. "He's waiting in there with my son." She stood in place.

Ann sat up carefully and swung her feet down. When they touched the floor, she knew for certain—she'd changed one part of her life completely, agreed to the change in this small house. She'd never be herself, not the one she'd known. No one else would know her either.

Yet the first thing she said in Bailey's car was, "Please leave me off at Miss Polly Drewry's house."

He accepted her clear directions in silence.

8

February 12, 1956

Dear Hutchins,

It's one day short of a month since you wrote to me. I trust you are not still stuck in New York in an ongoing blizzard and that England received you in the manner you hoped. I've been right here, making feeble attempts to fight back the cobwebs and strange living creatures that took a hold of my luxury apartment while I was with Rob. I've got it about back where it was in June when I left—just near-total chaos. I can't seem to get it much straighter than that, which must be how I want it. If I got really neat, I'd see what I have. And I might die laughing or howling (choose one).

Something that I do have is what you said—that you're glad I was present with Rob toward the end. I'm still not enough of a Scarlet Woman to refuse your thanks. I've also received, from Miss Eva as you warned me, the present from Rob. I walked straight down that morning and banked it, thinking I'd at least earned it. Then I had nights of thinking I must send it back, that you'd need it in Europe. But now I've decided—I'm keeping it to do something on my own that Rob never did. This summer I'm going to pack a small bag and head off to see some place that's not home. I've never spent more than three nights in a row more than sixty-five miles from my family's house (though I haven't lived there for nearly forty years). I guess that proposal will meet with your approval. I'd bow my head and add "Rob's too" if I hadn't, all my life, gone queasy every time some widow or mother would tremble and say "He of course still sees and knows and is pleased." Rob never watched me, even when I was all that was left to watch (except soda crackers in the cupboard and the dog); so I know he isn't now. I can count on viewing Montana in peace.

I hope you are peaceful. It can't have been anything but stunning to be called back from Christmas in Rome to see that, helpless. If I spoke hard to you—and I did, I recall—I was stunned myself, though I'd had more time than you to set my dials. Take my genuine regrets then please. But forget them before you have folded this letter, and find ways to clear your mind and life. Your father could never clear one line from his accounts once he wrote it down. There were whole years when he barely knew there was a present; he was solving the past. But the present killed him. Keep your eyes open then and aimed ahead.

Maybe we shouldn't correspond anymore now. I need a blank, I guess, like the one you tried.

But love, here, from
Min

February 19, 1956

Dear Hutch,

I've been waiting till I had something good to write, thinking you might be needing it. I certainly have. January always leaves me low as a mole. If only Christ would choose to be born in May, my year would go better. But I've got through, surprised as ever to notice time's main trick— it will not kill you. You can stand what it offers, though you may want to shut yourself in awhile and yell. I didn't have to yell after all this year, which is what I'm here to tell you.

Remember those pearls I was sewing on lace when you stopped here? The dress itself was meant to be made by the mother of the bride. It turns out she has a small problem with liquor, like being dead-drunk for days after Christmas. I understand why, as I said just now, but I wasn't quite set to be faced by the challenge of the bride herself coming in here on me four days before the wedding in serious tears with armloads of uncut satin and veiling. I was prepared if truth be told and glad to be busy. Didn't sleep for two nights but I gave that up eight or ten years ago, just lie down at dark since the air goes quiet. I finished in time and mostly by hand and it looked good on her. Gunny sacks would have looked good on her but I was pleased. So was she—Agnes Butters—and she paid me too much.

What surprised me was the phone ringing well before light on the wedding day. It was Mrs. Butters praising me and saying she wouldn't take No for an answer. She'd send a boy to get me at four o'clock for the candlelight service. I had never been to a wedding in my life and hadn't missed the pleasure but something said "Go" so I said "Thank you." The boy drove up at four as promised in a boiled shirt and swallow tails. He was slightly stiffer than the shirt himself. He said the stag party had never really ended and wouldn't till Monday. He didn't seem to know Richmond all that clearly. We drove through whole quarters I'd never seen before in fifty-odd years here but he finally found the church and we were still early. He turned me over to another dazed boy who was ushering. I whispered my name and he seated me in silence, though he smiled like a spaniel. I noticed I was sitting far forward—second row—but I figured he knew just where I belonged, so I kept in place and the church filled behind me and the music began. I never looked back. After maybe ten minutes they played a tune I knew—"O Danny Boy"—and my left eye seemed to catch a human bearing down. It was my same usher with Celestine Butters, the bride's ailing mother. I was in her pew! Or she was in mine. She greeted me warmly as any sister could have. Her chin was trembling but her breath smelled sober. I whispered "He put me in your pew, I'm sorry." She said "You're where you belong to be" (Mr. Butters is gone) and took my hand.

So we stayed there and looked and listened together. From hearing people talk and the radio, I knew a few words of what would be said. But I wasn't expecting the whole string of promises the old man would make those two children give. Being new to weddings I may have been the one person present who heard him. But I really heard. Could any two spirits in the safe midst of Heaven say confident Yesses to such good dreams? Well I want you to know Agnes Butters did and Fleetwood Wilmuth. When they turned round to face us at the end, Mrs. Butters said to me "You were born for this night." She was streaming tears. I knew she meant the dress. It would have held its own at a modest coronation if I do say so. But for one hot second I saw another meaning. I should not hold my peace. I should rise up and show them from the depths of my knowledge what lies they'd almost certainly told. I didn't, don't worry. I waited till the boy came and led me out—the second to leave after Celestine herself. By then I felt like I'd earned my seat.

I won't keep you any longer, knowing how you work. But I said I had something to cheer you up and I hope I have. I came home from church that night glad as any child to see my narrow bed and crawl in it single. I still thought as always when the light was out of the ones I've cherished and I thanked their memories. You're the one of them all that's alive so take extra care. There isn't really any other news right now. I won't wait for fire or flood but mail this at once. I can still read, remember, and digest all foods as calm as a goat so send me a word.

And take these two—
Long love—from
Polly

February 25, 1956

Dear Hutch,

I wrote to you awhile back, but the letter disappeared before I could send it. Now Mr. Grainger's big calendar here in the kitchen says you left six weeks ago yesterday. It seems a year longer, we have dug in so deep. Speaking of which, there was snow in the night and all day today. Mr. Grainger and I, being natives of The North, consider it a normal amount for the time; but your grandmother phoned us twice to say it was way past the record for her life here—a good foot everywhere, three feet in drifts. She was home without Sylvie, and Grainger got stuck when he tried to drive to her, but we knew it was coming and had stocked her with food, so she'll be O.K. Sun's predicted for tomorrow, I'm sorry to say. I wish it could stay like this at least a week. I went out after breakfast and took a long walk back into the woods, mostly the way you and I went last month. Very fine, every step. I can see why you left here when you left. I doubt I'll ever see why if you don't come back when you can and as soon as you can. I remembered when I got in as far as the creek that your father said one private sentence to me the morning I met him. You had stepped back into your empty house in Edom to turn off the power; so he and I were standing by his loaded truck, your life's possessions—I was standing, he was leaning both arms on the side like he couldn't stand alone but watching me close. I can face anybody I've met to date, but I'll grant he was hard. He'd seen that I knew you more than one way. That was as plain as how tired he was. He let me see both. Then when we heard your steps coming through the house, he said, "Will he ever come back, you think?" I looked and saw you forty feet away, and I said "No sir." I thought he meant Edom—would you come back there. I was sad to see you go too so I said No. You must not have seen him in that one minute. He looked like I'd cut him fast, gullet to groin. But he never called me wrong. I wish I'd known enough to lie to him then. Or you can prove me wrong.

I doubt I'll be here to welcome you. The Draft is cranking up to blow *my way. It took them awhile to notice I'd dropped out of college and was free to guard South Korea or West Berlin (why do we just get part of a place?). My cousin's on the Draft Board and has staved off action, but he won't hold for long—it's either a second shot at higher learning or they start shooting me. I may choose the latter. The Dean says I'm welcome back at Washington and Lee seven months from now, and I've told my father I'd swallow the pill. But the more I think, I think I'll look into joining the Navy. I've done two sizable unusual things for Americans my age— known you and had one gone child behind me. So I think I'm not ready, and may never be, to join the great Pussy and Grain-Liquor Talking-Club that waits outside. Not that I want to be any monk on a rock, staring out toward perfection; and not that I reckon the U.S. Navy offers a high-toned line of goods. But it might let me move, for three or four years. I'm gambling that if I could spend two or three more nights like that one we spent at Macbeth and after—if I could stand that near the fire again—then I could come back home tame and tuck my chin and find what I think I need and take it.*

I think I need what most people need. A place with enough quiet, a good wife and children—not a dozen but two or three to watch so I don't have just me and her to watch or trees. I can only look at trees so long, Shakespeare. I guess I decided that, walking this morning. You'd be welcome to visit anytime you could.

Didn't plan to go that far in when I started this. I mainly meant to say that up till the snow things here were going fine. Mr. Grainger has cleaned up a lot and turfed the graves. I've painted three-fourths of the back of the house. We read to each other at night and watch T.V. Hope you don't mind that, but we bought a used one to keep us in at night—me anyway. It cost thirty dollars and is big as my knee, but Grainger paid for it, and it seems to do the job. I've slept by myself every night, no guests.

I don't know whether that's good luck or bad, so I don't know whether to wish you the same. I'll entrust you to Fate then. I hope Fate thanks me. Let me have all the lowdown—and highdown—when you're free. I'll be here till I tell you.

Nearly suppertime now,
Strawson Stuart in person

March 1, 1956

Dear Famous Author,

Where's the poem you were going to make out of me? It's been all but nine months and I really think it's time. I'm getting quite nervous about my debut in English verse. I've been brushing my hair in case it gets mentioned.

Otherwise I've been knocking about as before. After seeing you I had a job in Swansea in a big wine merchant's. Unfortunately my electric skin drew in the owner's daughter, seventeen and all right. End of future in fortified wines. I'm thinking of getting treatments for the problem. Could they cancel my charge or reverse it or something? You're the one with training. Give a poor sod advice.

Then my mother got married which is quite another tale. Her third time and looks like the best chance yet. I was back for the wedding from Bristol where I'd gone and had many laughs. I told her "It only happens three times, Gwyn." She said "Says who?"

So I donned me bathing knickers, swam back to Canada and greet you from this thrilling spot, your side of the briny. I decided to taste city life for a bit and am serving hot meals at a place in Toronto, not quite the Savoy but I meet funny types and they plaster me with tips. Be wanting any dollars? Let me know right away. This may not last either.

That's all I can tell for now in writing. I doubt I shall ever see England —or Wales—again. I don't know how long I'll stay in these lodgings but I'd like to hear your voice on paper at least and to meet you some day over here where I'm better in control of my mind and words.

Your freezing mate,
Lew Davis

P.S. None of this means to say our summer voyages weren't absolute tops. It was Lew that was low. No regrets, just explaining.

March 1, 1956

Dear Hutch,

This card replies to two cards from you. Understand that I'm glad to get colored pictures of ancient stones, but I won't sit down and write lengthy news items or deep meditations to a charmer who tries to plead busyness. I'm glad you're busy. The world is busy. So am I, praise God— I've been painting again. Our trip set me off. The busiest soul has all the time it needs if it just sleeps less. So up with the cuckoo (have you heard the first one yet?) and do yourself justice. Then I'll tell you my story.

Stopgap love,
Alice

March 4, 1956

Dear Hutch,

A warm Sunday—68°. Just a week ago yesterday, we had calf-deep snow and the usual Three Stooges farce in the streets, us Dixiecrats skidding round like tigers in Finland; but here now it's spring or a blessed sample. No doubt we'll get bonked a time or two more, but I'm planning to live. I've always meant to ask you, Brother Hutchins—in your poring on the Laws of Sky and Land, do you find it's a sin to want to sleep in a hole at the root of an oak tree from December 25th at 10 a.m. till, say, March 21st? If it is I'm finally unredeemable. Bears have got the right idea. But have bears got souls? Let me know when you know.

That partly explains why my last few missives may have been a little bleak. The other reasons have to do with you and me—no major revelation but the same old gap we've been calling across (or refusing to call). Deep as it always was, I seemed to know the depth. Now your father's going—and all it caused in Rome and Richmond—has dug a new bottom, and I don't see it yet. You must have detected when you were here that I was more or less drowning politely. I mean, I didn't ask for rescue, did I? Or for you to drown with me? Let me claim those two small credits at least, in the face of big debts.

Am I saying more than that? Maybe just this much. I am trying to stop expecting you. I don't mean to sound like a thin-lipped martyr when I add that I doubt you're expecting me now or that you ever have. Or that either one of us will land in a hermitage if we never see each other again. I'd hate not to see you. I'd miss the eyes and the sides of your neck, though I also know my tendency to stare has been at least part of what sent you away.

You may never come back (partly a statement of possibility and partly permission—stay gone if you want). I may not be here. That's as much as I know now or ever knew. Why should that have to mean The End?

Love,
Ann

March 5, 1956

Dear Hutch,

We are all right and glad to know you are. Straw is working out better than I expected when he gets out of bed. Never saw one person need to sleep that much. I tell him he is going to root to the bed. He says that's the plan. Maybe I should have thought of that sixty years ago. Weather turned off good after a snow and I am thinking about planting us a vegetable garden. Straw talks about joining the Navy at night. Other times he looks like he plans to stay for good. He is a very neat house painter and drinks less than most any painter I know. Miss Eva well again from her cold and feeling mean. She told me today she was glad I moved out. Now she and Sylvie can argue all they want to. She laughed but she meant it.

Just one more news. Three weeks ago your friend Ann passed through here Saturday afternoon. I saw her five minutes. She was looking for Straw. That evening he told me she asked him did he know where to get a baby fixed. He got mad and she drove off still using your car. So Straw said. I was working on the graves. I write you this because I waited so long about Rob. If I had told you sooner you would be stronger now. Keep your toes warm

From
Grainger

March 8, 1956

Dear Hutch,

Your letter came yesterday and reminded me how the weeks had slid past, something I seldom expect them to do. Still it's nice to have one thing to prod me this late in my mortal pilgrimage—to where? I hardly thought you'd had time to unpack your socks, and here you are faced with Easter vacation. The English take a very loose view of work, don't they? How on earth did they ever rule the earth? Well, the earth was asleep at the time, I suspect. I'm a witness to that. I was twenty-seven years old— mother to a son more than ten years old—before I ever heard of real shots fired in serious anger, and they were in France and Belgium not here (I don't count the Spanish-American War, a schoolboy's outing though some boys stayed). I've still never heard such a shot with my own ears, never seen anybody struck or cut. But it seems all I'm told of—such restlessness, especially now that Negroes have got themselves noticed at last. I estimate I've spent a fourth of my life attending to claims on my mind from Negroes, none of whom was brought out of Africa by me or by anyone I've known. I cannot recall an unkind deed I've ever done to one—or one to me from them—but to read the Raleigh paper you'd think I was due to be strangled in bed any evening now. Well, let it come on, whatever's been earned. No stopping it surely, though I personally wish things would doze off again. The world, I mean, and you in its midst.

Maybe that would put you flat out of work. I'm not the biggest reader in the history of the Kendals—never liked to see other lives that close; that was Rena's choice—but I've gathered that however much peace may be got from reading a poem, the author gets little. Are you sure you've chosen well? In the short years I knew your Grandfather Mayfield, he wrote a number of commendable poems that he said were for me, several ways to say thanks. I knew I was giving him less than nothing; so I knew (even when I'd forgot most else) that the lines were for him, transfusions for his dream that would banish us all. I wish I had them here to show you, but I'm sad to say I burned them when I saw he would not consider taking me and Rob back (I tried to go back, which Rob never knew). What I know is—the reason I'm off on this tack—the poems gave even less comfort than I. But then he found Miss Drewry. I hope she helped him more. I saw in her eyes she had plenty left that nobody had used. I wonder, do I? I've meant to spend it all, in my quiet way here; but it keeps seeping up through my chest at night. I'd thought when you were old, you would wake up aching and stunned by the prospect. My hands are stiff for the first few minutes. In general though I wake up strong as a girl and as full with life to give. This morning after sunup I drifted back to sleep and saw I was standing at my bedroom window, looking down on the yard. The road had become a swift muddy stream; and you were standing on the far side, calculating the current. Or so I guessed—I guessed you were wanting to swim this way. The surface was broken by numerous creatures too fast to name. I knew they were nothing but freshwater fish; and I raised the window to tell you so, but of course I couldn't speak. I can very seldom speak in a dream, however important the news I have.

The waking news is slim, I can tell you. You'll have guessed it before me—a usual winter except for a deep snow and Rob's being absent. I believe he's gone now. For long days I didn't. Two separate times I had picked up the telephone and started on his number before I remembered he could not be there. I've even spoken out to him once or twice at night on the chance he can hear. I don't think he does. That would be the worst punishment God could arrange, to leave dead souls at attention to the world. So I'll say it to you, I loved Rob the best I possibly could. I think he grew to see that. I live in that hope. When he told me he was sick right after you left, I offered to nurse him from that minute on. He couldn't accept. The air he had finally got between us, that he got from you, wouldn't let him accept. So I wrote to Min. He never knew I'd told her, but she came posthaste and God bless her soul. I know you'd rather not have had her here at the end; blame me not Rob. I was helping finish something, which I haven't always done.

I have also tended to all your business for you. So far it just consists of paying Rob's bills. He cleaned behind himself the best he could, but a fair amount gathered in his last few weeks that's only now appearing. Dear God, you pay to die. The insurance will cover all but four hundred dollars of his medical expenses. I've paid for the funeral from my own money. I brought him here; I can surely see him off without strapping you. You'll have your own deaths. Please don't try to stop me. I'm going to let you handle the farm. Sam Jarrel stopped here last Saturday to ask did I need any more peanuts. I told him I doubted I could ever look a peanut in the face again. He had such a big crop last year, and Rob couldn't use them, so Sylvie and I did everything with peanuts but paint the walls. He also wanted instructions for planting. I said, "Just do what you've done all your life." He said, "Miss Eva, it ain't yours to say. Hutch may want it different." So I stood corrected and told him to write you (you'll think it's a ransom note if he does; he can barely print his name). If he doesn't and you want to make any changes, such as trimming back the peanuts or planting field daisies instead of tobacco, you know how to reach him. One daughter can read.

Sylvie's heading home now for her afternoon nap. She says it's the only time she sleeps, from three to five. I've offered to put her a cot in the dining room and save her the walk, cold as it is; but she says I'd bother her, "fumbling around." I still don't know if that's meant as a tribute to my afternoon vigor or a judgment of aimless on my present life. I don't plan to ask her to clarify, but she can mail this as she goes so I'll stop.

Whether you travel or stay, let me hear. When you're silent I never doubt you're there (Rena always thought people vanished when they left), but I will say the sight of your hand does help.

Your last grandmother,
Eva Kendal Mayfield

9

THE sun had survived all through their lunch. Even the breeze that had nudged at the river was gone on north; and when the publican's daughter looked out, the light struck her broadside there on the threshold and pressed one long coo of pleasure from her lips. Then she blushed ferociously to think they'd seen her and came forward primly with her tray to clear dishes. Mr. Fleishman ignored her, rose, crossed the terrace to the low river-wall, and looked across to the ruins of the nunnery lost in briars.

Hutch said to the girl, "More cider for both please."

Mr. Fleishman said "None for me," not turning. He'd finished his pint but had barely touched the pork pie.

The girl met Hutch's eyes at last and frowned conspiratorially.

He laughed. "Isn't this day a miracle?"

She paused to consider, glancing again at the sky—her auburn hair all but molten in the glow. "Not really," she said. "Often we get a few good days in March. May well snow tonight." But she ducked her head once more toward Mr. Fleishman, wrinkled her nose, and grinned as she left.

Hutch loosened his tie, unbuttoned his collar, then stood and went to Mr. Fleishman's side and said, "Fair Rosamond's dust breeds roses" (Henry II's mistress had repented and died in the Godstow nunnery, thirty yards away).

Mr. Fleishman gave no sign of hearing but took the last step till his toes touched the wall. He gazed another minute; then recited as drily as he'd just recited the rules for Hutch's thesis,

> " 'A boat beneath a sunny sky
> Lingering onward dreamily
> In an evening of July--' "

It was just past one on the tenth of March; Hutch was mildly baffled. "I can't name it yet."

Mr. Fleishman didn't turn but stood a moment, silent; then pointed his long arm straight at the ruins, the green bank below them.

> " 'Children three that nestle near,
> Eager eye and willing ear,
> Pleased a simple tale to hear—' "

Hutch said, "It's not Marvell; Marvell barely mentions children."

Mr. Fleishman turned then and slowly smiled, a labored rearrangement of all his lean face that finally seemed more pained than glad. "—The one great book ever written in Oxford, ninety-odd years ago: I knew men who knew him."

"Newman, Ruskin?" Hutch said. "Early Hopkins maybe?"

Mr. Fleishman's smile continued, rigid now; but his head shook hard, and the oiled hair slid like a wing toward his left eye. He pointed again—

> " 'In a Wonderland they lie,
> Dreaming as the days go by,
> Dreaming as the summers die:
>
> Ever drifting down the stream—
> Lingering in the golden gleam—
> Life, what is it but a dream?' "

The girl was back with Hutch's cider and paused, watching both men.

Mr. Fleishman turned. "May I change my mind?—a pint of bitter?"

She nodded, glanced to Hutch, then blushed again but persisted in saying what she knew. "It's *Alice*, that poem—*Through the Looking-Glass*. He wrote it there." She couldn't make herself point but ducked her head twice toward the opposite bank.

Mr. Fleishman said, "Thank you. Might I just have the beer?"

The girl frowned and left.

Mr. Fleishman said "She's half-right" and went to the table.

Hutch followed and sat.

"July 4th, 1862—" Mr. Fleishman said. "Young Mr. Dodgson and his friend from Trinity, Robinson Duckworth, rowed the three Liddell girls—Alice, Ina, and Edith—up the river for tea by the ruins at Godstow. They sat about there, I'm told, on the bank and were not back at Christ Church till half-past eight. It was here and while rowing that he made up the tale—*Alice under ground*—for the real child, you see."

So Hutch watched the bank and pulled at his drink, held as always by any revelation of the patience of objects (the willingness of grass and dirt and vines to sustain forever the energy of passionate gesture or speech—Tintagel, Castle Dore, Slaughter Bridge, all of Rome, Rob Mayfield's kitchen, the green slope at Godstow). Patient for whom? Waiting for what? He looked to Mr. Fleishman and said what that dry face and voice had stirred. "How old was Alice when she heard the tale?"

"Ten, I think—not older."

"I wonder if the notion of life as a dream could have come from her?"

"I shouldn't think so," Mr. Fleishman said, "—why?"

The girl was in sight again with the beer; but Hutch said, "Because when I was that age, I invented the notion entirely on my own. Nobody told me and I'm sure I hadn't read it."

"You must write to Dr. Jung; you may have an archetype." No sneer was implied.

The girl served in silence, took three steps back into one perfect hoop of direct sun, and said, "My dad says the old lady came back here twenty-five years ago when Dad was a boy."

Mr. Fleishman said "—Lady?"

"Miss Alice," she said, "Mrs. Hargreaves by then. She stopped here for tea, and Dad overheard her name, but he said she never even crossed the bridge."

Hutch said "Is she dead?"

"I should think so," the girl said, "wouldn't you?"

Mr. Fleishman looked to Hutch. "Twenty-odd years ago; she lived till near ninety. You were telling me a story—"

Hutch could see Mr. Fleishman was banishing the girl; she hung a moment, waiting. So he smiled up toward her and, for the first time since Ann's room in Richmond, felt the rush of desire—a thrumming in his ears. If he stood now and asked with an open hand, surely she'd follow him deeper into meadow grass and lend him all her competent body—barely contained in its milky walls, ready to stream. He wanted only that now, his mind a white blank of tender force.

The girl said, "I'm leaving. My dad has your bill." She pointed to the viney door.

"For where?" Hutch said.

She'd somehow won control of her face—no blush—but she looked toward Oxford across the flat pasture. "It's my half-day. I'll go in and buy my birthday present; Dad's given me five pound." She smiled at the scruffy ponies dozing.

Hutch said "What will you buy?"

"No idea really. I'll mooch through the shops till it finds me; it will." She turned to him then, open-faced as the sun itself, and quickly left.

Mr. Fleishman took a short swallow of beer. "You concluded that life was a dream—at what age?"

"Younger than Alice at the picnic at least; before I went to school, five or six years old. I grew up alone, no brothers or sisters, and in a small town with country round me. I spent a good deal of time talking to trees and dogs, whispering to rocks." He paused to check Mr. Fleishman for boredom; but the blue eyes were on him, patient, unblinking.

"Did they whisper back?"

Hutch laughed. "They said 'We're cold and old.' "

But Mr. Fleishman said, "I was not insulting you; don't insult yourself. Young Wordsworth, remember, walking to school would often grasp at a wall or tree to prove to himself the reality of matter."

Hutch nodded. "I never felt realer than the world. I only thought we were all being *dreamt*. We were simultaneous figures in a tale being dreamt by a giant asleep in a cave at the heart of a bare world, otherwise alone."

"Would you vanish if it woke? Did the prospect alarm you?"

Hutch laughed again. "I had a few cold moments, yes—the thought we might *phut* out with no word of warning some clear warm noon."

"—Or one by one," Mr. Fleishman said, "which appears to be the case."

Hutch thought awhile. "I never considered that. He dreamt us all together—my giant was a *he*—and we'd all stop at once if he woke or slept deeper."

Mr. Fleishman blinked, spread his spider fingers on the rusty table, and studied their knobbed length. Then he said "Your father died" (Hutch had told him briefly in January; they'd never discussed it). The fingers came together to form his hands again. "My skin is here in sunlight." He slowly pushed forward across the green iron and tapped Hutch's sleeve. "I am not dreaming you."

Hutch pushed against the finger; then raised his mug and smiled to the riverbank, the cradle of *Alice*, empty but stroked by gorgeous successions of glare and shade. He drained the cider and knew he was safe, suspected he was happy—awake now and free. "Thank you," he said to the whole real place.

Mr. Fleishman waited, then said "Not at all."

10

THE happiness lasted through the half-hour it took him to leave Mr. Fleishman back at his flat, drive into town, and park in Beaumont Street. As he walked in pure sun toward St. Giles, he felt the strangeness—that after the

shocks of the past three months (and Ann's cool letter had come yesterday), here he'd been lifted by a glimpse of spring, lunch with his bone-dry
tutor, and the memory of a childhood certainty. He walked ten steps believing that, then knew the truth—he wanted the girl and was hunting
her now, the girl from the pub with her birthday money. Surely he could
find her; she'd be in Elliston's or Marks & Sparks or maybe the record
shop. He pictured her gravely studying sweaters. She'd be alone or with a
girlfriend. He'd appear surprised at finding her, then invite them both for
coffee, the girlfriend would dissolve. Or he'd stride up and say no less than
the truth—"I'll be twenty-six years old in no time. I've waited too long"—
and she'd follow him. He knew he was half-wild with this bright day after
two months of work in all the strong wakes of his father's death; but he
walked straight on, famished and glad.

She was not to be found. The shops were crowded with grim-jawed
dowds still swaddled for winter and couples younger than he with babies,
fat as seals and solemn as clocks. But though he combed every aisle, she
was missing. He didn't know her name—he'd looked a good while when
he realized that. She'd never said her name; and in Mr. Fleishman's presence, he never could have asked. So beside the hills of flannel pajamas in
Marks & Sparks, his spiral of expectation collapsed. At first it seemed a
small disappointment. He'd head back to college, find a willing friend or
two, and drive down into the Vale of the White Horse—a ramble on the
chalk, then supper in Wantage or Farringdon.

But once he'd returned to the crowded street, the sun pressed harder
than before. He walked a long block, pummeled by shoppers in dense
winter clothes now reeking in the warmth; and by the time he'd reached St.
Michael's church, with its black Saxon tower, he'd convicted himself of a
deeper solitude than he'd known since the night-beach at Tresco. He didn't
want to yield though; he felt very strongly that he'd mooned enough in the
past year to last any two normal humans a long pair of lives. The steps of
the church were bare and in full light. He climbed to the top and sat,
vaguely hoping no vicar would shoo him off. None did. No passerby looked
his way. So he made himself a speech—"You were never meant for happiness." It tolled like a bell. He actually grinned. His grandmother had
trained him, at any low moment, to pause and count his blessings. A well-
made body that seemed to work. Four people that unconditionally loved
him (Eva, Grainger, Polly, Alice). The power of close attention to things,
visible things. The gift of words, not grown yet but growing. Sufficient
funds for this year at least, a home to return to. This present bright day.
No war to attend. A million smaller credits. *Therefore rejoice.* He smiled
again.

But—but, but. There were all the clues (a chain of hints beginning at
his birth, with his mother's death) that whatever giant was dreaming his
life was dreaming it solo—a solitary journey with skirmishes of company.

And any attempts by the characters to change the plot were foiled by the dreamer. The barmaid had vanished in the narrow heart of this one country town. Ann had sent him her letter, bathed in the thin air of distance he'd requested a year ago. Straw was bound for the Navy; Lew was in Canada. He would not hunt them out again, he somehow knew. Never meant for happiness—if happiness was permanent love, mainly calm. But who'd said it was (except ninety-nine percent of Western Man since love was invented in the eleventh century)? He should stand and return to his big dry rooms, stroke out his own calm with an ample hand, then sit at his desk facing Merton Field and the bare elms beyond and haul back the peace he'd known as a boy when any rough water could be stilled by a half-hour of patient sketching—any frazzled tree in the yard transferred to the hungry white paper in soothing lines: the happiness of power to see and transform, to dream a whole world in which he could sleep at least peacefully.

The girl passed then—he was almost sure—on the far sidewalk fifty feet away with a taller boy, as fine as she. They were holding hands but facing ahead as if they'd hardly met or were blind and assisted each other in desperate courtesy.

Hutch let them go. It seemed to cost nothing, no longing at least. He remembered he'd ordered a book from Blackwell's and rose to get it.

11

THE shop bore its usual Saturday freight of rural clergymen, embattled dowagers, graduate students in tweeds ripe as Stilton—all more intent on causing no sound and avoiding touch than on any book at hand. Hutch walked past the famous pair of ladies at the cash desk, rigid in their Radclyffe Hall impersonations, and climbed toward the English Lit. shelves at the back—the gnarled youth there who would have his book. As he passed the Art table, he smelled a faint trail of lemon and paused. It came from a small woman four feet beyond him in severe dark blue, her straight back to him. He thought he knew her hair—thin-textured, deep chestnut, half-down her tall neck. So he worked round the table, fingering the luxury of Phaidon folios, till he reached her profile. It was Vivien Leigh, slowly turning through a *Donatello* with spotless white gloves—the line of her own face from forehead to throat as splendid as any line caught in the book: the hip of the boy David, Judith with the sword. *The Helen of our days;* Hutch secretly fed on the sight for two minutes, preserving it for his own private gallery of perfections. Then she swung full toward him, set the book on its pile, and stared past his shoulder at the high sunny windows. The light showed her worn and too thin for safety, a webbing of shallow lines round her eyes. He knew that she and Olivier kept a house near Thame, ten miles from Oxford; he knew she had a stepson studying at Christ Church and was rumored to be seen dining with him at the George, but here she seemed suspended in an aimlessness as pure as her beauty till the madness smoked upward. He watched her frankly now; and though her eyes avoided him, she bore him calmly. Or was she only gathering the bottled rage of delicate bones to bellow like her Blanche at the end of *Streetcar?*—a hounded doe clawed down in a thicket, demanding aid. He could say, "Miss Leigh, I met you at Stratford last summer—*Macbeth.* Would you have coffee with me?" She seemed the one real chance in this dream-day. He cleared his throat softly.

Her eyes clicked toward him, searched him to the waist, returned to his eyes. Her long lips opened on small clenched teeth. Then she smiled. "Have you lost your glorious friend?"

Hutch was blank with surprise. "Ma'm?"

She laughed once, took two steps, and gave her hand—"Your Virginia gentleman."

He took the hand, nearly as broad as his own; then cupped the two with his free hand. "Yes. He's launched on his life."

She broke the touch easily, retreated a step—"Oh alas"—then took the Donatello and left. Her smile endured as far as the desk.

12

It was nearly three when he got back to college. The weather was holding and lunch was long over, so Front Quad was empty and stunned in the unaccustomed glare—no spare friends in sight to lure on a drive. He stopped in the Lodge for the second post—a wrinkled envelope addressed in Grainger's hand, his first from Grainger in more than a year. As he studied the tall script, he felt no conscious apprehension. But deeper he remembered the phone call in Rome, the news of Rob's dying; and he put the letter unopened in his pocket. Then he went toward his rooms. The meeting with Vivien Leigh still held him. He'd made her an offer—coffee at least—and she hadn't refused: turning away was not a firm No. Why hadn't he followed? To say what?—stage-door platitudes, English-teacher questions? When she'd charged her book and vanished through the door, he'd heard in his head but in her rich voice the plea of her Blanche—"I want to *rest!* I want to breathe quietly again!" The plea of a character but plainly her own too. He'd meant to answer that. Why? What rest had he to give, to her or anyone, who had never rested more than eight hours himself (and then in sleep)? As he entered his own quad—old Mob Quad, empty as the moon at full—all the questions found an answer. He had wanted to give the woman some short calm because—in her supreme beauty (fading daily), in the transitory force of an actor's work—she'd become a lucid emblem of his own destination or the long trip there: a life lived for others, though not at their request, ludicrously unneeded by them. No one else in Blackwell's had so much as glanced at a face the frank equal of any face known. He'd have told her that anyhow. Stale painful news to her.

He passed his own staircase, crossed the quad, and entered the Chapel. More vacant space—the vaulted gray belly of a grand whale, beached and drying for a century; a huge life lived out for whom, for what? *Well, for me,* he thought. But when he'd climbed to the choir and sat and faced the bare altar with its crowded but dubious Tintoretto, he could ask for nothing. He said her name silently, "Vivien Leigh." Then he waited and said, "Ann Gatlin. Strawson Stuart. Lew Davis. Hutchins Mayfield." The light in the windows dimmed as he sat. He'd go back and work, no trip today. He recalled Grainger's letter and opened it—the news on Straw's sleepiness, his Navy plans, then Ann's sudden visit, then *"she asked him did he know where to get a baby fixed."* Hutch saw their last night together in Richmond (her pressing him down to nurse at her source); he heard the last words of her letter again—*"You may never come back. . . . I may not be here. . . . Why should that have to mean The End?"* He made a quick calculation of dates. If they'd started a child in Rome and lost it, then she'd written her letter in the aftermath.

He stood to go to the Lodge and call her; it was just ten in the morning at home. He could hope to reach her—to say, God, what? At the door he paused by a swollen jasper urn donated by Czar Alexander I in memory of a visit here in 1814, a year before Waterloo. He looked toward the meadow, in brown shade now, and said what he'd said in the Pantheon—"Show me now please."

13

HE waited in the oak-and-glass cage of the Lodge while Victor the porter placed the call on the main college phone, a prewar antiquity massive as a dumbbell. When he finally signaled Hutch to enter the booth, there was thick fur and static on the line (not the unnerving clarity he'd heard in Rome under Grainger's voice). The British operator, a somber man, had reached Ann's house at least. Linda said "Yes."

"I have a call from England for Miss Ann Gatlin."

Linda waited. "Yes sir. She's gone now. I'm sorry."

Hutch said "Gone where?"—the grip of fright.

The man said, "You may not speak yet, Oxford." Then he said, "Is Miss Gatlin expected to return?"

Linda said, "Is it morning there where you are?"

The man paused as if that were also forbidden, a disastrous revelation; then conceded it. "Midafternoon."

"She ought to be back after suppertime Sunday, our suppertime here. Can you figure that out?" She seemed to laugh once. Was Bailey beside her?

The man said, "Oxford, you may try again tomorrow—at midnight perhaps: Greenwich time, of course."

Hutch said, "Can you ask if she's at her mother's please?"

"You could—for the full charge; yes you could."

Hutch said "I'll wait."

Linda said a clear "Yes" and was cut off at once.

Hutch didn't speak again—at her mother's and returning tomorrow for work. She was moving at least, that safe at least. She would not talk freely at her mother's. He must wait. But he had the small satisfaction of breaking the connection on the operator's dogged recital of rules.

14

WHEN he'd thanked the porter and tipped him to book a call for midnight Sunday, he stepped back out into the light, thinking only that he could not imagine any way—any series of harmless conscious actions—to kill the time, thirty-three clock hours. He didn't recall his recent plain prayer. But in those few minutes, the sky had cleared with the disconcerting speed of island weather. Now he'd have that to get through, a glorious day. Though he didn't know it, he strained in every fiber not to think the word *child*. Even his steps on the gritty pavement were gentle, unpercussive. He would sit in the deep musty chair by his window and do what Mr. Fleishman had suggested—read through the whole of Marvell's poems at a stretch. That should take him to dinner, with time for a nap (as always, in trouble, he was already tired). The night—he'd deal with that when it came, though Marleen Pickett's small face lurched up in his mind like a promise.

In the center of the hearthrug of grass in Mob Quad, a single figure stood, looking up toward the Chapel. A young man, middle-size, in clothes that were clearly not student clothes—clean and well-pressed and working-class: a light-blue gabardine suit, cheap and slick; the collar of a soft unbuttoned white shirt. The neck was almost as white, the hair black. The bells played their incomplete quarter-hour tune, which the man completed in a pure hum. Hutch thought he knew the voice but could summon no name; so he said, "You have a great future in music."

The man turned. "That's the first *good* news I've had."

It was James, James Nichols—in the pub last summer with the sleepy child, Nan. Hutch had forgot their quiet meeting and James's forecast of working on the stone here. He'd never recalled the dream he had (in Marleen's room) of finding James asleep at his father's, Nan smiling beside him. But he said, "You planning to restore all this?" He waved to the blistered walls around them.

James nodded. "Right. We're starting in Monday morning—tear it all down, remake it from the ground." He laughed. "You students will be billeted in tents—any luck, we'll have very little more snow. That's how the Americans would do it, right?"

Hutch walked toward him. "Then we'd dress you characters in medieval tights and let you give tours."

"Not me," James said. "Never show my legs."

"Why?"

"Drives the public mad. I learned that in prison." He spoke at normal volume, unashamed of his past, and continued smiling on the perfect teeth.

Hutch said, "We'll put you in monk's robes then."

"My poor feet'll freeze; don't they wear sandals?"

"Barefoot," Hutch said. "You'll need to toughen up."

James paused to think as though the plan were serious. Then he said, "I reckon I've toughened all I mean to. I'm easing down now."

"How's that?"

"Oh I don't know—saving my farthings for a holiday with Nan."

"Is she well?"

"Yes thanks."

"Still with you at your mother's?"

James shook his head once to show surprise. "You retain facts, don't you?"

"It's my trade, storing pictures. I can see her quite clearly."

James shook his head again. "Not the way she is now. She's grown half a foot." He measured her height in the air at his side, then studied the spot and raised his hand an inch. "I haven't seen her either since Boxing Day."

"She's back with her mother?"

"With her aunt in Reading. Her mother's in Yorkshire with a crippled bus-driver. I couldn't keep her here, me and my mum working."

Hutch squatted to the ground and combed in the cool grass. "But you see her when you want?"

James continued standing (he didn't belong here and took no liberties). "Right—well, no. I want to see her every day, but Reading's quite a journey when all you've got's a push-bike."

"You had a motorcycle."

James grinned. "Before prison—my mum sold it then. Just as well, I reckon; I'm dead most nights."

Hutch said, "We could drive down to Reading now."

James thrust both hands in his pockets and was silent.

"If you don't have plans."

"Not really," James said. "I was walking in the Meadow, thought I might find a girl in need on the river. They were all bespoke so I saw the old Chapel.here and thought I'd whip over the wall for a look. We'll be in early on Monday like I said."

"Aren't you late? In July you said you'd be here in autumn."

James leaned to the grass and brushed the tips slowly, then stood again. "Maybe so, maybe not. Everything in its time. I go where they tell me."

Hutch rose. "Then to Reading."

15

But they took the long way. Once they'd entered the warm car, James took up the *Guide to Berks. and Oxon.* and said, "Understand—I'm free till dawn Monday. If there's some place you'd rather be than Reading, I'll navigate."

Hutch said, "You'd rather not see Nan today?"

"Oh no. She can still be the goal by dark. She quite liked you—mentioned you more than once, asking her was she an owl. I just meant, if you had the time, we could roam."

Hutch cranked the engine—"I'm free till Sunday midnight"—then faced James's profile: its Italianate simplicity of line and depth (were Roman genes still afloat in British veins?—almost always working-class veins, untapped by Normans).

James accepted the look but still watched the street. "You turn into some kind of pumpkin then?"

Hutch laughed. "I may well. But sure, let's roam."

James opened to the maps in the guide. "Name a place."

"No. You. I'm tired of choosing."

James shut the book. "Inkpen Beacon, due south."

Hutch moved into gear—"What's that?"—and rolled forward.

"Highest chalk down in the British Isles."

"Anything else but chalk? Can we get tea for instance?"

"—Get hung," James said and frowned theatrically and strangled his throat with his broad left hand.

Hutch said, "I'm not sure I deserve that yet."

James looked over then and studied Hutch slowly. "Maybe not, not yet. But they've got a gallows there so mind yourself, eh?"

Hutch turned from Blue Boar Street into St. Aldate's, past Christ Church and Police Headquarters. They'd crossed Folly Bridge and the smooth brown river, when he said, "Keep me posted. I'm a very poor judge." But he felt nearly half-free again, to be rolling.

So they rushed on in steadily warming air, fast patches of cloud, through Frilford with its Romano-British cemetery; then the green eastern end of the Vale of the White Horse and dozing Wantage, the birthplace in 849 A.D. of Alfred the Great (its market-square garnished by Gleicken's white statue of Alfred as a Saxon in a boy's dream of Saxons); then little Great Shefford with its round-towered church ("owing to the prevalence of unworkable flint"); then Hungerford, a fiefdom of John of Gaunt ("who gave his fishing rights to the town; it remains an angling resort today").

They'd stopped nowhere and only slowed for traffic—the occasional Margaret Rutherford twin, heroically cycling in the narrow road. The talk had consisted of James's directions and readings from the guide, Hutch's questions on the story of what they passed. No personal words—only the weather and moderate speed, the consoling wallpaper of the scenes beyond them, the absence of thought.

Then open country, the start of the downs, scattered farms in mucky yards, a road like a path. James led now in silence with pointings and nods. Hutch said, "You know all this like your hand."

James waited. "Never seen any of it before. Never seen anything but Oxford and jail."

"Then you've got second sight."

James said "So I'm told."

Hutch said, "Did you know you'd see me in Merton?" He was watching the road.

"May have."

"What else?"

James waited, then faced him—"Eh?"—blank as paper.

"What else do you know?"

"That I've steered us right." He looked out his window. "That we're actually there." He pointed to a far tall pole on the ridge they were aiming toward. It bore a crossbeam at the top and two braces—cross from a Flemish crucifixion.

Hutch said, "Have you figured what I deserve?"

James said, "A short hike in the sun at least."

So he pulled as far off the lane as he could. James sprang up the bank and spread two strands of wire apart; Hutch crawled through and stood to return the favor. But James poised a moment on the narrow ledge of turf, vaulted the fence in one neat arc; and preceded him through the high grass, still wet despite the sun.

When James reached the gallows, he ringed it with his left arm and stared off south to the lunar downs of Hampshire. Hutch kept a little distance but turned in place, from the bare chalk view toward the greener north. For the first time since Oxford, he thought of his worries. They still seemed powerful—sufficient to end all his orderly plans for work, then life. But here now they seemed unable to find him; he felt he'd been rescued and buried in safety, though the prospect in every direction was endless. He pointed northwest at a distant hill. "What's that?"

James swung round, still hugging the pole, and consulted his guide. "That would be the backside of White Horse Hill."

"Ever seen it?"

James said "I'm seeing it now."

"The horse, I mean."

James said, "I never cared much for horses."

"It's a picture of a horse, prehistoric, cut in chalk."

"That's for you," James said. "You're the picture man."

Hutch grinned—"All right"—and looked to the east, another hill. "And that?"

James read slowly. " 'Walbury Hill, the highest chalk elevation in England, on the crest of which (975 feet) lies the Iron Age bastion of Walbury Camp.' "

Hutch nodded, walked past the gallows, looked southwest—Wiltshire, Dorset, Wessex, Hardy country. Then he came back and laid a flat palm on the post above James's arm (James was still facing Walbury, tracing the entrenchment). "Is the verdict in?"

"Eh?"

Hutch laughed. "—On the hanging. Do I hang?"

James said, "What's the worst thing you ever did?"

Hutch said "I refuse to testify."

James said, "I didn't. I sang like a lark. Of course they had a half-dead bloke I'd bashed and a dance hall of witnesses. Take your medicine, mate. You'll feel better for it."

"Do you?" Hutch said.

James waited, then laughed. "A new man—hark!" He turned the pole loose, stepped six feet away, consulted his book. Then he pointed to the gallows and read out clearly in the breeze that had risen—" 'The gallows, one of the last in England, is kept in repair as a term of the lease of the nearby farm. The third to stand upon this ridge, its predecessor was struck by lightning. On the first, a couple were hanged in 1676 for drowning the woman's two children in a neighboring dewpond on the downs.' "

Hutch said, "Is all that really in your book?"

James nodded. "Your book."

"You didn't just make it up?"

James shook his head and held the open guide out like a saint on an ikon. "This is England, remember? Everything's got a past as bloody as me." The light was blown across him in scraps by the strengthening wind; and though his hair ruffled and his eyes filled with tears, he stood now clean as any washed child.

Hutch took the largest key from his pocket and quickly scored *H.M.* in the post. There were many other names, carved deeper than his, and one small drawing—a man's profile, the mouth gapped open in laughter or pain.

James said, "You'd need a knife to make that last."

16

THE wind stayed behind them on into Reading, and the wall of Irish cloud had clamped evening down on their heads when James said "There, the ugliest house."

Hutch could see no difference. The row of attached houses—two-story, tan brick—was uniformly unredeemed, even by the yellow light of the street lamp which clicked on precisely as he killed the engine.

James turned. "You were thinking of how much time?"

"How much will you need?"

James thought. "Well, I'd estimate ten, twelve years. She'll leave about then." He stroked the steel dash.

"Shall I wait here?"

"For what?" James said, genuinely puzzled.

"Till you break the ice or finish your visit. I wouldn't mind."

James studied him. "You would. You'd die out here—bleeding Scott of the Antarctic! Follow me." He climbed out and knocked three times at the door before Hutch joined him.

Hutch said, "We could take her to dinner."

"She's eaten."

"Whose house is this?"

"Her aunt's, Helen's sister." James knocked again.

The letter slot opened from inside—silence.

James put in his forefinger gradually, smiling.

A child's voice said, "No. I'm here by myself."

James laughed. "You mustn't tell strangers that." He took back his finger. "It's your old dad, Nan. Now give us a look."

Her feet seemed to run away down a hall. Then she stopped and returned. "Say something else."

He said, "I've come a long way to see you."

Nan waited. "We leaving here?"

James squatted slowly and lifted the letter slot. "You turn the key. Ethel won't care. We'll play."

Another long wait as if she were balancing pain in a scale, anticipating loss. Then the sound of her struggle with the key, the bolt slid.

James stood and said "That's it." The door stayed shut. He opened it gently inward on air as dark as the street.

Hutch could see no one, a single dim bulb at the back by a stair.

James stepped forward, beckoning Hutch behind him. When they stood well inside, James shut the door. Nan was pressed in the corner by the hinges, facing out—grave as she'd been in the pub that first night. James said, "Say thanks to this man, eh?"

Nan looked to the worn mat. "Why?"

"He brought me—lovely new car. You remember him."

She shook her head fiercely.

"Course you do. He thought you was an owl, in Oxford the night you come to me."

Her head shook again.

"Where's Ethel gone?"

Nan looked up at Hutch. In the eight months her hair had darkened a little. Her ruddy face was purer now, luminous above her dark green sweater. Her eyes were dry. But every effort of her body, each cell, was aimed at James—to copy his shape.

Hutch squatted and met her gaze. "You had your tea?"

She nodded.

"Could I?"

She said, "I'm not allowed to touch the kettle."

James said "I am."

"You're not," she said. Her face had hardened astonishingly.

There were steps on the pavement, a knock at the door. "Nan, it's me."

James looked to Hutch, whispered "Ethel," and waved him backward down the hall.

Hutch retreated a yard.

James nodded to Nan.

She opened the door—a small woman sealed in a heavy gray coat, a small bundle wrapped in newsprint at her breast.

She saw Hutch first and stopped on the sill as if James were air. What seemed to be anger began in her eyes.

Hutch thought it was fear and smiled. "I'm with James. I drove him down."

That released her to see James; she studied him slowly. "You got a new outfit."

"New to you," he said and stepped from her path. Then he looked to Hutch. "Introduce yourself." He'd forgot Hutch's name.

Hutch said "Hutchins Mayfield."

Nan said "Hutch."

Ethel entered her own house. "She's mentioned you." She set her bundle on the table and hung her coat on a peg. Her face was still taut.

James said, "He's hoping you'll give him his tea." He thumbed toward Hutch.

Ethel picked at a stain on the sleeve of her coat. "Mick's working tonight. Nan's had her tea. I just got some fish and chips for myself. There's nothing else really." But she turned to Hutch. "You driving him back tonight?"

"Yes ma'm."

The *ma'm* surprised her (she was twenty-eight). The eyes half-relented. "You'll need something hot then, won't you?"

"I'm fine."

She waited. "You're not." Then she blushed. "*I'm* sorry—you just seem pale."

James said, "We came by Inkpen, the gallows. He's short on breath."

Ethel said, "James, you could fetch in more fish. I could make the tea." She searched in her coat and brought up a purse.

James looked to Hutch. "That suit you, eh?"

"By all means. But you stay with Nan; I'll go. Where's the nearest shop?"

Ethel forced a ten-shilling note into James's hand. "You know. You go. Bring some beer if you like."

James cupped the crown of Nan's hair but spoke to Hutch. "If I'm not back in twenty minutes, call the Constabulary—they've got me prints." He was gone like a bird, small evening bird.

Ethel said, "Our back room is shocking so brace yourself."

Nan led the way slowly, her arms out straight as if she were walking the thinnest wire.

The room was clean and no more disordered than any used space; but in its mute ugliness, it was mildly shocking—raw overhead light, wallpaper embossed with the ruthless pattern of old pressed-tin, three comfortless chairs, a dust-colored sofa, a chromo of dogs, a rotogravure in acid blues of the Duchess of Kent a-bristle with stones. No papers or books, no television, no sign of a toy. No trace of a child—but Nan herself, who sat on the floor and began to align eight thread-spools in silence.

Ethel lit a gas grate, poked the seat of a chair; and said, "You're

welcome to *try* it; don't break a hip." Then she vanished through another door, shut it behind her, and filled a kettle.

Hutch sat to watch Nan—or her shifting spools: he could hardly
watch her.

She made neat patterns in a regular order (arrows, stars), proceeding
through what seemed a list in her mind of all the permutations of eight.
No spool ever toppled and, though she'd clearly moved them many times,
they were spotless white. She made a big almond-shape the size of her
head, all perfectly placed. Then she looked up at Hutch. "What can you
do?"

He laughed. "With what?"

"These," she said. She touched a spool lightly.

"Nothing better than you. You work very well."

She nodded agreement solemnly. "You work with James?"

"Your father?"

"James."

Hutch tried to remember what she'd called James in July; but he
said, "Oh no. I'm a student—more boring."

Nan examined him carefully up and down. Then she said, "I never
get bored. Ethel asks me but I never do."

"You like school then?"

"I don't go to school yet. One more year." She held up a finger.

"Any playmates about?" There were muffled knocks from the kitchen
but still no other sign of children.

Nan shook her head firmly.

"Then what do you do?—beside that game." He bent and moved a
spool.

She set it back in place. Then she grinned broadly (James's great
sunrise-grin). "Nothing else," she said. "I'm a child, see?" She sprang
up and once more held out her arms, balanced now and still as the house.

Hutch sat back and said, "Do you ever miss James?"

Nan bore his look a moment, then quickly faced round—the kitchen
door.

Ethel had opened it and stood there broadside. "Run along up,
Nan, and put on your trousers—the new little blue ones. James'll like
those."

Nan was glad to obey.

Hutch rose. "Did he have far to go?"

Ethel said "Not really." She clasped her hands at her waist like a
singer. "Course he may have gone to Zanzibar. On my ten shillings!"

"Not likely," Hutch said. "He's got his job Monday."

"Had a job all his life, ever since he was Nan's age. I knew him then
but that never stopped him going his way."

"He loves Nan now."

"*I love Nan,*" Ethel said. "I've loved her right through; he drops in on her like bombs, now and then. Mick, my husband, loves her better than James. Mick'd spend every farthing he earned on her if I didn't hold him back."

Hutch said, "There aren't any other children here?"

She shook her head hard. "Can't be. Not with me here. The doctor says I can't." She crouched to the grate and lowered the gas; the room was crackling dry. Then she faced Hutch squarely, pale as he now. "Pardon me asking but aren't you American?"

"Yes."

"You're at college?"

"In Oxford. I met James there."

"You're quite influential with him, I can see."

Hutch smiled. "I've spent all of three hours with him."

Ethel nodded. "He worships Americans. He'd have *swam* there years ago if he could breathe water."

"You needn't worry; I don't own a diving bell."

She waited, then took one step too close and whispered the rest. "No, *take* him—please God. Get him out of Nan's sight."

Hutch eased back slightly. "Won't her mother send for her?"

Ethel laughed, her mouth as sour as if from spew. "Never, never. I'm safe from her."

"How's that?"

"—Men. Her eyes only focus on men."

Hutch said, "She's in Yorkshire now with a man?"

"She was last week. May be with a yak on the moon by now."

The noise of the front door opening—James. Nan calling to him from the top of the stairs. Laughter and some kind of scuffle in the hall.

Ethel said, "If he asks you, say she's better off here. She is and all; anyone can see that." Her eyes stayed on Hutch while she gestured round her, the blistered room.

Hutch nodded "Yes" and tapped her lean shoulder with his cool right hand.

James was on them—his arms full of fish and beer; Nan mounted on his shoulders, smiling fully at last. She had put on her owl sweater, outgrown but clean.

17

THEY'D eaten, heard Ethel's long rhapsody of trouble, then invented a game with Nan's spools and played it for half an hour on the floor while Ethel washed up. Then Mick returned from the biscuit works, and they talked uneasily with him awhile (he was in his late thirties and had a gimp leg). Then Nan lay by James's knees and fell asleep, sudden and mute as a plummet. James had tested her finally by bending to her eyes, brushing her lashes with his chin, and humming. She was thoroughly gone so he'd stood clear of her (not touching her again) and said, "We might as well go while we can." Mick had tacitly thanked them for going by laughing them off from the curb and standing till they'd vanished at the corner.

They'd ridden quietly the first twenty minutes with only occasional directions from James; but on the near side of Streatley, he said, "I reckon I should ask your pardon for that."

Hutch said, "I can't think of any offense."

James waited, staring off to his right. "Thanks," he said. "I just meant my muck—slogging you blind into all my muck."

"There at Ethel's? It seemed very tidy to me."

James sat through the whole of the town in silence; but when they reached country again, he said, "No—me, my sad little pile of mess."

Hutch said, "All I saw was that Nan has grown but loves you and that Ethel loves her."

James nodded at once but sat another long while, then faced Hutch's profile—"Where does that leave James?"—then quickly looked out his own window again.

Hutch could only think "Here, parallel to me" but he didn't speak. His own mind was aimed at tomorrow night, the chance of finding Ann and knowing what he must know—the size and nature of the muck he'd made.

James said "Well, *here*—eh?" and laughed.

Hutch said "What?"

"*Here.* I'm here in the valley of the Thames, still breathing, under stars as bright as my teeth, being chauffeured by a kind American gent of independent means toward my native heath and my proud profession. Only fifty more years of that—Christ, give me longer!" James laughed again, no bitter note.

Hutch said, "You want to hear where I'm driving *me*?"

James waited. "I don't mind. I said I was free."

"I think I may be too. I'll know tomorrow night."

"What happens then?"

"What I'm driving toward. I have to phone a girl in the States, in Virginia." Hutch stopped there, hoping to be led somehow.

"What will she have to say?"

"Where my child is maybe."

"Your child?" James said.

"One I made with her last Christmas in Rome. She met me there. I'm afraid she took the child."

James counted on his fingers. "It's not born yet."

Hutch nodded. "I'm afraid she's bought an abortion."

"You don't know for certain?"

"No. Her letters haven't said."

"She didn't ask for money?"

"No."

"It's not your baby."

Hutch managed to smile at the quick assumption. "It wouldn't be so simple."

"Is she rich?"

"Not at all—a lawyer's typist."

"Then—begging your pardon, guv—but you ain't the dad: no offense to the lady, who I never saw. At least I assume not."

"You haven't," Hutch said. "She's never been in England." But he pictured a face he hadn't recalled since late December—Rowlet Swanson's mountain vacancies, ready to speak whatever was asked.

James said, "Then she's had that much luck at least. Don't bring her here and wreck it."

Hutch said "I love her."

"Then why—" James quit. "Sorry. It's your life, I'm sure—carry on."

"No, ask any question. I may need to talk."

So again James stroked the dash as if to please it. "I was asking myself why you're here then and she's that far off, cutting out a child."

"Because I planned it."

"You just said you loved her."

Hutch nodded. "Very much."

James said, "I doubt I could understand not being with anybody I ever loved."

"We left Nan asleep."

"I'll go back," James said. "I'll take her when I'm settled."

"That's more or less what I planned," Hutch said. "I'd study here for two years, go home, get a better job, and marry."

"The job'll be what?"

"Teaching college, writing poems."

"Pay you for poems in America, do they?"

Hutch laughed. "No I throw in the poems for free."

James said "I should hope so" and that seemed to stop them.

They were quiet till Wallingford, the lights of its small heart. It was halfway to Oxford, and Hutch thought of pausing at the Lamb or the Feathers to stand James a beer. But when he glanced over, James seemed so embedded in the car's pure privacy—such a safe fair jury—that he drove on and then, in the stretch before Dorchester, said, "Who have you ever loved beside Nan?"

James thought. "Do I love Nan?"

"You said you did."

"When?"

"When I met you and her in the pub last summer. You said you and she fell in love with each other at St. Giles's Fair, the same day the gypsy told Helen she'd be the cause of blood in others."

James said "Christ," astonished; then sat awhile. "Is memory a qualification of authors?"

Hutch laughed. "Yes, the first."

"Then by all rights, mate, you're due to be Shakespeare." He turned to see Hutch for the first time fully. Then he laughed. "Just to show you what *I'm* due to be—I've forgot your name again."

"Hutch Mayfield."

"I like that," James said. "You'll go far with that."

Hutch said, "It's been a long way already. It may be tired."

"You're two hours older than me. Buck up."

"The name, I mean."

James said, "Have I the honor to be hauled by the heir to a noble American line?"

"—A line of deep thinkers and sensitive plants, if that's nobility."

"It's not," James said.

"Wrong again."

"You or me?"

Hutch said "Me."

James sat through a dark mile, the onslaught of wind from the west, the car rocking. Then he said "Never mind" with the same brisk warmth he kept for Nan. He spread both his hands in the panel light and spoke toward them. "The working class has its own slice of fun."

Hutch said, "I've laid a big bet on work."

"Start now."

"On what?"

"Your job," James said. "Make a poem right here." He scrawled in the air with his blunt forefinger.

"Pick a subject then."

James at once said "Me," then wrote on awhile in the chilling air before him. "—Why you've got me here. Why you've bothered with me."

Hutch thought he knew. "I suspect you're my father."

"Is that the poem?"

Hutch laughed once but realized it was, one of the oldest happiest poems—Jacob and Joseph, Odysseus and Telemachus, Lear and Cordelia. He turned to James—"It may well be"—then felt the foolishness.

But James thought it through. "I sort of doubt that. I mean, I've seen a fair number of oddities along my path; and I've known enough girls to be a bit vague—about *this* life, at least—but I doubt you're mine." When he looked round he grinned.

Hutch surprised himself with the confirmation—that something in the boy seemed identical with Rob, of the same good essence. Nothing ghostly or urgent but a gentle palpable return of the oldest presence he'd known and needed—the vulnerable potent needy youth who'd stood at the rim of Hutch's own childhood and asked for help. He faced the road and said, "No my father died a few weeks back. He meant a great deal. You look a little like him." He reached out his right hand and touched James's brow. "The eyes, just the eyes." That was not the case; but it seemed a fair way, on their windy progress up the black Thames valley, to honor the moment and its small consolation.

James looked forward also and nodded slowly. "Glad to help," he said. His strong delicate face, in its stillness, pressed on the night like an adequate prow through whatever waters might wait ahead.

18

THE operator was a man again but friendlier. When Ann answered through surges of static, the man said, "Ring off please, America. I'll try again." Then to Hutch, "Sounds like old Roosevelt, don't she?—I quite miss the war."

The second try she came through clear but small. "Am I better now?"

Hutch waited for the operator to speak, then realized he'd vanished. So he quickly said "Yes much better." He paused. "Are you really, Ann?"

"Oh sure." She laughed. "At least all the locals still *call* me Ann. I still recognize me in mirrors I pass."

"I got your letter."

"Good,' she said. "Then are you really Hutch?" She laughed again. "The same. At your service."

She held a long moment. "I'm glad, I guess."

"I also got a few words from Grainger. He said they'd seen you."

"I'd wondered if they did. I felt transparent."

Hutch said "You never are."

"I try," she said. "But I do seem to fade."

"Not for me. I see you every hour at least."

"Thank you," she said. "Is that any help?"

"To me?—a lot. Or it has been till now."

"What would change it now?"

Hutch thought for five expensive seconds. "You wanting me gone."

"Never. I told you."

"You didn't tell all."

Ann said "What's missing?"

"I'm here to ask that. Grainger's note has me worried."

She waited, then saw no way to move but straight. "What did Grainger say?"

"That you asked Straw to help you find an abortion."

"Grainger's more or less right."

"—And that Straw got mad."

"Well, *hurt.* I seemed to hurt him." Her voice still sounded with real regret.

"Did you find it though?"

"Yes."

"Who helped you?"

"Bailey, Linda's Bailey."

"Was Bailey involved?"

"Just in helping," she said, "—finding the woman."

"It was ours, right?"

"I hope not," she said. Hard as it was, she'd never planned to lie.

Hutch said, "Should I know who else was there?"

"Not here—in Rome. After you went—once, for fifteen minutes. I was lost when you left me."

Hutch saw Rowlet's face again, asking his question in the ruins by the river—how to act once he and Ann were alone, "two orphans in Rome." Hutch recalled he'd never answered more than "Good luck." So now he didn't speak Rowlet's name. He suspected he might be fatally cut in some vital part; but he said, "It was not a good time for anybody."

"Awful."

"Are you safe?"

"I hope so," she said.

"Your health, I mean."

"I hope so, yes."

Hutch said, "Was it a real doctor Bailey found?"

"No a colored woman. She was gentle as she could be."

"Have you seen a doctor since?"

Ann said "No."

"When was it?" Then he knew he was multiplying questions in confusion, for balance. "I'm sorry," he said.

"February eleventh, a Saturday night, four weeks ago." Her voice had begun to balk toward the end.

Hutch wondered where he'd been at the actual moment. But then he heard her tears—restrained as they were, still plain through the buried leagues of wire. He said, "Have you managed to work right along?"

"Never missed a day."

"Good."

"I guess so." Her voice had firmed but was suddenly tired.

"Do you want to come here?"

She waited. "For what?"

Hutch laughed. "The sun! The royal palms! No for me, for a rest."

"Have we ever been a rest?" It seemed a dumb riddle, but she didn't revise it.

And Hutch said "Sure," then searched for examples—Rome, Christmas day on the Palatine, the shape of her body laid on the trees at the Great Mother's shrine: a feasible goal. He also saw Lew beside him on Tresco, fervent in loss; Straw bare and cold from his nocturnal swim. Different goals. Or all one center? He said again "Sure."

"Not for me," Ann said.

"That can't be true."

She waited again. "It's true—about *rest*. I've loved more than half our minutes together; but I can't recall resting, not if we were awake."

"Why not?"

"I could never stop wanting you. I could never believe you meant to stay."

Hutch thought "Oh I did" but once more saw the places that had drawn him to their various hearts (the places were people). Could he choose one now? He said, "Is the ring still buried in your powder?"

"I took it home Friday to Mother's. It's safe there, no burglars for years."

"I asked you to wear it." That still seemed his choice, made a year ago nearly.

Ann laughed. "In my nose? We never had it sized."

It fell in on him then, a shoal of regrets that tasted like revulsion. "Ann, the child may have been part mine. Is that much true?"

"Yes."

"And what happened in Rome was a kind of accident?"

"Yes," she said, "a kind of revenge."

"And you still think you want me to stay in your life?"

"Most days, yes. I think it most days."

"Then get back the ring, wear it on a chain till I'm home again, and believe I mean to stay." He believed himself.

Ann said "Let me wait."

"For what?"

"Myself. For me please, Hutch. I've been on a whole long outing of my own—I don't mean Rome—and I wasn't really ready, and I'm not home yet. The main thing I need to believe right now is that I'll get back. When I do I'll know."

"What?"

Her stillness was total but she didn't think. She was locked in the midst of a brown fatigue. Then she said, "I'll hope to know what to want."

Hutch saw no way to ask for more, though the one request that rose in his mind now was *ending*—an honorable mutual walking away. Had he ever felt that with anyone else? Maybe Rob toward the end when the pain of witness exceeded the love. He said, "I'll be here, I guess, when you know."

"I'll write you a letter tomorrow at lunch."

"I live for the mail." He laughed. "Ann, I want to send you the money."

"Please no."

"I owe it."

"You don't," she said. "You've already paid. We're both paid-up."

Hutch thought, hot and fast, "You owe me a life"; but he said "All right." The heavy old receiver in his hand was strong with the scurf of two generations of similar breaths, scattered and gone. He flicked it with his tongue, trying unconsciously to summon her sweetness—the presence against him of skin warm as his with identical intentions: endlessly generous, courteous, conversant through whole long nights.

Ann seemed to say "Thanks."

19

Hutch thanked the porter for managing the call, then entered the dark Front Quad, still raked by wind that had held since Saturday night. High clouds tore past toward what?—White Russia, Mongolia, Alaska. Behind them the sky was uniformly light but starless and no sign of moon. He hoped he'd meet no one but could navigate the fifty yards to his room in silence, then read Rob's posthumous letter again. He'd stored it carefully after the first time, too painful then. Now its memory promised at least counter-pain to the news from Ann—and maybe more. A map toward what he still meant to have, the life Rob missed; a chart-by-omission. A grown man's life, aimed straight toward a goal and proceeding there. A *waking* life, dreamed by no one but his open-eyed self—truthful enough to know its few needs and fill them, if no other body stood to suffer. Even here, Ann's voice five minutes behind him, there seemed no big impediment to that. He felt as stripped as he'd felt in Cornwall or in the wrecked boat on the black beach on Tresco—solitary pilot-and-crew combined—but peaceful now and safe to the end.

No one crossed his path. The glum handful of students who'd lingered to study through Easter were shut in asleep, no light at any window. The dons (surely brandied as Christmas peaches) were snoring in the chill, though his own steps made the sole human sound. The college—five acres of the most fruitful ground ever consecrated to harmless work—was his to roam. But he wanted his own room—the charged souvenirs that mapped his past (the pinebark man carved by old Rob Mayfield, the stones from Castle Dore and Cybele's altar, the magnifying glass from Archie Gibbons, the pages written four thousand miles from here by a man who'd finished eleven years of high school in no blaze of anything brighter than the worship in Min Tharrington's eyes).

His staircase was dark so he started the dozen high steps slowly, boards soft as flannel. In the moments of climb, he discovered this much— that even he had not expected a year mined like this with cuttings and space. He knew it had stunned him and knew he was flat exhausted now; he'd have the whole six weeks of Easter to gauge the damage and feel it deep. And stop it—repair his life and whoever else he'd agreed to hurt. Who else but Ann? Yet Ann had known of Rob's speeding death and kept the secret for her private purpose—to join him, unhindered and smiling, in Rome. A free choice of hers, to lie and face the ends of a lie. What blame should he bear?

His door was half-open. He remembered he'd shut it. Other nights he'd have quickly assumed a flying visit from English friends, with their universal indifference to the warmth he painfully nursed from his two-bar heater. But the friends were gone. He froze two steps below the landing and listened hard. Steps in his bedroom, the low sound of music (jazz from Radio Luxembourg); then steps and radio moved toward the sitting room. Hutch stayed in place. From there in the dark, he could see his desk five yards away, his eyes exactly level with its top. A man came over and stood beside it—back turned, dark clothes, portable radio in hand. He set down the radio and touched an open notebook (Hutch had tried today to revive his Tristan poem—Gorvenal's version, what the butler saw).

The man was James almost certainly—the broad white plane of neck above his back collar, the short black curls. James had known the time of the call to Ann. Hutch had never been robbed, never heard of anyone in college being robbed—no one ever locked a door—so he felt both the standard symptoms of rape (his room, his psychic body, rummaged in) and the second great cave-in of the night. A cheerful likeable acquaintance unmasked as a scheming thief. *"Fool,"* Hutch thought. "He told me from the start." He'd also nearly killed a man. Should Hutch go for help?

The radio had stopped—dead batteries? James thumped it gently twice with no success. All his movements were slow as if underwater or in cold oil. He opened the center drawer of the desk. Rob's letter was there.

Of all that had happened today—this year—Hutch could not stand that. He took the last steps loudly, entered the room.

James looked round, smiling calmly. "I found you then. I was scratching about in here to find your name—didn't know your room, picked the one with lights."

Hutch nodded. "It's mine."

"But your wireless is dead." James tapped at the dial again, sudden music. "Hullo, I'm a healer!"

Hutch said "Can I help you?"

James flushed crimson; his eyes crouched incredulous. He took a step back. "I was thinking I might just manage that for *you.*"

Hutch frowned a mute question.

"—A bit of help," James said. "I thought you might want it."

"I'm still up and moving."

"—Your call to the States; it sounded like a killer."

"You heard it?"

"Course, not—what you told me last night, your girl and that kid."

The desk drawer still hung open. Hutch closed it, closed the notebook and squared it neatly, then switched off the music. "Well, a *maimer,*" he said. "I doubt it killed me." He flexed his right hand in the air between them.

James said "I was wrong."

"How?"

"The kid was really yours." He looked to the seat of the chair but stayed upright, an unwelcomed guest.

Hutch had not faced him for two minutes now; he watched the worn carpet and nodded to that. "You were wrong."

"Did you thank her?"

"No."

"You will and all."

"Why?"

"Christ, look at *me.*" James struck his own breastbone hard with a fist.

Hutch heard it as an order and looked up then. It had been a sad admission—James's pallor was a firm luminescence in the air, stronger than the lamp and desolate. Rob again, a thousand times in memory. Moth to his own flame, dying and fed. Hutch said, "Send for Nan. I'll take you to get her."

As slowly as he'd moved when Hutch spied on him, James thrust out a flat palm—enough, have mercy. "She's Helen's or Ethel's or Mick's— or the Queen's. Anybody's but mine."

"Where does that leave you?"

"In me skin." James drew back his palm and scrubbed a cheek. Color flooded again, the ready blood. "In your room here."

Hutch said "How'd you get in?"

A sizable gap. "Oh now, mate, *my* little crime was assault. I never stole a tanner."

Hutch nodded. "The porter didn't see you, right?"

James smiled. "No I soared in silent from the river." He pointed out the black uncovered windows. "On me bat-leather wings."

Hutch said "Sit down" and turned to draw the curtains. The big horse-chestnut was loud in the wind.

James sat on the edge of the chair he'd touched.

"I could do up some cocoa."

James said "No thanks."

"I might have a little whiskey left."

James said "No thanks." Then as Hutch knelt to open the battered cupboard, he said "You got any sleep?"

Hutch turned.

"Sleep—you know, what humans do at night." James shut his eyes and snored.

Hutch said "I might." When he stood, empty-handed, he felt a great calm.

20

March 12, 1956

Dear Hutch,

I promised to write you a letter at lunchtime today so here I am. It was not that restful a night, as you can guess; and Monday in the office is always nervous as a jumping bean. And I said, on the phone and in the letter last week, almost everything I know. Please remember that, if you want information on Ann Gatlin still. I like to watch you better than anybody I've known. I like to be with you day after day, even if it keeps me sweating with hope. I'm fairly dry now and I guess you must be after last night, but—well, but what? Nothing right now. I'm trying to curb the prophetess in me; she was so scared of all she thought she saw and was also wrong more than half the time.

Can I stop there for now? Just for now, understand—with this one postscript. In every word I've said since Christmas (I reviewed them all in the dark last night), there was just one lie. I want to correct it. Your ring is not at Mother's house. I had it with me on February 11th; and after the day, I asked Bailey please to take me to Polly's. I told her the story—the only person beside you and Bailey (he hasn't told Linda). She took it the way rocks seem to take rain, so I asked her to hold the ring for safekeeping. It felt like the right thing then and still does. So it's there with her.

I have to go out now and try to find a new dress in thirty-five minutes. Mother made me vow to come home for Easter and gave me a check

*to refurbish my looks. Did you notice Easter falls on April Fool's Day this
year? The Prayer Book says it hasn't done that since 1945 and won't again
in the twentieth century. Is that some kind of blessing? Please advise.*

*Love,
Ann*

March 18, 1956

Dear Ann,

*I waited till your letter came so as not to babble before you spoke. It
came yesterday. I thought a lot of course, this way and that; but like you,
I don't have much worth saying. You rein in your sibyl; I'll silence my
own tin-horn Jeremiah. That's to say I don't have or feel any trace of
blame, and that's not to ask for the year's Big Heart Prize. You must have
done all you saw to do. I've been doing the same. My lie was, that doing
what I saw to do has included touching several people other than Ann.
I'd have told you sooner if I'd known it mattered.*

*All it means now is, I don't claim pride of place over you and that
I'm still open to more of the world than I planned to be. You remember
Grandmother telling me last year that, at twenty-five, I was over the hill.
In less than two months, I'll be one year farther over—on the skids, by her
schedule. And I hoped to be dug in better by now, a hill camp at least
from which I could see the line of the route and stock my provisions.*

*I'm not—dug in, as you well know. So I think I should stop predicting
the route. And if I do, don't I stop—like you—knowing who I can ask to
share the wait? None of which means I don't remember our numerous
best times as grand—long unblemished days—and hope there will, some
way, be more of them (well-spaced through whatever lives we get).*

*Love always,
Hutch*

March 20, 1956

Dear Polly,

*Isn't this the first day of spring? I ask because I'm a shut-in here—
the third straight day of rain, the air's solid water. I wonder how I'm
breathing; gills would seem called for. And in fact there were long welts
under my jaws when I looked just now—I'm evolving to last in a new
world, I trust.*

*It's Easter vacation, six long weeks of it. After Easter I'll probably
spend a week or so in Cumberland and Scotland; but with the trip home,
I got well behind in my work and must scramble. Reading, reading—slow
progress, wearing these deep-sea goggles.*

I'm also too far behind with the mail. Your letter, with the word on Agnes Butters' wedding, came three weeks ago and cheered me as intended. But even more so in the past ten days when I read it more than once. I had a note from Grainger, then telephoned Ann and learned her sad news. I'm sorry you had to have one more load of my family's mess left at your door, but I'll always be grateful you were there and ready. She seemed fairly strong when I heard her voice, and I've since had a letter which sounds O.K. She said she would go to her mother's for Easter; but if you have an extra few minutes some evening and could stand the thought, please give her a call and check on her for me. I may have hurt her worse than I've hurt anybody since Rachel died. She won't come here —I asked her plainly—and I can't go there.

I've thought a lot lately of something you said in a letter last summer, that the men in my family had all been warmers. I've wanted to be, God knows, and have worked at it overtime since my eyes focused. But so far I've failed—and over long stretches. I don't know why. Sometimes I think it has to be involved with never having known or even seen my mother. You and Rob and Grainger, Grandmother, Aunt Rena were as kind to me as St. Francis to birds; but I knew about Rachel and wanted her there and kept a place for her that no one else was allowed to fill. Not ten days ago I dreamed her again more or less the way I've always dreamed her. I'm loafing in the woods behind Grandmother's house; and suddenly I see Rachel standing by a creek, on the far side—young and healthy as a straight spring tree. I always tell her "Wait" and run for the others to share my luck. Through the years several roommates have claimed I really called "Wait" in my sleep. The other night a friend was here while I dreamed; and I didn't seem to speak out, didn't wake him at least. I'd lost it when I woke (the end of the dream), but I think she may have stayed, and I crossed over and saw her close at least. Anyhow it's past time to move on from that. What I didn't get from her, I still have to give. And all I know to give is what I seem better at than anything else —the patience to watch things (people mainly) and copy their motions. I hope that will somehow prove a means of love, of finding the place where each thing is still and will no longer leave.

Which brings me to something important at the end. Ann wrote me she'd left the ring with you. I want you not only to keep it but have it. You're the only one left who knew all the men involved in handing it on —old Rob, Forrest, Grainger, young Rob, me. You spoke of Agnes Butters and her groom making outlandish vows at their wedding, just the normal perfect vows. Well, I tremble for them too. But it seems to me you've kept them, out of everyone I've known—steady love for whole lives. I had the ring stretched to fit some years ago; but if you'll wear it, you could have it sized easily. Let me know the cost.

Whatever, now it's yours. When and if I ever need one, please let me start anew. I tried to write a little poem to send with the gift, but poems are in hiding right now. Maybe later.

I'll be here another eighteen months or so. Then who knows where? —but on the same side of the ocean as you. A warming thought. Stay strong and be there always.

Love,
Hutch

March 28, 1956
Dear Hutch,

That ring was offered to me by your grandfather on Christmas eve 1904 for thanks not love. I could not take it then and am honest when I say I have not spent ten seconds wanting it since. But I will take it now and thank you for it here, not wait to see you. It fits my right hand, these knobby old fingers. I won't wear it though. My neighbors would faint then ask fifty questions. I have taped it to the bottom of a slat in the bed your great-grandfather slept and died in. He must have paid for it. Everything in this house is yours in my will. But if I am not here when you get back or have lost these remnants of my great mind, you will know where it is. The ring not my mind.

What means even more is what your letter said, that I kept promises. I hope I did. People just kept asking for things I seemed to have so I can't take any credit for responding. I was lucky there were askers, all men with fine eyes. I still cherish eyes and am glad mine have lasted.

That reminds me to put them back to work now. It is seven a.m. and I have undertaken three Easter dresses that are still lying here in pieces staring at me. One of them is for Ann who seems to be well. She just needs time. So do you, don't worry so much, you're happy. All the men in your family were happy men. Not one of them knew it till I said so. I have said it to you and I know I'm right.

Believe me,
Polly Drewry

REYNOLDS PRICE

Born in Macon, North Carolina in 1933, Reynolds Price attended North Carolina schools and received his Bachelor of Arts degree from Duke University. As a Rhodes Scholar he studied for three years at Merton College, Oxford, receiving the Bachelor of Letters with a thesis on Milton. In 1958 he returned to Duke where he is now James B. Duke Professor of English. His first novel A Long and Happy Life *appeared in 1962. A volume of stories* The Names and Faces of Heroes *appeared in 1963. In the ensuing years he has published* A Generous Man *(a novel),* Love and Work *(a novel),* Permanent Errors *(stories),* Things Themselves *(essays and scenes),* The Surface of Earth *(a novel),* Early Dark *(a play), and* A Palpable God *(translations from the Bible with an essay on the origins and life of narrative). His books have appeared in fourteen languages.*